Psychology of Aging

To Grandma

Although you are no longer Earth-side, I know that you see what I've accomplished and are proud of me. You were the first to show me what successful aging looks like. With your leopard-print shoes, your wish to go skydiving for your 80th birthday, and your feisty nature that continued to shine through into your 90s, you were always the life of the party, and the one we all looked up to. Your wisdom, your grace, and your positive outlook taught me so much—I will be forever grateful. Thank you for showing me that growing old is beautiful and a miraculous part of walking this life.

This book is for you, my fellow bookworm. I love you so much.

As a global academic publisher, Sage is driven by the belief that research and education are critical in shaping society. Our mission is building bridges to knowledge—supporting the development of ideas into scholarship that is certified, taught, and applied in the real world.

Sage's founder, Sara Miller McCune, transferred control of the company to an independent trust, which guarantees our independence indefinitely. This enables us to support an equitable academic future over the long term by building lasting relationships, championing diverse perspectives, and co-creating social and behavioral science resources that transform teaching and learning.

Psychology of Aging

A Concise Exploration

Sara J. Margolin

SUNY Brockport

FOR INFORMATION:

2455 Teller Road
Thousand Oaks, California 91320
Email: order@sagepub.com

1 Oliver's Yard
55 City Road
London EC1Y 1SP
United Kingdom

Unit No 323-333, Third Floor, F-Block
International Trade Tower Nehru Place
New Delhi – 110 019
India

18 Cross Street #10-10/11/12
China Square Central
Singapore 048423

Acquisitions Editor: Adeline Grout

Editorial Assistant: Julie Mangoff

Production Editor: Vijayakumar

Copy Editor: Melinda Masson

Typesetter: TNQ Tech Pvt. Ltd.

Indexer: TNQ Tech Pvt. Ltd.

Cover Designer: Candice Harman

Marketing Manager: Victoria Velasquez

Printed in the United States of America

Library of Congress Control Number: 2024014623

ISBN: 978-1-0718-5216-3

This book is printed on acid-free paper.

24 25 26 27 28 10 9 8 7 6 5 4 3 2 1

BRIEF CONTENTS

DETAILED CONTENTS

LETTER TO THE READER

Dearest Reader,

When I set out to write this book, I was aiming for a few things. First, I wanted to create a book that you'd want to read. Nobody has ever learned anything from a book sitting on a desk. Second, I wanted to work toward dispelling the myths of aging that are so pervasive in Western society and that perpetuate the fear of growing older. And finally, I wanted to help you understand the reality of the aging process, both in others and in yourself.

Too many times, people fall into the trap of believing what they always have believed, and only seeking evidence to confirm those beliefs (aka confirmation bias). This is not how science works, and it certainly doesn't help progress. To move forward is to learn new, disconfirming evidence and to grow from that knowledge. I do hope that you learn something useful here, and that you can join the movement to change the perspective on aging to something more positive and more realistic. Together, let us help the world see how special it is to be granted the gift of growing older.

Warmest regards,

Your friendly, neighborhood gerontologist,

Sara J. Margolin, PhD

PREFACE

I'm not going to lie; the public view of aging is not a positive one. Everywhere we look, we see people doing anything and everything to avoid aging: advertisements for face creams to stop skin aging (e.g., snail mucin—don't google it, it's gross), social media influencers selling supplements to "make them younger" (e.g., green juice), and crash dieting to turn back time before a high school reunion (e.g., carnivore diets and water fasts). We see individuals not hired for a job because they are "too old," or world leaders being criticized as unable to lead their country because they also are "too old" and must be senile. Privately, we may wonder when we'll each lose our capability to think, drive, or live independently; or perhaps we witness one relative (out of many) diagnosed with Alzheimer's disease and begin to fear and/or expect its inevitability in ourselves. The problem with these concerns is that they are not true, not needed, and not part of the typical, healthy aging process. But how would we know that, if not for books like this one?

Fortunately, aging is not a negative experience in and of itself. It isn't a disease to be prevented or cured. And it isn't something to be feared. In fact, aging is a positive process of growth—or it can be, if we let it. But, the falsehoods we believe about aging perpetuate myths and fear . . . or at least that's how it goes in Western societies. In this book, readers will get a peek into the positive experiences of aging, and the changes that science shows are positive ones (or, at the very least, not as negative as we fear they are). The doom-and-gloom perspective has no place in aging. Additionally, this text highlights that change is change and, while it does occur, not all change is decline or loss. Change can be positive, beautiful, and special all throughout our lives.

Importantly, this book acknowledges that aging happens in many ways. Aging happens in our bodies, our minds, our relationships, and our roles in our social world. And any one of these affects the others. That is, changes in our bodies can affect our relationships or our mental health, and changes in our relationships can affect our bodies. As such, this book takes a bio-psycho-social approach to aging, addressing all three components in an integrative way to give a holistic view of the aging process with truth, compassion, and positivity—with real-life examples and a bit of humor sprinkled on top.

When we adjust our expectations of the aging process and clear the misconceptions, we will be able to dispel the fear that surrounds it. Many times over, students have told me that they were afraid of aging before taking my class, but came out the other side with a clearer understanding of aging, less fear, and some confidence to move forward in their own lives.

Acknowledgments

Thank you to the reviewers of the first edition:
Melissa S. Atkins, Marshall University
Kristin August, Rutgers University, Camden

Lisa Emery, Appalachian State University
Ashley Ermer, Montclair State University
Madhavi Menon, Nova Southeastern University

ORGANIZATION AND RESOURCES

In this text, you'll find five units, each with one to three chapters within. This organization is intended to address some popular myths that many believe to be true (including myself at one time) with concise coverage of the research in that area. In some cases, one chapter is enough to bust the myth, but for others (e.g., older adults lose their memory and intelligence, and they become unable to remember to do basic daily tasks), there are several topics to tackle and a few chapters needed to do it. This myth-versus-fact approach is new in the field and addresses the misconceptions about aging head-on. Many books present facts and science, but this one does so with a focus on adjusting our mental framework to accommodate the new (ahem, accurate) information.

Moreover, each chapter is organized in a clear and concise way, explaining the topics and the research with applications to real life through approachable, conversational language. This was important to me when writing this book (and is important to me when I'm teaching in the classroom as well) because what good is learning information if you aren't going to use it? That's not to say that every student who takes a course on the psychology of aging is going to use this information in their professional life (though many will become psychologists, social workers, or nurses). But, aging is a part of life that we all experience—if we are granted the blessing of living long enough to do it. So, the information can and should be used to process pieces of our own aging as well.

Within chapters, there is also organization to facilitate learning. Real-life examples start each chapter and are presented throughout the text, relating new concepts, research, and theories to information that is familiar and relatable (cognitive science tells us that this is an effective strategy for learning new information). The beginning of each chapter also presents a list of learning objectives. Presenting these first allows for mental organization and foundation building, after which readers more easily learn and organize the chapter ahead (another learning strategy we can trace back to basic cognitive science). Key terms are presented for emphasis on important concepts. At the end of each chapter, comprehension questions allow for metacomprehension reflection, and additional recommended readings are listed for students to dig deeper on topics from that chapter.

ABOUT THE AUTHOR

Sara J. Margolin, PhD, received her doctoral degree in cognitive and sensory processes with a certificate in gerontology from the University of Florida in 2007. Since then, she has been a full-time faculty member in the Department of Psychology at SUNY Brockport teaching classes in cognitive processes, sensation and perception, research methods, and (of course) the psychology of aging. Her research emphasizes cognition and aging, specifically how reading processes may change (or in some cases be preserved) with age and the inclusion of negated sentence structure, and has been published in journals such as *Educational Gerontology* and *Experimental Aging Research*. In her spare time, she loves to read (we aren't surprised), cook (though this is a skill yet to be perfected), and spend time camping with her husband (the biggest goofball), two sons (mini goofballs), and three very large dogs (fuzzy goofballs).

UNIT I

MYTH: OLDER ADULTS LOSE PHYSICAL CAPABILITIES

In this unit, you'll learn about how the body naturally ages—inside and out—and how those physiological changes can impact us psychologically. Specifically, this unit will focus on the distinction between normative aging processes and those determined by disease. What's important here is that normative aging is not disease—though I think we all fear that they are one and the same.

Additionally, you'll see that aging does not equate to physiological downfall or nursing home residence. And aging does not automatically push you into the role of "burden." Independence is not always lost (in fact, this is rarely the case), and many older adults remain fully functioning for the majority of their days.

It's my hope that you see physiological changes as just that—changes. They are not burdensome or problematic. And just in the way we adjust to life as we move from adolescence to adulthood, we adjust to changes from adulthood to older adulthood. Gradually. And hopefully without fear.

iStockPhoto/supersizer

1 PHYSICAL AGING

LEARNING OBJECTIVES

1.1 Explain the normative age-related changes that occur in physical appearance, cellular aging, neurological aging, and hormonal aging.

1.2 Describe the chronic disease and disability progression in osteoporosis, cardiovascular disease, and arthritis.

1.3 Explain how quality of life is defined by ADLs and IADLs, disability, and the impact of the socioeconomic health gap.

1.4 Describe the large array of settings for elder care, and how elder mistreatment might occur.

In the 1990s and early 2000s, if you fell asleep while watching TV and woke up in the middle of the night, it was not to a notice from Netflix asking you if you were still watching—Netflix didn't exist yet. Rather, you likely awoke to an infomercial (i.e., informational commercial lasting 30 minutes or more) for some "As Seen on TV" product that nobody actually needs. One of my favorites was a device designed to slim your neckline and remove sagging and aging skin from the bottom of your chin. It was a spring-loaded device you put under your chin, and you moved your chin up and down to squish it and "exercise" your double chin and sagging skin away. I wish I was kidding. This thing has stuck with me for all these years because of its ridiculousness, and how it perfectly epitomizes the lengths people will go to in order to avoid "aging." Now, as I write this, I see a headline in *Page Six* where "Kim Kardashian says she'd 'eat poop' daily if it made her look younger" (Zilio, 2022). I mean, you can't make this stuff up. If I thought the neckline slimmer was ridiculous, this claim is on a whole other level. But this is how extreme many in Western culture are with youth and the appearance of youth. What they aren't realizing is that physical aging is normal, and that the process of aging *is* beautiful. Changes to our appearance, body systems, cells, neurology, hormones, and other systems occur. That doesn't mean these fail us, and it doesn't mean we become ugly, disabled, or ineffective as humans. However, products like the neckline slimmer play into our fears and beliefs about aging and speak to the desperation that people feel to avoid the things they fear the most—and they don't even work. You can't exercise your chin skin away (is that really a sentence I just wrote?). In this chapter, we will address the normative changes that occur in our body with age, as well as what can happen when illness strikes and leads to disability. The chapter will also discuss nursing homes as just one alternative to senior living situations, and the risks and potential for elder abuse.

NORMATIVE AGE-RELATED CHANGES

In discussing normative age-related physical changes in our bodies, it's important to recognize that *normative* means that these changes happen to many of us, and that these changes are not the result of disease. Most of the time, normative changes are minor and gradual, are not the same as disease, and do not impair daily functioning (Whitborne, 2002). This is an important distinction to make: Normative changes do not usually impair daily functioning, but disease-related changes can impair daily functioning dramatically. Let us first address some physical changes that occur in many of our body systems as the aging process progresses. Many of these changes are not noticeable at all, and others are only noticeable after they have progressed for many years. Changes can happen on a large scale, like in our height or weight, or on a small scale at a cellular level in our DNA.

Physical Appearance

The first of these aging processes we'll discuss involves the changes that happen in our physical appearance. Unfortunately, in Western culture, with changes in physical appearance comes a very clear gender-based double standard (e.g., England & McClintock, 2009; Lauzen & Dozier,

2005). You are probably familiar with this bias. When women age, their *beauty is lost*. However, when men age, they appear *distinguished*. This is not only inconsistent messaging, but it clearly tells women that they are no longer desirable when they are older. This is **ageism**, plain and simple. Changes that occur in our bodies with age are similar across genders (though there are some differences by biological sex, as will be discussed in just a bit), but they are not perceived in a similar way. This perpetuates fear (e.g., McConatha et al., 2003) and can lead to behaviors intended to avoid the physical aging process (hello, neckline slimmer). But what are the normative changes that one can expect with age, and do they really cause such devastation in our physical appearance? No. Really they don't. But let's discuss what those specific changes are.

One of the most noticeable physical changes is our body weight. Typically, we see a pattern of weight change throughout adulthood that is an inverted *U* shape (Hutfless et al., 2013). That's to say that adults typically will gain weight slowly and steadily throughout adulthood until about age 60, and then weight begins to decline. For me, this is noticeable when my friends (now middle-aged) complain about having put on 15 or so pounds in the last 5–10 years. I tell them that it's normal, but they fight me on it, because this is not the predominant idea in Western culture. This isn't limited to either biological sex, but rather is related to changes in activity level (e.g., Di Pietro et al., 2004), nutrition needs and metabolism (Amarya et al., 2018; McCrory et al., 2002), and hormonal changes (more on hormonal changes in just a bit). Importantly, the weight changes that are normative in our aging process are small—approximately 10% of our body weight. Changes that are larger than this have been associated with disability (e.g., Busetto et al., 2009) and may be the result of other health and health behavior changes such as changes in thyroid function (e.g., Michalaki et al., 2006), lowered activity levels/desk jobs, and more.

Changes in height can occur as well (see Figure 1.1). Commonly, across the years of older adulthood, individuals can lose between one and two inches (or two to four centimeters) in height (Fernihough & McGovern, 2015)—this makes me wonder if I'll remain over five feet tall into my older years. There are biological sex differences here, where women tend to lose a bit more in height than men due to differences in how hormonal changes impact bone density. That is, postmenopausal women lose bone density at a higher rate due to shifts in estrogen levels (Frost, 1999). This bone density loss is normal; however, it can become abnormal if density gets too low. When bone density is sufficiently low, it results in osteopenia (i.e., small loss in bone density) or **osteoporosis** (i.e., larger loss in bone density that can cause irreparable damage and lead to injury, fracture, and/or disability). These are not normative aging, but rather disease, and are atypical in the general population. (We'll discuss this in more detail later in the chapter when we talk about chronic illness.) However, bone density is just one variable that impacts this loss in height; changes in musculature, posture, and simple gravity also play a role. Compression of the cartilage discs in between the vertebrae of the spine can contribute as well (Kimura et al., 2001). This compression impacts posture, and over time impacts an individual's height. Interestingly, I was speaking with an EMT recently, and she mentioned that when she asks patients their height, many older men respond with "I used to be" such and such height rather than their current height. She also specifically said that her observation was that only men tended to make these comments. So not only are they aware of this physiological change, but they are resistant to it as well—even in a medical situation.

FIGURE 1.1 ■ Changes in Height With Age

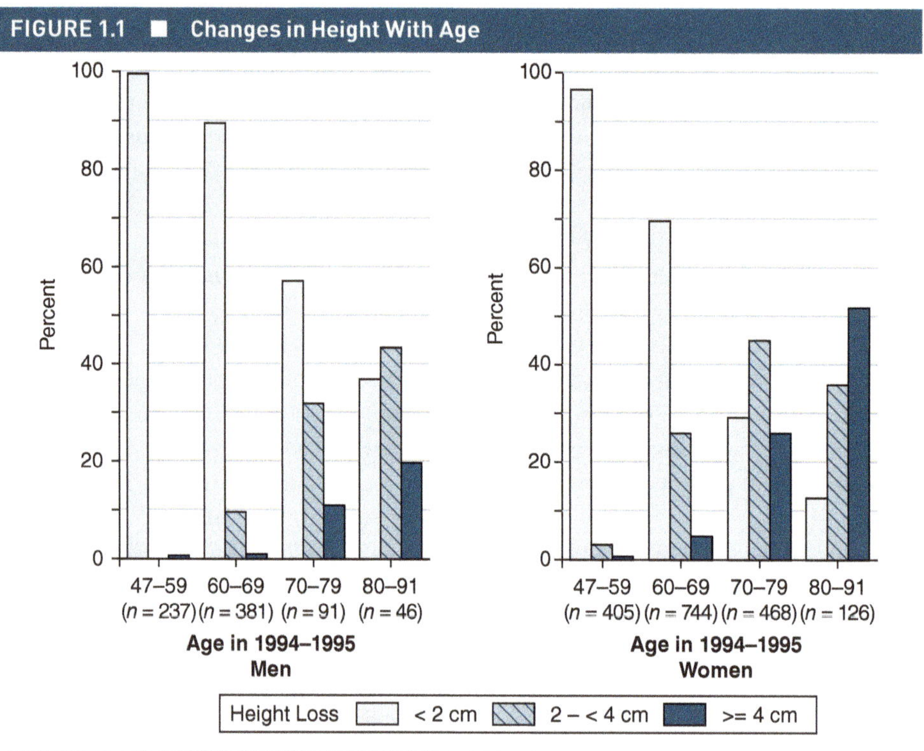

Source: Masunari, N., Fujiwara, S., Kasagi, F., Takahashi, I., Yamada, M., & Nakamura, T. (2012). Height loss starting in middle age predicts increased mortality in the elderly. *Journal of Bone and Mineral Research, 27*(1), 138–145.

While there are no published data that support this emotional toll, specifically of a decrease in height, this does make sense. And, research does show that older adults tend to overestimate their height (Cawley et al., 2017). Evolutionarily speaking, height and strength are associated with a man's traditional responsibility in hunting and protecting (Archer, 1996). To lose that is to lose one's evolutionary role, at least to some degree. Additionally, some research has connected the reduction in height to increased mortality, such that when height begins to decrease in middle age (rather than later in life), there is an increased risk of mortality by illnesses such as coronary heart disease, stroke, and respiratory illness (Masunari et al., 2012). To be sure, these data do not definitively dictate mortality via decreased height, but do signal that as a culture, we are not OK with the changes that occur with age, even if they don't mean anything in terms of our functioning or our well-being. And, if the changes signal anything regarding end of life, the fear of the change can become even greater.

In addition to changes in our height can be changes in our musculature. Muscle changes can contribute to our height changes, but some happen to our overall body composition. Commonly, as we get older, we experience some muscle loss. This muscle loss, called **sarcopenia**, is not initially dramatic, and it doesn't typically become noticeable until age 80 or older (Walston, 2012). Instead, it is a small, gradual change that can slowly impact our posture, strength, and mobility. We may gradually become slower, less flexible, and less mobile over the course of 20 or 30 years. However, weakness that occurs suddenly is not normal and is not a part of the typical aging process, but rather may signal a disease process. Walston (2012) argues that normative changes in musculature are usually the result of changes in hormones, inflammation (see Chapter 10 for a further explanation of how inflammation impacts aging), activity levels, or neurological changes. They can certainly be exacerbated by disease and poor nutrition, which would make a loss of function more likely. However, maintaining function can be achieved through directed exercise and good nutrition (e.g., Timmerman et al., 2012).

Other changes in our physicality that we notice as we get older are in our skin and hair. They vary dramatically from one individual to another, but changes do occur. We may see wrinkling in the skin, skin dryness, lightening of the skin tone, and loss of elasticity and fullness in the skin (e.g., Farage et al., 2010). Our hair can become dry, change its texture, and stop producing its color (i.e., turn gray). These changes are normal and cannot be reversed or halted. However, this is not what the beauty industry wants you to think. *Try this cream, and your skin won't age. Try this shampoo, and your hair will be soft like a baby's.* While moisture is good and can help protect aging skin, neither of these products can stop or reverse the changes that occur with age. Moisture from a cream or a shampoo can minimize the look of some of the lines that we see in our skin and some of the brittleness that happens in our hair, but it will not address what is happening under the surface. Underneath the skin's surface, there is a breakdown in the collagen and structural layers within the skin. Because the top layer (i.e., the epidermis) is getting thinner, it becomes more susceptible to damage and is more likely to lose moisture (see Chapter 2 on how skin changes contribute to changes in our sense of touch). To be sure, there are loads of individual differences in how these changes occur, as they are influenced by a variety of factors, including genetics, sun exposure, diet, and smoking (e.g., Gupta & Gilchrest, 2005). And some research does support that supplementation with marine collagen can reduce the appearance of the skin wrinkling (e.g., Evans et al., 2021). Nevertheless, some change does happen eventually. And that's OK. It is normal and doesn't mean that the skin is unhealthy or that anything bad is going on. This is a reality that's hard for many to handle, because of the value placed on youth in Western culture.

iStockPhoto/Mario Arango

The value that youth is better and more attractive is not new. Studies dating back to the 1980s and 1990s have demonstrated that not only do others value youth and equate youth to beauty (e.g., Koblenzer, 1996), but older adults also do the same about themselves (e.g., Graham & Kligman, 1985; Kligman & Koblenzer, 1997). Kligman and Koblenzer (1997) describe a cyclical effect that occurs when an older adult sees their "youth and beauty fade." If they interpret this as a negative experience, their willingness to continue to treat themselves well (make doctors' appointments, exercise, eat well, etc.) wanes. The poor treatment exacerbates the changes in their appearance, because now they aren't just aging; they may become unwell. They then see their appearance as even worse, and so the cycle continues. Rather, others who maintain self-esteem in the face of changing skin may better care for themselves. The difference here is a health concern as the result of differential psychological reactions to the physiological aging process.

So what exactly are the psychological implications of these physical changes? As we saw with the neckline slimmer and Kim Kardashian's claim that she'd "eat poop" if it kept her looking young, some individuals will take age-related changes in their appearance very seriously, which can negatively impact their body image (Becker et al., 2013). And some resort to extreme, ridiculous, or ineffective behaviors in their pursuit of maintaining youth. This is reasonable given the avoidance and negative social interactions that come in our society when one is deemed unattractive (e.g., Gupta & Gilchrest, 2005; Gupta & Gupta, 2003). One study even demonstrated that caregivers in a nursing home and a hospital were less nurturing toward patients who were visibly older or unattractive in some way (e.g., Gupta & Gupta, 2003). It is awful to be treated this way based on one's appearance, especially in a setting where you need care—but then again, all humans need care. And the potential for neglect and lack of support makes the reaction to avoid looking older or unattractive understandable to some degree. Who would want to be avoided and deprived of nurturing? The implications of a lowered quality of life because of one's appearance include symptoms of depression and anxiety and lowered self-esteem and are a very real outcome for many (e.g., Farage et al., 2010).

As someone who knows that being older doesn't equate to being unattractive, I find this a hard pill to swallow. These acts of "grasping at straws" to remain young seem sad and unnecessary but may be indicative of a culture shift that is needed in our Western world. This is not to say that doing anything cosmetically is bad. There is nothing inherently bad about changing your hair color, putting on face cream, or getting plastic surgery. However, the reasons for engaging in these behaviors are important. Are we putting on face cream because it makes us feel good, or are we putting it on in an attempt to prevent aging? Are we coloring our hair because we like the way we look with brown hair instead of gray? Or are we coloring it because gray hair means we're getting older and we feel we need to hide that? Are we doing it to gain and/or maintain social acceptance? This is an important distinction to make, and one that can give insight into our own beliefs about physical aging.

Cellular Aging

While we may see changes to our appearance—height, weight, hair color, wrinkled skin, and so on—easily with our eyes, there are aging processes happening below the surface on a cellular level that are not visible to our naked, human eye. Rather, changes happen to our cells and our DNA over time and with exposure to stressors in our environment (e.g., Epel et al., 2004; Lin et al., 2012; see Chapter 10 for more information on how stress affects our cells). With normative aging, cells can be impacted in two ways: through oxidation and/or through limitations in cell division. We will discuss the impact of each of these here.

First, cellular **oxidation** is a process by which cells can be damaged through use and exposure to **free radicals** in our environment. Oxidation is not damage by disease, but rather just something that happens by use over time. I like to think about the oxidation process like rusting (because the process is chemically very similar to what happens when metal rusts). No matter our environment, simply living exposes us to free radicals—that is, substances that are missing electrons in their outer atomic layer. When these free radicals come upon our cells and see available electrons, they take them to complete their outer atomic layer and become more stable. While sharing is good in human relationships, this type of sharing is not. When our cells give up their electrons, they become unstable and can no longer survive. The cell dies (it essentially becomes rust), and its leftover bits get absorbed into the surrounding cells. This is a normal process, but if it happens too much or too often, cells cannot regenerate fast enough. The good news is that **antioxidants** can help slow down this oxidative process. Antioxidants, found in foods rich in color like espresso, berries, cloves, and kale (e.g., Carlsen et al., 2010), can intercept the free radicals before they take electrons from our cells. Instead, they provide the electrons (rather than allowing them to be stolen from our body's cells) and keep the free radicals' attack at bay. They won't stop the oxidation process from happening but can minimize its impact—that is, less rust. And while the full mechanism behind oxidation is more complex than this, involving enzymatic activity, internal oxidation, and the influence of stress (e.g., Cutler & Rodriguez, 2003), a large amount of data suggests that oxidation is at least part of the mechanism behind the cellular aging process (e.g., Kuznik et al., 2022). This is one reason why eating foods rich in antioxidants can be beneficial (e.g., Beckman & Ames, 1998; Liguori et al., 2018; see Table 1.1), although some research demonstrates that we can also produce some of our own antioxidants naturally (e.g., Junqueira et al., 2004).

TABLE 1.1 ■ Foods With High Antioxidant Value

Fruits	Vegetables	Beverages	Herbs and Spices
Indian Gooseberry	Curly Kale	Espresso	Clove
Plums	Okra	Black Coffee	Cinnamon
Blueberries	Broccoli	Red Wine	Mint
Dates	Black Olives	Pomegranate Juice	Nutmeg
Mango	Artichoke	Green Tea	Ginger
Apricots	Red and Green Chili	Grape Juice	Rosemary
Strawberries	Pecans	Black Tea	Sage

Source: Carlsen, M. H., Halvorsen, B. L., Holte, K., Bøhn, S. K., Dragland, S., Sampson, L., Willey, C., Senoo, H., Umezono, Y., Sanada, C., Barikmo, I., Berhe, N., Willett, W. C., Phillips, K. M., Jacobs, D. R., Jr., & Blomhoff, R. (2010). The total antioxidant content of more than 3100 foods, beverages, spices, herbs and supplements used worldwide. *Nutrition Journal, 9*(3), 1–11.

Another process that inherently determines aging at a cellular level occurs in our cells' division process. All throughout our lives, our body's cells replicate and replace themselves to keep things fresh; however, there are limits to how many times each cell can do this. This idea is not new—clues of scientists' suspicions that cells cannot replicate indefinitely date back to the late 1800s. However, Leonard Hayflick determined these limitations to be centered on the ends of the cells' DNA in the mid-1900s (e.g., Hayflick, 1968). These ends, called **telomeres**, shorten each time a cell divides. And, like ripping paper in half to get two pieces, the telomeres can only shorten so many times before the cell cannot be "ripped in half" again. This limit has been termed the **Hayflick limit** (Burnet, 1974), and while the limit is different for different types of cells, it defines that the cell can only divide so many times before it will no longer replicate. This means that there is an inherent end to cell replication. Like oxidation, the shortening of the telomeres eventually results in cell death and can be accelerated by stress (e.g., Lin et al., 2012; see Chapter 10 for more details on the impact of stress on telomeres). However, the Hayflick limit indicates that cell division (and replacement) progresses for much of our lives. This refreshment of cells is positive, even if we can't do it indefinitely (this isn't *Fame*, and we aren't going to live forever). To be sure, there are cells whose telomeres maintain their length—through enzymatic activity of telomerase—but these cells are cancerous and grow and divide with no boundaries, constraints, or limits (e.g., Olovnikov, 1996). Those are not the cells any of us really want to have around.

Neurological Changes

Cellular changes don't just happen in the cells of our skin or internal organs; they also happen to our neurons. These neurological changes can have implications for our speed of cognitive processing, memory, and executive function (see Chapters 3 and 4 for more details on the changes in those processes; and here's a preview: they aren't all bad). Importantly, in normative aging processes, neurological changes are mild, slow, and general (e.g., Burke & Barnes, 2006). This is different from changes that occur as the result of disease processes, where changes are faster, more specific, and usually more dramatic overall. Changes in neurons can happen through growth or through **pruning** (i.e., eliminating) in the neural networks of the brain. Yes, I said *growth*. Our neural networks change and grow each time we learn something, creating new neural connections (e.g., von Bernhardi et al., 2017). These connections form for anyone at any age. While it may take more time to change the network and grow a new connection, an older adult can learn new tricks and create new connections (Burke & Barnes, 2006). Alternatively, pruning unused or unnecessary neural connections happens as well (Craik & Bialystock, 2006). Use it or lose it, I always say. And it's true. If you don't need a connection and haven't used it in a long time, there's no sense in using energy to maintain it. Humans maintain **neural plasticity** and adjust and change their neural networks into older adulthood (e.g., Disterhoft & Oh, 2006).

Research here supports these ideas. In one study, Soshi et al. (2021) investigated factors that contributed to neural plasticity in older adults' frontal lobes, and its relation to memory function. Here, older adults were assigned to an aerobic exercise intervention and compared to their age-matched controls not engaging in the exercise program. Brain scans indicated growth in the frontal cortex and hippocampus of older adults in the exercise intervention group, suggesting that the exercise was a mitigating factor in encouraging new neuronal growth (see Figure 1.2).

FIGURE 1.2 ■ Changes to the Frontal Cortex and Hippocampus, Resulting From Physical Exercise

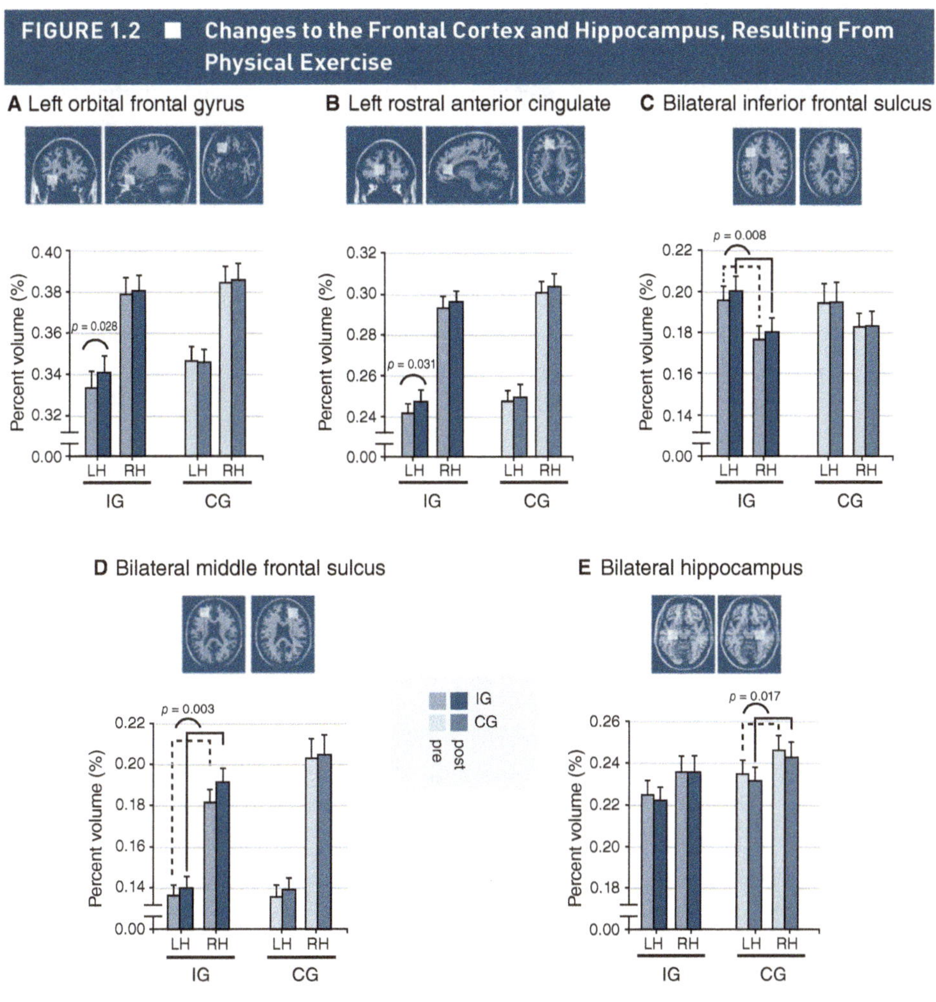

Source: Soshi, T., Andersson, M., Kawagoe, T., Nishiguchi, S., Yamada, M., Otsuka, Y., Nakai, R., Abe, N., Aslah, A., Igasaki, T., & Sekiyama, K. (2021). Prefrontal plasticity after a 3-month exercise intervention in older adults relates to enhanced cognitive performance. *Cerebral Cortex, 31*(10), 4501–4517.

Importantly, the increased brain volume in these areas was also associated with improved performance on working memory tasks, indicating that the growth in neural connections was leading to enhanced cognitive functioning for this group of older adults. The same was not true for individuals who were not in the exercise intervention group. These results are supportive not only that neural plasticity is possible in older adulthood, but also that physical movement is a facilitator of that benefit. And since exercise can help our bodies as well, it can feed two birds with one grain.

Other research has examined brain structures in the oldest old (i.e., adults over 85), and how changes here may mimic some of those seen as the result of disease processes (e.g., Balasubramanian et al., 2012). While this may be seen as negative, and some try to use this as evidence that we will all just get Alzheimer's eventually anyway, this is absolutely not the case. Some normative neurological changes, however, do overlap with changes seen in Alzheimer's disease. Specifically, Balasubramanian et al. (2012) showed neuritic plaques in the oldest old who did and others who did not meet the criteria for Alzheimer's disease. However, these changes did not preclude individuals from learning. The difference (discussed in further detail in Chapter 8) for individuals with Alzheimer's disease is that the neuritic plaques and neurofibrillary tangles (i.e., neurological changes) occur at a younger age, are more widespread, develop at a more rapid pace, and result in impaired functioning. While Balasubramanian et al. demonstrated that some neurological changes occur even for those who do not have Alzheimer's disease, change over time is normal. A brain of a 70-year-old shouldn't be the same as one of a 25-year-old. These are different people with different experiences, knowledge, motivations, relationships, and so on, and these differences are reflected in the physiology of the brain.

Hormonal Changes

Physiological changes occur to our hormonal and reproductive systems as well. The most well-known such change is menopause, but this is not the only change that occurs. Changes occur before, during, and after menopause. And, changes occur for both biological men and biological women (e.g., Horstman et al., 2012)—though biological men do not have the obvious demarcation from fertile/able to bear children to not fertile. Let us examine the hormonal shifts as biological and evolutionary mechanisms.

Shifts in hormones for biological women occur throughout adulthood, with drops in estrogen and changes to the menstrual cycle occurring as early as one's 30s (e.g., Bachmann, 1994; Dunson et al., 2002; see Figure 1.3). This begins the changes that will eventually impact fertility

FIGURE 1.3 ■ Changes in Estrogen Levels With Age

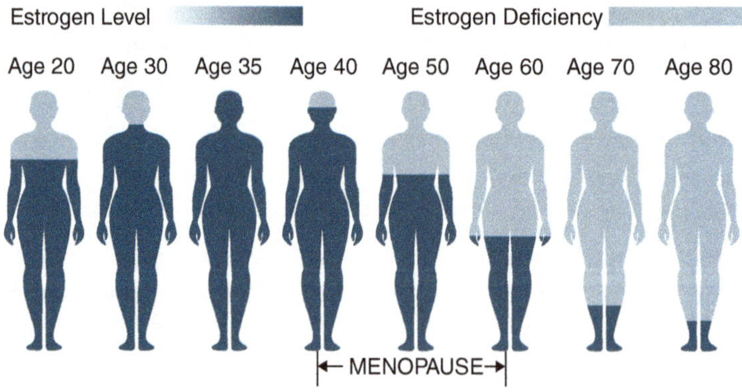

Source: USF Health Diabetes and Endocrinology Center. (n.d.). *Menopause and post-menopausal hormone therapy*. https://health.usf.edu/care/diabetes-endocrinology/services-specialties/hormone

through "the change" during menopause. The shifts in estrogen levels can result in changes in bone density and, without proper nutrition (and with the right—ahem, wrong—combination of genetics and environmental factors), can result in osteopenia or osteoporosis (e.g., Horstman et al., 2012). But more on that in just a bit.

Shifting from one who can bear children to one who can't, evolutionarily, is crucial for the survival of those young. It's important that the one who bears and rears those children is strong and able to do those jobs, and that their hormonal health supports the bones that are needed to do that job. That is different from the biological male, who needs to spread his DNA far and wide to perpetuate the species (e.g., Birkhead, 2000)—no matter the current status of his strength or youth. Evolutionarily speaking, he would not be bearing or rearing the children anyway. The result here is that while, biologically, men do experience some changes to their hormones that lower their sperm count (e.g., decreases in testosterone; Wang & Stocco, 2005), this does not stop them from continuing to reproduce.

If we look closely at the differentiation here between biological women and men, it's clear that fertility and reproduction are important. For women, youth is the time of fertility. This evolutionary predisposition may be the impetus for valuing youth in women but not in men—although we now know that this not the only value women provide. In more modern life, the social roles have evolved (we'll discuss social roles later in this book), and thus the perspective on menopause as the end to female reproduction is a bit different; however, the negativity surrounding it often remains. For example, Kelly (2011) argues that menopause is viewed by many as a demarcation between a "normal appearing" woman and one who acts overemotional and unsteady—and that life postmenopause is viewed as having nothing to look forward to. This delineation could make sense in the evolutionary view that life is to create more life. However, modernity and cultural changes show that there is more to life than making more life. And this textbook shows that there is plenty to look forward to postmenopause. So, I would argue that the claim of normal/not normal à la Kelly isn't a fair or legitimate point to make; we just need to spread the word.

Shifts in hormones impact other body systems, including sleep, protein metabolism, and muscle mass, as well as cognitive function and mood (e.g., Horstman et al., 2012). For instance, changes in hormones can interfere with temperature regulation mechanisms, making individuals feel hot when there is no heat around (i.e., hot flashes). I remember one such instance with my mother where she was so uncomfortable, she just sat under the ceiling fan and cried in frustration. If this is the "unsteadiness" Kelly (2011) was referring to, I can understand (though these claims should be situational and not dispositional; but more on those in our discussion on social cognition in Chapter 7). Who would be rational or pleasant when they are so uncomfortable? Additionally, Horstman et al. (2012) explain that these changes can lead to a low level of inflammation in the body, leaving the older adult more susceptible to autoimmune diseases, cancer, diabetes, and cardiovascular disease. While not part of the normative aging process, an increased risk of these disease processes exists and should prompt an individual for regular check-ins with their doctor to ensure any disease is detected early and treated properly (Pradhan et al., 2002). We'll discuss the specifics of some of these diseases next.

CHRONIC DISEASE

When aging processes don't go as expected, are accelerated, or impact our functioning, they are often the result of disease, rather than normative aging. This is an important distinction. Aging does not equate to disease. Ever. In this section, we'll discuss some common (though still not normal) chronic disease processes that may impact functioning in older adulthood. These diseases may be ones you've heard of, witnessed, and maybe thought to be normal in aging. I assure you they are not.

The first of these diseases was mentioned earlier in this chapter: osteoporosis. Osteoporosis is a condition where bones have lost so much of their density that they become brittle, putting the individual at a high risk for fracture and injury (see Figure 1.4).

This condition is more common among women than among men (and more common among white individuals than Black); rates reported by Sozen and colleagues (2017) are that one in three women and one in five men will be affected. Additionally, increased risk falls on those with family history of osteoporosis. Fortunately, these rates do not indicate that everyone will develop osteoporosis, nor do they indicate that everyone diagnosed will lose function in their day-to-day lives. Most individuals with osteoporosis live normally, with regular bone density scans to monitor progression (e.g., Silverman, 2005). Additional precautions should be taken to minimize the risk of falls around the home (better lighting, no loose cords or rugs, demarcation at the edges of stairs, etc.), and in some cases, medication can be prescribed to slow the progression of the disease as well (e.g., Solomon et al., 2005). However, dietary calcium sources (milk, yogurt, broccoli, kale, etc.), as well as weight-bearing exercise (pushups, bicep curls, etc.), can help prevent onset and progression in some individuals (e.g., Schmiege et al., 2007; Shanb & Youssef, 2014).

Cardiovascular disease (i.e., heart disease) is another common occurrence in older adulthood, encompassing atherosclerosis, cardiac arrest, coronary artery disease, high blood pressure, and more (Halter et al., 2014). To be sure, these are scary to think about for many of us, but it bears repeating—these are not a guarantee in older adulthood. However, many older individuals live with high blood pressure (often controlled with diet, exercise, and/or medication) or are at risk of cardiac arrest. Interestingly, although cardiovascular disease is the leading cause of death in both men and women (e.g., Mosca et al., 2011), the absolute numbers of women have surpassed the

FIGURE 1.4 ■ Comparison of Osteoporotic Bone to Healthy Bone Tissue

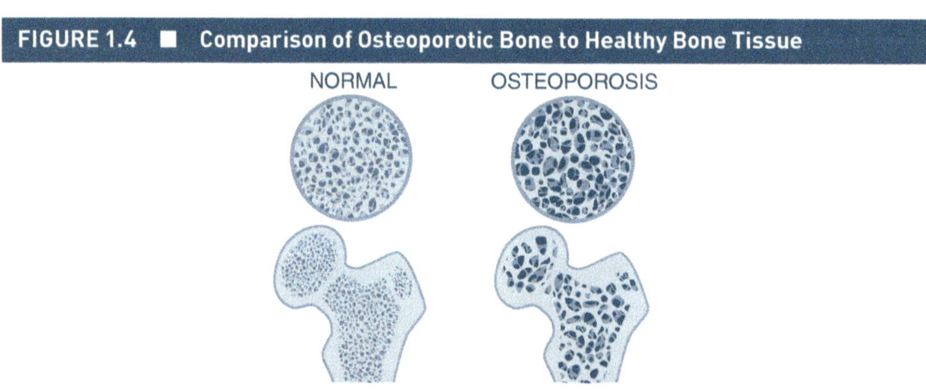

Source: iStockPhoto/Bigmouse108.

numbers of men dying from cardiovascular and related diseases since the mid-1980s. One reason for this discrepancy has to do with awareness of the differential symptom displays. I suspect that, like most people, you relate heart disease and cardiac arrest symptoms to chest pain, shortness of breath, and shooting pain in the left arm. While you are correct, those are the typical symptoms displayed by men (see the American Heart Association for more information). Women, on the other hand, tend to show different symptoms—which seem to be more consistent with "just not feeling well." Women often report feelings of nausea, fatigue, upper back pain, and malaise. Not identifying these symptoms early can end in catastrophic results. Spreading awareness of these symptoms has been a goal of the American Heart Association's Go Red for Women initiative, in the hopes of reducing these rates and improving women's heart health outcomes.

A third common illness in older adulthood that we'll address here (though there are certainly others) is arthritis (see Figure 1.5). Importantly, we'll distinguish between **osteoarthritis** and **rheumatoid arthritis** and the functional outcomes of each (see the Arthritis Foundation for detailed information about the many different types of arthritis—there are over 100!). Osteoarthritis is known as "wear-and-tear" arthritis. That is, it is a type of arthritis resulting from using a joint over a long period of time. That exceptional use can result in the wear-down of the cartilage in the joint, resulting in pain when the bones rub against one another without the cushion that was once provided by the cartilage. This is different from rheumatoid arthritis, which is an autoimmune disease that results from an inappropriate immune response. In rheumatoid arthritis, one's immune system mistakes joints and their surrounding synovial fluid for foreign bodies and attacks them, creating inflammation of the joint and breakdown of the bones themselves (e.g., Majithia & Geraci, 2007).

As you would expect, using joints over a lifetime could put one at a higher risk of developing osteoarthritis. This long-term use, often stemming from one's occupational choice (e.g., Cooper, 1995), along with any additional wear and tear that can come from injury, high-impact sports or running (e.g., Lane et al., 1993), and so on, can increase these risks. However, risks of osteoarthritis are mechanical, and are fundamentally different from risks associated with rheumatoid arthritis. Here, risks include genetic factors (i.e., a family history of rheumatoid arthritis and/or other autoimmune disorders), as well as other factors like exposure to tobacco smoke and female biological sex (e.g., Bax et al., 2011; Deane et al., 2017). Additional considerations for the development of rheumatoid arthritis come from changes in the immune system that are associated with aging. Here, immune changes can include shifts in the distribution of T-cells, B-cells, lymphocytes, neutrophils, and so on (e.g., Fali et al., 2018), as well as an increase in pro-inflammatory cytokines, like tumor necrosis factor (TNF) or c-reactive protein (CRP; Franceschi & Campisi, 2014). These changes can make an immune attack against oneself more likely—though young people do also experience rheumatoid arthritis and other autoimmune diseases (e.g., Horiuchi et al., 2017), so this is not definitive.

Both instances of arthritis can impact an individual's functioning over time, but the likelihood of more pain and diminished functioning is higher in rheumatoid arthritis than in osteoarthritis (e.g., Affleck et al., 1999), given that this is a systemic issue rather than one isolated to a couple of joints that have been worn down over time. Therefore, we should consider a saying that I heard from a woman in one of the group fitness classes I taught years ago. She told me, "Motion is lotion." She speaks truth! Research on exercise has demonstrated that gentle,

FIGURE 1.5 ■ Comparison of Osteoarthritis and Rheumatoid Arthritis With a Healthy Joint

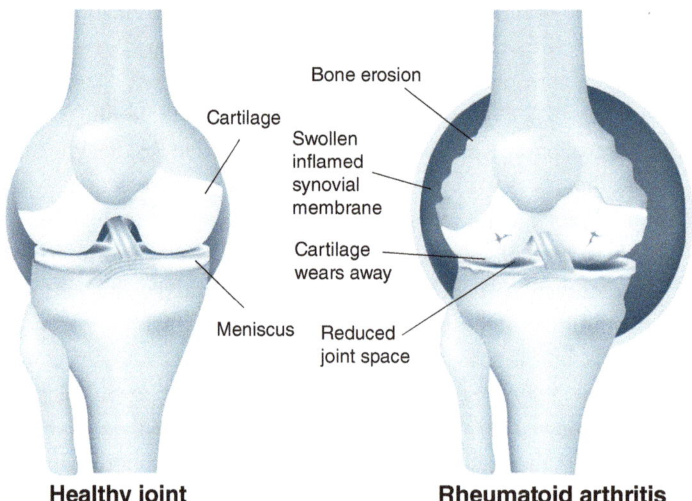

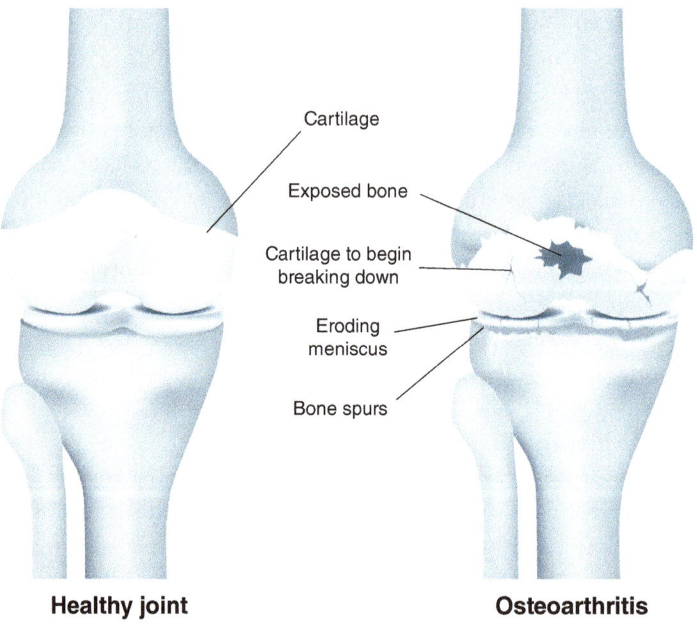

Source: iStockPhoto/ttsz

consistent activity is helpful in reducing pain in osteoarthritis (e.g., Fransen et al., 2015) and maintaining range of motion and muscle strength in the muscles that support the joints in rheumatoid arthritis (e.g., Cooney et al., 2011).

At this point, you may be wondering: Why discuss these health concerns in a book about psychology? My answer to you is because it's all connected. These health concerns specifically impact our fears about getting older as well as our functioning and well-being as older adults. And, some research shows that any tendency to catastrophize (i.e., think badly about) conditions like arthritis can increase the struggle with these diseases (e.g., Edwards et al., 2006). Functioning (discussed next in terms of quality of life and disability), and our ability to continue to lead independent lives, is important to leading a good life in older adulthood.

ADL PROBLEMS AND DISABILITY

In relation to disease, we will discuss the impact that these diseases have on our **quality of life (QoL)** and any functional limitations that can impact our ability to lead our daily lives. Exploring these issues is important for a health care practitioner to be able to identify the extent to which an individual is impacted by their specific health concerns. For example, someone newly diagnosed with rheumatoid arthritis may have no issue cooking meals or dressing themselves, but as the disease progresses, they may start to notice that opening jars or buttoning a shirt becomes difficult. And, while these specific examples are easy to accommodate with jar openers and shirts without buttons, some functional limitations can lead to difficulties in day-to-day tasks and independent living (e.g., climbing in and out of a bathtub or up and down stairs).

Measures that are often used in determining the extent to which an individual is impacted by disease are the **activities of daily living (ADLs)** and **instrumental activities of daily living (IADLs)**. Measuring ADLs and IADLs through both observation and self-report can help a practitioner determine how effectively an individual can carry out activities of daily life (e.g., Elsawy & Higgins, 2011; see Table 1.2).

TABLE 1.2 ■ Activities of Daily Living (ADLs) and Instrumental Activities of Daily Living (IADLs)

Activities of Daily Living (ADLs)	Instrumental Activities of Daily Living (IADLs)
Bathing/showering	Transportation
Toileting	Preparing food
Continence	Managing/taking medications
Dressing	Paying bills
Feeding	Communicating with others
Ambulating	Mental support and relationships

Source: Adapted from Zallio, M., McGrory, J., Berry, D. (2020). How to Democratize Internet of Things Devices: A Participatory Design Study to Improve Digital Literacy. In: Di Bucchianico, G., Shin, C., Shim, S., Fukuda, S., Montagna, G., Carvalho, C. (eds) Advances in Industrial Design. AHFE 2020. Advances in Intelligent Systems and Computing, vol 1202. Springer, Cham. https://doi.org/10.1007/978-3-030-51194-4_19

For example, ADLs are activities that address basic needs, including things like feeding oneself, dressing, bathing, and toileting. Alternatively, IADLs include activities that allow an individual to live independently, such as paying bills, doing laundry, and cooking meals. These activities can be impacted by any one of several disease processes (stroke, arthritis, Alzheimer's disease, etc.), but are not negatively impacted by normative aging itself (e.g., Baltes & Smith, 2003). A healthy older adult should be able to accomplish their ADLs and IADLs with little trouble, even if the tasks are completed more slowly than they were in young adulthood. These measures are important in identifying early functional impairment, which can allow for early intervention (e.g., Brach et al., 2002). However, early intervention isn't always an easy feat. In a study by Brach et al. (2002), a group of older adults was measured on their ADLs and IADLs, as well as their perception of their own daily functioning. The comparison of perception and actual functioning demonstrated that these individuals were less aware of declines that were just beginning and were therefore less likely to report difficulties to their health care providers. That is, they reported tip-top functioning, though their IADLs were less than stellar. And, unfortunately, a delay in reporting any difficulties in functioning could mean the difference between timely intervention and more severe functional decline/lowered QoL. Moreover, if a goal of our older adult years (even within the context of disease) is to maintain independence, then accurate assessment and functional intervention is necessary earlier rather than later.

In instances where functional decline becomes too great, and difficulty in carrying out ADLs and IADLs is too large, the result is **disability** (Colón-Emeric et al., 2013)—that is, substantial limitation in at least one major life activity (see the Americans with Disabilities Act [ADA] for more information). Disability is not a death sentence, nor is it an indicator that one needs to resort to living in a communal living space or nursing home (more on that later). Rather, it is an indication that support is needed (e.g., Wilson et al., 2009). The type of support can be small, such as a meal delivery service rather than cooking one's own meals, or large, like having a home health aide come a few times a week to help with bathing. These supports can allow for better overall well-being (e.g., Murphy et al., 2009)—a factor that contributes to QoL.

While QoL is potentially different for everyone, there are some commonalities. A good QoL usually constitutes things like social and emotional health, physical well-being, life satisfaction, and happiness (e.g., Power et al., 1999). These components are arguably universal across individuals and across cultures, and because they are so pervasive, it seems logical to assume that we'll want to find ways to maintain and/or improve them for all. Drewnowski and Evans (2001) explored this idea through the relationship between physical activity, nutrition, and QoL. They argued that the impact of physical activity and nutrition on QoL is just as important as their impact on physical health measures, such as blood pressure and muscle strength. Additionally, a sense of personal control over dietary choices (and perhaps being able to cook them oneself, if that is something they enjoy), as well as enjoyment of physical activity, is important. This makes sense—we won't carry on eating or doing anything that we don't want to do for very long. Anecdotally, I can tell you that when older adults love their exercise, they will carry on for years and years. When I was a group fitness instructor, attendees of my classes were primarily women over 60. These women loved our classes and had been taking them for upwards of 20 years. In the class, they found physical activity, as well as positivity and friendships—contributing to social and emotional well-being and a good QoL. However, the extent to which an older adult's physical activity benefits their QoL is at least partly due to what they view as the importance of that physical activity (e.g., Stewart & King, 1991). That is, Stewart and King (1991) showed that physical activity is most impactful on the factor that is of most concern for the individual. If the older adult is already doing well physically/health-wise, then their perception of the impact of physical activity may be primarily on cognitive and socioemotional well-being. However, when health-related factors are of higher concern, those are the factors to receive the perceived benefit. Regardless, the QoL benefit is clear.

iStockPhoto/kali9

Disability and Compression of Morbidity

With functional changes seen in common disease processes in older adults (remember these are not a guarantee but are more likely to occur in our later years), there is also an increased likelihood of disability (e.g., Gill et al., 2006; Quiñones et al., 2016). However, the longer an older adult can stave off that decline in functioning, the less time one will spend in poor health. This **compression of morbidity** is the result not only of advances in health care that extend our life expectancy, but also of health care improving overall health at a higher rate than the extension of life expectancy (mostly due to the treatment and eradication of highly contagious diseases, like polio and tuberculosis; e.g., Chatterji et al., 2015; Fries, 2003). However, we should consider the difference between life expectancy and healthy life expectancy—with that difference largely due to the QoL during the time when one deals with illness and/or disability. Chatterji et al. (2015) suggest that health treatments and interventions have usually been aimed at fatal diseases, leaving other diseases to remain. While this is positive in the sense that we'd be keeping an individual from dying from a specific disease, it also means that when that individual has more than one illness (e.g., heart disease *and* arthritis), the other disease remains and can become the source of functional limitations. Therefore, lifestyle changes become increasingly important to maintain QoL and healthy life expectancy. For example, if treatment focuses on an individual's heart disease and cardiovascular function, that is fantastic. But their arthritis may not be treated with the same gusto, because arthritis is not fatal. This individual could then face limitations in mobility and difficulties opening jars and chopping vegetables (i.e., making nutritious meals). Not only would these limitations lower their ability to carry on with activities they once loved, reducing their QoL, but they also could backfire and impact the individual's heart disease—as would be the case in preparing nutritious meals. Ideally, then, treatment would focus more holistically on the entire well-being of the individual, rather than just the things that could lead to the end of life. Unfortunately, we aren't there yet.

Socioeconomic Health Gap

Interestingly, compression of morbidity seems to be specific to countries with higher incomes—though data from lower-income countries are scant (see Chatterji et al., 2015). However, the data that do exist suggest that developing countries see more poverty and insufficient access to proper health care. Compound those issues over a lifetime, and we get a scenario where disability in old age is more likely (Chatterji et al., 2015). Therefore, developing countries tend to report an expansion of morbidity (i.e., a larger amount of time spent ill or disabled before the end of life), rather than a compression of morbidity that we see in more developed countries (of course, this may change as we move forward into post-COVID-19 life). This distinction is just one example of the health discrepancies between individuals of different socioeconomic status, but there are certainly others.

ELDER CARE

With the concerns of the possibilities of functional limitations in older adulthood, in cases where illness strikes, the issue of continuing independent living becomes a very real question. For many, needing assistance for daily life is a very scary idea, especially for those in Western culture, as we place high value on our independence (e.g., Plath, 2008). Needing assistance is also difficult for us because of the way we see popular culture/media portray one of the few options of older adulthood—a nursing home—in a very negative light. If you remember the 1980s–1990s sitcom *The Golden Girls* (Harris et al., 1985–1992), two of the four women were a mother-daughter duo: Dorothy and Sophia. Dorothy jokingly threatens her mother, Sophia, with sending her to a nursing home each time Sophia annoys her. She says "Shady Pines, Ma," as if this nursing home is the worst of the worst places to be and Dorothy would leave her there to be neglected until she dies. While meant in a comedic context (and very sarcastic—definitely my love language), this is a fairly real fear embedded in how Western culture views older adulthood: When we get older, we either live with our child, or, if they don't want us, we go to "a home." However, this is far from the truth. There are many living options during older adulthood, including independent living. And nursing homes are usually reserved for those who need actual nursing care. From nurses.

Moviestore Collection Ltd/Alamy Stock Photo

Living options for older adulthood include independent living in one's own home, living with an adult child, retirement communities, assisted living, and skilled nursing facilities (e.g., Glaser, 1997; Tomassini et al., 2004)—though these options and the preferences for these options seem to be somewhat culture and income dependent (e.g., J. R. Beard & Bloom, 2015; Edmonds et al., 2005; Kamo & Zhou, 1994). These options are in gradation of care, from independently living in the home one always has lived in to living in a dorm-like facility with around-the-clock nursing care, and everything in between. For example, many older adults choose to live in retirement communities. These are ordinary neighborhoods whose residents are all over 60 (sometimes over 50). Here, residents need to do no upkeep on their property, but have all the independence they have always had. The difference is that their community is comprised of individuals like them, and the physical work of mowing the lawn, tending to the swimming pool, and so on is no longer their responsibility. Additionally, many of these communities have a clubhouse or community center, where activities are available for the residents, making community connections easier and allowing for older adults to stay active and engaged.

When an individual needs a bit more than just someone to take over the lawn and outdoor maintenance of their home, assisted living is helpful. Here, an older adult usually lives in an apartment-style community, where services are available as needed. These services range from light cleaning or meal prep to assistance with all IADLs. Usually, nursing care is not provided in an assisted living facility, but sometimes individuals can have home health aides come help with bathing and such a few times per week. However, when more medical assistance is needed and a nurse would be ideal, a nursing home is the place to be. Here, medical care and real licensed practical nurses (LPNs) and registered nurses (RNs) are available to administer medications, check vital signs, communicate with doctors, and so on (e.g., Bedin et al., 2013). In a nursing home, individuals also benefit from the same services that other living arrangements do—meals, cleaning, and help with bathing and other IADLs and ADLs. It is important that we understand that the fact someone is in a nursing home doesn't mean they aren't able to do *anything*. Rather, they need medical care that can't be administered in their home, or they have a medical condition that makes it unsafe for them to be alone in their home (Sherwin & Winsby, 2011). Importantly, Sherwin and Winsby (2011) explain that a nursing home *isn't* a complete loss of autonomy—this is an important distinction for patients, families, and nurses to understand. Allowing for considerations for what an individual *can* do, as part of their medical condition, cognitive capabilities, and social and emotional functioning, should be a top priority. Allowing for autonomy for the nursing home patient is important in their willingness to be there and their QoL overall (van Thiel & van Delden, 2001).

Along with loss of independence, admission to nursing homes is a specific point of fear for older adults (e.g., Quine & Morrell, 2007), though most older adults will not need to live in a nursing home. One of the factors that plays into this fear is the media's portrayal of nursing homes and the news stories we hear about horrible things happening in nursing homes (e.g., H. Beard & Payne, 2005)—including elder abuse and neglect. While vivid and scary, the instances of elder abuse we hear about in nursing homes are not the norm. Nor is elder abuse confined to nursing homes. We'll discuss this issue next.

Elder Mistreatment

Like any other group of people, older adults can be subject to abuse—physical abuse, psychological abuse, emotional abuse, sexual abuse, financial abuse, and even neglect. While not universal, or even very common, elder mistreatment (EM) happens enough to be of concern. The World Health Organization (WHO, 2015) reports rates between 2% and 14% worldwide. However, as you may suspect, it is very likely that these estimates are lower than what actually occurs because instances of abuse are often not reported due to their sensitive and/or personal nature. For instance, a victim may be reluctant to report financial abuse because their abuser was their adult child who took money out of entitlement (e.g., Bagshaw et al., 2013). Alternatively, the abuser may hold power over the older adult, as in the case of a caregiver—either at home or in a nursing home. Or, perhaps the older adult is married to the abuser, the individual is emotionally abusive, and they do not recognize it or classify it as abuse. All these scenarios and more can prevent reporting and/or recognition of EM (e.g., Schmeidel et al., 2012).

But, if this happens at least as often as is reported, what are the factors that put an individual at risk for abuse or abusive situations? And can we do something to intervene? Joosten and colleagues (2017) tell us that poor physical and mental health, functional dependence, cognitive impairment, or disability increase the risk of EM. Additionally, Johanneson and LoGiudice (2013) suggest that when caregiver stress and strained familial relationships are thrown into the mix, the risk gets higher. The New York State Elder Abuse Prevalence Study (Lachs & Berman, 2011) showed that individuals living in urban areas were up to 50% more likely to be victims of abuse, in any form. That said, there are some interventions that have been demonstrated to be effective, including Enhanced Multidisciplinary Teams (E-MDTs). These teams are comprised of accountants, lawyers, mental health providers, and law enforcement. This multifaceted approach allows for any type of abuse to be handled and provides support for the victim at the same time (Morano & Berical, 2022). To be sure, this type of intervention is effective, but prevention is also important (e.g., Stark, 2012). As individuals in communities across the world continue to get older, there will be more and more cases of EM, if the proportion of instances remains the same. Education about the occurrence and risk factors can help aid in prevention, though there is very little research on prevention, in comparison to that on intervention (Pillemer et al., 2016). However, along with education, Pillemer et al. (2016) offer additional suggestions for prevention of EM, including caregiver interventions (including respite care), money management programs, helplines, emergency shelters, and multidisciplinary teams (as described earlier for intervention). Recognition and understanding are the first steps in tackling this difficult problem.

AGING WELL: PHYSICAL CHANGES

Aging well physically happens when we understand the physical changes that occur normally, and how they differ from disease processes. Changes that occur with normative aging are small, and if we remain physically active (within reason), our body will do what it needs to do. The psychological ramifications of this, though, are a different story. It is common for those in Western culture to fight the aging process—from denying its existence (pluck those gray hairs, they never happened) to desperately doing anything to reverse it (Kim, please don't eat poop). Regardless, aging is going to happen. Allowing it to happen, changing our perspective toward it, and understanding that aging is normal, natural, and beautiful will help.

KEY TERMS

activities of daily living (ADLs)
ageism
antioxidants
compression of morbidity
disability
free radicals
Hayflick limit
instrumental activities of daily living (IADLs)
pruning
neural plasticity
osteoarthritis
osteoporosis
oxidation
quality of life (QoL)
rheumatoid arthritis
sarcopenia
telomeres

COMPREHENSION QUESTIONS

1. Explain some of the normative physical changes that occur with our appearance in older adulthood. Include changes in height, weight, skin, and hair.
2. How does aging occur at a cellular level? Describe the Hayflick limit and the oxidation process.

3. What are the hormonal shifts that occur during the aging process, and how do they impact fertility, reproduction, and other body systems?
4. How do neurological changes in aging occur, and how do they compare to those occurring in Alzheimer's disease?
5. How do chronic illnesses like osteoporosis and cardiovascular disease impact older adults?
6. Distinguish between osteoarthritis and rheumatoid arthritis, also addressing their specific impact on functional limitations.
7. How do ADLs and IADLs contribute to day-to-day functioning, and how are they used as a measure of functional limitations?
8. How does disability impact quality of life?
9. Explain the compression of morbidity and how it relates to disease, disability, and socioeconomic status.
10. Distinguish between senior living options.
11. What are the factors that contribute to the risk of elder abuse? What are options for intervention and prevention?

ADDITIONAL READINGS

Agnati, L. F., Zoli, M., Biagini, G., & Fuxe, K. (1992). Neuronal plasticity and ageing processes in the frame of the "Red Queen Theory." *Acta Physiologica Scandinavica, 145*(4), 301–309.

Akamigbo, A. B., & Wolinsky, F. D. (2007). New evidence of racial differences in access and their effects on the use of nursing homes among older adults. *Medical Care, 45*(7), 672–679.

Erickson, K. I., & Kramer, A. F. (2009). Aerobic exercise effects on cognitive and neural plasticity in older adults. *British Journal of Sports Medicine, 43*(1), 22–24.

Farage, M. A., Miller, K. W., Elsner, P., & Maibach, H. I. (2013). Characteristics of the aging skin. *Advances in Wound Care, 2*(1), 5–10.

Gosselink, C. A., Cox, D. L., McClure, S. J., & De Jong, M. L. (2008). Ravishing or ravaged: Women's relationships with women in the context of aging and Western beauty culture. *The International Journal of Aging and Human Development, 66*(4), 307–327.

Jiang, C., & Jiang, S. (2021). Elder mistreatment and life satisfaction of older adults: Mediating roles of emotional closeness with children and loneliness. *Journal of Elder Abuse and Neglect, 33*(5), 351–367.

Kirchengast, S., Peterson, B., Hauser, G., & Knogler, W. (2001). Body composition characteristics are associated with the bone density of the proximal femur end in middle- and old-aged women and men. *Maturitas, 39*(2), 133–145.

Leamnson, R. (2000). Learning as biological brain change. *Change: The Magazine of Higher Learning, 32*(6), 34–40.

Shay, J. W., & Wright, W. E. (2000). Hayflick, his limit, and cellular ageing. *Nature Reviews Molecular Cell Biology, 1*(1), 72–76.

iStockPhoto/funstock

2 SENSATION AND PERCEPTION

LEARNING OBJECTIVES

2.1 Discuss normative, common, and abnormal changes in vision.

2.2 Identify the limits of normal hearing as well as the psychosocial implications of hearing loss.

2.3 Discuss how touch, proprioception, and balance change with age.

2.4 Explain the interplay between taste and smell, their limited changes in older adulthood, and their link to cognitive impairment.

I was once in a book group at the public library. Every month, we would all check out the same book and then meet back up at the library to discuss the book. One member of the group, an older woman, would always check out an audiobook version of each month's selection to compensate for her visual deterioration caused from macular degeneration. However, one month, the book selection was not available on audiobook. So, her husband sat and read the book to her—all 500 pages of the historical romance novel (notably, this was not his preferred genre, nor is it mine). This was a sweet demonstration not only of the love he had for his wife, but of one of our fears surrounding the myth of sensory aging: that we'll inevitably lose our eyesight. This is a myth, fully and deeply. In this chapter, you will read that while there are some changes that occur with our eyes and vision as we age, losing our sight to the point of being unable to read even with the assistance of glasses is not a part of normal aging.

VISION

As we age, there are some normative changes that occur with the structure of the eye. And, while common, none of these inevitably lead to blindness. In fact, many of them require only small adjustments to our day-to-day life to approximate near-youthful eyesight.

First, we'll discuss the changes to the basic structures of the eye (see Figure 2.1). To address these, as well as the lifestyle and psychological impacts these changes may have, we should first review the basic flow of light information in the eye. When light from our environment comes to our eye, it first passes through the **cornea**. This structure is the clear outer coating of the eye itself. Its purpose is to protect the eye and maintain a balance of moisture, but also to focus light further into the eye. Next, light will move through the **pupil**, which necessarily dilates or contracts to allow more or less light into the eye (as needed, depending on the lighting in the environment). The pupil is controlled by the iris, the colored part of the eye, which dictates

FIGURE 2.1 ■ Anatomy of a Human Eye

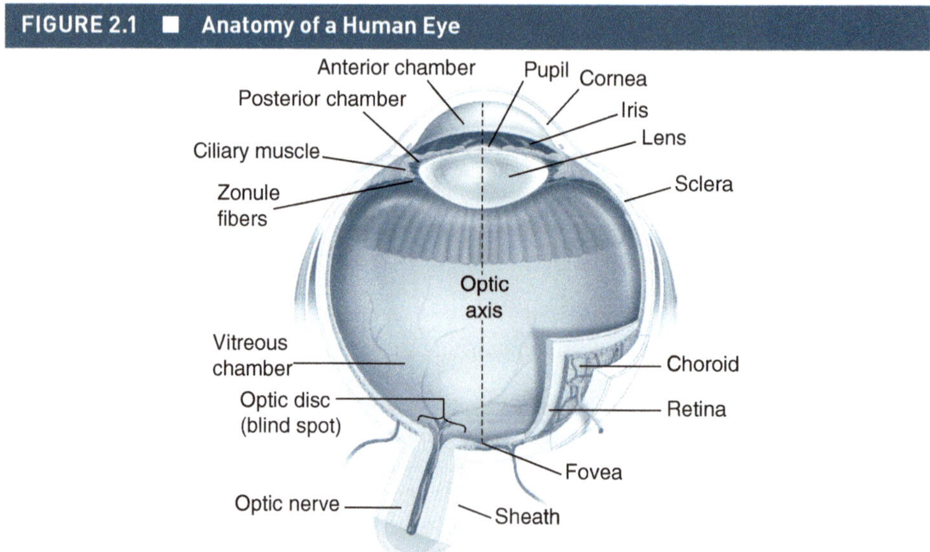

Source: Schwartz, B. L., & Krantz, J. H. (2023). *Sensation and perception*. SAGE, p. 69.

how much light the pupil should let in. Directly behind the pupil is the **lens**. The lens serves to complete the focusing of the light that is moving into the eye so that it can land properly on the back of the eye. To do this, the pupil will change shape, a process known as **accommodation**. It will get short and fat or long and thin or anything in between to do its job. Once the light lands on the back of the eye, an area known as the **retina**, receptors (called **rods and cones**) are waiting to transduce the light stimulus to neural signal. When **transduction** occurs, the environmental stimulus has changed format into something that the neurons and the brain can understand.

Now that we understand what happens to light as it moves through the sensory organ for vision, we can ask the question: What changes are reasonable to expect with age, and how might they affect day-to-day functioning?

Changes in the Cornea, Pupil, and Lens

The cornea, pupil, and lens serve to adjust and funnel light into our eye in a specific way that deals only with the stimulus itself. That is, these structures function early on in the process of taking in visual stimuli. As you can imagine, when changes happen to the structures that are responsible for focusing light, letting light in, and allowing for clear vision, a potential for noticeable vision changes arises.

With the cornea, there are a couple of small changes that an older adult may encounter. The first is dryness. Dry eyes can occur at any time during the lifetime, but in older age this is more common because of an inefficiency in the maintenance of hydration in the body (e.g., Lavizzo-Mourey, 1987; Walsh et al., 2012). The second change that can arise in the cornea has to do with ultraviolet (UV) exposure over time. Since an older adult has lived a longer life, it is likely that they have been exposed to more UV rays than, say, someone in their 20s. The impact of UV rays on the cornea is in its coloring (e.g., Lombardo et al., 2015; vanKujik, 1991)—making the cornea turn a bit yellow, like an old newspaper. This does not affect the function, per se, but does impact the type of light wavelengths that can move through the cornea and into the eye. With a yellowed cornea, an individual may prefer to see colors like red, orange, and yellow. However, besides mismatched clothes (e.g., a red shirt with yellow pants, because those are the colors someone with a yellowed cornea may prefer), the majority of integrity and functionality of the cornea remains intact. In addition to color changes, many older individuals may experience a thickening of the cornea (e.g., Hayashi et al., 1995). This may lead to incorrect focusing of the light entering the eye, and ultimately a need for contact lenses or glasses to adjust the light and compensate for the changes occurring in the cornea.

Similar to the cornea, the lens may also be impacted by UV light (e.g., Lindsey & Brown, 2002). Research demonstrates that exposure to UVB rays over time increases the **lens bruescence**, where lenses tend toward absorbing shorter wavelengths (blue) and allowing longer wavelengths (yellow and red) to pass through (e.g., Kessel et al., 2010; Lindsey & Brown, 2002), and can result in a lens nearly three times as dense in adults over 60 years of age as those under 60 (e.g., Pokorny et al. 1987). Like many normative changes within the eye, each of these is not a particular problem, but transmission of light through the lens as a whole spectrum may be problematic. Colors may look a little yellowed and less true than in younger eyes, and less light overall may get through. Less light overall through the lens can be problematic in dim-light situations in particular (e.g., Watson, 2001). With less light in the environment, even fewer light waves enter the eye. And, since light is information, the older adult will receive less information to their eye than is ideal.

Additionally, aging lenses may become harder. This hardening of the lens, known as **presbyopia**, starts as early as age 40 and can easily diminish the lens's ability to do its job (e.g., Patel & West, 2007). For a lens to focus light onto the retina, the lens needs to accommodate (i.e., change shape). A dense, hardened lens won't change shape easily, and the individual will experience blurry vision. You may notice an older adult (or yourself) stretching an arm out with a book or restaurant menu to get a "good look" at it. This isn't being dramatic, but rather the outstretched arm is holding the reading material at a place where the lens can focus it. Any closer, and the hardened lens can't fully adjust to focus the letters appropriately. The good news is that presbyopia is easily corrected with the use of glasses or contact lenses (e.g., Mercer et al., 2021; Wolffsohn & Davies, 2019). As long as the individual is willing to wear them, correction is easy.

Light entering the eye needs to pass through not only the cornea and the lens, but also the pupil. In fact, the pupil is the opening in which the light gets through to the lens. Any changes here can affect the flow of light to anything beyond it. And changes do occur. In older age, the ability of the pupil to dilate and allow more light into the eye can diminish (e.g., Bitsios et al., 1996; Daneault et al., 2012). The reason this occurs is the weakening in the ciliary muscles whose job it is to control the dilation (i.e., enlargement) and contraction (i.e., shrinking) of the pupil. When weakened, the pupil does not adjust properly to the changes in environmental light stimuli. In a bright situation, like outside in the middle of the afternoon, the sun can be particularly bothersome. The result of a pupil that does not fully dilate in dim light? Poorer vision. Light is information in our sense of vision, and as such we need the light to tell us what is in front of us. No light, no information. Less light, less information. The impact of the changes in the pupil can be difficulty in driving at night (though older adults' driving will be addressed more fully in Chapter 3), potential trip-and-falls from walking around one's home in the evening and night hours, and trouble in power outage situations (e.g., McMurdo & Gaskell, 1991).

Changes in the Retina

In addition to changes in the front portion of our eye, we can see some small changes to the back of our eye. The most common change here is one where the peripheral area of the retina thins out, resulting in a reduced concentration of the rods in our eye (e.g., Freund et al., 2011; Sturr et al., 1997). The purpose of the rods is to transduce light (i.e., convert light signal to neural signal), primarily in dim lighting situations. Fewer rods means less transduction (i.e., conversion to neural signal) in dim light. Couple this change with the reduced dilation of pupils discussed earlier, and we can see a significant impact in vision in dim-lighting scenarios. While there is not much we can do about preventing this change, as would be the case in preventing UV exposure and its impact on the cornea and lens, the solution here is adjustment to lighting in one's environment. As with the easy adjustments made to manage difficulty resulting from pupils' inefficient dilation, adding lighting around one's home can be achieved and can make a tremendous impact on visual experience.

Atypical Changes

While the changes described in the previous section are considered normative changes to aging eyes (I was reminded of presbyopia at my most recent trip to the optometrist: "You know what happens over age 40, right?"), there are some other changes that may represent something entirely different that are the result not of aging, but rather of illness. The experiences described as follows are not normative but may be common. And you may know many individuals who experience instances of cataracts, glaucoma, or macular degeneration. But anecdotal evidence aside, these are not universal, nor are they to be expected with advancing age. Aging does not equal disease.

Cataracts

If you have ever heard someone describe that they see "floaters," they are more than likely describing cataracts (see Figure 2.2). According to the University of Michigan Kellogg Eye Center (n.d.), "By age 65, over 90 percent of people have a cataract and half of the people between the ages of 75 and 85 have lost some vision due to a cataract." Cataracts (the most common of these atypical changes) result from protein buildup in the lens. This protein buildup can cause light to reflect incorrectly off the protein and become unfocused when finally landing on the retina. Alternatively, the cataracts may be sufficiently large as to block some light from going through the lens altogether. As you can imagine, both of these will result in poor vision. However, this change is something that simply slipping a pair of glasses on cannot reasonably fix. Treatment for cataracts is more involved, including lasers to break up the protein in smaller bits so as to not cloud the vision and/or complete lens replacements. These surgeries can help restore vision for an individual who has been struggling with the impact of cataracts, and can be a great relief (e.g., Stuen & Faye, 2003).

FIGURE 2.2 ■ Healthy Lens Compared to a Lens With Cataracts

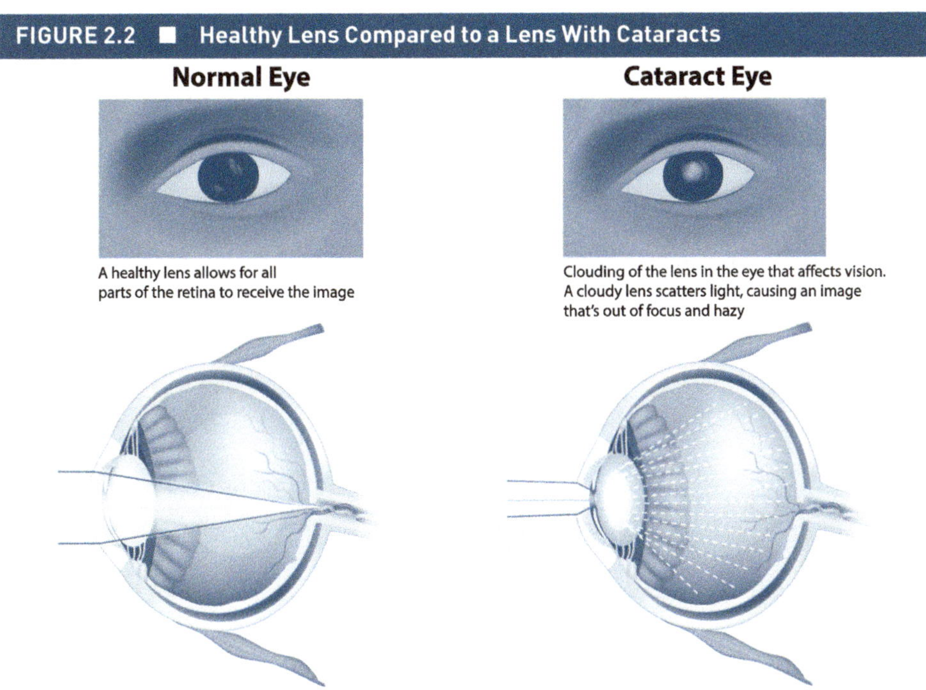

Source: https://glaucomaassociates.com/wp-content/uploads/2017/10/Cataract-cloudy-vision.jpg

Glaucoma

Like cataracts, glaucoma can occur in conjunction with any or all normative vision changes. According to the National Institutes of Health, National Eye Institute (2010b), Black Americans are most at risk for developing glaucoma (compared to white Americans, Hispanic Americans, or those identifying as *other race*), with nearly 6% of Black Americans over the age of 60 inflicted. This rate increases to 12% for individuals over the age of 80 (National Institutes of Health, National Eye Institute, 2010b). In this illness, an individual experiences increased pressure within the eye (i.e., intraocular pressure). Some amount of pressure pushing outward from the inside of the eye is good. It allows the eye to keep its shape and allows for fluid exchange around the eye. However, too much pressure can cause problems in the retina, and for the optic nerve. Pushing too hard on the optic nerve can result in the delay or cessation of sending signals from the eye to the brain. Checking the pressure in your eye is a regular part of a thorough eye exam, and you likely have experienced it with a small tool (called a *tonometer*) applied to the front of the eye (Icahn School of Medicine at Mount Sinai, 2024). Most individuals come away from this exam with a clean bill of health and return in a year or two to check again. If pressure is too much, the optometrist or ophthalmologist may prescribe treatment to bring down the pressure before damage to the eye and/or optic nerve occurs. Adjustment here for eye health is (once again) more than just a pair of glasses or contact lenses. Often, eye drops designed to lower and maintain proper pressure in the eye are given (e.g., Xalatan or Rescula; Sponsel et al., 2002), along with continual checkups by an optometrist or ophthalmologist to monitor any future changes in pressure or progression of glaucoma or vision loss.

An older adult is getting an eye exam, which often includes a test for glaucoma.

Macular Degeneration

This final of the eye-related illnesses we'll discuss is one that affects the retina. This is the one that affected my fellow book club member, ultimately preventing her from reading books the way she always had. Age-related macular degeneration, in both its wet and dry forms, affects approximately 2% of adults over the age of 50, with the largest proportion of these individuals experiencing dry macular degeneration (see National Institutes of Health, National Eye Institute, 2010a). In macular degeneration, an individual's **macula** begins to deteriorate. The macula is the center of focus on the retina, where the main object in a scene (e.g., the letters on a page or screen as you read) is focused. As it deteriorates, the receptors (i.e., rods and cones) in the macula no longer serve their function to transduce light into its corresponding neural signal. Over time, the area of the retina that is affected expands, moving outward from the center of focus. In macular degeneration, an individual loses vision in their center of focus that slowly moves beyond the center and begins to impinge on the periphery.

Approximately 90% of instances of age-related macular degeneration are what are called dry AMD (e.g., Salvi et al., 2006). In these cases, individuals experience damage to and atrophy of the cells in the center of focus. Vision is gradually distorted and progresses toward vision loss. The other approximately 10% of cases of age-related macular degeneration are referred to as wet AMD. Here, fluid leakage (hence why it's called *wet*) from abnormal vessels in the retina lifts and separates the layers of the retina at the macula area. As leakage progresses, so does vision loss. Individuals with a family history of macular degeneration (as well as those with a history of smoking behaviors) have an increased likelihood of developing AMD in their later years. However, research suggests that quitting smoking, eating dark leafy vegetables (such as spinach or kale), and supplementation with vitamin C, vitamin E, and beta-carotene can mediate the risk of progression to advanced AMD (e.g., Salvi et al., 2006). The Amsler Grid, pictured in Figure 2.3, is one tool that the optometrist/ophthalmologist will use to test for macular degeneration.

Effects of and Adjustments to Visual Changes

The effects of changes in vision can range from small wonderings about needing glasses to large changes in lifestyle. However, as we'll see, the psychological and behavioral implications can be significant, even in the most subtle of normative eye changes.

Driving at Night

With the changes that we commonly see in the pupil and reduction in the concentration of rods, we may see a significant impact on an individual's ability to see in the dark. This has a large behavioral impact in their ability to drive at night (e.g., Gruber et al., 2013; West et al., 2003). Imagine guiding a large motor vehicle down a highway at 70 miles per hour, only to realize that you can't see the lane lines or the cars that are stopped up ahead. Not only could that be terrifying for the driver, but it would also be dangerous for all involved, including the other drivers on the road. The discovery of changes to night vision could necessarily impact someone's desire to or ability to travel after the sun goes down. The trickle effect of this change could mean

FIGURE 2.3 ■ Amsler Grid

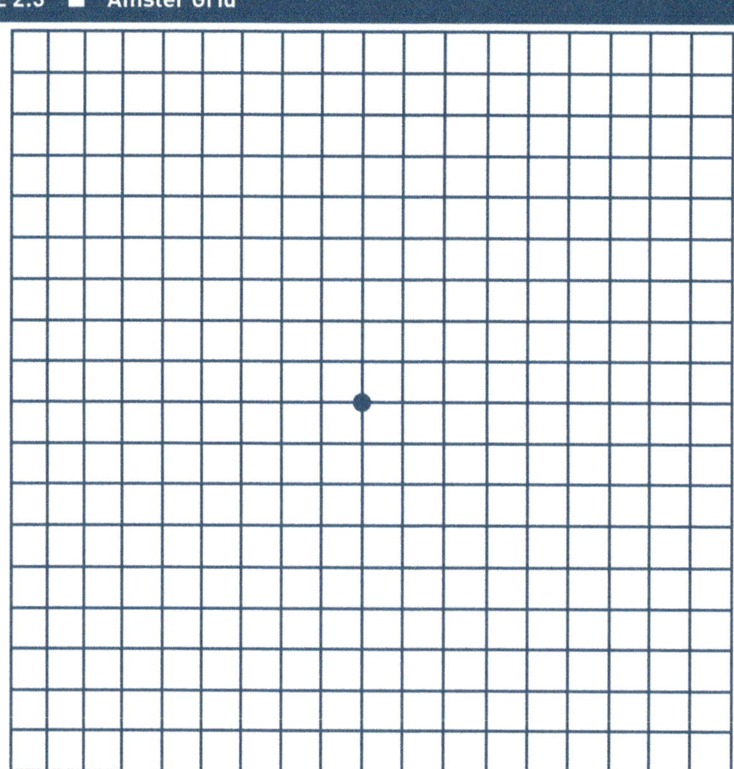

Source: https://www.aao.org/image.axd?id=4a0d828b-c698-47cf-9455-e265332e7968&t=635998033438800000

disengagement from their community (e.g., no more evening club or town meetings), or a feeling of losing independence and "becoming a burden" on friends and family (e.g., Burmedi et al., 2002). While neither of these are always necessary, some amount of creativity in working around this limitation is needed (e.g., Gottlieb & Gillespie, 2008) to avoid the negative mental health and socioemotional outcomes that may result from that sort of disconnection (e.g., Burmedi et al., 2002). However, vision is just one contributor to success, confidence, and safety while driving; further discussion of this topic can be found in Chapter 3, where we'll address perception and attention (the next steps in information processing) with respect to driving as well.

At Home

A reduction of visual capacity in dim lighting doesn't just affect driving. Hazards can also exist within the home, impacting how one moves around their living space (e.g., Lord, 2006). Poor lighting or getting up in the middle of the night to use the restroom could be dangerous. Imagine not seeing the edge of the stairs. Yikes! Fortunately, night lights are an inexpensive tool to plug in and increase the lighting around your home. They are even available with an automatic sensor that turns on and off depending on how much ambient light is available in the area. Additionally, marking the edge of the stairs with brightly colored tape can enhance them, even when light is scarce (e.g., McMurdo & Gaskell, 1991). Creativity and adaptability are key here, though. Being able to adapt to changes allows for independent living, rather than limiting behavior (e.g., Steinman et al., 2009)—and, truth be told, many of these adjustments are great for people of all ages and ranges of abilities.

Changes in Reading Behaviors

Reading behaviors can be severely impacted by even just a small, normative age-related vision change (e.g., Goertz et al., 2014). For individuals who've lived with typical/healthy vision their whole lives, this can be quite impactful. Remember our discussion on presbyopia from earlier in this chapter? Presbyopia can put a damper on an individual's reading behavior because the hardening of the lens limits the lens's ability to do its job to focus the small letters onto the retina, leaving the reader to do it on their own—moving the reading material further and further away from their eyes until it is in focus. The problem here is that our arms are only so long, and at some point we're putting additional strain on the lens and increasing the likelihood of a headache (Patel & West, 2007). Moving to a point where an older adult needs glasses to adjust for presbyopia can signal to a person that they are getting older. Admitting to the need for glasses (and actually using them) and an option for books in large print are reasonable accommodations for this normative vision change (e.g., Whiteside et al., 2006).

HEARING

There are several different types of hearing changes to anticipate with advancing age, but many of them are not noticeable until far into our old age (e.g., age 80 or beyond)—researchers often refer to individuals in these age groups as the oldest old (e.g., Solé-Auró & Crimmins, 2013; VonFaber et al., 2001). This section will discuss normative and non-normative age-related changes in hearing, accommodations and adjustments we can make as speakers or listeners, and the impact changes in hearing may have on relationships and social interactions.

Presbycusis

One hearing change that we may experience is called **presbycusis**. Presbycusis occurs when an individual loses detection of high-frequency hearing (i.e., sounds that come in at a higher pitch). This type of hearing loss, which occurs when years and years of listening to loud sounds add on to a genetic predisposition (Gates & Mills, 2005), can begin as early as age 60 (though it isn't often noticeable until many years later) and is quite common past the age of 80 (Walling & Dickson, 2012). The loss of high-frequency hearing can significantly impact speech perception—an important part of life as a human. And, interestingly, Gates and Mills (2005) report that many of the complaints of those encountering presbycusis are not that they can't hear, but that they can't understand what's being said. I'm sure you can imagine that the social implications of hearing loss are large (and we'll address those in just a bit). And while presbycusis is specific to high-frequency hearing, many individuals use this term interchangeably with age-related hearing loss because, when progressed, presbycusis can ultimately move toward lower-frequency ranges of hearing. And, when it does, it encroaches on speech perception and communication, especially in noisy environments (Gates & Mills, 2005). But the result is the same: loss of hearing. The cause can be one of many.

Changes in the **cochlea** (in the inner ear, shown in Figure 2.4) and in the **auditory nerve** (carrying signals out of the ear to the brain), as well as changes in the **tympanic membrane** (i.e., the ear drum) and neurons in the auditory centers in the brain, can result in a markedly increased **auditory threshold**—where the quietest sound an individual can detect is louder than it was at a younger age (see Figure 2.5). Thresholds can increase as much as 40 decibels for the high-frequency range of sounds (Gates et al., 2008; Wiley et al., 2008). Individuals most at risk for developing presbycusis are those with a family history of age-related hearing loss, those who are exposed to loud noises as part of their occupation, those who smoke, and those with hypertension (i.e., high blood pressure) or kidney disease (e.g., Gates & Mills, 2005). Moreover, some medications may accelerate and/or exacerbate high-frequency hearing loss (Joo et al., 2020). Any neural loss that occurs as the result of stroke, injury, or general atrophy can also impact the progression of hearing loss (e.g., Kuo et al., 2016; Walling & Dickson, 2012).

One common presentation of age-related hearing loss is the result of hardening or stiffening of the membranes in the ear (Purdy, 2001), including the tympanic membrane or the basilar membrane in the cochlea. Regardless of which membrane begins to harden, the result is the same: The membrane doesn't move the way it should, to progress the sound waves into the ear

FIGURE 2.4 ■ Anatomy of the Human Ear

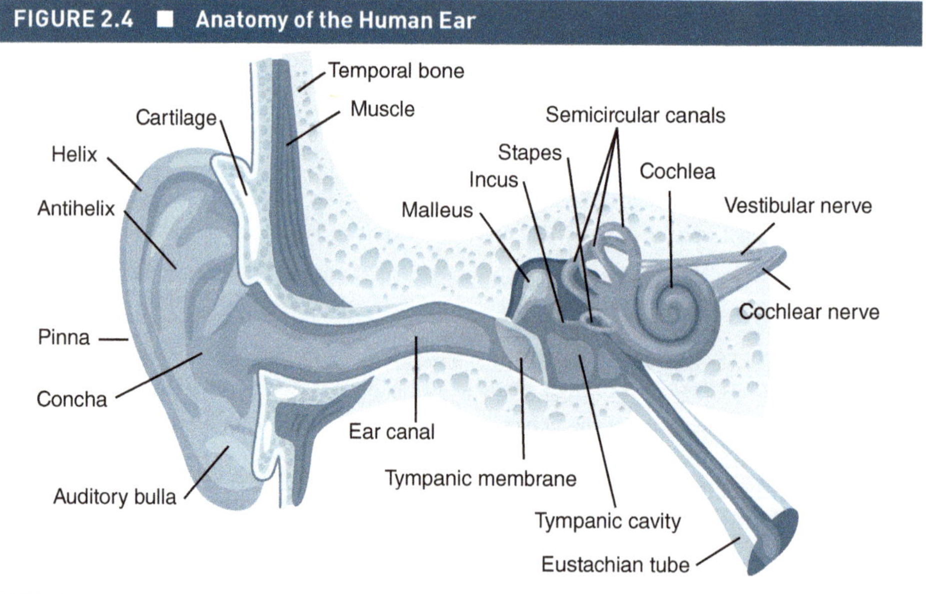

Source: https://media.istockphoto.com/id/1150305939/vector/human-ear-anatomy-ears-inner-structure-organ-of-hearing-vector-illustration.jpg?s=612x612&w=0&k=20&c=6BNBHTPNY9ZkGgTWHFU7-or-UKRrPSKjYH_2Tlzzfu4=

FIGURE 2.5 ■ Threshold Changes for Older Adults

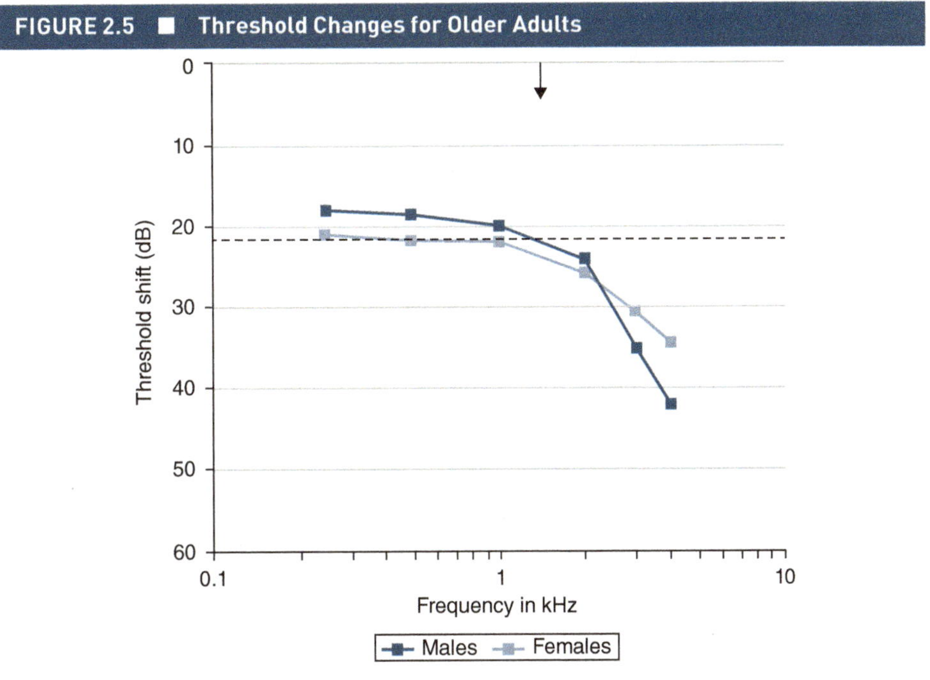

Source: Gates, G. A., & Mills, J. H. (2005). Presbycusis. *The Lancet, 366,* 1111–1120.

to be transformed into a neural signal for the brain. Those sound waves are the stimulus we need to hear, and without the membrane moving them into the auditory system at a sufficient amplitude, hearing won't occur.

Other types of hearing changes that an older adult may experience are the result of damage to hair cells or changes in neurons (Walling & Dickson, 2012). Damage to hair cells often comes from prolonged exposure to loud sounds, which can happen over a lifetime and affect the onset of hearing loss (e.g., Cruickshanks et al., 2010). When hair cells are damaged, they cannot serve their purpose: to transform sound waves into neural signal (i.e., transduction). So, the sound signal will never get past the ear. Only neural changes happen after that point in the hearing process, as degradation of the auditory nerve, atrophy of neurons in the brain stem, or even **apoptosis** (i.e., programmed cell death) of neurons in the temporal lobes and beyond (e.g., Eckert et al., 2019; Golub, 2017). Once sound gets transduced into neural signal—any changes that can happen in the auditory nerve, in the brain stem, or into the hearing centers of the brain—the temporal lobe can impact hearing at the neural level. Neural changes can be the result of atypical aging (e.g., Alzheimer's disease or stroke) or advanced age (i.e., those in the oldest-old group). Regardless, the result will be a loss of hearing that simply raising the volume cannot remedy.

However, there are instances when presbycusis is not only *not* harmful, but maybe useful. One example is the implementation of the *mosquito tone.* A Welsh security firm first developed the mosquito tone to combat young people taking over a shopping district. More older adults liked to shop in that shopping district, but the young adults and teenagers would create problems, mischief, and ruckus, and the older adults would be annoyed. Since these businesses' target clientele was the older adults, the younger individuals were driving away their sales opportunities. In response, the security firm decided to play a very high-pitched (high-frequency) tone, which bothered the young people—they left. The older people, some of whom dealt with presbycusis, didn't feel the effects because they didn't hear the sound. It's sort of the same premise as a dog whistle. It's high enough for dogs to hear, but not in the range for human hearing so humans don't get bothered by it. The mosquito tone was high enough to be within the range that younger people could hear but many older people couldn't. According to my students, this sound has more recently been developed into a cell phone ringtone—presumably so the younger students can hear their phones and their older teachers won't. Nobody has yet to admit using it in my class (ha ha!).

iStockPhoto/kali9

Effects of and Adjustments to Hearing Changes

As with changes in vision, living a whole life with healthy hearing and then experiencing changes can be quite challenging. I know this to be true from personal experience—as I am now the proud owner of significant hearing loss in my right ear. While I use this to my advantage, needing to cover only my left ear when I want it to be quiet, it is also difficult. I often find myself asking my family and my students to repeat themselves, and then feel bad when I've asked them to do so several times in a row. I know it's frustrating for them too. And certainly, conversations are interrupted, are misunderstood, or at the very least lack the flow that they once did. Social implications for hearing loss are large because, as humans, it is in our very nature to communicate through speech—and when that's how we've done it our whole lives, and it needs to change, the adjustment can be difficult.

Social Isolation

In many cases, the result of hearing loss can be unnoticed for a very long time. We can compensate for many things in our life—ask our friends and family to speak louder, ask people to repeat themselves, and turn up the volume on the television and radio. Add this to the social stigma associated with getting older and hearing aids (e.g., Wallhagen, 2010), and we can see that an older adult may be resistant to using this tool. In fact, some estimates are that only 30% to 40% of individuals who have a hearing aid actually use it (Barker et al., 2016; Hanratty & Lawlor, 2000).

However, at some point, the resistance becomes problematic (who wants to ask their friend to repeat themselves 16 times? That's where I was at. And it's hard), and without compensation we can experience things like social isolation (e.g., Maharani et al., 2019; Mick et al., 2014; Shukla et al., 2020). When we can't engage in conversation with more than one person because following the conversation across a large group or incorporating lipreading becomes too complex, we give up.

Social isolation is the last thing we want to happen in our later years. Social support is important, and without it, many older adults decline quickly (e.g., Mick & Pichora-Fuller, 2016). Social support (discussed in Chapters 8 and 10) can help with coping (Krause, 1986) and cognitive stimulation (e.g., Adams et al., 2002) and can even contribute to maintaining physical well-being through activity (e.g., Fransen et al., 2015). But, the loss of hearing can make social situations difficult, frustrating, and unappealing (e.g., Ciorba et al., 2012). Additionally, hearing loss can result in the degradation of the quality of life (e.g., Ciorba et al., 2012; Mosnier et al., 2015).

Research on the relationship between hearing loss and social isolation further demonstrates that self-reports of hearing loss are associated not just with isolation, but with the psychological ramifications of that isolation (e.g., depression and mood changes; Saito et al., 2010; Tambs, 2004). In a longitudinal study on hearing loss, social isolation, and cognitive function, Maharani and colleagues (2019) examined the relationships between these variables. Specifically, these researchers investigated what they called the "cascade hypothesis" in adults over age 50—that hearing loss cascades down the line to social isolation, loneliness, and cognitive decline. This hypothesis was supported by the data, demonstrating that the worse an individual's hearing status, the more likely the same individual would score high on the social isolation and loneliness measures. Additionally, results showed that when an individual showed severe loneliness, they also were likely to demonstrate cognitive impairment. Moreover, data showed a direct connection between hearing impairment and cognitive function, which the researchers explained could be the result of poor input. Without stimulation going in through hearing stimuli, the brain becomes starved of information, resulting in cognitive impairments. This explanation is supported in neuroimaging studies that show clear brain atrophy in individuals who've had long-term uncorrected hearing loss (e.g., Peelle et al., 2011).

There is good news, however: Remediation works. That is, research has also demonstrated that corrected hearing—whether by hearing aid (e.g., Weinstein et al., 2015) or by cochlear implant (e.g., Mosnier et al., 2015)—can create positive change to the cognitive capabilities, quality of communication with others, social and emotional well-being, and overall quality of life. In practice, Weinstein et al. (2015) evaluated patients at an audiology clinic before and after hearing aid fittings. These patients averaged 80 years of age and were getting hearing aids for the first time. Measures of social and emotional loneliness as well as perceived social isolation demonstrated some positive changes after just four to six weeks of hearing aid use. At postmeasure, patients with moderate or severe hearing loss demonstrated significant improvements in their social and emotional loneliness measures as well as their perceived judgments of social isolation. These results clearly demonstrate that the hearing aid was beneficial for these individuals and may serve as a tool to help reverse the social and emotional implications of hearing loss.

Impact on IADLs

In day-to-day life, individuals who have lost even some of their hearing can feel an impact on their ability to complete the activities they are used to doing. For example, someone experiencing hearing loss may not be able to make a phone call to the bank when they see a discrepancy on their bank statement because hearing the bank representative on the other end of the phone will be difficult. The result? Their bank account discrepancy remains, or they must rely on others to do this for them. Certainly, this instance is unappealing and requires disclosing private information. Tasks such as these are known as IADLs, or instrumental activities of daily living, introduced in Chapter 1 (Elsawy & Higgins, 2011). While these activities are not required for survival (as are activities of daily living, or ADLs, like eating and drinking), tasks like balancing a bank account, going grocery shopping, doing laundry, navigating public transportation, and other daily tasks required for independent living are still important. Loss of hearing can impact these tasks (e.g., Borda et al., 2019; Keller et al., 1999) and result in a lower quality of life. Research on the impact of hearing loss on IADLs shows that individuals with significant hearing loss who do not use a hearing aid show marked impairments in their performance on IADLs compared to individuals without hearing loss (e.g., Borda et al., 2019).

Strategies to Help

Perhaps one of the most common, and obvious, ways to help an older adult with hearing loss is with a hearing aid. Hearing aids can be quite helpful in increasing the volume/amplitude of the incoming sound. Research on the impact of hearing aids demonstrates that their use can improve older adults' execution of IADLs, making their performance comparable to that of an individual without any hearing loss (e.g., Borda et al., 2019).

How could something so small have such a profound impact? If the individual's hearing loss is the result of stiffening of membranes (tympanic and/or basilar), increasing the amplitude of sound (and thereby increasing the force with which the membranes are pushed) can be an effective way of getting the membranes to move the way they need to in order to get the sound stimulus into the auditory system. However, with every solution comes some pitfalls. Hearing aids can increase sounds' volume, but when we increase both the sounds we want to hear and the sounds we don't want to hear, we may still have trouble. The trouble here is being able to differentiate between the target sound and the background noise. Luckily, modern models of hearing aids have been able to adjust and accommodate for that, allowing the devices to amplify speech sounds and not amplify sounds occurring in other frequency ranges (Hear.com, 2023).

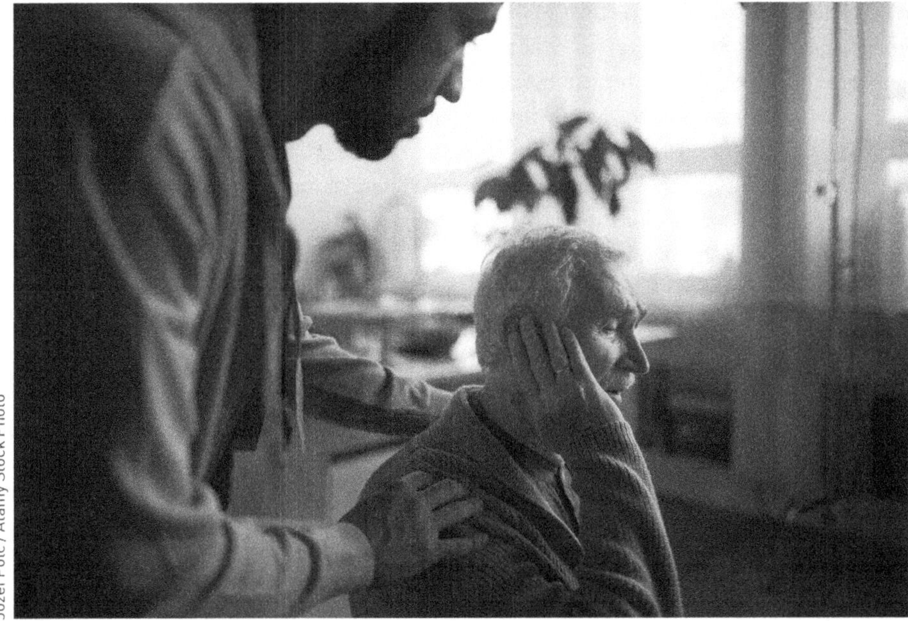

Jozef Polc / Alamy Stock Photo

Listening to others in a crowded environment can be difficult.

Unfortunately, like much of the thought surrounding the aging process, there is a stigma surrounding the use of hearing aids (e.g., David & Werner, 2016; Wallhagen, 2010). There is an idea that "hearing aids are for old people," and if we need one, we may be reluctant to use it, lest we accept that we are aging and no longer a desired "youth." The truth of the matter is that hearing aids can be very useful in any individual (young and older) whose hearing loss comes from a mechanical issue like a hardening of the membranes in the ear (e.g., Walden & Walden, 2004). The hearing aid will amplify the sound waves, making a louder volume of sound. The louder volume will push more forcefully on the hardened membranes in the ear and can be particularly helpful in situations where you can't turn up the volume (e.g., a family dinner conversation). However, in instances where hearing loss is due to damage to hair cells in the cochlea or a neural issue, as may occur in the auditory nerve, the temporal lobe, or the hearing centers of the brain or brainstem, increasing volume isn't helpful. Compensation here is more challenging.

In response to a loss of hearing function from problems at transduction (the hair cells), a cochlear implant may be suggested. A cochlear implant stimulates the auditory nerve, instead of allowing the hair cells to serve that function, thus bypassing the mechanical portion of the auditory system (F. R. Lin et al., 2012). While older adults are eligible for cochlear implants, a cochlear implant is not always an ideal solution for an older adult. The rationale here is that a cochlear implant provides an electrical impulse to stimulate the auditory nerve but isn't the same as a sound stimulus. Therefore, a degree of learning about this new kind of stimulus is necessary to adjust to the implant (Glennon et al., 2020). This works well in a younger person's neural system that has not already spent half a century learning sounds and wiring the brain to those connections. Learning for an older adult can be slower and more effortful (as you'll learn in later chapters). Adding this effort to our later years may be beneficial for some individuals, but for others it may not be worth it. The additional time, energy, and mental effort to adjust to the new kind of sound stimulus, alongside the risks associated with the surgery of implanting the cochlear implant itself, need to be weighed against the benefits of regaining hearing function. For many, the benefits don't outweigh the costs. That's not to say that age should eliminate one from considering a cochlear implant, but some considerations of just how much improvement can be made over the long term should be had (e.g., Hiel et al., 2016). Other adjustments can also be included in remediation for hearing loss, such as speechreading, closed captioning, and auditory training (Dubno, 2013). Assisted listening devices, including vibrating alarm clocks, flashing-light doorbells, and the like, can also be helpful for individuals adapting to hearing loss.

The good news is that aging alone does not cause hearing loss, and hearing loss is not universal (F. R. Lin et al., 2011). F. R. Lin et al. (2011) report that only about one-third of adults between ages 65 and 75 experience notable hearing loss, and this statistic only jumps to about half of older adults over the age of 75. Much of the hearing loss individuals experience is minor and manageable with things such as the closed-captioning function on the television or leaning on the support of friends and family (e.g., Moser et al., 2017). These social supports can do things like turn down the background noise and speak directly to you so you can see their lips to facilitate speechreading. They can speak clearly, being careful not to "dumb down" the language—this is termed **elderspeak** and can be condescending and insulting to an older adult (Kemper, 1994). The individual has lost hearing, not cognitive capacity. Here, support matters and can help in the compensation and adaptation for an older adult (Williams et al., 2005). In the context of social support, not only can older adults with hearing loss manage, but they can thrive. There is no need to limit oneself when there are supports and tools.

TOUCH, PROPRIOCEPTION, AND BALANCE

Touch, proprioception (i.e., limb and body position), and balance are discussed together in this section because of their relationship with one another. Additionally, changes in the mechanisms in the skin, and the skin itself, are related to temperature regulation (e.g., Blatteis, 2012; Kenney & Munce, 2003). What we may have heard or experienced, anecdotally, is that older adults are always cold and are most certainly at risk for falling and breaking their hips. While some individuals are in line with this myth, like many things discussed in this book, it is not the default or inevitable way of aging. Understanding changes in the skin, the touch receptors, and the other related mechanisms will help us distinguish typical aging from disease-related changes and further understand the simple modifications we can make to help an older adult adapt to minor or moderate changes. Adaptation isn't necessarily negative.

Skin

Much like the other sensory organs, skin has receptors to help take information from the environment and turn it into neural signal (i.e., transduction). In the skin, these receptors are called **mechanoreceptors** (see Figure 2.6) (Hao et al., 2015). Four types of mechanoreceptors in the

FIGURE 2.6 ■ Mechanoreceptors in the Skin

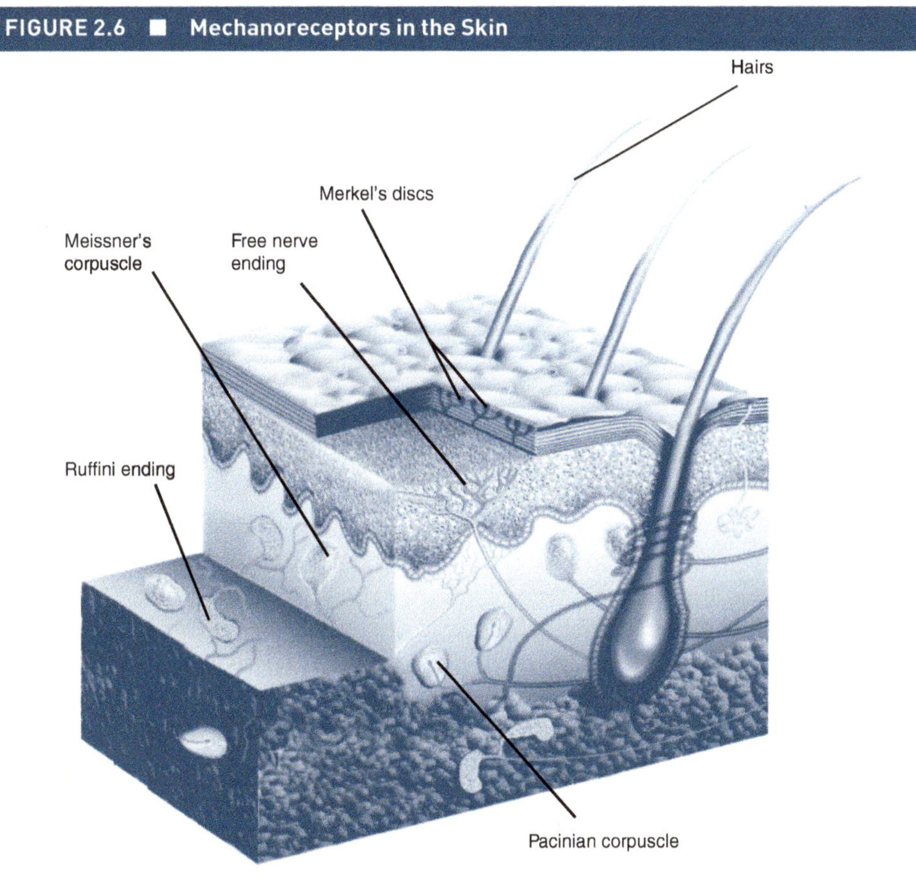

Source: Schwartz, B. L., & Krantz, J. H. (2023). *Sensation and perception*. SAGE, p. 454.

skin differentially respond to different types of stimuli. For example, one type of mechanoreceptor might respond to heat, while another would respond to pressure. The distribution of mechanoreceptors in our skin is dependent on the sensitivity of the area of the body, and the necessary precision needed within the sense of touch (e.g., Vallbo & Johansson, 1984). That is, there are more tightly packed mechanoreceptors in the fingertips than in the back of the leg to more precisely define the touch in the fingertips—as would be necessary in a task like typing. The back of the leg doesn't need that level of specification.

With age, we can see a change in mechanoreceptor distribution along with a thinning of the layers of the skin. Together, these can have implications on an older adult's ability to discriminate and identify by touch (e.g., feeling the difference in the shape and size of an object), temperature regulation, hydration levels, and sensitivity to pain and heat (e.g., García-Piqueras et al., 2019).

However, these changes need not be limiting. In fact, some research has demonstrated that maintaining attention to touch throughout the lifetime, as does someone who is blind and reads Braille with their fingertips or someone who plays the piano proficiently and often, can allow an individual to retain precision in this sense (e.g., Legge et al., 2019). Other research has shown that older adults simply need to change their strategy. Norman et al. (2013) asked young and older participants to judge the curvature of an object using either static or dynamic touch (i.e., touching when holding an object still vs. manipulating it in the hands). When using static touch, older adults performed more poorly than young adults. However, when using dynamic touch, older adults were able to judge the curvature of an object just as effectively as a young adult. The shift in strategy to moving the hands along the object changed which mechanoreceptors were responding (and in which proportions) as well as began to involve the muscles and joints (and their corresponding neurons). The additional information facilitated their judgments and resulted in better task performance. This is consistent with previous research demonstrating additional proprioceptive (limb position) information from active touch, providing support for object and shape perception (e.g., Gibson, 1962; Heller & Myers, 1983).

Temperature Regulation

With the thinning of the skin, an older adult may be more susceptible to some physiological changes that can make temperature regulation more difficult (Blatteis, 2012). One of the reasons for this is that when skin thins, it loses moisture more easily, leaving the older adult more vulnerable to dehydration (e.g., Farage et al., 2008, 2013) as well as other outside influences like weather. When an individual becomes dehydrated, their ability to maintain internal temperatures in the context of more extreme hot and cold temperatures becomes more difficult (e.g., Calleja-Aguis et al., 2007; Gross et al., 1992). This might be why older adults may be more inclined to adjust living situations to make themselves more comfortable and ease the strain on their body's temperature regulation system (see Figure 2.7). That is, when they have the financial means to do so, older adults may want to stay in their northern home in the summer and a southern home in the winter (for an individual in the United States or Canada)—individuals engaging in this type of shifts in residency are commonly called *snowbirds*. In fact, rates of this temporary migration show Florida, Arizona, and Texas as common locations for older adults to spend their winters (e.g., Smith & House, 2006), where weather is consistently warm through most months of the year. This pattern allows individuals to escape both extreme cold (as they'd experience in the northern winters) and extreme heat (as they'd experience in southern summers).

Alternatively, an older adult may wish to simply stay inside more often, where they can control the temperature of their home with the use of central air-conditioning and heat. However, there are implications to this with regard to social relationships. Staying in one's own home constantly removes the individual from social situations in which they are likely to engage with others in conversation, and other more physically active hobbies (e.g., Barrenetxea et al., 2022; Cornwell & Waite, 2009). Not only could this be detrimental to an older adult's social relationships, but it could play a negative role in their physical health as well (e.g., Cornwell & Waite, 2009; Farrell et al., 2022; Holt-Lunstad, 2017).

The positive aspect of these changes is that it really is relatively simple to be able to maintain temperature regulatory systems, or assist them, with the right preparation. Hydration is important; drinking water from a special cup—many people find using a straw an effective way of

FIGURE 2.7 ■ Older Adult Migratory Behavior, Based on Temperature Changes Throughout the Year

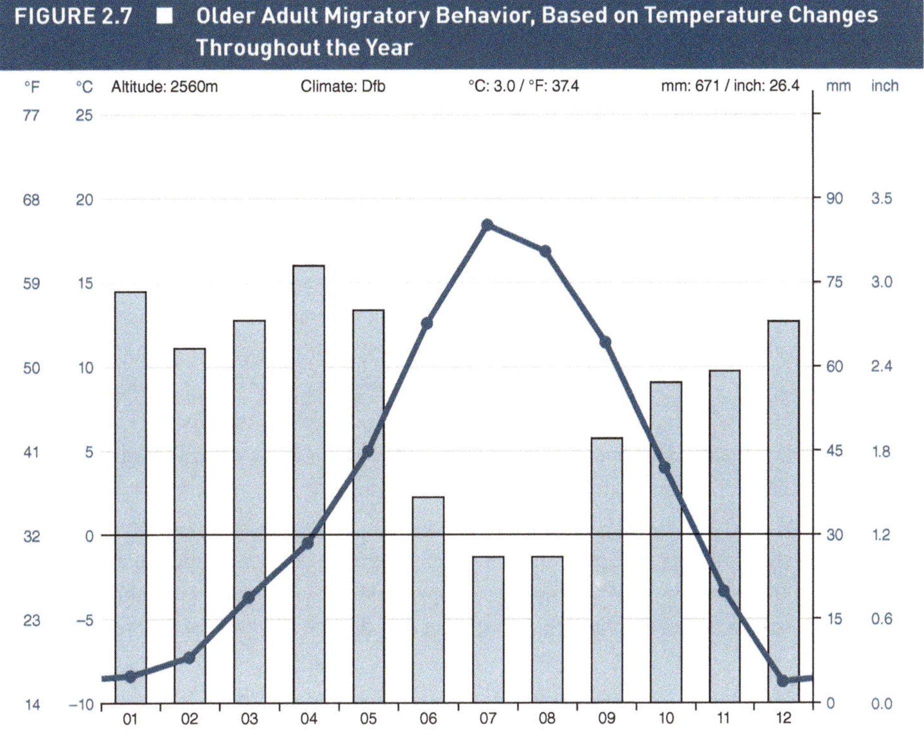

Source: https://images.climate-data.org/location/124464/climate-graph.png

drinking more water (see Williams Integracare Clinic [n.d.] for more information)—or keeping a pitcher on your kitchen counter to pour from all day can make this easy. Taking advantage of resources to maintain cooler temperatures in the summer and warmer temperatures in the winter may be easy with central air-conditioning and heat but may be more difficult without these resources available in the home. And, of course, these are not available to everyone at every income level. However, free community resources like a library are not only readily available in most every town and city, but they have temperature regulation to make their patrons comfortable and provide mentally and socially stimulating contexts in which to continue to engage with one's community.

Vestibular System

Relatedly, the **vestibular system**—the multi-organ system that helps one maintain balance in the body—can be of concern in an older adult. In a typically aging individual, there are some changes to the vestibular system having to do with the interplay of the functioning in the inner ear, the vestibulo-ocular reflex, and postural reflexes (e.g., Hall & Meldrum, 2016). Within the ear, the fluid in the inner ear needs to be balanced and pressurized properly to maintain good balance throughout the body. The tilt of the body, natural sway, and interaction with the environment needs to be accounted for by redirecting one's gaze. And, the reflexive reaction to rebalance the body posture should respond. Without these three, one may feel dizzy or like they could fall at any moment (called **vertigo**), and dizziness is known to be a large predictor of fall risk in older adults (e.g., Herdman et al., 2000). Typically, these instances of vertigo are largely benign and easily treated with physical therapy. Resolving them, however, is important for reducing fall risk and increasing quality of life (Lindell et al., 2021).

It's important that we recognize that vision and redirecting your vision to allow the information to guide you (albeit automatic and below your level of consciousness) is a substantial component of the functioning of the vestibular system. If you are able, and feel like you can do it safely, try this: Stand up and stand on one foot. Then, close your eyes. You likely will find that you lose your balance and feel like you're about to fall over, and instinctively put your foot down. You can correct by opening your eyes, and your body will respond. But what happens if you lose a bit of your visual function from a common illness like cataracts? You are not able to just open your eyes and correct your faulty balance. The good news is that vision is not the only system that contributes to balance, nor are typical visual changes (as described earlier in this chapter) the changes that contribute to loss of balance or mobility.

Other systems, like the touch system, play a role as well. In healthy aging, we can see normative declines in the sensitivity in haptic (touch) input through the bottoms of the feet (e.g., Shaffer & Harrison, 2007), and while this may not seem impactful in terms of maintaining postural balance, it can be quite influential. That is, the input received through the soles of the feet can signal the nervous system to invoke a reflex to play out in the legs and feet (e.g., Peters et al., 2016). In one study, researchers at the University of British Columbia aimed to determine how this decline in input can be used to predict older adults' risk for balance impairments and postural stability problems (Peters et al., 2016). Here, young and older adults were stimulated on the bottoms of their feet with vibrations lasting one to two seconds. Participants were asked to report whether they felt the stimulation. Stimulations were presented at different amplitudes until their thresholds (i.e., minimum intensity to detect) were determined. Once thresholds were determined, stimulation on the bottom of the foot was given, and recordings from the corresponding leg via surface electrode pads were taken to measure reflex output. Results showed that older adults not only had higher thresholds for detecting stimulation (i.e., they needed more stimulation to notice that it was happening), but also had lower reflex output (i.e., less outgoing response to the stimulation). Researchers indicated that these findings demonstrate a relationship between the input sensitivity and the reflex output. The impact of these decreasing reflexes can be found in the risk of balance impairment in older adults. That is, if reflexes aren't working quickly enough in response to input coming through the bottom of the foot, an individual is less likely to be able to recover from an impediment in their path or more likely to lose footing in a rougher terrain (e.g., on a beach or a walking trail). The good news is that there are minor modifications, as well as practice, that can mitigate these limitations inherent in an aging nervous system that will be discussed in the next section.

Safety Concerns and Modifications

Balance impairment in an older adult seems like a terrible hazard and one we could see causing a path toward disability—the likelihood of which is not that large, and only increases when co-occurring with other physical or cognitive declines (e.g., Tu et al., 2022). The changes we see in the vestibular system and postural reflex difficulties are usually minor, and safety may just be a matter of simple environmental adaptations (like those provisions provided by the Americans with Disabilities Act, or ADA) and additional practice in movement (including physical therapy and tai chi; Komagata & Newton, 2003; Leung et al., 2011; Maciaszeck & Osiński, 2010; Silsupadol et al., 2006). Research in this area has investigated community-based exercise programs, specifically utilizing tai chi for its slow, low-impact qualities. In several studies (e.g., Jones et al., 2006; M. R. Lin et al., 2006; Taylor et al., 2012), results of tai chi as an intervention for balance impairment and fall risk have demonstrated significant improvement. Even in the instances where individuals do not show changes in muscle mass or bone density, improvements in balance, gait, posture, and risk for falling have been demonstrated in a matter of two to three months. Moreover, this type of exercise, occurring in a community setting, can be beneficial for older adults' social and emotional well-being as well. In fact, when I think back to my time as a group fitness instructor, I remember that many of the older women in my classes formed relationships and social bonds that resembled those they'd have with their own siblings, and the comments they made about those relationships told me that these were some of the most supportive and enduring friendships I'd ever seen.

Within the home, there are practical environmental changes that can be made to mitigate fall risk and help one maintain their freedom of movement. Checking the edges of rugs (and taping them down); removing cords from crossing walking paths; adding night lights in hallways, stairwells, and bathrooms; and applying brightly colored tape to the edges of stairs are all easy and cost-effective ways to improve the environment in one's home, as it relates to everyday contexts in which falls may occur. Additionally, one may add textured mats to the bottom of a bathtub or shower to minimize slipping and add a handrail to the side of the shower as well. The more of these little tweaks one can make, along with adding physical training (like tai chi) to regular exercise routines, the better the independence and lower the risk of falls. None of these modifications need to be specific to an older adult, either. People of all ages can benefit from any one, or all, of these minor changes—and that alone can help development through adulthood and minimize the stigma and fear of getting older.

TASTE AND SMELL

While the senses we've already discussed are important to interact with our world and get information, they are not the only ones. We gain information through our senses of taste and smell as well, and these are impactful on many levels—as we may have seen if we lost either or both of these during a recent COVID-19 infection. Typically, in a textbook such as this, taste and smell are addressed in tandem, mostly because these two senses work together all throughout the life span. Together, they give you an experience of **flavor**, with smell carrying most of the weight here. If you've ever tried to eat something while having a head cold and noticed that you don't taste much, you know what we're talking about here. Or, if you've ever referred to a candle's *flavor* instead of its *scent*, you also know what we're referring to here (a candle manufacturer would refer to it as *scent*, but by saying *flavor*, you really aren't that far off). With regard to aging, we tend to notice the same sort of thing. That is, while we do tend to lose some taste buds as we move through adulthood, this loss is not noticeable until late adulthood (after 80 years old; Doty, 2018). However, the sense of smell can contribute to some changes in flavor and eating experiences (e.g., Tuorila et al., 2001). Specifically, researchers in Finland (Tuorila et al., 2001) asked young and older participants to give intensity and pleasantness ratings for a variety of flavors. Analysis of the ratings showed that older adults were more impacted by the sweetness and saltiness of the flavors. Importantly, the participants' ability to rate the intensity of what they were smelling was not related to their ability to identify what they were smelling. These two mechanisms may be different, and therefore may be impacted differently by aging and/or disease processes.

iStockPhoto/monkeybusinessimages

Other research suggests that the sense of smell can be linked to Alzheimer's disease and cognitive impairment in more than one way (e.g., Dintica et al., 2019; Goette et al., 2019; Kreisl et al., 2018; Park et al., 2018; Stamps et al., 2013; Swan et al., 2002). First, research shows that individuals who are less able to identify a smell are more likely to develop a cognitive impairment or Alzheimer's disease later (e.g., Goette et al., 2019). And, while this speaks to the sense of smell, it also loops in the memory component of pulling a name that labels the smell from one's memory storage. Other research shows detection of smell directly links to cognitive impairments. In a study investigating this link (Stamps et al., 2013; see Table 2.1), participants demonstrated a right nostril deficit in the detection of the smell of peanut butter in individuals with a mild cognitive impairment—before it turned to a more severe case of dementia. Here, participants with a mild cognitive impairment needed the peanut butter sample to be at nearly half the distance from their right nostril compared to their left and compared to their healthy counterparts before they could detect that the smell was present. The results here demonstrate an inexpensive test that can be used to detect Alzheimer's disease early, at a time when more

TABLE 2.1 ■ Olfactory Detection Distance Asymmetry for Individuals With Cognitive Impairments

	Symmetric	Asymmetric (Left worse)	Asymmetric (Right worse)
Alzheimer's Disease	0	18	0
Mild Cognitive Impairment	11	10	3
Other Dementias	15	0	11
Older Controls	21	2	3

Source: Stamps, J. J., Bartoshuk, L. M., & Heilman, K. M. (2013). A brief olfactory test for Alzheimer's disease. *Journal of the Neurological Sciences, 333*(1–2), 19–24. https://doi.org/10.1016/j.jns.2013.06.033

options are available for a patient to slow down progression of the disease. Interestingly, other research has demonstrated that olfactory training (OT; regularly smelling specific odorants at predetermined concentrations) can improve connections and benefit those experiencing cognitive decline (e.g., Oleszkiewicz et al., 2021).

AGING WELL: SENSORY CHANGES

Adaptability is important. Changes happen all throughout our lives. Making them positive can be simply a matter of how we adapt to them. Sensory changes are no different. Many of the sensory changes that occur as a part of normal aging processes are small, and as such, small adjustments can make a big impact. For example, reading large-print books instead of regular print or zooming in on your computer screen can ease the strain on your eyes as your lens begins to harden, and won't restrict what you like to read or stop you from reading at all. In addition, using closed captioning on the television while you're watching it and asking your friends and family to speak more slowly and clearly are easy accommodations that can make adapting to life's sensory changes easier, with very little effort. And, they are accommodations that we can make for our loved ones as well. Consider these limitations when planning your next event—maybe a wedding or birthday party. Perhaps lower the volume of the music during dinner to allow those with difficulty hearing to participate fully in conversation. Or, we can help locate ramps and handrails for our loved ones. These small actions may mean a world of difference.

KEY TERMS

accommodation
apoptosis
auditory nerve
auditory threshold
cochlea
cornea

elderspeak
flavor
lens
lens bruescence
macula
mechanoreceptors
presbycusis
presbyopia
pupil
retina
rods and cones
transduction
tympanic membrane
vertigo
vestibular system

COMPREHENSION QUESTIONS

1. In the absence of disease, explain why seeing at night while driving may be difficult.
2. What are some simple changes one can make to adjust to minor vision changes? Why do these work?
3. Identify three ways in which vision may change that are not consistent with healthy aging.
4. In what ways does smell change with age? How can these impact how an older adult eats?
5. Why can hearing loss lead to social isolation?
6. How can hearing loss be corrected? And why are individuals resistant to these modifications?
7. Is balance a particularly large problem in an older population? How can physical fitness help maintain or correct balance?
8. How are touch and temperature regulation related?
9. How is touch related to balance?

ADDITIONAL READINGS

Aimonetti, J. M., Deshayes, C., Crest, M., Comuault, P. H., Weiland, B., & Ribot-Ciscar, E. (2019). Long term cosmetic application improves tactile discrimination in the elderly: A new psychophysical approach. *Frontiers in Aging Neuroscience, 11*, 1–7.

Bott, A., & Saunders, G. (2021). A scoping review of studies investigating hearing loss, social isolation and/or loneliness in adults. *International Journal of Audiology, 60*(2), 30–46. https://www.doi.org/10.1080/14992027.2021.1915506

Calkins, D. J. (2013). Age-related changes in the visual pathways: Blame it on the axon. *Investigative Ophthalmology and Visual Science, 54*, ORSF37–ORSF41.

Castaglione, A., Benatti, A., Velardita, C., Favaro, D., Padoan, E., Severi, D., Pagliaro, M., Bovo, R., Vallesi, A., Gabelli, C., & Martini, A. (2016). Aging, cognitive decline, and hearing loss: Effects of auditory rehabilitation and training with hearing aids and cochlear implants on cognitive function and depression among older adults. *Audiology and Neurotology, 21*(1), 21–28.

Hay-McCutcheon, M. J., Reed, P. E., & Chelmarlio, S. (2018). Positive social interaction and hearing loss in older adults living in rural and urban communities. *Journal of Speech, Language, and Hearing Research, 61*, 2138–2145.

Leandri, M., Campbell, J., Molfetta, L., Barbera, C., & Tabaton, M. (2015). Relationship between balance and cognitive performance in older people. *Journal of Alzheimer's Disease, 45(3)*, 705–707.

Liang, X., Ding, D., Zhao, Q., Wu, W., Xiao, Z., Luo, J., & Hong, Z. (2020). Inability to smell peppermint is related to cognitive decline: A prospective community-based study. *Neuroepidemiology, 54*, 258–264.

Meng, Q., Wang, B., Cui, D., Liu, N., Huang, Y., & Chen, L. (2019). Age-related changes in local and global visual perception. *Journal of Vision, 19*(1), 1–12.

Stevens, J. C. (1992). Aging and spatial acuity of touch. *Journal of Gerontology, 47*, 35–40.

UNIT II

MYTH: OLDER ADULTS LOSE THEIR MEMORY

It is scary to think that there'll be a point at which we won't be able to think, process, remember, converse, or engage in other mental processes when we've been doing it effectively our whole adult lives. However, this is not usually the case. In fact, most older adults function just fine mentally.

In this discussion, I'll address different types of attention and memory and how they may be impacted by the typical aging process. Information processing will also be addressed, as well as limitations associated with age-related slowing and inefficient memory resources. Importantly, these discussions will show that the experience of older adults often outweighs slowing and difficulties we may have regarding our memory. And clear distinctions will be made between healthy aging and changes resulting from disease processes.

Additional discussions will include intelligence, creativity, and wisdom in later life, as well as strategies for staying mentally sharp throughout the life span. Examining these concepts in depth will help us to understand that normative aging does not include the loss of memory or mental faculties.

iStockPhoto/FG Trade

3 ATTENTION AND MENTAL PROCESSING

LEARNING OBJECTIVES

3.1 Discuss normative and non-normative limitations in attentional processing, including selective and divided attention as well as automaticity.

3.2 Explain how older adults may allocate their attentional resources differently, but still effectively as compared to their younger counterparts.

3.3 Discuss how older adults' speed of processing relates to their intake and use of information.

I often hear from older adults (and those in middle age) that they are fearful of losing their mental faculties as they move through the later part of their lives. Once, an individual told me that they didn't remember whether they closed their garage door when they left the house, so they had to turn around and drive all the way back home to check. And their garage door was, in fact, closed. They just didn't remember closing it. And then they told me that this must be a sign that they are developing dementia. It is not. This is a common occurrence, even for younger adults (I do this *all* the time), and is simply the result of not paying attention. If your attention is not focused on something you are doing, you won't have processed that you did it. In this chapter, we'll discuss how attentional resources are allocated, and how automatic processing can be beneficial for preserving resources that are best used for other tasks. You will also learn how older adults' attentional resources are used differently, but not more poorly than those of young adults. Moreover, even older adults can learn to have automatic processes that don't require much attention at all.

TYPES OF ATTENTION

To understand what normative age-related changes in attention are and what may be the result of atypical processes, we must first understand the different types of attention and different ways of using attentional resources. Attention can be used to select certain components of our environment (and filter out or ignore others), and attention can also be used in an automatic way to allow processes to work quickly, efficiently, and under the radar, so to speak.

Selective Versus Divided Attention

In our day-to-day lives, we are constantly being bombarded with stimuli. There are sounds, sights, touches, tastes, and smells. All of them, all the time. Think about right now, for example: You've got this text in front of you, papers rustling next to you or behind you, air-conditioning or a fan blowing on you, your clothing touching you, and maybe even the taste of gum or a drink in your mouth. There's so much going on, but you are still able to focus on what you're reading. The reason is your attentional resources.

I like to think about attentional resources like mental energy: You have some that you can give to any given stimulus or task at any given moment. Sometimes, you have a lot of mental energy available. Sometimes, not as much. But, because attention is the first step in the information processing system (Atkinson & Shiffrin, 1968; I'll discuss more about information processing in Chapter 4), it's important to determining what you need to focus on—that is, what is relevant for you in that context. This determination allows you to appropriately allocate those attentional resources to the most important thing(s), because those are the things that'll be shepherded into your information processing system. This determination is important because everyone (young and older) has limited resources. Resources are not endless, and so we need to be strategic in how we are doling them out. When you select the task or stimulus you are going to focus on, you filter out what you don't need. This filtering process (Broadbent, 1956), called **selective attention**, uses some attentional resources in and of itself, leaving fewer resources available for the task at hand (e.g., Treisman, 1969; see also Table 3.1). Therefore, we ideally like to work in a "distraction-free" environment when our task is important or requires a lot of

TABLE 3.1 ■ Types of Attention

Selective Attention	Focusing on the task at hand, while filtering out unneeded information	Studying while ignoring the others talking in the coffee shop
Divided Attention	Splitting mental energy among two or more tasks	Talking on the phone while cooking dinner

attention. If we don't, we spend too much of our resources on selecting our task/filtering out distractions and don't actually have enough mental energy to do the task we need to do.

This leads to a subsequent realization—what if there are multiple tasks or multiple stimuli that need our attention? Can we handle focusing our attention on more than one task at once? The answer to this question is that it depends. Our ability to divide our attentional resources, called **divided attention** (e.g., Somberg & Salthouse, 1982; Spelke et al., 1976), is dependent on how many resources a task or a stimulus needs. If a task requires much of our mental energy, we will likely not have enough left over to add another thing to our "attentional plate." However, a task that is simple, is automatic, or doesn't require a lot of attention to complete likely can be added on to another. Here's an example: Reading this text, and filtering out irrelevant stimuli around you, likely needs most of your attentional resources. Therefore, you probably don't have any left over to have a conversation or watch television. However, folding laundry doesn't usually require a lot of attentional resources. So, you are probably able to also watch television, listen to an audiobook, or chat with a friend at the same time.

The good news is that while our attentional resources are limited, they are also flexible. We can allocate and reallocate those resources regularly (e.g., Kahneman, 1973; Kahneman & Henik, 2017; Posner & Petersen, 1990), updating our mental energy needs as the task demands change or our environmental stimuli or emotional contexts change (e.g., Meinhardt & Pekrun, 2003). We can switch from one task to another easily, by simply reallocating our mental energy to the new task. For example, if your phone rings while you are reading, you can answer the phone and redirect your attention to the phone conversation and back to reading once you've hung up the phone.

Automatic Processing

Some tasks happen with so few resources that there is no real need to consciously allocate attention to them at all. That is, they are well practiced and therefore don't need our constant attention to execute. This can happen with time and experience with the task (e.g., Logan, 1992; Logan et al., 1999; Servant et al., 2018). For example, when you learned to drive, there was an initial period where you were consciously and decidedly attending to each and every step (turn the car on, adjust the mirrors, fasten your seatbelt, look around, place the car in gear, turn the wheel slowly, release the pedal, etc.). Over time, and with more experience driving, you can complete many of these steps without even realizing you are doing them (e.g., Charlton & Starkey, 2011)—like the story at the beginning of this chapter, where my friend didn't remember that they closed the garage door. The processes became **automatic processes**, and therefore no longer needed a tremendous amount of attentional resources devoted to them (e.g., Logan, 1992). This can become dangerous in the case of driving, where we may need resources at the ready to pull into our processing in the case of unexpected circumstances like an abrupt weather change or another driver cutting in front of us. These instances are not automatic processes, but instead require more controlled attention. Controlled attention needs more resources. Having those resources ready, rather than tied up doing another task, like talking on the phone or eating, is needed for our safety.

Not all processing can become automatic processing, like driving, or benefit from automatic processing. Nor can all individuals practice a task enough to make it automatic. Can older adults? That is, are their resources efficient enough and available enough to maintain and/or create automaticity in their attentional allocations? The answer is yes (e.g., Jenkins & Hoyer, 2000), but it is dependent on the familiarity with the tasks as well as the complexity of the tasks (Hertzog, 2008). One task commonly used to measure the automatic/controlled distinction in the laboratory is the Stroop task (Stroop, 1935, 1938). The classic Stroop task (different from more modern variations on the task) presents color words (e.g., *blue, red, yellow*) to a participant written in a conflicting color ink (e.g., the word *blue* written in red ink), and asks the participant to name the color ink the word is written in (e.g., Stroop, 1935).

This task is difficult because an adult participant must suppress the automatic response of reading the word in favor of a more controlled response of naming the color. Typical measures of response time show that naming the color ink takes longer than reading the word (or what would occur if the word and the ink color matched), indicating that there is more mental energy (i.e., attentional control) needed to complete the task. This task is used across the ages for children, young adults, and older adults to gain some insight into attentional processing (e.g., Uttl & Graf, 1997; Williams et al., 2007). We'll see it alongside other tasks next.

RESOURCES IN OLDER ADULTS' ATTENTIONAL PROCESSING

With any concern about maintaining mental faculties, it becomes reasonable to ask whether any amount of mental resources/attention/mental energy will work the way it always has. Unfortunately, there is no short answer to this question (or else, this chapter wouldn't exist). However, there are some patterns in differences in attentional operations with age.

Attentional Control

The first of these differences can be seen within the context of the Stroop task, examining attentional control. Some research in this area argues that older adults slow down in response times during the Stroop task, and that this slowdown is related to a general slowing in processing that comes with age (e.g., Rey-Mermet & Gade, 2018; Salthouse, 1996), which will be discussed more in depth later in this chapter. However, more detailed analyses show a slightly different pattern. These analyses show that not only do older adults slow down overall, but they are further slowed in the conflicting version of the Stroop task, where the color of ink does not match the color word presented (e.g., Nicosia et al., 2021). That is, when they are asked to discard an automatic response and give a controlled response, a more exaggerated slowdown is revealed—above and beyond the slowing that may come with normative aging. Specifically, when Rey-Mermet and Gade (2020) gave young and older adults a series of attentional control tasks, the Stroop stood out as one in which older adults had more difficulty in adjusting their attentional control, trial after trial, to shift from an automatic response to a controlled one. This pattern of data demonstrates that older adults' attentional control can be more limited—not to the extent that they are unable to complete an attentional selection task, but rather that they are slower when shifting to using more control.

One explanation for this additional difficulty was outlined by Hasher and Zacks (1988) in the **inhibition deficit hypothesis.** This hypothesis suggests that older adults are less able to rid their information processing system from irrelevant information. That is, the individual will be unable to keep information that isn't needed for the task at hand from using up already limited mental resources. The result? Even fewer available resources to use.

For example, Connelly et al. (1991) asked older and younger participants to read text that had italics interspersed throughout. The instructions during reading were to attend to one font and ignore the other. So, in the way that we might filter out the rustling of papers or the hum of the air conditioner, participants were supposed to ignore irrelevant text—the text in the different font. As shown in Figure 3.1, older adults were less able to ignore the irrelevant text, especially when it was meaningfully related to the other text they were reading. Connelly et al. concluded, then, that there was something happening with the selective attention of the older adults; there was an inhibition deficit.

However, there can be a positive perspective on this research if we look closely at the type of information that the older adults were less able to ignore—information that was meaningful. Perhaps there is a limitation in older adults' efficiency in selective attention, as the inhibition deficit hypothesis suggests. Or perhaps older adults are using their

FIGURE 3.1 ■ Mean Reading Times for Young and Older Adults in the Context of Irrelevant or Relevant Text

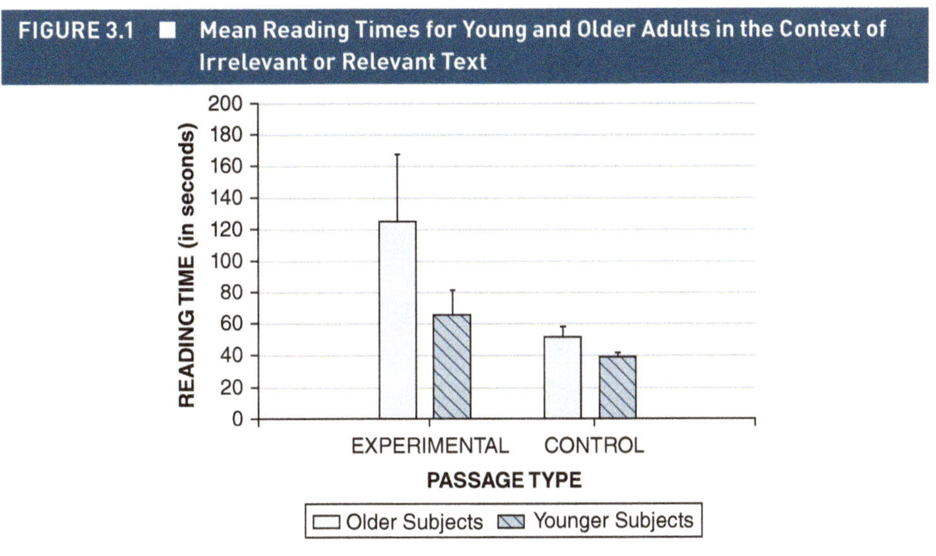

Source: Connelly, S. L., Hasher, L., & Zacks, R. T. (1991). Age and reading: The impact of distraction. *Psychology and Aging, 6*(4), 533–541.

experience to choose not to select out information that may be relevant, from their perspective. Research related to the idea that older adults' experiences color their goals for retaining and using information shows that older adults' goals may simply be different (e.g., Trunk & Abrams, 2009). In a series of two studies, Trunk and Abrams (2009) measured the communication goals of young and older adults in their expression of memories of their own life (i.e., autobiographical memories), aiming to determine whether any off-topic speech during storytelling was the result of an inhibition deficit or the result of different communicative goals. Here, researchers found that both young and older adults produce off-topic speech (what could be deemed irrelevant to answer a question or express the topic at hand). However, older adults maintained that their goals in communication were comprehensive and included things like expressiveness. While young adults demonstrated similar goals sometimes, their goals changed depending on the type of communication in which they were engaging. That is, when young adults aimed to be concise, they were in fact concise. However, older adults' goals in this study were consistently to be comprehensive and expressive, no matter the type of information being communicated. This may be strategic in allowing irrelevant information (i.e., the off-topic information) to be maintained in the attentional system, rather than inhibited. But that is just one argument, and there seems to be research to support both inhibition deficit (e.g., Arbuckle & Gold, 1993; Gold & Arbuckle, 1995; Hasher & Zacks, 1988) and purposeful maintenance of seemingly irrelevant information (e.g., Giles & Coupland, 1991; James et al., 1998). So, more research may be needed to determine the circumstances under which an individual is maintaining "irrelevant information" on purpose compared to those under which an individual may be maintaining it unknowingly due to an attentional deficit.

In some cases, the differences here may be task dependent. Sometimes, a task may allow for experience to easily override one's ability to inhibit, where an individual sees value in

iStockPhoto/kali9

holding on to meaningful information—as in reading (e.g., Connelly et al., 1991) or telling a story about one's life (e.g., Trunk & Abrams, 2009). In other tasks, including the Stroop, Simon (as in the game where one must replicate increasingly longer patterns of pressing colored buttons), and flanker tasks (which involve choosing or directing attention via pointing arrows around a computer screen), experience and a long life lived are not helpful in overriding limitations (e.g., Aschenbrenner & Balota, 2017) because those tasks are not naturalistic or encountered outside the laboratory. Here, similar difficulties to those described in the Stroop task earlier in this section arise, and demonstrate the underlying difficulties associated with inhibition, selective attention, and limited attentional resources (Aschenbrenner & Balota, 2017).

These effects are not born out in other types of attentional control, such as with divided attention. In divided attention, as we explained earlier, an individual must divide up and allocate their mental energy to multiple tasks, sometimes running out of resources needed to complete a task before the task is complete (e.g., Somberg & Salthouse, 1982; Spelke et al., 1976). Here, we could reason that an older adult may run out of resources sooner, if their attentional resources are already partially used up with holding on to additional/irrelevant information, as the inhibition deficit hypothesis would suggest. Research in this area provides support for this suggestion (e.g., Anderson, 1999; Tun & Wingfield, 1995). In much of the research on divided attention, researchers ask participants to complete two tasks—known as a **dual task paradigm** (e.g., Anderson, 1999; Huang & Mercer, 2001; Tun et al., 1991). One of the tasks is the primary task, where participants should work to the best of their ability. The secondary task should then be completed with whatever resources are left over. In this paradigm, it should be the case that the secondary task will suffer from limited resources, because if there aren't enough available, this task won't get completed. Any differences in age comparisons between young and older adults should play out here in this secondary task.

Anderson (1999) examined the secondary task performance, comparing young and older adults' response times in completing four-choice visual memory tasks. Here, older adults' response times were significantly longer overall, demonstrating general slowing (see the speed of processing section later in this chapter for more details on how speeds slow as we age). However, analysis of response times also demonstrated an even larger age difference in the secondary task in the divided attention condition. That is, older adults were slower regardless, but when also confronted with reaching the limit of their attentional resources, their performance slowed even further. Moreover, when asked about the difficulty associated with divided attention, Tun and Wingfield (1995) demonstrated that older adults perceive the difficulty that plays out in their performance. In a series of self-ratings, shown in Table 3.2, older adults rated combinations of tasks as more difficult than the tasks completed individually and rated them more difficult than young adults. Additionally, when tasks were newer to them, they also rated them as more difficult—demonstrating that without practice a task will use more attentional resources than tasks that are familiar and/or practiced. However, difficulty ratings did go down when older adults were asked about more familiar tasks, like

TABLE 3.2 ■ Mean Difficulty Ratings (on a scale of 1 to 5) for Routine and Combination Tasks for Young, Young-Old, Older, and Old-Old Ages

	Young	Young-Old	Older	Old-Old
Routine tasks (e.g., walking, doing chores)	1.32	1.61	1.64	1.86
Monitoring tasks (e.g., driving while reading road signs)	2.02	1.90	2.17	2.65
Speech tasks (e.g., talking while watching TV or playing cards)	2.73	2.87	3.10	3.24

Source: Tun, P. A., & Wingfield, A. (1995). Does dividing attention become harder with age? Findings from the Divided Attention Questionnaire. *Aging, Neuropsychology, and Cognition, 2*(1), 39–66. https://doi.org/10.1080/13825589508256588

speech, suggesting that familiarity and experience relieves some of those limited attentional resources.

What all of this means is that older adults can use their attention strategically, as they once did, but only to a point. They will likely be a bit slower, use up resources more quickly, and perceive tasks to be more difficult if they are unfamiliar. A relief from this difficulty can come if tasks become more familiar or automatic or rely on tasks they've done for many years.

Automaticity

But then, a question arises: Can an older adult create new automatic processes and/or benefit from automaticity with attentional resources? The answer is yes! It is possible to achieve automaticity (e.g., Jenkins & Hoyer, 2000), though some research will argue differently (e.g., Maquestiaux et al., 2010). When a task is repeated, and each component of that task is repeated, the entire task can become automatic and be completed without using many of the attentional resources available for that individual. For example, when learning to knit, each stitch is repeated over and over again with the same procedure: needle in, wrap the yarn, needle out, stitch off. With enough iterations of this procedure completed, the motions needed to create one knit stitch use less and less attention, eventually relieving the knitter from using these attentional resources. Then, those resources are free to be allocated to some other task.

iStockPhoto/Rawpixel

Creating a new automatic process is age-related in that we are working within the confines of the limitations of attentional resources described earlier. However, these limitations can be sidestepped if an individual can rely on previously well-rehearsed skills for the task they are trying to do. Research in this area demonstrates that part of an individual older adult's ability to create automaticity is dependent on how difficult a task is (Hoyer & Touron, 2003), and that automaticity can be preserved when a task relies on something like language, which older adults are adept at using (e.g., Lien et al., 2008; Rawson & Touron, 2015).

For instance, in a series of two experiments, Jenkins and Hoyer (2000) asked young and older adult participants to complete a visual search task, counting the number of target letters they saw on a computer screen. Both young and older adults (though not everyone) were able to reach automaticity in this task, demonstrating that it was possible to do so. However, when tested 18 months later, the older adults did not maintain their skill level. That is, they were no longer quick and automatic the way they were when they first reached that level of performance. This result tells us that while automaticity is possible, it isn't easily maintained—at least in the context of a laboratory task. If a task is more realistic, like reading or word-based tasks that would be used and/or practiced day to day, there may be more likelihood of retention of the automaticity of the skill. However, research in this context is scant. Anecdotally, I can tell you that it is possible. When I taught dance fitness classes years ago, there were many older women in my classes. New attendees often had to learn some of the common dance steps they'd encounter during my classes. At first, those steps were awkward, and I could see the women mouthing the footwork and order of the steps as they executed them. By the next class, or even the end of their first one, they'd have them down. All I had to do was call out the name of the step and they'd do it, automatically. And if they missed class for a week or two, or even longer, they would be able to come back and do the step with very little review—demonstrating retention of their newly acquired automatic skill.

SPEED OF PROCESSING

In examining speed of processing, we must first look at the measures used in this type of research. This is important because the measures are meaningful in interpreting the results discussed here. In speed-of-processing research, you will see researchers describe response times or reaction times, usually measured in milliseconds between the presentation of a stimulus and the response to that stimulus. This is a fairly precise measure of how much mental processing is happening. The interpretation? Longer response times usually mean more mental effort used in getting to the end response.

The types of responses expected from an individual can vary depending on what kind of information is needed to answer a research question. We may get a **simple reaction time** measure, where we just want to know how fast an individual can respond to a prompt. For example, if we ask someone to press a button on a computer keyboard every time they hear a bell, this is a simple reaction time. It is a good baseline measure to compare other types of responses to because there's no real cognitive work that needs to happen here. It's just a measure of their psychomotor response, or the time between the presentation of a stimulus and the reaction to that stimulus (e.g., Wilkinson & Allison, 1989; Woods et al., 2015). A **choice reaction time** is different. This one asks a participant to make a choice before they respond. Here, you may ask someone to respond one way to one stimulus and differently to another (e.g., Stone, 1960; Teichner & Krebs, 1974). For example, they could press a button on a keyboard when they hear a bell but repeat out loud every time they hear a word. Finally, we could measure a **complex reaction time**. This measure is one where many decisions and many different responses are expected in the same context (e.g., Wei & Prater, 1962)—like in driving, which we'll discuss in more detail later in this chapter (Stanisław Jurecki et al., 2017).

As you would expect, based on what we have discussed to this point, older adults are indeed slower in their reaction time measures, as compared to younger adults (e.g., Tun & Lachman, 2008). Interestingly, we know that the slowdown comes not from the motor response of pressing a button or slamming on the breaks, but in the decision to make that response (e.g., Ratcliff et al., 2001). That is, the slowing happens in the cortex, not the peripheral motor neurons that execute the response (though there is some evidence of the slowing in the initiation of movement originating in the motor cortex; Frolov et al., 2020). This is interesting and useful information to be sure, but we need to look closer at the research to determine whether that slowdown is harmful or potentially beneficial in terms of the final outcome of the task they are asked to complete. For instance, an individual may slow down to regain accuracy in the tasks they are working on, rather than going the same speed they once did at the expense of accuracy. This is known as a **speed-accuracy trade-off** and can benefit performance when accuracy is more important than the speed at which it is completed (e.g., Brébion, 2001). You may do this when you slow down on your exams so you can answer more questions correctly or when you slow down while giving directions to make sure you give the details correctly.

One important caveat to consider in the discussion of reaction times in older adults is the issue of individual differences, or the difference from one person to the next. There is a tremendous amount of variability from person to person in any reaction time measure, but when you look at reaction time measures among groups of older adults, you will often find even more individual differences than you do among groups of young adults (Hultsch et al., 2002). One reason for this is the wider range of ages—in a young adult research sample, the group often ranges from 18 to 24 years of age, whereas in an older adult research sample, the ages range from 60 to 90 years. The wider window means a possibility for much more change within the group. Moreover, when a group has as much variability within it as we may see in an older adult research sample, we may not be able to detect subtle differences in our reaction time measure—the statistics are not in our favor. So, with that in mind, we can discuss possible age-related slowdowns in processing times, as well as what could cause them and what they mean for performance, but with some caution in the conclusions we draw from the discussion.

Earlier suggestions on age-related slowdowns tell us that general slowing occurs across different functions because of general neuronal loss and weakening in the connections between neurons (e.g., Somberg & Salthouse, 1982). That is, throughout adulthood brain cells eventually just die. Not a lot of them, but little bits all over the brain—not concentrated in any one area, but just a thinning out. With that, we see signals sent throughout the brain becoming slower (e.g., Birren et al., 1980). I liken this to an aging computer. That is, it still does all the work you need it to do but takes more time to do it. It just runs slower. In our modern world, we may want to discard the computer (as some people want to do with the aged—entirely disrespectful and fear-based—and something I aim to change with the education provided in this book), but we just need some patience. Given a bit more time, the program will open, and the files will save.

Myerson et al. (1990) agree with the computer analogy and suggest that the overall neural weakening interferes with necessary steps needed to complete a task—some more complex tasks require more steps and have an opportunity to "lose steam" or lose a piece as the process goes on. The more pathways that disconnect or lose a piece, the less efficient the messages are going to be getting sent from beginning to end. If latencies get longer in one section of a process, the whole process will slow down. Research supported this idea up to this point, where researchers could predict an older adult's slowdown as a direct projection from a young adult's response time (e.g., Cerella et al., 1980).

One of the top researchers in this area of gerontology, Dr. Timothy Salthouse, suggested that older adults are slower to process information through the information processing system—from attention to short-term memory to long-term memory (but more on that progression in Chapter 4; e.g., Salthouse, 1980, 1996)—and that this slowing can and does hinder the extent to which information is successfully used later. The reason that Salthouse (1996) gives for this hindrance is that the completion of processing more rapidly (and in the case of repetition for rehearsal) and in rapid succession does not allow the trace to fade before the next repetition. However, when slowed, this process doesn't work the same way—allowing incoming information to fade before it can be strengthened by another go-around. The differences here between slow speed and faster speed could mean not just differences in speed, but also differences in the strength of the information moving into the information processing system, with the result being poorer performance. That is, with this permutation of the idea of cognitive slowdowns, there is an assumption that the slower processes are less effective (e.g., Bryan & Luszcz, 1996). But what happens when older and younger adults use the same strategy, and one group just performs more slowly? Bryan and Luszcz (1996) aimed to determine just that using a paradigm that asked individuals from both age groups to complete a couple of recall tests as well as speed-of-processing tests and determined that this indeed was the case (see Figure 3.2). Their research supported the idea that slower isn't just slower, and there's more to the story.

What is the larger picture here with respect to a cognitive slowdown? That is, is slower always less effective, or could some of these slowdowns be specific to the task or context in which they are tested? The Baltimore Longitudinal Study of Aging aimed to get some very specific details on the breakdown of age-related slowing (Fozard et al., 1994). In this study, a large sample of over 1,200 adults were tested over the course of eight years. During this time, researchers measured consistent slowing beginning even in young adulthood. Additionally, errors increased across this time, indicating that at least in the tasks completed here, the slowing was not the result of a speed-accuracy trade-off. The researchers concluded that reaction times do slow down over adulthood, but there was a large influence of task difficulty. That is, the more difficult tasks slowed more than those that were easier.

With respect to skills that are well practiced, we see that slowdowns do still occur, but those slowdowns are not indicative of poorer performance necessarily. For example, Salthouse (1984) examined the speed of typing for well-experienced typists. These individuals were measured on both choice reaction time and speed of motor response (not in reaction to anything), as well as speed of typing. Results showed that older adults were slower than young adults on both the choice reaction time task and the motor response but did not show a slower typing speed. What was different here? Expertise. Older adult typists were able to use their knowledge of typing to anticipate what was coming. They leaned on a **span of anticipation**, or a window ahead of what they were currently typing, to plan out the next moves they would make on the keyboard. In comparing types of errors, speed, and comprehension of the messages being typed, Salthouse

FIGURE 3.2 ■ Mean Number of Words Recalled for Different Amounts of Rehearsals

	One rehearsal		Two rehearsals		Three rehearsals	
Age group	*M*	*SD*	*M*	*SD*	*M*	*SD*
	Number of words recalled					
Younger	6.03	2.06	7.31	2.06	7.81	2.74
Older	4.61	1.78	5.19	1.70	4.99	1.42
Across age group	5.33	2.09	6.29	2.31	6.49	2.85

Source: Bryan, J., & Luszcz, M. A. (1996). Speed of information processing as a mediator between age and free-recall performance. *Psychology of Aging, 11*(1), 3–9.

demonstrated maintenance of skill for older typists despite lowered processing speed. This evidence answers the question of how an older adult can persist with relatively normal/consistent function in real-world activities but show poor performance on lab tests.

iStockPhoto/SDI Productions

In real-world tasks, at which older adults are particularly adept because of a lifetime of practice, their experience reigns supreme and allows for compensation with no dip in performance. My own research shows the same (Margolin, 2018). In a study of older adults' comprehension of text, data showed that those who maintained reading practice as frequent patrons of the public library scored comparably to or even higher than their younger counterparts in a comprehension assessment. In the realm of cognitive aging research, this is a win. Not only does it paint a positive picture of a very real outcome of the aging process, but it also tells us that there is sometimes more happening than standard laboratory tasks can tell us.

Additionally, other research has demonstrated that while some processes do slow down, there are training activities that can improve or even reverse these slowdowns. The result? Improved day-to-day function, particularly when the practice can extend to other related tasks. Much of this research has trained older adults on speed-of-processing tasks and has demonstrated its success in extending that training to a daily activity like driving (e.g., Ball et al., 2010; Edwards et al., 2009; Edwards et al., 2012; Vance et al., 2007). This research and its implications are discussed in the next section.

Processing Speed and Driving

News media have covered many stories over the years regarding older drivers in car crashes. In some cases, they argued that the older driver couldn't see, and so arguments about checking older adults' vision before allowing them to drive a car ensued and even became law in some states (see the National Highway Traffic Safety Administration's [NHTSA, 2020] *Safety Outcomes of Licensing Procedures for Older Drivers*). As we saw in Chapter 2, normative changes in vision are usually in the range of reading (as opposed to distance) and so are unlikely to affect seeing road signs. To be sure, good visual acuity (or corrected-to-good visual acuity) is important for driving, but it isn't the only factor in determining safe driving (e.g., Anstey et al., 2005; Dawson et al., 2010; Schwebel et al., 2007). As discussed earlier, we know that driving is a task that, once acquired, can become automatic. However, it is good practice to have additional attentional resources left over for instances where you'll need them, like when another driver swerves into your lane or when quick weather changes occur. A driver is responsible not just for the automatic processes involved in maneuvering their vehicle but also for so much more: expecting the unexpected driver to pull out in front, estimating the speed of other cars on the road when needing to turn, switching attention from the road to the road signs and back again, and many more minute-to-minute tasks. Controlling attention, as well as using multimodal sensory information, is important (Anstey et al., 2005).

From what we've learned in the present chapter, one may be concerned about how less efficient attentional allocation and slower processing speeds could affect older drivers, and if they do, could we remediate? Moreover, what would this remediation look like, and could it extend or apply to other related tasks? Driving is a task that clearly involves many decisions to be made, often very quickly, with the potential for dangerous outcomes. However, research does show that older adults are less likely to be involved in serious car crashes (e.g., Scialfa et al., 1991; see also Table 3.3). In fact, as of 2020, the NHTSA reported that older adults contributed to just 14% of fatal car crashes, compared to 38% of those aged 16–20. Regardless, there can be some difficulties associated with driving that can cause concern, fear, or even a potential for a loss of independence if an older adult is unable to drive or is restricted in their ability or willingness to drive.

Research in this area has developed an interesting measure to help in its investigations: the **useful field of view** (UFOV; Wood & Owsley, 2014). Since we know that visual acuity is only

TABLE 3.3 ■ Rates of Car Crashes by Age in 2021

Age range	Fatalities by Car Crash
< 15	1,190
15–24	7,117
25–34	8,493
35–44	6,752
45–54	5,820
55–64	6,037
65+	7,529

Source: National Center for Statistics and Analysis. (2023, April). *Early estimates of motor vehicle traffic fatalities and fatality rate by sub-categories in 2022* (CrashStats Brief Statistical Summary, Report No. DOT HS 813 448). National Highway Traffic Safety Administration. https://crashstats.nhtsa.dot.gov/Api/Public/ViewPublication/813448

one small component to competent driving, researchers developed the UFOV to measure how much visual information is actually taken in and attended to in one glance. This is important because we can look at something with our eyes (and our eyes can see it clearly), but unless we direct our attention to it, we won't actually *see it.* I'm sure you have experienced this while driving. You go to look over your shoulder to your blind spot before changing lanes of traffic, only to turn your head back toward the road ahead of you and realize that you don't know what you saw in that quick glance. Obviously, your eyes looked, but your attention did not. This is important for the safety of you and others on the road—young and older. The UFOV measure also assesses components of divided attention, selective attention, and processing speed. Researchers have used this measure for years for measuring the outcomes of speed-of-processing training as it pertains to day-to-day tasks, including driving (e.g., Ball et al., 2010; Edwards et al., 2013).

Researchers have trained older adults to increase processing speed on tasks of variable complexity (e.g., Ball et al., 2010; Edwards et al., 2013; Roenker et al., 2003). This speed-of-processing training can be useful under a variety of contexts, both in the lab and in everyday life. In one study, Edwards et al. (2005) trained participants on a series of processing speed tasks, including timed instrumental activities of daily living (IADLs), road sign selection, letter and pattern comparisons, and Wechsler Adult Intelligence Scale—Revised digit substitution (a component of the WAIS intelligence test, discussed in more detail in Chapter 5). Participants trained for a total of 10 hours over the span of five weeks. Additionally, during the training sessions, participants were able to discuss topics related to speed of processing in their daily lives, such as driving and mobility. After training, participants showed an increase in UFOV performance as well as improvements on the timed IADL tasks. These results showed that the participants were able to transfer their improvements across domains to other, related activities, including those that contribute to their living independently.

iStockPhoto/Wavebreakmedia

In other research, data comparing participants who trained specifically on a driving simulator to those who trained on increasing processing speeds more globally, Roenker et al. (2003) demonstrated that more global training was transferable to other contexts, like driving. These participants also demonstrated better UFOV measures and executed fewer dangerous driving operations in a road test than those trained specifically on driving. And, when tested 18 months later, participants had maintained their increased performance in processing speed as it related to driving and visual search tasks (like finding road signs). However, it is important to recognize that speed-of-processing measures trained in this research are not universal and will not transfer to just any task (e.g., Vance et al., 2007). That is, a speed-of-processing measure that is applicable for driving may not be useful for reading (and vice versa), and as such, the training given may not transfer to increased performance on an unrelated task. However, it is promising that speed of processing can be trained and improved upon for older adults. Practice doesn't make perfect, but it can make improvement. These improvements are paramount for maintaining independence throughout adulthood.

Reading and Processing Speed

Reading is an area of cognitive research where speed is measured quite frequently (e.g., Kemtes & Kemper, 1997; Rayner et al., 2013; Stine, 1990; Stine-Morrow et al., 2008). Reading speed often indicates how quickly a reader can take in information from a page. However, it is usually interpreted along with recall or comprehension data because, much like anything else, speed means nothing if there is no meaningful outcome. That is, if you read quickly, but don't remember or understand what you've read, what good is it? In this instance, a speed-accuracy trade-off may be beneficial.

Like other reaction time measures, reading speed is measured in milliseconds, as pausing to identify a word or phrase and moving on in the text happens very quickly. These measures are often taken using an **eye-tracker device** (e.g., Rayner et al., 2013) and the **moving window technique** (e.g., Kemper & Liu, 2007). The eye-tracker device uses infrared light to reflect off the eyes and back to a computer screen to follow and map where the eyes move, how far they move, and how long they fixate in any one location before moving on to the next. The moving window technique determines how a text is presented to the individual. Wherever a reader pauses and fixates on the presented text, a window around that point of fixation is revealed. When their eyes move to the next point of fixation, the window moves as well, so that wherever the individual looks, they will see text to read. This allows the researchers to control how much text is presented to their participants at any one time while they are tracking where they look and how much time they spend there.

The moving window technique can be modified to be used without an eye-tracker device, as I have done in my own research (Margolin & Abrams, 2009). Here, readers were revealed a window of text, but instead of moving the window based on the movement of the eyes, the participants were to press a button on the computer keyboard to move to the next portion of text. Reaction time measures were taken from these keypresses, and while these keypresses add a motor component to the measurement, we know that much of the slowing that comes with aging does not come

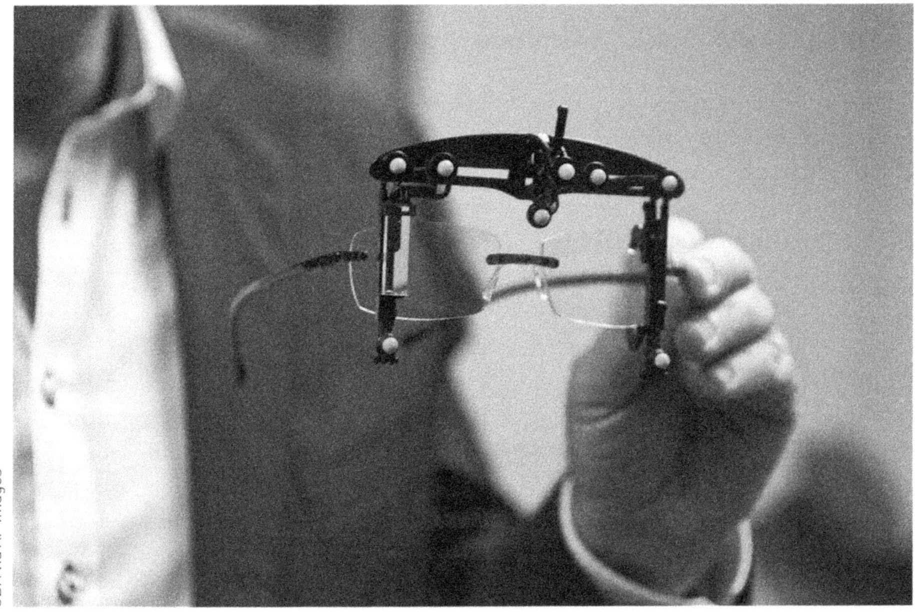

from the motor response. Additionally, any slowing from the motor component of pressing the button would be consistent across all responses, so the *difference* in reading times between conditions will remain the same when this component is factored out. Importantly, as you can see from this description, these methods involve self-pacing. That is, the reader controls the speed at which the information comes in. This is important because it allows for a slowdown to occur and is different from a technique where a participant may be presented with text at a predetermined rate of speed (which may or may not be one at which the reader thrives).

Patterns of reading time data consistently show older adults' reading times as slower than those demonstrated by young adults (e.g., Margolin & Abrams, 2009; Stine, 1990; Stine-Morrow et al., 1996; Stine-Morrow et al., 2000), and there is evidence to show that these slowdowns happen not just because older is slower. Rather, older adults may be more strategic in their allocation of mental energy when reading—perhaps based on their experience or perhaps based on their awareness of their own limitations. For instance, Stine (1990) examined whether older and young adults were similar in their allocation of time spent reading and if they allocated time at similar locations. Of particular interest was how older and young adults would spend their time at clause and sentence boundaries, places where wrap-up and integration with text that was read earlier is likely to occur. Results showed that, while both age groups spent more time at clause boundaries (i.e., ends of clauses, often marked by commas) and sentence boundaries, young adults allocated more time to sentence boundaries than did older adults. Instead, older adults spent their extra time pausing at clause boundaries, where they may have been breaking up the sentence into more manageable pieces for processing, enabling older adults to work within their limited constraints. When reflecting on the differences in reading times and their impact on recall and comprehension of text, we see that slower reading times do not always coincide with poorer overall memory for text (e.g., Margolin, 2018), but we'll discuss more on memory in Chapter 4.

AGING WELL: ATTENTION AND MENTAL PROCESSING

Aging well in terms of attention and processing speed comes from two directions. The first are things one can do actively to improve cognitive performance, and the second is a change in perspective regarding our expectations and fears associated with changes in attention and speed of processing.

In our lives, there is rarely an event where time matters, or we run out of time to complete it. Think about an individual sitting down to pay their bills or fold their laundry. These take as long as they take, with unlikely situations for time constraints—except in the case of driving, where speed may matter more. However, research shows that experience can compensate, and older drivers are less likely to get into accidents than younger drivers for a few reasons: (1) Older adults usually drive less, without commutes to work once they retire; (2) their experience outweighs their slower processing speed; and (3) they are usually aware of their limitations (e.g., seeing at night, as described in Chapter 2, or slower attentional speeds).

Aging well in the case of attention and speed can really be as simple as experience and practice. Cohen-Shikora et al. (2018) demonstrate that older adults can be flexible in their attention and perform similarly to their younger counterparts. Here, researchers allowed participants to gain experience with the Stroop task and measured their performance on a subsequent Stroop task. While one may have predicted that older participants would be unable to shift control and subsequent strategy based on cues given before each trial, participants did demonstrate flexibility. These results suggest that experience with a task can assist in guiding an older individual in their further task performance. We saw this play out earlier in this chapter as well in our discussion of older typists. These individuals guided their way and compensated for any potential loss of speed with solid grounding in their area of expertise. The advice is clear here: Use experience and build on what we already know.

KEY TERMS

automatic processes
choice reaction time
complex reaction time
divided attention
dual task paradigm
eye-tracker device
inhibition deficit hypothesis
moving window technique
selective attention
simple reaction time
span of anticipation
speed-accuracy trade-off
useful field of view

COMPREHENSION QUESTIONS

1. What is the difference between selective and divided attention?
2. Why might selective attention be difficult in an older adult?

3. How could limitations in inhibition be beneficial for an older adult?

4. How would a typical older adult perform in a dual-task paradigm?

5. Where is a slowdown important for older adult task performance? When is performance hindered, and when does it benefit?

ADDITIONAL READINGS

Argiris, G., MacPherson, S. E., Della Sala, S., & Foley, J. A. (2020). The relationship between dual-tasking and processing speed in healthy aging. *Psychology and Neuroscience, 13*(3), 375–398. http://doi.org/10.1037/pne0000189

Bashore, T. R., Ridderinkhof, K. R., & van der Molen, M. W. (1997). The decline of cognitive processing speed in old age. *Current Directions in Psychological Science, 6*(6), 163–169. https://doi.org/10.1111/1467-8721.ep10772944

Butler, K. M., & Weywadt, C. (2013). Age differences in voluntary task switching. *Psychology and Aging, 28*(4), 1024–1031. https://doi.org/10.1037/a0034937

Chambon, C., Herrara, C., Romaiguere, P., Pabon, V., & Alescio-Lautier, B. (2014). Benefits of computer-based memory and attention training in healthy older adults. *Psychology and Aging, 29*(3), 731–743. http://doi.org/10.1037/a0037477

Lima, S. D., Hale, S., & Myerson, J. (1991). How general is general slowing? Evidence from the lexical domain. *Psychology and Aging, 6*(3), 416–425.

Sliwinski, M., & Buschke, H. (1999). Cross-sectional and longitudinal relationships among age, cognition, and processing speed. *Psychology and Aging, 14*(1), 18–33. https://doi.org/10.1037//0882-7974.14.1.18

iStockPhoto/nkbimages

4 MEMORY

LEARNING OBJECTIVES

4.1 Explain the information processing model, including how processing speed changes can impact information processing.

4.2 Explain how the different memory systems may be differentially impacted by age-related variables.

4.3 Contrast normative and atypical memory changes.

Years ago, my sister called me very upset about an incident with her grandmother-in-law, Nana. She said, "Nana forgot how to make the blueberry muffins. That means she's developing dementia, right?" After I got my sister to calm down, I helped her understand that while Nana is getting older, and she forgot a recipe, it doesn't necessarily mean that she is developing dementia. But that's the fear, right? When we get older, we lose our mental faculties, and it's because we're all getting dementia eventually? Nope. That's most definitely not how it happens. What Nana was experiencing could have been the start of dementia, but it also could have been very typical, normative age-related changes in her memory function. Moreover, there were other things to consider surrounding Nana's forgetfulness: How long had it been since she last made those muffins? Was she making them in her own kitchen, where context could help her remember, or was she making them at her daughter's house? Was she in a time crunch? Was she distracted or tired? Obviously, I encouraged my sister and her mother-in-law to seek medical consult for Nana, because any concern should be assessed by her doctor. However, there really shouldn't have been much cause for concern over one isolated incident. We all forget things all the time. Human memory is fallible.

In this chapter, you'll learn what may have happened for Nana. I'll discuss how information moves into the human memory system, including how it is stored and retrieved from storage. Additionally, I'll discuss how normative age-related changes in things like attention and processing speed (as discussed in Chapter 3) can impact parts of the information processing system further down the line. Finally, you will learn how disease and nutrition can affect memory function—beyond what we may see with normative changes—recognizing that these additional losses are not the norm and do not happen universally to everyone.

THE INFORMATION PROCESSING PERSPECTIVE

As you learned in the previous chapter, we are constantly exposed to information in our environment—stimuli from sights, sounds, smells, and so on. When we direct our attention to that information, it is funneled into the **information processing system** (what you may have heard of as the Atkinson and Shiffrin model; Atkinson & Shiffrin, 1968; see also Figure 4.1). It is here that we can use information, discard information, or save information for later. Each step of the information processing system allows for distinct types of processing for a specific purpose, and each step can be affected by normative age-related changes differently than the previous step or the step to follow.

Sensory Memory

In this first stop in the information processing system, known as **sensory memory**, our sensory systems provide a landing zone for incoming information. Here, information comes in passively and in its raw, unprocessed form to allow for our attention to grab it. A trace of the

FIGURE 4.1 ■ Information Processing Model

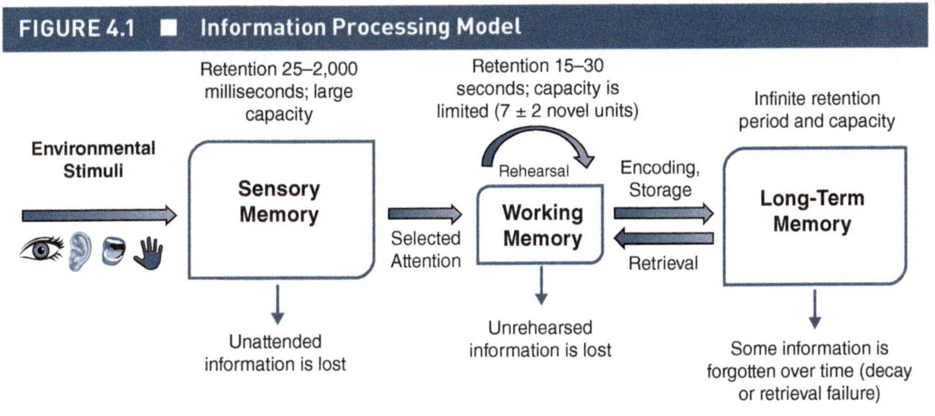

Source: Based on Atkinson, R. C., & Shiffrin, R. M. (1968). Human memory: A proposed system and its control processes. In K. W. Spence & J. T. Spence (Eds.), *Psychology of learning and motivation* (Vol. 2, pp. 89–195). Academic Press.

information remains there for a short amount of time and then dissipates. But during that short time, we get a second chance to attend to the incoming information. That is, visual sensory memory (known as iconic sensory memory) allows for a space for visual information to come in and time for our attention to be directed to it. If attention is directed to this information, it will get moved from sensory memory to the next stop in the information processing system. This does not just happen for visual information, however. It happens for all types of sensory information—auditory (i.e., echoic) sensory information coming in through the ears, haptic (i.e., touch) information coming in through the skin receptors, and even taste and smell information coming in through the chemical sensory organs. You may have even noticed this type of memory when you see a visual trace behind a firework sparkler. That trace is your iconic sensory memory, lasting only about 0.5 second past the initial stimulus exposure (e.g., Bradley & Pearson, 2012; Sperling, 1960; Tye, 2006). There is no need for longer-term storage at this sensory stage. Rather, either an individual will attend to it (if they deem it important or relevant), or it will fade away.

Importantly, as you learned in the previous chapter, our attention is limited—and it's not just limited for older adults; it's limited for everyone. Therefore, the extent to which information coming into our sensory memory **buffer** (i.e., storage bucket) can be moved further into the information processing system is limited to what we pay attention to. If we do not allocate our mental energy to a stimulus, it may not make it further into the information processing system (although there are instances that may bypass this limitation). Older adults, however, are only limited further to the extent that their sensory systems limit them. That is, visual changes like presbyopia or auditory changes like presbycusis can limit what information comes into sensory memory. The good news is that beyond specific sensory input limitations or changes (e.g., presbyopia or presbycusis), sensory memory is not usually limited by any normative age-related changes (e.g., Walsh & Prasse, 2014).

Victoria Lesniara/Alamy Stock Photo

Working Memory

Once information has been attended to, it will move on to the next step in the information processing system. This next stage is called **working memory**—you may have also heard this called **short-term memory**. This storage buffer is used primarily to store information we need to use right now. I like to call it our "right-now memory." If we are referring to this buffer as short-term memory, typically it is referring to information that we are simply holding on to for a moment, like holding a phone number until we dial it. Alternatively, when it's called working memory, we're incorporating the idea that we may also be manipulating or working on the information we are holding in this storage buffer—such as when we do mental math. Whichever we call it, short-term memory or working memory, the storage is limited both in capacity and in time, and in many instances these terms are used interchangeably (even though the concepts are slightly different).

With respect to capacity, we have long known that a healthy individual can hold approximately seven items in their working memory buffer at any one time (e.g., Miller, 1956), and those items can only remain in that buffer without rehearsal (or before transferring to long-term storage) for 20–30 seconds (e.g., J. Brown, 1958). This is very different from what people will colloquially refer to as short-term memory. You may have heard people in conversation say that their short-term memory is failing because they can't remember what they had for breakfast that morning. To that, I would say that (1) anything that happened hours ago is no longer short-term memory because more than 30 seconds has passed, and (2) not remembering what you ate for breakfast is not a signal that your memory is failing (but more on non-normative changes later in this chapter). This is common, though. We even see this conversation play out in children's movies like *Finding Nemo* (Stanton & Walters, 2003). The character Dory has what she terms "short-term memory loss." By that terminology, we'd think that she has no ability to hold on to information for use right now, which would indicate that she can't even have a conversation because nothing is available for her to use in the moment. Rather, Dory is unable to transfer information to her long-term memory (the third stage of the information processing system). She cannot move information from immediate availability to long-term storage, resulting in an inability to recall what happened earlier that day or a previous conversation because it was never stored for later use. This is not short-term memory loss, but rather an encoding (i.e., input) problem. That's to say Dory's short-term memory seems fine, and likely her long-term memory is fine, but the information she is trying to remember never made its way to long-term storage.

For older adults, we do see changes in the efficiency and usage of this working memory/short-term memory buffer (e.g., Balota et al., 2000; Craik, 1994; Erickson & Barnes, 2003), just not in the same way that Dory does. This second buffer in the information processing system is where we begin to see some normative changes in the system, resulting from a variety of causes.

First, if you think back to the discussion on speed of processing in Chapter 3, you'll remember that older adults tend to process information at a slower rate of speed (Salthouse, 1996). In typical day-to-day functioning for most tasks, this is not an issue of concern because most of the time we can do tasks at whatever speed we need to with no inherent time limit. However, this is not necessarily the case when we consider the input of information through the information processing system. If information can only be held in our working memory buffer for less than 30 seconds before it fades or needs to be moved to long-term storage, but information is still coming in (slowly) when the beginning of that set/message is starting to fade, something will be lost. That is, by the time all the information is in, some is already leaving. As you can imagine, this can be problematic when we need the whole and not just bits and pieces. Research conducted out of Japan showed support for the impact of processing speed on working memory (Kunimi & Kojima, 2014). In this study, Kunimi and Kojima (2014) asked participants to complete a digit span test and a processing speed test. In the digit span test, participants were presented with a series of digits either visually or auditorily and asked to repeat back the digits forward and backward. That is, if they were presented with the digits 1-2-3, they would repeat 1-2-3 in the forward condition and 3-2-1 in the backward condition. If correct, they would be presented with a string of digits one longer than the previous one again and again, until the string was too long to remember and repeat back—presumably at the individual's upper capacity limit. For the digit substitution task (measuring processing speed), participants saw a code where the digits 1–9 were assigned a symbol (see Figure 4.2). Then they saw a string of digits and needed to write the corresponding symbol as quickly as possible. Once completed, the participants additionally spent some time copying symbols from the top of the page, and speed for this was measured as well. Data were analyzed to determine if working memory could be predicted from digit span and processing speed measures, while incorporating age as an additional variable. Results showed that this was indeed the case. Additionally, results showed a negative correlation between processing speed and working memory, suggesting that as processing speed (i.e., length of time) goes up, working memory goes down. While we can't argue from this research that processing speed causes the lowered working memory capacity (nor would we want to), we can see that there is a predictable relationship with increasing age.

FIGURE 4.2 ■ Digit Substitution Task

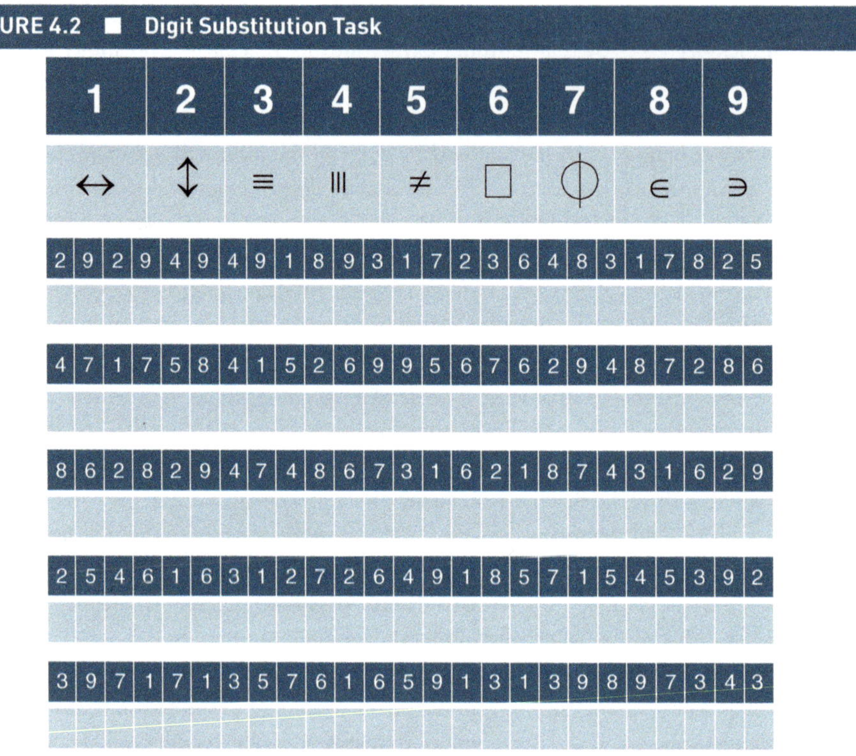

Source: Gilmour G., Porcelli S., Bertaina-Anglade V., Arce E., Dukart J., et al. Relating Constructs of Attention and Working Memory to Social Withdrawal in Alzheimer's Disease and Schizophrenia: Issues Regarding Paradigm Selection. Neurosci. Biobehav. Rev. 2019;97:47–69. doi: 0.1016/j.neubiorev.2018.09.025.

Alternatively, we could consider the research discussed in Chapter 3 supporting the inhibition deficit hypothesis (Hasher & Zacks, 1988). This research supported the idea that older adults were less efficient at inhibiting or discarding irrelevant information from their information processing system (e.g., Connelly et al., 1991). Arguments for and against the information being irrelevant were made, but regardless of whether the information is relevant, it holds space. When it holds space in one's working memory buffer, there is little space left (from what is already limited) to be used for the task at hand. Connelly et al. (1991) demonstrated this easily when they asked participants to ignore text presented in a different font. Not only were older adults less adept at ignoring it, but they found inhibition even more challenging when the information was meaningful. This affects the capacity of one's working memory in that the reader would be holding target text as well as distractor text in their working memory—or at least attempting to do so. This not only will impact how much relevant information can fit in the now-more-limited buffer, but also will impact the individual's understanding of the text as they begin to move the information further into the information processing system.

We can also consider that many older adults have been out of practice of using memory and working memory strategies for some time—at least in the same way that young adults are using them. These strategies are useful and quite well practiced among young adults still in school, for example, when listening to lectures and taking notes on what they are hearing. However, older adults have potentially been out of the school environment for a long time and are likely not as well practiced at the strategies needed to be successful at these specific types of working memory tasks. That said, it is possible for strategies to be helpful, but we need to consider that the strategies themselves use resources if they are not automatic/well practiced.

The good news is that research on working memory strategies suggests that training older adults on working memory strategies can be beneficial. That is, older adults can improve their working memory performance using strategies such as verbal encoding and mental imagery (e.g., Bailey et al., 2008; Borella et al., 2017; Brehmer et al., 2012; Carretti et al., 2007). In one study, Borella et al. (2017) trained participants on an adaptive working memory task or an adaptive working memory task along with mental imagery strategies and compared their performance to an untrained control group. In the adaptive working memory task, participants worked on training to remember longer and longer lists of sentences. The group also training with visual working memory was trained to create mental images to help during their training sessions. Results showed that not only did older adults improve their working memory performance on the specific tasks they trained on, but participants also transferred some of the improvements to related tasks, such as forward and backward digit span tests. Anecdotally, I have seen this play out in my laboratory as well. Commonly, as a working memory measure, I will assess participants' forward and backward digit spans. And usually, I see the measure to be somewhere in the range of 5 to 9 items, depending on age and whether it is the forward or the backward measure. In one instance specifically, I had an older man score a 13. This is well out of the range of what I typically saw, and I was confused (and frankly, impressed, because my digit span measure isn't that high)—until he told me that he was a retired accountant. His practice—"training" if you will—using numbers for his entire career transferred to his ability to remember numbers in other contexts.

As you would imagine, declines in working memory with age are somewhat task dependent. That is, if tasks are more difficult, involve more information, or are unfamiliar, we'll see measurable differences between young and older adults in a laboratory setting (e.g., Craik et al., 2010; Iachini et al., 2009; Peich et al., 2013)—much like in the research described here. However, in real life, where context and tasks are familiar, we can (and do) see instances of older adults functioning just fine because their context and experience can provide support (e.g., Margolin, 2018). A healthy older adult can easily read a book, carry on a conversation, or follow a recipe—all tasks that require much of their working memory resources—demonstrating that laboratory tasks may get at a basic efficiency issue in their *right now memory*, but in real life, with real tasks, there is likely no issue at all.

Long-Term Memory

Once information has moved far enough in our information processing system to be used by our working memory, we may deem it important or useful enough to hold on to for later use. If that is the case, we will engage in some type of rehearsal (i.e., practice) and move the information from our working memory buffer to our **long-term memory** buffer. The long-term memory buffer is a seemingly endless storage unit for information. While some may argue that there are limits to its storage capacity, this is not exactly true. Rather, the limits here are in retrieval (e.g., Kane & Engle, 2000; Unsworth et al., 2012). That is, unlimited amounts of information make it in. Not all of it can make it back out. What determines whether something that has been stored can be retrieved and used again is its connection to other information within the long-term memory buffer (Collins & Loftus, 1975).

In 1975, Collins and Loftus developed a basic theory of how this information is stored, called the semantic network model (Collins & Loftus, 1975), which prompted the further development of these types of theories since that time (e.g., Carpenter, 2001; McClelland & Rogers, 2003; McClelland et al., 1986). These types of memory storage theories are called **nodal network theories** and are based on the original premise that information is stored in long-term memory as a network, with related information connected to each other (see Figure 4.3). To get from one piece of information to another, something needs to be used or activated, and then the activation spreads to the next, related piece of information. In relation to the idea of retrieval, we can get information out if a connected piece of information (usually some type of cue or reminder) is activated. However, if nothing is connected, it won't be retrieved. With that in mind, we could consider that something could exist in long-term memory without ever being used or retrieved.

So the questions here would be (1) can older adults get access to the information they have stored in long-term memory, and (2) can older adults form new long-term memories? The answers here are yes and yes, albeit with more effort and more opportunities for mistakes. According to one nodal network theory, node structure theory (NST; MacKay, 1987),

FIGURE 4.3 ■ Network Model

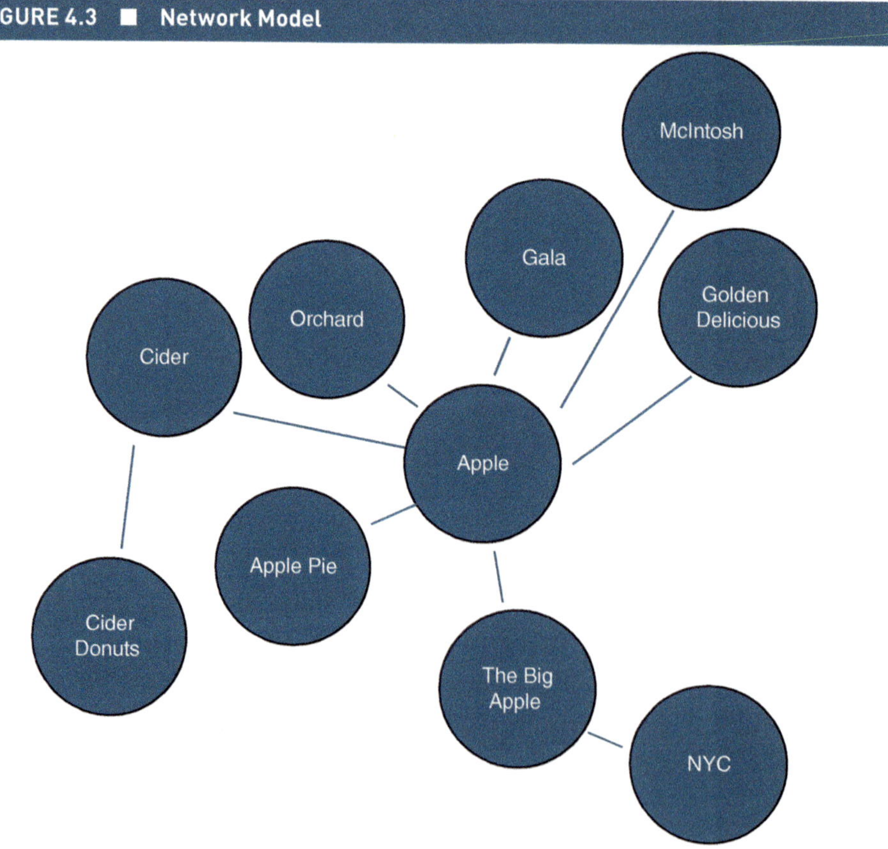

connections between nodes (i.e., pieces of information) can be strong or weak. If they are weak, there is a lesser chance of activation spreading to the connected node. Interestingly, Burke et al. (2000) proposed a corollary to this hypothesis that describes what happens to the network with aging: It weakens (transmission deficit hypothesis, or TDH). TDH tells us that the connections between all pieces of information weaken throughout the system as we get older. This is not normally a problem, and really goes unnoticed most of the time. However, when compounded by fewer connections (leading one to rely on only one or two weak connections), infrequent use, or a long time since the last use, we may see retrieval failures.

The typical weakening proposed in TDH may explain what happened with Nana and the blueberry muffins. If she hadn't made the muffins in a while, it is possible that her connection to the information about the recipe was weakened beyond what would generally occur with aging, resulting in an inability to retrieve that information. It is not disease related, but rather just a compounding of two small amounts of weakened connections to create something larger. Alternatively, if this was a repeated forgetting that couldn't be refreshed by reading the recipe, or one that was repeated for more information than just that one recipe, we could start to be concerned about Nana. However, I'll discuss these concerns in more detail later in this chapter. I should also note here that while these theories are older, they align quite well with the newer neuropsychological research (e.g., Bassett et al., 2018; Sporns, 2014; Sutterer & Tranel, 2017), where nodes compare to neurons and connections between nodes compare to neural connections/synapses. Altogether, the theoretical nodal network approaches approximate the physiological neural network.

Semantic, Procedural, and Episodic Long-Term Memories

Within the long-term memory buffer, we see that there is a systems approach to organization (e.g., Rutherford et al., 2012). That is, there are different types of information that we'd be likely to store in our long-term memory stores: **semantic memory**, **procedural memory**, and **episodic memory** (see Table 4.1). As these are separate systems within the long-term memory buffer, evidence shows that normative aging affects each differently and that declines are not the pattern for all these types of long-term memory (Zacks & Hasher, 2006).

The episodic memory system is one of these long-term memory systems, which includes memory for information about "episodes" or events. Memory about a day at the beach or a trip to the store would be episodic because this is an event that occurred. As you can imagine, such memories contain multiple components. For example, a memory about a trip to the store may

TABLE 4.1 ■ Types of Long-Term Memory

Semantic Memory	Memory for information	Facts, definitions, trivia
Episodic Memory	Memory for an event	First day of school
Procedural Memory	Memory for how to do something	How to ride a bike

Source: Tulving, E. (1987). Multiple memory systems and consciousness. *Human Neurobiology, 6*(2), 67–80.

include what time of day you went, some of the items that were on the shopping list, whether you saw anyone you knew at the store, if you used a shopping cart, and more. And, because there are usually many components to an episodic memory, there is ample opportunity for a piece or pieces of a memory to be forgotten. Memories aren't stored as films in our mind, but rather are stored in individual, separate pieces. So, if a connection to a piece of that memory is weak (as NST and TDH could predict), that piece of the memory will be lost. As such, episodic memory is particularly susceptible to forgetting as we grow older. Weaken one connection, and a piece of the memory can be forgotten. That doesn't mean the whole memory is gone, but just a piece of it. However, weaken enough of them, and potentially the whole memory can be forgotten.

Research on episodic memory in older adults supports the idea that this is the case (e.g., Kausler, 1994; Shing et al., 2010); even in healthy aging, adults show differential decline in episodic memory (e.g., Korkki et al., 2020). Specifically, older adults show most difficulty in retrieving episodic memories for recent events. These are things that have happened in a time where they are already in their older adulthood. During this time, Shing et al. (2010) suggest there is difficulty in association mechanisms, and binding the bits of the episode together is important for cohesive memory retrieval (e.g., Murre et al., 2006; Treisman, 1996). That is, there is difficulty connecting the recent events into the network of what already exists in their memory systems. Taken together with what I discussed earlier regarding weakened connections, it makes sense that if an older adult is not able to create a strong connection to a recent episode, they will have trouble retrieving it later.

Semantic memory works differently, however. This type of long-term memory refers to knowledge and meaning of information. Facts. Trivia. Knowledge. Vocabulary. Unlike episodic memory, semantic memory does not usually consist of multiple components. As such, bits and pieces need not combine together for one memory to be retrieved. Connections to each piece of information can be weak, to be sure, but successful recall of a piece of knowledge is not dependent on the recall of other bits of knowledge. Moreover, because of older adults' extensive experience in the world, their knowledge base is just as extensive. Semantic memory is one area where we don't see normative decline in older adults' performance—but often see comparable performance when compared to their younger counterparts (e.g., Federmeier et al., 2002; Lövdén et al., 2004; Margolin, 2018). Simply put, older adults just know more stuff.

Difficulties can arise here in semantic memory, but usually those difficulties are related to when speed to retrieve is involved (Salthouse, 1996). Think about playing *Jeopardy*. This is pure semantic memory retrieval. Older adults likely know more of the clues to those answers, but the speed to buzz in and provide their response hinders older adults in performing as top contenders on the show. Rather, you see middle-aged contestants winning big. These individuals are usually old enough to have a substantially wide knowledge base and diffuse semantic memory connections. However, they are not yet old enough to have experienced a slowdown in their processing speed, which would inhibit their "trigger finger" in responding before their opponent. The result? Lots of knowledge and a fast response time. In *Jeopardy*, that's the winning combination (pun most definitely intended!). But, I'll discuss more about *Jeopardy* and knowledge in Chapter 5.

Obviously, real-life situations don't require that an individual "buzz in" to answer a question or have a conversation. And so, time-related retrieval difficulties are rarely an issue. However, there are instances where difficulties in semantic memory retrieval can prove to be very frustrating—the case of word retrieval failures. Word retrieval failures are best known as the **tip-of-the-tongue phenomenon** (e.g., Abrams et al., 2007; R. Brown & McNeill, 1966; Burke et al., 2004; Burke et al., 1991; see also Figure 4.4). Everyone has experienced this phenomenon, young and older. You know the feeling: You are trying to think of a word, but you just can't. You know you know it, but it just won't come. Sometimes you know the first letter or the part of speech (noun, verb, etc.), but you just can't think of the word. It's frustrating, to be sure, but not harmful. Nor is it indicative of anything other than normal memory functioning. Here's what we think is happening: weakened connections. That's it. The word is there, stored in your semantic memory, but the connections are weak enough that you can't access the pronunciation of the word at the time you need it. For young adults, this is usually because the words haven't been frequently or recently used or are less familiar to start. For older adults, that weakening is compounded by age-related weakening.

In 2007, my colleagues and I presented the theory behind the phenomenon, as well as the rates and rationale for older adults' increased rates of occurrence (Abrams et al., 2007). First, we argued that the reason for tip-of-the-tongue occurrence can be easily explained through TDH. With weakened connections, activation can't spread from the definition of the word to the word itself, or to the pronunciation of the word in our semantic memory system. That said,

FIGURE 4.4 ■ Transmission Deficit Hypothesis and Tip-of-the-Tongue

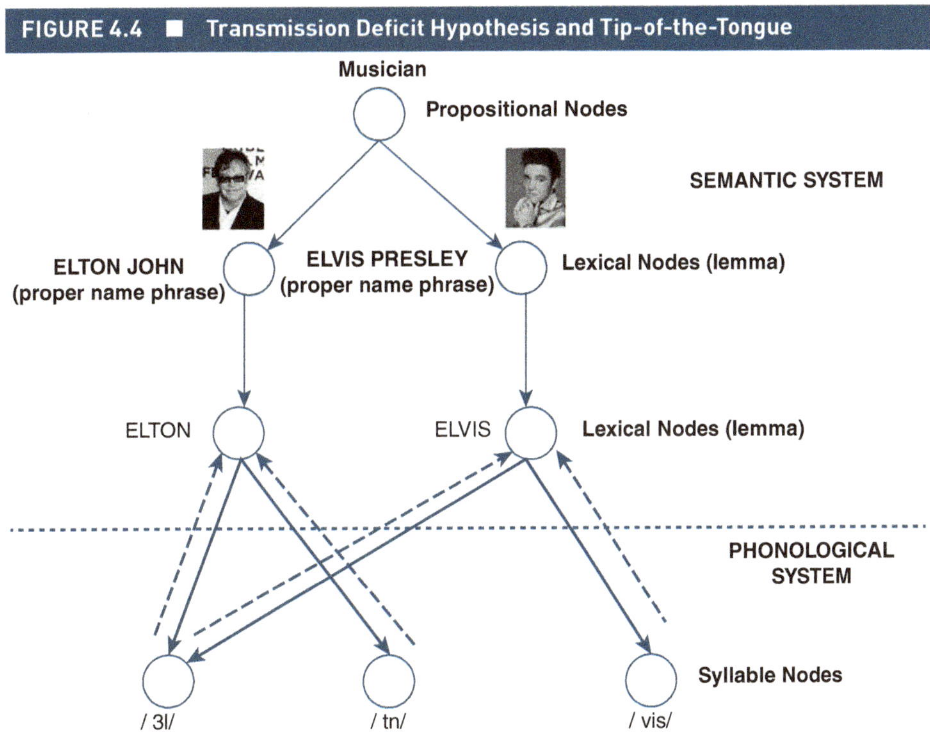

Source: White, K. K., Abrams, L., & Frame, E. A. (2013). Semantic category moderates phonological priming of proper name retrieval during tip-of-the-tongue states. *Language and Cognitive Processes, 28*(4), 561–576.

if connections are weaker for older adults, as predicted by TDH, we can (and do) see an increase in the rate of occurrence. This is documented both in the laboratory and in real-life diary studies (e.g., A. S. Brown & Nix, 1996; Burke et al., 1991; Farrell & Abrams, 2011; James & Burke, 2000), and confirmed in neural imaging that showed atrophy of left insula gray matter (Shafto et al., 2007). Moreover, the tip-of-the-tongue phenomenon more often happens for proper names (e.g., Burke et al., 1991) and for words not frequently or recently used (e.g., Abrams et al., 2007), again suggesting weakened connections. Connections can, however, be strengthened by accessing some of the information contained in the nodes—most effectively with the sounds of the beginning of the words (e.g., Burke et al., 2004; James & Burke, 2000; White & Abrams, 2002). This is positive and is likely what happens in day-to-day life when a tip-of-the-tongue event automatically resolves itself—often very quickly. Usually, frustration lasts a few minutes, and is either resolved or forgotten as the individual moves on in their day. Sometimes, carrying on in their day results in encountering the sounds of the word they were trying to think of (in another context or in another word), and resolution occurs.

The advantage that an older adult has here is their vast semantic memory. While knowing more words provides more opportunity for a tip-of-the-tongue event to occur, it also provides many opportunities for alternative words or synonyms to take the place of the word we are having trouble accessing. In some cases, those alternatives are called *blockers, interlopers*, or *persistent alternates* because they can block the retrieval of the so-called right word (and really it's not until an individual can release that alternative that they can get the word they originally wanted; Meyer & Bock, 1992; Perfect & Hanley, 1992). However, in some cases, that's OK. And, the individual will carry on with the alternative word because it fits the bill just fine in the context in which they wish to use it. In the case of a proper name, that doesn't always work. However, for other kinds of words, it is definitely an advantage. It's also important to put these word retrieval failures in perspective. While these instances are frustrating, they are not usually life threatening, nor do they really interfere with normal day-to-day functioning.

A third type of long-term memory is known as procedural memory. This type of long-term memory is also fairly resistant to forgetting, as it is a very different type of memory than the other two, and as such likely uses very different components in the brain (e.g., R. M. Brown & Robertson, 2007; Karni & Korman, 2011). Procedural memory is "how to" memory that allows us to remember how to do something, like how to ride a bike or play bridge. These types of memory are less reliant on bits and pieces like episodic memory and are also less reliant on language. Think about how you might attempt to verbally explain how to ride a bike—that'd be very difficult to communicate (but probably very funny to try). Positively, procedural memories do not seem to fall victim to normative age-related changes, making it distinct from episodic and semantic memory (e.g., Churchill et al., 2003; Mitchell, 1989; Nilsson, 2003). Instead, research on procedural memory shows that not only do procedural memories seem resistant to the impact of normative age-related changes; they also seem to persist longer than other types of long-term memory (e.g., Mitchell et al., 1990). It really is just like riding a bike.

It should be noted here that we may have semantic, episodic, and procedural memories for the same information, and those pieces will be impacted differently as we age. For example, we may have a procedural memory for how to ride a bike, but we also may have episodic memories surrounding when we learned to ride it as well as semantic memories that are factual about ourselves that we know how to ride one. One of these memories can inform the other and act as a cue in the case of weakened connections when something is forgotten, and for this reason (as well as others such as context, distraction, and hearing or visual impairments) we may not see these specific patterns of diminished episodic memory, bolstered semantic memory, and intact procedural memory play out exactly this way all the time in day-to-day scenarios.

OTHER TYPES OF MEMORY

Sensory memory, short-term/working memory, and long-term memory are not the only ways we use our memory. That's to say there are instances where we remember things that may be longer in term but don't fit easily into the categorizations described earlier—but are frequent uses of our memory systems. Sometimes, we must remember to do something later, or we recall information without trying to think back and recollect. These too can be impacted by limitations in our information processing system and are explored next.

Prospective Memory

Prospective memory is an interesting one, and not one you read about or maybe even hear about outside of cognitive science research. However, it is one that we use every day, perhaps without even realizing it. Have you ever said to yourself, "I can't forget to pick up milk at the store on the way home from work today"? That's **prospective memory**. It is memory for our future intended actions, which require an individual to remember to respond in a specific way when something in the future is encountered (McDaniel & Einstein, 2007).

As you can imagine, this type of memory can be impacted in various ways—the first of which is attention. Like other types of memory, paying attention and directing your mental energy to the information is necessary if it is to be encoded for later use. As such, we often see prospective memory correlated negatively with a busy lifestyle (e.g., Cuttler & Graf, 2007)—the busier you are, the less likely you are to remember to pick up the milk. This is normal, and expected, based on what we know about attention. Busy = less attention paid to each individual task. The same pattern holds true for older adults. That is, older adults also tend to show difficulties with prospective memory (e.g., Brom & Kliegel, 2014; Einstein et al., 2000; Kamberis et al., 2021; Scarampi & Gilbert, 2021; Strickland et al., 2022; Varley et al., 2021; West & Craik, 2001). While not indicative of anything other than normative aging processes, the implications of a decline in prospective memory can be impactful if they are surrounding something important, like taking medication (e.g., Zogg et al., 2012).

Interestingly, there is a distinction between the links created to attempt to remember the prospective memory—that is, the cue. For instance, if the prospective memory is time-related or if it is event-related, we may see differences in the success in retrieval and subsequent action taken (though research does show that working memory also plays a role in successful execution of the intended action, which may put older adults at a disadvantage above and beyond the prospective memory requirements; Park et al., 1997). Think about needing to take a medication in the evening. An individual could make this a time-related event and cue the medication to be taken at 6:00 p.m., and that would be just fine. However, 6:00 p.m. is only one cue, and nothing really signals that it is 6:00 p.m. (distinct from 5:30 p.m. or 7:00 p.m.). Because of this ambiguity, an individual could reasonably miss it. The time could come and go, and no medication would be taken. Alternatively, you could make this an event-related prospective memory and tie the medication to *dinnertime*. Here, you have many more cues to link to the task: setting the table, preparing the food, sitting down, eating, cleaning up, and so on. These are helpful, because if you miss one cue or one cue is weak, you have others to help you remember to take your medication. This is particularly helpful for an older adult whose prospective memory is mediated by factors such as processing speed and working memory (e.g., Park et al., 1997; West & Craik, 2001). Providing ample time to reach the desired response is helpful and, in the case of taking a medication at dinnertime, would provide more opportunities to take it. After all, dinnertime may last for 60 minutes or more, but it's only 6:00 p.m. for 60 seconds.

iStockPhoto/FG Trade Latin

Additionally, older adults and busy people alike would benefit from external cueing and memory aids in these instances (e.g., Schryer & Ross, 2013). There is nothing bad about doing things like setting an alarm, leaving sticky notes, keeping a running list, or anything else that can help remind you of the prospective memory events you intend to take action on. For example, if you need to take medication at 6:00 p.m., you could take it at dinnertime, or you could set an alarm to remind you to do it at 6:00 p.m. Either would be helpful, and either would result in your successful self-administering of the medication. I use external memory aids all the time—putting a sticky note on the front door to remind me to grab something on my way out of the house, or setting an alarm in my phone to remind me to send an email in the morning (this is fantastic for those moments when you are trying to go to sleep and you suddenly think of something you need to do the next day. Just ask Siri to remind you to do the task, and you will get a reminder alert at the time you request). The trick is to recognize that using these tools is just that: using tools. You are not cheating the system. You are providing support for yourself to work within the constraints of normal memory function. The other trick is to recognize that forgetting to do something later is also a part of normal memory function. It is part of a typical busy life and part of a typical healthy aging process.

Implicit Versus Explicit Memory

The types of memory we've described to this point could be generally classified as **explicit memory**—that is, memory for information that is purposefully encoded and purposefully retrieved. Explicit memory is notably poorer in older adults (e.g., Jelicic, 1996; Ward et al., 2013), especially when involving episodic memories and/or strain on limited processing speed, attentional resources, or even executive function (i.e., directing and allocating the resources to where they need to go). Additionally, explicit memory can be fed by a belief that memory is poorer in older adults—a stereotype. I'll discuss this further in Chapter 7, but the belief that one will have memory impairments in older age can negatively impact functioning (e.g., Eich et al., 2014; Hess et al., 2003). It's a self-fulfilling prophecy. It's almost as if the individual thinks, "Well, I'm older, so I'm not going to do well on this memory test, so why bother trying?" And, then they do poorly. To be sure, there are other mechanisms beside this self-fulfilling prophecy, because research does support the idea that older adults' explicit memory is indeed less accurate and less efficient than that of their younger counterparts and is often less accurate compared to implicit memory (discussed next; e.g., Drury et al., 2000; Light & Singh, 1987) because of the difficulties already described.

Implicit memory, on the other hand, describes a type of memory that is automatic or not effortfully encoded or retrieved. That is, an individual retrieves information without actively trying to remember. For example, say your roommate is going to the store and asks you what kind of cheese you want for your sandwiches this week and you respond quickly with "feta." This is not a typical type of cheese for sandwiches, but you had been on TikTok earlier and saw a recipe with feta cheese baked with tomatoes and mixed with pasta. By responding "feta" to your roommate's inquiry, you were remembering the TikTok recipe without trying to remember the TikTok recipe. The main difference between explicit and implicit memory is the intention to remember.

Interestingly, implicit memory is often very resilient. Like what we'd see in amnesic patients, older adults do not seem to show consistent deficits in this type of memory (e.g., Light & Singh, 1987). That is, implicit and explicit memories seem to operate on two different systems—one that can be easily and consistently impacted by variables such as age and amnesia and at least one other that is not necessarily impacted by these variables. Research on implicit memory with older adults, and research on implicit memory more generally, demonstrates that changes and age differences demonstrated in this type of memory are small and may be task-dependent (e.g., Chiarello & Hoyer, 1988; Drury et al., 2000; Maki et al., 1999; Mitchell & Bruss, 2003; Schacter et al., 1992). For example, Mitchell and Bruss (2003) asked participants to complete a series of five implicit memory tests and three explicit memory tests. In the implicit memory tests, participants were asked to complete word fragments (e.g., *e_e__a__*) or word stems (e.g., *ele-*) with the first words that came to mind, as well as completing pictures and naming pictures. Each of these implicit memory tests required participants to respond to the test stimulus itself, rather than intentionally thinking back to remember. In the explicit tests, participants were asked to think back to recall based on a cue or without a cue (which looked like the words and pictures that needed completing in the implicit task). Data from these tests showed comparable implicit memory scores when comparing the young and older participant groups, consistent with the idea that implicit memory is well maintained across the life span.

Source Memory

Another type of memory in which there may be some concern with an older age group is **source memory** (e.g., Bröder & Meiser, 2007). This is memory for where the information came from—that is, what is its source? Ordinarily, where we learned information isn't necessarily cause for concern. However, there are some instances where not knowing the source can be problematic. For instance, did you think about taking your medication, or did you actually do it? Did you pay the handyman already, or did you just write the check? You may have mental images of these events taking place, but are those images sourced from the actual event or from the daydream/thought of the event? You can see the potential for problems here: taking medication twice or not at all, paying the handyman twice or not at all, and so on.

The question is this: Are older adults able to accurately monitor the source of their memory? The answer is not so much (e.g., Dywan & Jacoby, 1990; Schacter et al., 1991; Siedlecki et al., 2005; Trott et al., 1997). This makes sense in the context of what we've already discussed here. As you can imagine, the source of the information is simply additional information about the event in which we are learning it. It is the context component of the episodic memory. Given weakened connections for older adults as well as the susceptibility for losing pieces of episodic memories, there is also a likelihood of missing pieces of the source of the information. For example, in one study, Dywan and Jacoby (1990) showed young and older adult participants a list of fictitious names, and then showed them a second list of names that included some from the first list and some famous names. Participants were asked to identify the famous names. However, older adults mistakenly identified the names from the first list as also being "famous." Their decision was based on familiarity rather than actual source. That is, they were unable to remember where the name came from—did they remember the name from a movie or magazine, or did they remember it from the list they read? The result was that they based their judgment on whether or not they knew the name—that's all the information they had available.

This example is very typical of what we see in the examination of source memory in laboratory tasks, where older adults show difficulties in remembering and using source information. However, this isn't impactful for day-to-day functioning. Specifically, given older adults' vast life experience, the source of information is usually not needed, and may be discarded to preserve limited memory resources for what *is* needed. This is positive in that we understand that while we may be able to demonstrate deficits in a controlled lab environment, there is something about an older adult's life experience and familiar contexts that can override any difficulties we may be able to expose in the lab. Let us not lose the forest for the trees—the small bits of source memory not remembered are the trees, but the forest is much more valuable. And, the forest is the independent functioning of an older adult.

AGE-RELATED VERSUS ATYPICAL MEMORY CHANGES

To this point, this chapter has discussed primarily normative age-related changes in memory. All of these are common, minimal, and gradual and don't typically disrupt day-to-day functioning. This is positive for our perspective on aging as it pertains to cognitive function. However, there are instances when memory changes occur beyond the typical—due to illness, injury, stroke, and other factors. These changes are usually larger, occur more quickly, and more obviously interfere with normative day-to-day functioning. To be sure, any change that is concerning should be explored with a health care provider.

Clinical Memory Assessments

First, we could discuss how we might go about determining whether memory deficits exist beyond what is normative for an aging adult. Memory assessments are a good way to start. These can consist of standardized assessments, self-report measures, family/caregiver questionnaires and interviews, and task-based assessments. One common standardized measure of memory and cognitive function is called the Mini–Mental State Examination (MMSE; Folstein et al., 1975; see also Figure 4.5). This test asks about orientation to space and time, short-term memory for items, ability to follow simple instructions, and attention. While older, this test is still a good first pass for screening to determine if there may be something further to assess. Additionally, the MMSE can be used on psychiatric populations (e.g., Lamarre & Patten, 1991) and those who have suffered head injury (e.g., de Guise et al., 2011) to determine mental status.

Beyond the MMSE as a screening tool, clinicians may ask for self-report. This can be helpful in early stages of clinical memory issues, but not necessarily later ones. That is, early on, one might be aware of memory difficulties; however, once progressed, the individual may not remember that they can't remember. In these instances, a clinician may choose to ask an individual to perform a memory task for them to see their performance to something specific in that moment. These tasks are not usually difficult (digit span tests, etc.) but do bring about some of their own unique problems. For example, the clinician should consider the context in which they are conducting that memory test. Is it a loud emergency room? A quiet, unfamiliar doctor's office? In the presence of a loved one or not? Any of these can be worrisome, scary, or anxiety-provoking to an older adult who is already potentially scared about what is happening to them and fail to consider that the individual may perform better when in the familiar context of their home or day-to-day life, where they have contextual memory cues to help. Other alternatives involve the family members or caregivers. These individuals can watch for and record daily difficulties they see in completion of activities of daily living (e.g., feeding, dressing, bathing) and instrumental activities of daily living (e.g., laundry, preparing meals, paying bills) using a

FIGURE 4.5 ■ Mini-Mental State Examination

MMSE Sample Items

Orientation to Time

"What is the date?"

Naming

"What is this?" [Point to a pencil or pen.]

Reading

"Please read this and do what it says." [Show examinee the words on the stimulus form.]

CLOSE YOUR EYES

Source: Reproduced by special permission of the Publisher, Psychological Assessment Resources, Inc. (PAR), 16204 North Florida Avenue, Lutz, Florida 33549, from the Mini-Mental State Examination, by Marshal F. Folstein, MD and Susan E. Folstein, MD, Copyright 1975, 1998, 2001 and the Mini-Mental State Examination-2, Copyright 2010 by Mini Mental LLC, Inc. Published 2001, 2010 by PAR. Further reproduction is prohibited without permission of PAR. [Copyright@parinc.com].

diary. Questionnaires and checklists in this vein can also be helpful in identifying troublesome memory losses.

Memory and Dementia

Once the clinician has the data, though, how are distinctions made between normative age-related memory changes and those that are indicative of something more serious? This can be tricky in early stages of clinical memory loss and the different types of dementia (there are several, but I'll discuss those in more detail in Chapter 8). What is important to recognize, both for a layperson and for a clinician, is how much the memory impairment is impinging on daily functioning. It is also important to remember that not everyone develops dementia. In fact, rates are lower than many think they are. The National Institutes of Health (NIH) reported dementia in 7% of individuals aged 71–75 in 2002 (Plassman et al., 2007) and only 9.5 cases per 1,000 people as of 2016 (Ponjoan et al., 2019), and suggested that these low rates are likely within a context of ever-increasing streams of education. With that in mind, when a clinician is evaluating an individual, it is likely that they will rule out other factors before considering a dementia diagnosis.

For example, when Nana forgot the blueberry muffin recipe, we could see that while it worried my sister, it was not necessarily a sign that she was developing dementia. She had forgotten *one* recipe *one* time (and to be honest, most people can't remember a whole recipe, no matter their age or cognitive status). There are some questions that the doctor would need to ask before even approaching thinking about dementia for Nana. When was the last time she made those muffins? Had it been a while? Was she making them in a different context or different time of day than she normally would? How had Nana been sleeping and eating? Did other memory issues also occur? Did other behaviors change? Did those change suddenly or over time? And so on the conversation would go. A complete evaluation of her day-to-day function would need to be assessed, and dementia cannot be diagnosed based on one memory retrieval failure incident. Nor should it.

Importantly, extreme memory loss or confusion is *not* typical, and *not* a sign of normative aging processes, particularly if it happens quickly. These can be signs of something medical that can and should be treated quickly, such as stroke or delirium.

Memory and Nutrition

Nutrition should also be considered when discussing memory changes in older adulthood. In some cases, deficits in nutritional status, such as dehydration, electrolyte imbalance, and hypocalcemia (i.e., low blood calcium levels), can mimic memory impairments as can dementia or even delirium (e.g., Amanullah & Seeber, 2010; Fernandez-Romero & Spica, 2021). However, these are hardly problems of the mind. They just display as such. Rather, a clinician should test to rule out these medical causes of memory dysfunction and then work to remedy them. Changing hydration, prescribing medication, or treating underlying kidney or parathyroid illness can adjust these causes to help improve memory function.

iStockPhoto/Kiwis

Moreover, in the same way that we can nourish our minds with information to strengthen the connections that weaken with age, we can nourish our brains with good nutrition. This can be difficult in the case of dental problems, changes in taste or smell, and abilities/resources to prepare good meals (see earlier chapters on physical and sensory changes). However, research in this area demonstrates that eating foods with omega-3 fatty acids, like salmon or walnuts, can reduce the risk of cognitive decline in older adulthood (e.g., Loef & Walach, 2013; Moore et al., 2018). In my house, we call this "brain food," and it makes me happy that we all can feed our brains something good.

AGING WELL: MEMORY

Declines in memory function are a large source of fear surrounding aging and may be the one that makes people most fearful. However, as this chapter has discussed, aging well, and preserving memory function, isn't just possible—it's common. Typical changes that occur in the human memory system are not large, nor should they be feared. Often, older adults know more, function well, and do *not* commonly develop dementia. In fact, rates of dementia have been declining over the last 20 years in large part thanks to increases in educational levels (see National Institute on Aging, n.d.). So, instead of thinking about what goes wrong with memory, let us think about what goes right, and what we can do to increase those odds. The first of these is to feed our brain what it wants. More education (formal and informal), practice using that knowledge (to strengthen the connections), and experiences (of all kinds) can provide the support that our information processing system needs. Add in nourishment for your brain in the forms of hydration and omega-3s, and we've got a recipe for something good.

KEY TERMS

buffer
episodic memory
explicit memory
implicit memory
information processing system
long-term memory
nodal network theories
procedural memory
prospective memory
semantic memory
sensory memory
short-term memory
source memory
tip-of-the-tongue phenomenon
working memory

COMPREHENSION QUESTIONS

1. What parts of the information processing system experience age-related changes?
2. What are some reasons for forgetting in older adulthood?
3. Explain how processing speed can impact memory.

4. How would one differentiate between normative and atypical memory changes?
5. Explain the impact of inhibition deficit on working memory limitations.
6. How does context impact older adults' memory encoding?
7. Why would episodic memory be impacted more than procedural memory?
8. Explain the impact of weak connections across the information processing system.
9. How does aging impact prospective memory, and how can this be managed?

ADDITIONAL READINGS

Brédart, S. (2019). Strategies to improve name learning: A review. *European Psychologist, 24*(4), 349–358. https://doi.org/10.1027/1016-9040/a000363

Denburg, N. L., Buchanan, T. W., Tranel, D., & Adolphs, R. (2003). Evidence for preserved emotional memory in normal older persons. *Emotion, 3*(3), 239–253. https://doi.org/10.1037/1528-3542.3.3.239

Guillaume, C., Clochon, P., Denise, P., Rauchs, G., Guillery-Girard, B., Eustache, F., & Desgranges, B. (2009). Early age-related changes in episodic memory retrieval as revealed by event-related potentials. *NeuroReport, 20*(2), 191–196. https://doi.org/10.1097/WNR.0b013e32831b44ca

Henry, J. D., Hering, A., Haines, S., Grainger, S. A., Koleits, N., McLennan, S., Pelly, R., Doyle, C., Rose, N. S., Kliegel, M., & Rendell, P. G. (2021). Acting with the future in mind: Testing competing prospective memory interventions. *Psychology and Aging, 36*(4), 491–503. https://doi.org/10.1037/pag0000593

Laukka, E. J., Köhncke, Y., Papenberg, G., Fratiglioni, L., & Bäckman, L. (2020). Combined genetic influences on episodic memory decline in older adults without dementia. *Neuropsychology, 34*(6), 654–666. https://doi.org/10.1037/neu0000637

Mitchell, K. J., & Johnson, M. K. (2009). Source monitoring 15 years later: What have we learned from fMRI about the neural mechanisms of source memory? *Psychological Bulletin, 135*(4), 638–677. https://doi.org/10.1037/a0015849

Müller, N. C. J., Genzel, L., Konrad, B. N., Pawlowski, M., Neville, D., Fernández, G., Steiger, A., & Dresler, M. (2016). Motor skills enhance procedural memory formation and protect against age-related decline. *PLOS One, 11*(6), e0157770. https://doi.org/10.1371/journal.pone.0157770

Mullet, H. G., Scullin, M. K., Hess, T. J., Scullin, R. B., Arnold, K. M., & Einstein, G. O. (2013). Prospective memory and aging: Evidence for preserved spontaneous retrieval with exact but not related cues. *Psychology and Aging, 28*(4), 910–922. https://doi.org/10.1037/a0034347

Nyberg, L. (2017). Functional brain imaging of episodic memory decline in ageing. *Journal of Internal Medicine, 281*, 65–74. https://doi.org/10.1111/joim.12533

Ortega, A., Gómez-Ariza, C. J., Román, P., & Bajo, M. T. (2012). Memory inhibition, aging, and the executive deficit hypothesis. *Journal of Experimental Psychology: Learning, Memory, and Cognition, 38*(1), 178–186. https://doi.org/10.1037/a0024510

Park, D. C., & Festini, S. B. (2017). Theories of memory and aging: A look at the past and a glimpse of the future. *The Journals of Gerontology: Series B, Psychological Sciences and Social Sciences, 72*(1), 82–90. https://doi.org/10.1093/geronb/gbw066

Zuber, S., Ihle, A., Loaiza, V. M., Schnitzspahn, K. M., Stahl, C., Phillips, L. H., Kaller, C. P., & Kliegel, M. (2019). Explaining age differences in working memory: The role of updating, inhibition, and shifting. *Psychology & Neuroscience, 12*(2), 191–208. https://doi.org/10.1037/pne0000151

Amanda Edwards/Getty Images

5 INTELLIGENCE AND WISDOM

LEARNING OBJECTIVES

5.1 Identify the different types of intelligence.

5.2 Describe how intelligence is assessed across the life span, including psychometric and cognitive-structural approaches.

5.3 Describe and contrast fluid and crystalized intelligence, including the changes demonstrated in older adulthood.

5.4 Explain how an older adult may remain mentally sharp and agile well into their older adult years, including influences of physical health and mental exercise.

5.5 Describe postformal thought and how older adults can accept and think through ambiguity.

5.6 Explain how differences in knowledge and experience can inform wisdom.

As a child, I was what you'd call a nerd (who am I kidding? I'm still a nerd). But, as a nerd, one of the things I loved was a family tradition of watching the game show *Jeopardy* every evening after dinner. We loved it so much that one time, my sister and I made up our own version of the show and forced our parents and grandparents to play the game with us—I was the host. But every night, when 7:30 rolled around, we'd all cuddle up in the living room, and we'd race to provide the question to the answer. Every time I got one right, I'd be elated. My favorites were when they had a college tournament or a teen tournament, because that meant the clues would be a little easier and I'd have a better chance of getting them right. Then, in high school, I was finally old enough to try out for the show. Home internet access was new, and I had a dial-up connection, so it was slow to load, but that didn't deter me. I waited patiently and filled out the form to try out. I was so excited. But somehow, kids at school found out and mercilessly teased me (though I told nobody except my parents, so I have no clue how they found out). So, I abandoned my desire to try out for the show.

Fast-forward to a few years later, when I learned that a college tournament tryout was to be held within only a two-hour drive from my college. I was *in*. My boyfriend (now husband) took me, with faith that I'd be great. I went into that hotel conference room and took my seat, pen in hand, answer sheet in my lap. Clues came up on a screen in front of us, and I quickly jotted down my questions/answers. I was sure of every response; I knew I had nailed it. Until I didn't. I had a tip-of-the-tongue moment. Who *was* that actor who played opposite Mel Gibson in the *Lethal Weapon* movies? I could picture his face and repeat his lines, but for the life of me, I could not remember his name. Then that was it. It was over. And I missed my chance with that one response. Was I still intelligent? Yes. Is this how we measure intelligence? Sometimes. But what we'll learn in this chapter is that intelligence isn't just knowing random facts about history and movies. It's all different things. It's knowing not to tease someone for wanting to be on *Jeopardy* (social intelligence), it's knowing how to comfort your partner when they can't remember the answer (emotional intelligence), and it's sharing your experiences with others to help them learn through your knowledge (wisdom). We'll also see that with age, we gain more of these than we lose, because with older adulthood comes life, knowledge, experience, relationships, and so on. With age comes wins and losses and desires to share what we've learned with others so they don't have to learn the hard way. Measurement can get tricky, for sure, but we'll discuss that too, along with ways we can maintain our ability to retrieve information, keep our function, and remain sharp for as long as possible.

MULTIDIMENSIONALITY AND TYPES OF INTELLIGENCE

If there is one thing that the layperson and the expert agree on about intelligence, it is that it is multidimensional. There are many components and many types of intelligence. Is there consensus on how many? No. But, the idea that people can be intelligent in many ways is widely accepted in and out of the research lab. Some suggest that there's social-emotional intelligence, verbal intelligence, and informational intelligence, while others suggest additional groupings, such as intelligence for problem solving or decision making, artistic intelligence, entrepreneurial intelligence, or even moral intelligence (e.g., Paulhus et al., 2002; Schlinger, 2003).

Importantly, we recognize that intelligence is more than just a fixed set of factors, but rather groupings of characteristics that help us motivate, act responsibly, communicate, and share our knowledge with others (e.g., Pfeifer & Scheier, 2001). This combination of factors is uniquely human, and while attempts at reproducing intelligence with computers are impressive (i.e., recent advances in artificial intelligence, or AI), there are still many aspects of human intelligence that scientists haven't gotten computers to replicate.

What scientists *have* been able to do, however, is examine intelligence as it changes across adulthood. Age-related changes are usually variable by individual and by type of intelligence, and intelligence can change through experience and/or training (e.g., Masunaga & Horn, 2001; Schaie & Willis, 1993). Some research has examined potential for intelligence changes as the neuroanatomy of an individual changes in older adulthood (e.g., Jäncke et al., 2020; Raz et al., 2007; see also Figure 5.1 [Giorgio et al., 2010]). In a longitudinal study, Jäncke et al. (2020) examined change over the course of four years. Their measurements of neuroanatomy included grey matter volume, white matter volume, and lateral ventricular size, while their measures of intelligence included verbal and nonverbal psychometric IQ measures (see the following section for more information on psychometric IQ testing). Analyses showed that while grey matter

FIGURE 5.1 ■ Age-Related Changes in Grey Matter

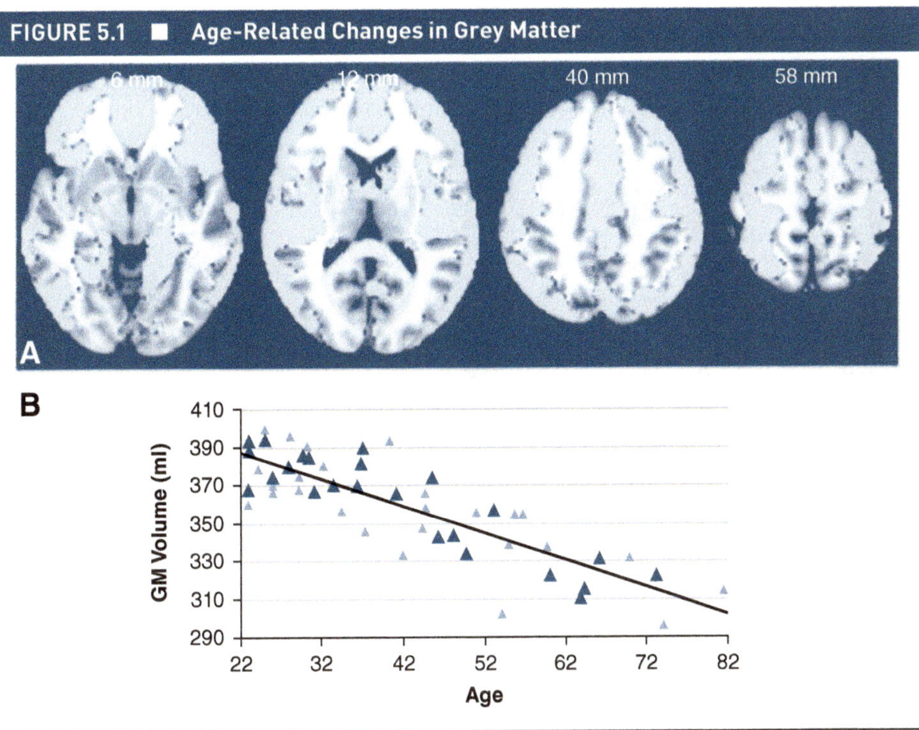

Note: Light blue triangles represent women, and dark blue triangles represent men.

Source: Giorgio, A., Santelli, L., Tomassini, V., Bosnell, R., Smith, S., De Stefano, N., & Johansen-Berg, H. (2010). Age-related changes in grey and white matter structure throughout adulthood. *NeuroImage, 51*(3), 943–951. https://doi.org/10.1016/j.neuroimage.2010.03.004

volume and white matter volume appeared mostly normal, they did decrease just under 1% per year, and the lateral ventricular size also changed, by increasing 4% per year. These changes could have indicated changes in intelligence measures, but they did not. Rather, participants' psychometric measures remained stable over the time of the study, indicating that while some physiological changes happen during our older adult years, they are not necessarily indicative of functional change. With respect to intelligence, it is possible that little to no change occurs, though that is dependent on how it is measured and what type of intelligence is examined.

In some cases, demonstrations of intelligence are dependent on speed, such that speed to access information indicates that the information was stored and retrieved well and/or that the individual can reason through and respond in the allotted time (e.g., Lindenberger et al., 1993; Robitaille et al., 2013). Lindenberger et al. (1993) measured five components of intelligence, including speed, reasoning, memory, knowledge, and fluency. These measures were conducted as a series of cognitive tasks, such as animal fluency, digit–symbol substitution, picture matching, word finding, and so on, while researchers also measured speed. Data analyses showed that speed negatively impacted all four of the remaining measures. Moreover, analyses showed that decrements in performance specifically related to age were small, but the relation to speed was larger. That is, age itself wasn't responsible for the declines seen in these intelligence measures; rather, the individual differences in speed were the more likely culprit (which themselves may change with age, as we remember from Chapter 3; Salthouse, 1996; Tun & Lachman, 2008). So, given the sensitivity to how we measure different types of intelligence, it makes sense to examine that specifically, and how those measures may reveal age-related or speed-related changes that occur.

MEASUREMENT

There are multiple ways to measure intelligence, as would be logical given the different types of intelligence. Some types of testing are **psychometric**, which focus on the answers to the tasks only. Standardized intelligence testing is often psychometric because it is easy to score—the answers are correct or incorrect. These types of tests put a focus on the responses given, rather than how the individual arrived at their answer. Alternatively, **cognitive structural approaches** to testing examine why or how an individual came up with their response. That is, what was their rationale or thought process in getting there? Was it creative? Did it consider a "grey area" of morality? Was it common among others their age? Examining via cognitive structural approaches can give some insight as to an individual's reasoning skill, developmental progress, and moral intelligence, as will be discussed later in our sections on postformal thought and wisdom.

Importantly, to have a valid test of intelligence, one must first **operationalize** what intelligence is—that is, define intelligence in measurable terms. And, because there are many types of intelligence, a valid test of emotional intelligence would operationalize intelligence differently than would a test of crystallized intelligence (i.e., content knowledge; see section on fluid and crystalized intelligence for more information). When we properly operationalize our measure, we can be more confident that we are measuring what we want to be measuring, making it more likely that our measure is **valid** (Gravetter & Forzano, 2018)—and a valid measure will give accurate information about the type of intelligence we're exploring. Oftentimes, individuals refer to intelligence in terms of knowledge and skills associated with that knowledge—and call it **general intelligence** (i.e., *g*). And, *g* has been linked to academic achievement (e.g., Roth et al., 2015), with predictor correlations ranging from .30 all the way up to .70, depending on the study (Costa & Faria, 2018; Naderi et al., 2010). This connection, as with my connection with *Jeopardy*, assumes knowledge is intelligence. Is that a valid measure? Maybe. But it also leaves a lot out of the explanation of the construct of intelligence.

However, in Western culture, knowledge is valued and opens the doors to access additional education and opportunities, so its measurement receives a lot of attention. One of the most common ways we've (as a society) seen a measure of intelligence is IQ (e.g., Brody, 1997; Eysenk, 2012; Mackintosh, 2011). IQ (i.e., intelligence quotient) allows for a numerical score as a measure of intelligence. These measures have shown high rates of heritability, though that heritability does not determine IQ fully (Dickens & Flynn, 2001; Plomin & Von Stumm, 2018). Rather, Dickens and Flynn (2001) argue for a large influence of environment on one's IQ scores as well. This environmental influence is important in the case of how perhaps an older adult would differ from a younger adult in their intelligence measures, having differential access to education, nutrition, health care, and other resources—and perhaps would influence my intelligence through my nightly ritual of *Jeopardy* watching.

Wechsler Adult Intelligence Scale

Perhaps the most well known of all IQ tests is the Wechsler Adult Intelligence Scale (WAIS) (Wechsler, 1981, 2008). This test has been widely used to measure four components of intelligence, including verbal comprehension, perceptual reasoning, working memory, and processing speed, and has gone through several revisions since the 1980s. (Note the lack of emotional intelligence, social intelligence, artistic intelligence, entrepreneurial intelligence, and moral intelligence components here. Those are measured elsewhere, using different assessments.) As shown in Table 5.1, there are four subsections of this assessment, each containing several tasks. For example, the verbal comprehension subsection contains tasks about word meaning and similarities between words, whereas the working memory subsection contains span tasks (i.e., list how many items you can remember) as well as organization tasks (e.g., given an alternating list

TABLE 5.1 ■ Categories and Subtests Within the WAIS

Verbal Comprehension	Word Similarities, Vocabulary
Perceptual Reasoning	Block Design, Matrix Reasoning, Visual Puzzles
Working Memory	Digit Span, Arithmetic
Processing Speed	Symbol Search, Number/Symbol Coding

Sources: Wechsler, D. (1981). *Wechsler Adult Intelligence Scale-Revised* (WAIS-R). Psychological Corporation.

Wechsler, D. (2008). *Wechsler Adult Intelligence Scale-Fourth Edition* (WAIS-IV). Pearson.

of letters and numbers, reorganize the numbers in sequential order and the letters in alphabetical order). Other tasks include arithmetic from story problems, visual puzzles, matrix reasoning, symbol searches, and number/symbol coding. Together these tasks give insight into general intelligence, and the clinician conducting the test can come up with an intelligence score (i.e., IQ).

The WAIS has also been adjusted to be used in a shortened form for individuals with lowered stamina (e.g., psychiatric populations, individuals with low IQ, and even older adults who've been referred for further neuropsychological evaluation; Blyer et al., 2000; Meyers et al., 2013; Silverstein, 1985). The shortened form of the test has demonstrated appropriate validity and **reliability** (i.e., consistency; Gravetter & Forzano, 2018) for examining the same intelligence constructs in many other populations (Meyers et al., 2013). For some (not all), however, there were some differences in intelligence score outcomes between the shortened and full versions of the test. Therefore, the shortened form should be used with caution.

Interestingly, newer questions regarding the use of the WAIS in healthy older adults suggest that there may be some differences in how intelligence is measured and described in adults over 65 (e.g., Borella et al., 2020; Salthouse & Saklofske, 2010). In one study, Borella et al. (2020) examined how working memory limitations can impact the measures of intelligence through the tasks used in the WAIS. If you remember from Chapter 4, we learned that working memory is multidimensional, so depending on the component of working memory examined, intelligence measures may be impacted differently. Borella et al. suspected that components of working memory that necessitated more control (e.g., a backward span test would need more control than a forward span test) would have the largest impact on measures of intelligence. To determine whether this was true, participants ranging from young adult to older adult completed the full version of the WAIS, including five working memory measures (a variety of span measures). Results showed correlations between working memory measures and components of the WAIS, such that correlations were stronger the older the participants got. Additionally, data showed higher correlations between working memory and intelligence for the working memory measures using the highest amounts of control, as was predicted. This is important in considering intelligence measures in older adulthood—working memory limitations play a role and should not be ignored. Older adults' intelligence measures should not be interpreted without working memory, because lower measures of intelligence may not actually be lower intelligence at all, but rather may be a reflection of differences in working memory. From studies like this, we can understand that older adults' intelligence must be examined carefully and in full detail. Let's examine one such study next.

Seattle Longitudinal Study

In the world's longest-running, largest longitudinal study of intellectual development, Schaie (1996) examined the multifaceted nature of older adults' intelligence and gave us a new window into how intellectual function changes. Remember that in a **longitudinal study**, the same individuals are followed over a period of time. This gives us information about how these individuals change—that is, age changes. This is different from a **cross-sectional study** that compares different age groups to tell us how those groups are different from one another; this can only tell us about age differences, which may be mediated by other things like cohort effects. Longitudinal studies, while more of a time investment, do give us better insight into the changes as they occur. However, they are not without their limitations (investment of time and money, practice effects from measuring the same individuals, unlikelihood of incorporating many age groups, participant attrition, etc.). To combat these limitations, Schaie created a complex design (later known as a **sequential design**) that incorporated some new participants along the way, creating some cross-sectional groups within the longitudinal design. This unique combination allowed for some comparisons between age groups across a wider age range, and some replacement from participant attrition. Later in the study (after about 25 years), additional qualitative data collection methods as well as assessment of cognitive interventions were added (see Schaie & Willis, 2010).

The Seattle Longitudinal Study measured several components of intelligence to observe how those changed over time, examining adult developmental changes. The components of intelligence were divided into two main categories: primary mental abilities and secondary mental abilities. Primary abilities included numerical ability, verbal ability, inductive reasoning, spatial orientation, perceptual speed, and verbal memory, while secondary abilities included fluid and crystallized intelligence (there's a full section on these specific types of intelligence in just a bit), visual organization, auditory organization, and short-term and long-term acquisition and retrieval. Measurements took place in six testing cycles, where Schaie hoped to capture intellectual change as it occurred (unless, of course, it happened suddenly in the middle of the gap between measurements—but that type of change would be more likely the result of disease, rather than normative aging, as it would be sudden and not gradual).

Data from these measures showed some interesting patterns (Schaie & Willis, 1993, 2010). From the cross-sectional data (i.e., comparisons of age differences), data showed large age differences between the youngest old and the oldest old in measures of inductive reasoning, spatial orientation, numeric ability, verbal memory, verbal meaning (but not Educational Testing Service [ETS] measures of vocabulary knowledge), and perceptual speed. However, we interpret these age differences with caution because they are focused at the high and low ends of the ages tested, and do not show the progression of change from one end of the age spectrum to the other. Longitudinal data give us that piece. Those data showed similar changes, though, confirming the suspicions from the comparisons. The longitudinal data showed that there is very little change in intellectual ability in the earlier years of older adulthood. Larger, more substantive change is evident really only after age 75. Participants demonstrated increases in primary abilities during young and middle adulthood, but some declines occurred in later adulthood. Within those declines, it was common for individuals to show declines in one or two abilities but not across them all. That is, intellectual decline was not large, nor was it widespread. Additionally, there was no uniform pattern of decline that applied to all participants, but most participants showed at least some amount of change. Several moderators were identified as having influence over the change that did occur. These moderators were cohort differences, perceptual processing speed, personality/sense of internal control, and health (more on the impact of health on intelligence later in this chapter). Importantly, other research has demonstrated success in modifying and training to reverse declines to some degree (e.g., Willis & Schaie, 1986).

Mayer-Salovey-Caruso Emotional Intelligence Test

Emotional intelligence (EI) is conceptualized in an entirely different way than the intelligence we discussed in the previous section. Instead of examining mental processes like language, perception, knowledge, and reasoning, EI examines identifying emotions, facilitating thought, and understanding and managing emotions (in yourself and others; see Table 5.2). Like general intelligence, EI can be measured with a formal assessment measure, in this case, the Mayer-Salovey-Caruso Emotional Intelligence Test (MSCEIT; Mayer, 2002). This assessment contains several components, which gather information about the different pieces of EI. These tasks ask participants to identify emotions from an individual's facial expression, consider hypothetical emotional situations, draw conclusions based on appropriate emotional reactions, and so on, and an intelligence score can be calculated and interpreted.

Research on EI has examined its development across the life span. In one such study, Cabello et al. (2016) compared EI in men and women (transgender and gender-nonconforming individuals were not included) across three age groups: young adult, middle-aged adult, and older adult. Here, each of the four components of EI were examined as per the MSCEIT, and results showed higher overall EI for women compared to men, and higher EI for middle-aged adults compared to young or older adults. However, this age comparison did not hold for the subcomponent of understanding emotions. In this instance, older adults showed lower scores than middle-aged or young adults, and middle-aged adults showed lower scores than young adults (i.e., it was a linear relationship that went down with age). These data suggest that gender and age both impact EI, and at least in this case, the effect of gender was larger. Regardless, this leads us to question why lowered EI would occur for older adults given their lifetime of experience to put emotions and their interpretation into perspective. And, is there anything we can do to help change those patterns?

To address this first question, we could look to EI theory, which does suggest that EI grows and develops with life experiences (e.g., Mayer et al., 1999). This pattern plays out in the data described in the previous paragraph to the extent that it increases from young adulthood to middle adulthood. However, this increase does not continue into older adulthood. Bisiacchi et al. (2008) suggest that the reason for this may be due to changes in cognitive function in older

TABLE 5.2 ■ Components of Emotional Intelligence

Perceiving Emotion	Perceiving and identifying emotion from others
Assimilating Emotions	Combining different emotions into one meaningful mood, perception, or occurrence
Understanding Emotions	Reasoning about emotions and combinations of emotions
Managing Emotions	Regulating one's own and managing others' emotions

Source: Mayer, J. D., Caruso, D. R., & Salovey, P. (1999). Emotional intelligence meets traditional standards for an intelligence. *Intelligence, 27*, 267–298. http://dx.doi.org/10.1016/S0160-2896(99)00016-1

adulthood. Aha! Working memory and processing speed—evil supervillains strike again! Well, not really evil so much as the normative changes we see in these cognitive components *can* influence how and how much information, even emotional information, is processed—ultimately impacting EI. However, there is a positive here. Research has demonstrated interventions that can assist (e.g., Delhom et al., 2020, 2022). Delhom et al. (2020) implemented an intervention focusing on attention, clarity, and emotional repair, as recommended by Mayer and Salovey (1997). The intervention went for 90 minutes of training each week for 10 weeks, using introspection and cognitive behavioral techniques. Outcome measures involved EI as well as measures of life satisfaction and emotional resilience. Data showed that EI increased via this intervention, as did self-reports of life satisfaction. Delhom et al. (2020) suggested that the attention that was paid to emotions during the intervention allowed for more awareness and clarity surrounding those emotions, the situations in which they arise, and the consequences of them. The result was an increase in the understanding of those emotions and a higher likelihood of using them to adapt to difficult or different situations. Cognitively speaking, the intervention allowed for practice and additional resources to allocate for processing the emotions as information. As we would expect from what we learned in Chapters 3 and 4, information processed with more attention receives more processing and is more likely to make its way through the information processing system. In an older adult, who has some additional limitations on their information processing system, this additional time and the opportunity to allocate more resources can compensate for any normative age-related changes and, in this case, result in better processing of emotions.

FLUID AND CRYSTALLIZED INTELLIGENCE

Since midway through the 20th century, types of intelligence known as fluid (*f*) and crystallized (*c*) intelligence have been explored. According to Cattell's (1943, 1963) theory, these types of intelligences are distinct from one another. **Fluid intelligence** allows one to use mental flexibility, solve problems, think creatively, draw conclusions, and understand the relationship between real and make-believe. Alternatively, **crystallized intelligence** is the accumulation of knowledge and information over a lifetime (e.g., what we'd need to know for a game of *Jeopardy*). Research in this area has developed over the last 75 years and has demonstrated that changes in our fluid and crystalized intelligence coincide quite nicely with the findings we already know about memory and information processing (see Chapters 3 and 4 for in-depth information). Processing becomes slower, and inhibition of irrelevant information is hindered, ultimately clogging the system. Together, these could negatively influence fluid intelligence and our ability to be flexible. Alternatively, semantic memory grows over time—with experience comes knowledge—and leads to increases in crystallized intelligence. Could these interact? Absolutely, they can (e.g., Thorsen et al., 2014).

When I think back to my years watching *Jeopardy*, I remember that many of the contestants who won big were those in middle age. At that age, adults have increased crystallized intelligence to a point that trivia knowledge is large but have not reduced their processing speed to a point where it hinders their buzzer-pressing skills (i.e., their speed of retrieval and response).

This played out with my family members as well. My parents were middle-aged at the time, and responded well to the questions, but my grandparents would not get them in time. They'd often comment "I knew that" when the contestants answered or when the host revealed the correct response. They probably did know that, because they had a lifetime of experience to have accumulated that knowledge, but they were unable to retrieve it in time.

Zimprich and Martin (2002) explored how changes in processing speed can directly predict changes in fluid intelligence (see Figure 5.2). In this study, older adult participants completed two measures of processing speed (a number connection task and a symbol substitution task) as well as two measures of fluid intelligence (a picture completion task and a block design task). Participants completed this battery of tests twice, where testing times were separated by four years. Data analyses revealed a .53 correlation between changes in processing speed and changes in fluid intelligence measures. While not a perfect correlation by any means, this *is* a strong correlation as far as developmental research is concerned. This is positive in that we can reasonably

FIGURE 5.2 ■ Influence of Processing Speed on Fluid Intelligence Measures

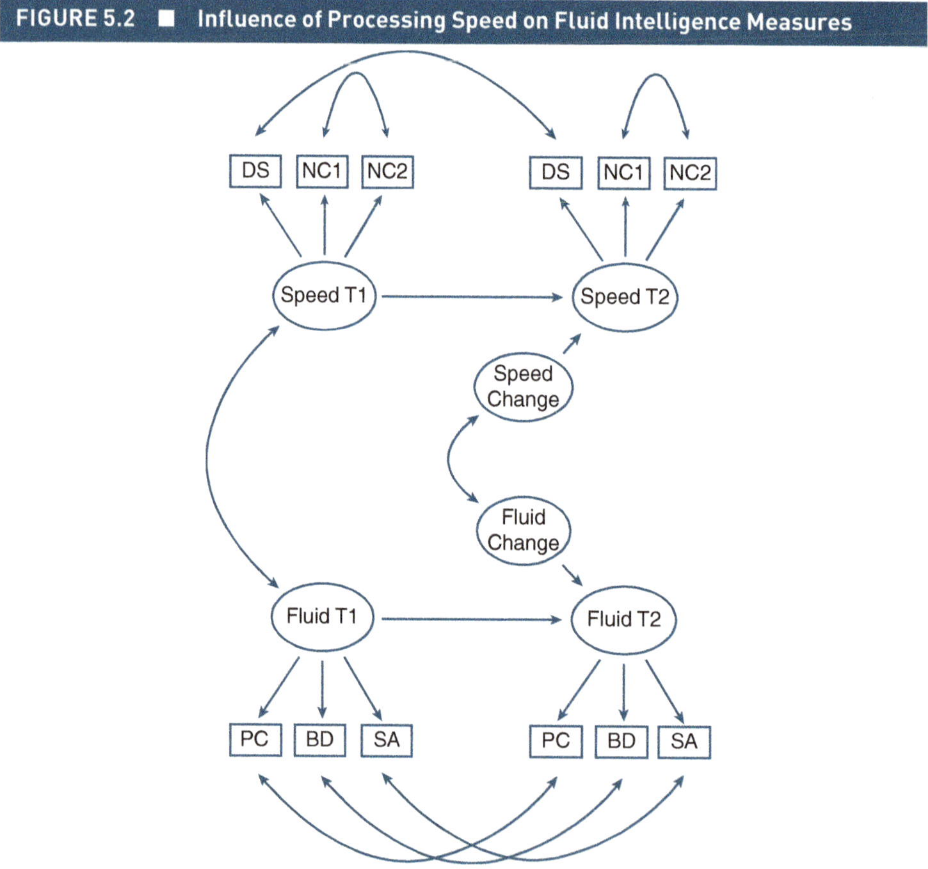

Source: Zimprich, D., & Martin, M. (2002). Can longitudinal changes in processing speed explain longitudinal age changes in fluid intelligence? *Psychology and Aging, 17*(4), 690–695.

explain that a large component of fluid intelligence changes that occur in older adulthood aren't necessarily due to intelligence changes at all, but rather are a result of other changes in our information processing system. That is, intelligence isn't declining, but *measures* of intelligence are declining because of the power that processing speed has over those measures.

Other research on fluid intelligence has demonstrated similar results (e.g., Horn, 1982; Lindenberger et al., 1993; Thorsen et al., 2014); however, more recent research has identified that while these changes can be measured, the older adult may not be aware of the changes as they are occurring (e.g., Fastame, 2022; Shakeel & Goghari, 2017). In their study, Shakeel and Goghari (2017) measured fluid intelligence, working memory, and cognitive flexibility in a sample of older adults. These measures included Raven's Advanced Progressive Matrices (Raven et al., 1973), digit span sequencing, and a trail-making task (Delis et al., 2001). Additional measures of creativity, planning, and self-perceptions of cognitive functioning were also included in the battery of tests. Data analyses showed that measures of working memory, creativity, and cognitive flexibility were significant predictors of fluid intelligence (though together only predicted about 20% of variance in fluid intelligence). Additionally, there was very low predictive ability for other measures, including self-reports of cognitive functioning. These results suggest that measuring other variables as a roundabout way to get at fluid intelligence is not the way to go. Rather, measuring it directly is much more effective. And, while there seems to be a relationship between fluid intelligence and other cognitive variables, as you would expect, this relationship is not the be-all and end-all. As for self-report and -awareness, it seems that if fluid intelligence declines, it does not decline in a way that is dramatic enough for self-reports to reflect it. That is, it is likely not noticeable enough to be problematic or to interfere with daily functioning. Regardless, any decline is decline (even if it is the result of the influence of another variable), and we may want to investigate whether intervention can be helpful.

As you would expect, crystallized intelligence can grow over time and expands every time we learn something new (which is hopefully often). However, fluid intelligence isn't directly trained in school or Western culture—somehow knowing facts is valued over flexible thinking or problem solving in many ways. However, even in older adults, research shows that fluid intelligence can be trained and improved (e.g., Baltes & Willis, 1982; Gard et al., 2014; Tranter & Koustaal, 2008). Engaging in cognitively stimulating tasks above and beyond what one typically does in a day can allow older adults to improve their mental flexibility and fluid intelligence. Tranter and Koustaal (2008) asked older adult participants to engage in a 12-week intervention. Before and after intervention, participants' fluid intelligence was measured via the Cattell Culture Fair test (Cattell & Cattell, 1960), as well as other measures of intelligence and cognition including the WAIS block task (Wechsler, 1981, 2008), an adult reading test, and the Mini–Mental State Examination (MMSE; Folstein et al., 1975). During the intervention, participants completed problem-solving activities such as word manipulation, creative drawing, dot-to-dot puzzles, and mystery picture identification. Participants also completed tasks as group tasks, where they solved puzzles using creative building and origami. Assessments of fluid intelligence of the group of participants who engaged in these mentally stimulating activities, compared to those who had not, showed evidence that those who challenged their thinking patterns in completing these tasks improved in their fluid intelligence measures. Participants who maintained the status quo in the control group during those 12 weeks did not show change. This is positive in that using your mind, maintaining challenging activities, and working your mental processing resources can improve fluid intelligence over time. And, while this may be the source of the false claim that many online "games for seniors" can "prevent Alzheimer's," there is a kernel of truth here. Of course, we'll discuss more on those games and what really can help us stay sharp in just a bit—but, spoiler alert, fully preventing Alzheimer's isn't possible.

Creativity

One concept related to intelligence that can help in solving problems and maintaining flexibility is creativity. Creativity isn't just being crafty with paint and construction paper, though. When we conceptualize **creativity** in psychology, we are referring to individuals coming up with novel ideas, useful propositions, and unique solutions to problems—and thinking logically to make those solutions work (Sternberg, 2006). Creativity needs originality, fluency, and mental flexibility to work (e.g., Runco & Jaeger, 2012). To be sure, art can be included here; however, often, it isn't. Rather, thinking "outside the box" is a better way to consider it. For example, if you are locked out of your house, you may simply wait until your partner gets home to unlock the door or call a locksmith. However, using creativity, alternative solutions could be found, such as searching for an open window or using a nail file or hairpin to pick the lock. As you can imagine, there would be curiosity around how this type of creative thinking would be affected by changes in processing speed, working memory, and fluid intelligence in older adulthood, as well as how it could be measured overall.

iStockPhoto/justhavealook

Measurement of creativity is possible through psychometric testing, where individuals are often asked to generate original ideas for open-ended problems (e.g., alternative uses for a brick—which, funnily enough, would be a creative way to get into your locked house; Kaufman et al., 2008). Research in this area has demonstrated that there is a positive relationship between fluid intelligence and creativity (e.g., Batey & Furnham, 2006; Jauk et al., 2014). Specifically, Jauk et al. (2014) found that in addition to a personality variable, there were two markers of creativity that predicted fluid intelligence measures: originality and fluency. These markers predicted creative activity—not necessarily whether those creative activities turned into something publishable/publicly acknowledged as a creative product, but creative activity all the same.

The question remains, though, what happens to these creative activities in the context of limited efficiencies of working memory and/or slower processing speeds in older adults? We would predict that these limitations could hinder the fluency (at least) of those creative ideas. Consider that inhibition difficulties could take up room in an older adult's already limited working memory stores (see Chapter 4 for more details on this discussion). Then, when those resources are needed to generate creative ideas, there is little left to hold those ideas. Alternatively, fluently generating creative ideas sometimes requires that one discards unreasonable, or unworkable, ideas as well as previously generated ideas. Difficulties with inhibition could put one at a disadvantage in doing so, and ultimately result in coming up with fewer ideas overall. A similar limitation would be in place with processing speed. Slower speeds could interfere with one's ability to fluently generate new ideas at all. Taking time, losing steam, and losing those ideas in the long run would make for poor creative activity outcomes. Research supports these logical predictions, showing that inhibition significantly predicts creativity, creativity is significantly related to fluid intelligence (e.g., Benedek et al., 2014), and declines in processing speed can negatively impact creativity measures in older adults (e.g., Sharma & Babu, 2017). Does this mean that older adults aren't creative? No. In fact, some research shows that, in some instances, older adults can generate more creative solutions to a problem, compared to younger adults (e.g., Carpenter et al., 2020). However, training and bolstering their fluid intelligence skills and mental flexibility may be beneficial for creativity to truly flourish. We know that this training is possible, as per our earlier discussion (e.g., Tranter & Koustaal, 2008), and we'll address more on training in just a bit.

Decision Making

To the extent that higher-level cognitive processing such as creativity and problem solving is influenced by fluid intelligence, working memory, and processing speed, we would do well to also consider another higher-level process: decision making. Making decisions happens on large and small scales every day—from what to eat for breakfast to purchasing a car or even whether we choose to sign a do-not-resuscitate order for ourselves, and everything in between. Being able to make good decisions is an important factor in independent living, and so considering how we make decisions, the role of intelligence, and how it is influenced by normative cognitive changes in older adulthood is important.

Measuring decision making can happen in a variety of ways, but one of the ways we may be most curious about is those decisions that are relevant to leading life outside the laboratory. After all, that is what we need when we wish to remain independent. Ramachandran et al. (2020) aimed to investigate the role of intelligence in decision making in a financial context, as financial decisions are some of the hardest ones to make for many individuals, including older adults. Here, older adults were asked to complete the Iowa Gambling Task, where they were asked to consider monetary selections, track gains and losses over time, and make decisions in a real-time, ambiguous, and risky context. Participants needed to choose cards from a deck, where they would win or lose "money," and learned over time which choices would allow them to experience monetary gain or loss. This description sounds cognitively demanding just to read, let alone complete. Participants also completed tasks of fluid intelligence and emotional intelligence. Results showed that measures of fluid intelligence predicted performance on the Iowa Gambling Task, but measures of emotional intelligence did not. Ramachandran et al. (2020) concluded that age-related changes in fluid intelligence may be more powerful in determining how daily financial decisions are made than emotional intelligence. Additionally, they suggest that stability in emotional intelligence with age may allow for some support and moderation of the changes we may see in fluid intelligence when measuring it directly.

Of course, there are other factors involved in intellectual change, including working memory and processing speed (e.g., Henninger et al., 2010), cohort differences, social and lifestyle factors, mental activity levels, nutrition, education levels, personality, and more (Schaie, 1994). In the next section, we'll consider some of the factors that may influence our ability to maintain high function and what could influence change for the positive in intelligence and mental processing in older adulthood.

STAYING MENTALLY SHARP

It's common for me to spend downtime reading or playing puzzle games on my phone (this should come as a surprise to absolutely nobody). Recently, I was playing a game on my phone and had an advertisement for a different game come up that claimed to "prevent Alzheimer's." And then another said it could tell me "how old your brain is." My first instinct was to roll my eyes and turn off my phone, but I didn't. The thing is, while these claims are clearly clickbait and on the surface seem like fearmongering at its finest, they actually do hold some weight if we strip them of their clickbait-y marketing tactics. The basic underpinnings of these claims are true: If you remain active cognitively, your mental processing will stay sharp. And, while we can't fully prevent Alzheimer's disease, we can buffer the effects of it (should it hit) if we have strong, plentiful neural connections—which would only come if we were continuing to use our brain. Research in this area also demonstrates that training in older adults can bolster spatial orientation and inductive reasoning (e.g., Willis & Schaie, 1986), knowledge over the life span accumulates toward expertise (i.e., Masunaga & Horn, 2001), and physical health can influence how these variables play out over time (e.g., Raz et al., 2007). In this section, we'll explore how these additional factors can help us maintain positive mental capacity, flexibility, and performance.

Physical Health

In earlier chapters, we've discussed in great length how physical health can change via normative aging and disease processes that are common in older adulthood. From these discussions, you could conclude that brain health is important in maintaining good cognitive function.

You'd be correct. But, beyond attempting to avoid Alzheimer's disease (which isn't entirely possible, as it's the result of so many different factors, nor is it normative aging), what would good physical health do for us in terms of cognitive function and intelligence? Not only would nutrition influence the health of our neurons through vitamin B12 and omega-3 fatty acids (see Chapter 8 for more information here; Féart et al., 2010), but vascular health can impact intelligence as well (e.g., Raz et al., 2007).

Raz et al. (2007) followed white matter hyperintensities (WMH; i.e., brain matter lesions) over time for adults with hypertension (i.e., high blood pressure). Over the course of the longitudinal study, those individuals who had hypertension, who developed hypertension, or whose blood pressure measures went up showed increases in WMH; increases were almost double during this time frame. This increase was most notable in the frontal and parietal lobes, areas known to be important for executive function (i.e., cognitive resource allocation, planning, and other higher-order cognition) and attention. Additionally, measures of fluid intelligence were correlated with the WMH increases, such that fluid intelligence measures declined as the WMH volumes increased. These suggest that the physical changes that occur alongside hypertension can negatively impact intelligence measures in older adults. Other research has connected increases in WMH to declines in overall cognitive and functional decline (e.g., Silbert et al., 2008). Maintaining good blood pressure through diet and exercise (and medication, if needed) can minimize these changes, at least as they exist through WMH volumes. And notably, the Mediterranean diet, a diet high in vitamin B12 and omega-3 fatty acids, has demonstrated significant positive impact on blood pressure (e.g., De Pergola & D'Alessandro, 2018). And, since this diet is also known for its contributions to brain health (e.g., Féart et al., 2010), among other things, it may be one to discuss with your doctor.

iStockPhoto/marilyna

Mental Stimulation

Use it or lose it. This phrase is important when it comes to maintaining cognitive function, as we've seen in the previous two chapters. But, what about when we're considering normative age-related changes? Do we just settle in for the ride? Or can we work to reverse normative changes? Do those games we see advertised work? While I can't speak to the specific games, as there isn't research testing their efficacy specifically (and therefore the claims they make in their advertising can't be trusted), we can look to the research on *brain training* and see how training interventions can improve fluid intelligence. Since this is what has been most impacted by age-related changes in processing speed and working memory limitations, it may be the one to benefit most from training.

In series of publications, spawned from a large study on intelligence interventions—Project ADEPT (Baltes & Willis, 1982)—Willis and colleagues explored the impact of training for older adults (e.g., Blieszner et al., 1981; Willis et al., 1981; Willis & Nesselroade, 1990; Willis & Schaie, 1986). These studies investigated many aspects of intellectual functioning in older adults, from the young-old (in their 60s) to the old-old (in their late 70s and 80s). In one of these training interventions, Willis and Nesselroade (1990) compared data collected over the course of almost a decade, investigating figural relations and perceptions in adults in their 70s (older than had been studied in research before this). The training was directed toward a fluid ability, targeting comparisons between figures and their relationships to one another—a task that requires mental manipulation. Throughout the seven years of training and measurement, data showed steady improvement in this fluid training, and landed the older adults at a skill level higher than before training after those seven years. That is, adults in their late 70s were performing better than those in their late 60s/early 70s. And, this isn't the only context in which research has demonstrated efficacy in training. Willis and Schaie (1986) showed similar improvements in spatial orientation and inductive reasoning tasks (see Table 5.3). Here, participants from the Seattle Longitudinal Study who had been identified as declining in spatial or inductive reasoning measures over the course of the previous 14 years received training in those skills. The training was successful in returning these individuals to predecline status. These results show that

TABLE 5.3 ■ Mean Scores for Inductive Reasoning and Spatial Orientation Trainings

	Inductive Reasoning Training		Spatial Orientation Training	
	Pretest	Posttest	Pretest	Posttest
Inductive Reasoning	50.25	55.49	49.87	52.37
Spatial Orientation	51.23	54.38	49.23	53.71
Perceptual Speed	50.40	52.91	49.32	51.93
Numeric	51.22	52.75	48.42	50.12
Verbal	51.57	52.27	49.06	49.94

Source: Willis, S. L., & Schaie, K. W. (1986). Training the elderly on the ability factors of spatial orientation and inductive reasoning. *Psychology and Aging, 1*(3), 239–247. https://doi.org/10.1037/0882-7974.1.3.239

while there is possibility for normative age-related decline, there is also possibility for working toward reversing or preventing that decline through mental stimulation training.

Expertise

In Chapter 4, you saw that in some cases, older adults can compensate and override declines in processing speed by way of their expertise. Salthouse (1984) showed this effect with typists whose typing skill did not decline despite declines in processing speed measures. These typists demonstrated that their expertise was helpful in maintaining skill, despite age-related changes. What's happening there? And how does it relate to intelligence? When we have expertise, we have increased knowledge in one specific area, and all the skills necessary to use the knowledge in that area. For example, a ballet dancer has great skill in execution and knowledge of dance steps. And, while they may maintain normal working memory for most information, they may have increased working memory and speed of processing for dance moves and music specifically because those skills are necessary in the context of their area of expertise. To the extent that adults accumulate knowledge and expand crystallized intelligence throughout adulthood, we could predict that their knowledge would buffer any cognitive deficits, at least as they relate to the expertise that they have (e.g., Zaval et al., 2015). That is, an individual whose expertise has expanded neural connections within a topic area would not notice neural changes nearly as soon as someone who has fewer or weaker connections. The extra connections would cushion that blow, so to speak.

iStockPhoto/skynesher

Research on expertise in older adulthood confirms this prediction (e.g., Baltes, 1997; Masunaga & Horn, 2001; Morrow et al., 2001). In one study, Masunaga and Horn (2001) measured fluid intelligence, working memory, and deductive reasoning within one's area of expertise (in this case, Japanese Go, a strategy-based board game). While measures of working memory more generally may decline along with measures of fluid intelligence, speed of processing, and so on, within the context of Japanese Go, the decline did not occur. This seems to happen outside of the laboratory as well. For example, have you ever noticed your professors teaching beyond the typical average American retirement age of 65? It's because they are working in their area of expertise. Barring any illness, injury, or disability, their intellect remains intact. And often, according to Baltes (1997), an older adult can retrieve information better and faster than a younger adult, if working within their niche. This knowledge and specialization comes over the course of a lifetime. The more years lived, the more knowledge (aka crystallized intelligence). These connections create a rich neural network that can buffer any normative declines that may come. Moreover, this cognitive development allows for individuals to progress into advanced levels of thinking, and perhaps pass their knowledge on to the next generation. I'll discuss these possibilities next.

POSTFORMAL THOUGHT

Throughout our lifetime, our capacity for more advanced cognitive processes develops. You probably discussed this in your introductory psychology class or your child development class. As an infant, your capacity for understanding is very different from that of a school-aged child, which is different from that of a teenager. This is clearly described in Piaget's theory of cognitive development (Piaget, 1929). Individuals develop from sensorimotor understanding and object permanence, to understanding conservation and mental reversal/manipulation, to understanding hypotheticals and abstract thought. However, Piaget's theory stops describing the progression of cognitive development past age 12. But, even intuitively, we know that a 12-year-old is very different from a 65-year-old. The question is, how are they different? Cognitively, the difference is in **postformal thought** (e.g., Sinnott, 1981, 1984). Postformal thought goes beyond what we learned in school, what is dictated by law, and formal thought through scientific logic. Postformal thought goes toward understanding and tolerance for the grey areas in life—the fuzziness—understanding that there is ambiguity in different situations, and we should/can consider context when thinking about a problem or making a decision. For example, we could consider the recent Supreme Court decision to overturn *Roe v. Wade*. In formal thought, we could agree or disagree with the decision to allow abortion, but we would think about it in absolutes. That is, it would always be *right* or always be *wrong*. Alternatively, thinking about the issue using postformal thought, we would consider nuances of different circumstances—understanding that some contexts might make abortion an option, while others might not—or at least understanding that there is some ambiguity in the discussion and some balance between emotion and logic, and some inherent self-reference in the perspectives that one takes in their thoughts.

Measuring postformal thought addresses this ambiguity. Rather than absolutes in right and wrong, as we'd see mostly in psychometric measures, measurement here often (though not always) uses cognitive structural approaches to testing to explore how and why an answer is what it is. Sinnott et al. (2020) demonstrated that postformal thought requires that an individual work within constraints of an ill-defined problem, requiring interpretation and selection of what type of logic to use. This may be something difficult for individuals to accomplish if they have not reached the level of postformal thought in their cognitive development (and many adults simply do not). Additionally, Sinnott et al. demonstrated a link between postformal thought and cognitive flexibility, such that individuals need to adjust their problem-solving strategies on the fly when they encounter new information or a shift in context, as would be the case in a real-life dilemma like that of *Roe v. Wade*. This is where **moral intelligence** comes into play as well, where moral intelligence is an understanding of how values and universal human truths are put into action (e.g., Lennick & Kiel, 2007). Understanding that morality does not always align with law is also a sign of moral intelligence. That is, what is right and what is wrong *morally* is not necessarily what is dictated by the law of a particular country/state/city. For example, consider the case of a 10-year-old girl whose parents requested she have an abortion after she became pregnant as a product of rape. The law in her state dictated that abortion was illegal. Period. But what about this circumstance? Is the law in line with what is morally right here? Measures of moral intelligence can show whether one can understand these nuances and have been used in contexts such as education (e.g., Toprak & Karakus, 2018), business (e.g., Lennick & Kiel, 2007), and nursing (e.g., Arshiha et al., 2016), contexts in which working with moral perspective is important.

But what can moral intelligence do for us as we move through older adulthood? One might consider that understanding and acting morally, with values, is to use one's crystallized intelligence for good (and not evil). This altruistic giving of information for the betterment of others in the next generation is what we'd consider wisdom.

WISDOM

Unlike creativity, moral intelligence, crystallized intelligence, or emotional intelligence, wisdom is something that we almost universally associate with age. It's demonstrated all over pop culture from Yoda in the Star Wars empire to Professor Dumbledore in the Harry Potter series to even Cinderella's fairy godmother. Each of these examples is older in age and may make us assume that with age comes wisdom. While that is not necessarily the case, because wisdom requires more than age, it is more likely that an individual who is wise is older. That is, wisdom requires vast, broad knowledge (i.e., crystallized intelligence), experience (older adults have lots of that), and capacity for postformal thought (only achieved after other stages of cognitive development have been achieved). The giving of this informative combination of factors to others makes for wisdom.

Research on wisdom shows us that wisdom can inform problem solving and decision making as well. Worthy et al. (2011) showed that older adults were able to use their experience and wisdom to change and use different problem-solving strategies than young adults, who did not use previous outcomes to inform their strategies. Additionally, other research has shown that wisdom can contribute to emotional well-being (e.g., Etezadi & Pushkar, 2013). In one study, Etezadi and Pushkar (2013) demonstrated older adults' higher ratings of perceived personal control and life satisfaction were statistically related to measures of wisdom. This suggests that with the experience and perspective that contribute to wisdom comes a positive outlook on life. Being older isn't negative, and when we have the wisdom to see that, life becomes positive and satisfying.

AGING WELL: INTELLIGENCE

We've seen that speed of processing and working memory color our demonstrations of intelligence. However, while these limitations (and changes associated with them) can negatively impact the demonstrations of intelligence as we get older, given the time, space, and experience to accommodate for those limitations, intelligence isn't a large concern. Rarely do healthy older adults show declines in more than a couple of areas of intelligence (as per the Seattle Longitudinal Study), and even those are not noticeable for many years. Aging well in intelligence means giving yourself grace and time to use the lifetime of knowledge gained. Even working toward training for use, retrieval, and flexibility is possible. And knowing that you have the ability to pass on to a future generation is a beautiful thing.

KEY TERMS

cognitive structural approaches
creativity
cross-sectional study
crystallized intelligence
emotional intelligence
fluid intelligence
general intelligence
longitudinal study
moral intelligence
operationalize
postformal thought
psychometric
reliability
sequential design
valid

COMPREHENSION QUESTIONS

1. Describe the multidimensionality of intelligence.
2. Distinguish between psychometric and cognitive structural approaches to measurement.
3. What factors influence and/or moderate measures of intelligence? How?
4. How is the WAIS used for older adults?
5. Describe the findings of the Seattle Longitudinal Study.
6. How is emotional intelligence measured? What patterns of change and/or stability exist in older adulthood?
7. Distinguish between fluid and crystallized intelligence. What patterns of change and/or stability exist in older adulthood?
8. How can intervention impact fluid intelligence? What power does training hold in older adults' intelligence measures?
9. What can expertise do for maintaining intelligence?
10. How can postformal thought and moral intelligence inform wisdom in older adulthood?

ADDITIONAL READINGS

Ashton, M. C., Lee, K., Vernon, P. A., & Jang, K. L. (2000). Fluid intelligence, crystallized intelligence, and the openness/intellect factor. *Journal of Research in Personality, 34*(2), 198–207.

Ball, K., Berch, D. B., Helmers, K. F., Jobe, J. B., Leveck, M. D., Marsiske, M., Morris, J. N., Rebok, G. W., Smith, D. M., Tennstedt, S. L., Unverzagt, F. W., Willis, S. L., & ACTIVE Study Group. (2002). Effects of cognitive training interventions with older adults: A randomized controlled trial. *JAMA, 288*(18), 2271–2281.

Benovenli, L., Fuller, E., Sinnott, J., & Waterman, S. (2011). Three applications of the theory of postformal thought: Wisdom, concepts of God, and success in college. In R. L. Piedmont & A. Village (Eds.), *Research in the social scientific study of religion* (Vol. 22, pp. 141–154). Brill.

Carpenter, S. M., Peters, E., Västfjäll, D., & Isen, A. M. (2013). Positive feelings facilitate working memory and complex decision making among older adults. *Cognition and Emotion, 27*(1), 184–192.

Chu, C. H., Nyrup, R., Leslie, K., Shi, J., Bianchi, A., Lyn, A., McNicholl, M., Khan, S., Rahimi, S., & Grenier, A. (2021). Digital ageism: challenges and opportunities in artificial intelligence for older adults. *Gerontologist, 62*(7), 947–955.

Delhom, I., Gutierrez, M., Lucas-Molina, B., & Meléndez, J. C. (2017). Emotional intelligence in older adults: Psychometric properties of the TMMS-24 and relationship with psychological well-being and life satisfaction. *International Psychogeriatrics, 29*(8), 1327–1334.

Isingrini, M., & Vazou, F. (1997). Relation between fluid intelligence and frontal lobe functioning in older adults. *The International Journal of Aging and Human Development, 45*(2), 99–109.

Sligh, A. C., Conners, F. A., & Roskos-Ewoldsen, B. (2005). Relation of creativity to fluid and crystallized intelligence. *The Journal of Creative Behavior, 39*(2), 123–136.

Vaughan, F. (2002). What is spiritual intelligence? *Journal of Humanistic Psychology, 42*(2), 16–33.

UNIT III

MYTH: OLDER ADULTS ARE PUSHED OUT OF SOCIAL RELATIONSHIPS AND WORK

This unit will discuss the social roles in later life, including the transition from one to another. Discussions on grandparenting, intimate partnerships, friendships, and retirement/retiree status will show how older adults are far from isolated from their world. The rewards and difficulties of these relationships and roles will also be addressed, as well as how we (both young and older) think about the roles and responsibilities often held throughout older adulthood.

In addition, this unit will discuss how people think about and are influenced by social rules, biases, and their associated constraints—just like the myth described earlier. These chapters will explore how even older adults hold similar beliefs to younger adults about the older generations, and how these beliefs may impact their own performance on (specifically cognitive) tasks. Importantly, there will also be discussion on the positive impact of social interactions on older adults' cognition.

iStockPhoto/Lisa5201

6 SOCIAL ROLES AND RETIREMENT

LEARNING OBJECTIVES

6.1 Discuss the role of grandparents in child-rearing as well as the physical, emotional, and cognitive benefits of this role.

6.2 Describe the progression and characteristics of long-term marriages as well as the concerns of divorce in older adulthood.

6.3 Identify the functions that different friendships serve, including intergenerational friendships.

6.4 Explain the transition from the worker role to retirement, the value in older workers, and the role of leisure for happiness in retirement.

Not long ago, I was chatting with my sister-in-law, and a topic came up in our conversation that was shocking to us both. The topic was more of a realization, and that was that we were both technically at the age where we could be grandparents—without either of us needing to have become parents as teenagers. This realization was unsettling for both of us, and not because we're afraid of getting older. Rather, neither of us feel like we are ready to take on the role that we saw our grandparents play. My grandparents were kind, wise, silly, and fun. As a child, I remember often going to sleepovers at my Neno's house (our version of Nana). Nothing spectacular or wild happened when my sister and I slept over at Neno's house, but it was still special. It was a time for card games, warm blankets, and pink plum applesauce. Neno was never harsh with us, but we always listened. She parented without parenting, you know? And the thought that I could be in that position for someone else? It's just an odd feeling. My sister-in-law felt the same way.

The thing about being in a grandparent role is that expectations for behaviors are different than the expectations for a parent. My sister and I expected that Neno and Mopsie (our version of Poppie) would be there with their full attention all the time when we were at their house. I remember Neno being so concerned about us being cold when we got out of the shower that she'd crank up the heat and pull fresh towels from the dryer to make sure we stayed warm. I remember bread dough tucked into the blanket in the guest bedroom to rise. I remember slow afternoons watching old movies in the living room with Mopsie or running through the sprinklers in the backyard. It was just peaceful. This was very different from home, where our parents were pulled in a million directions from worrying about our schooling, work, bills, cleaning, and so on, and were always doing something. Time with Neno and Mopsie was like time suspended. Nothing else needed to happen. And while, looking back, I'm sure my sister and I went to their house because our parents needed a break from their role as parents (as a parent now, I can't blame them), we didn't know that. We just knew that we had time with our grandparents. The saying is that "it takes a village," and it really does. Every family member plays a role in the raising of children, and I am reminded of it every time I make Neno's pink plum applesauce for my children—not grandchildren . . . yet.

In this chapter, we'll learn about the role that grandparents play in a family, and how that role can be socially, emotionally, and even cognitively beneficial for everyone—including the grandparent. Additionally, we'll explore how relationships change, the role friendships serve, and how our social roles shift as we move into and through older adulthood. We release previously held positions (e.g., worker) and take on new ones (e.g., grandparent or retiree). These changes are not negative, nor are they the loss of our place in our family or in our society. Instead, they are a shift in how we live and are expected to live (both by others and by ourselves). To be sure there are positive and negative components to these changes, but much of the negative is simply a result of how we view aging in Western culture, rather than actual negative outcomes at all.

GRANDPARENTHOOD

There is no one specific age at which we become a grandparent. Sometimes this happens in middle adulthood (as my sister-in-law and I realized), and other times it occurs later in life. And sometimes it doesn't happen at all (and that is OK), but it is by far the most common role for an older adult to take on. In fact, a recent report from Bowling Green State University showed that over 70% of older adults in the United States are grandparents (Westrick-Payne, 2023). And because it is so common, there is a preconceived idea of what a grandparent is, what they look like, and what they do. These societal expectations of attitudes and behaviors comprise the **social role**. Think about the television show from the '80s and early '90s, *The Golden Girls* (Harris et al., 1985–1992). These women were *older* and looked like stereotypical *grandmothers*. And they all *were* grandmothers. It was clear that their characters were designed to embody the grandparent role, from their look (hairstyles and dress) to their relationships and behaviors (except for maybe Blanche!). But they were only in their 50s. Alternatively, Jennifer Lopez is in her 50s, but doesn't "look like a grandmother." So, what is the difference here? The expectation that an individual fills a specific social role. J.Lo is not expected to fill the role of *grandparent*, whereas Sophia, Dorothy, Rose, and Blanche were. Their outward appearance, actions, and attitudes reflect that. Do all grandmothers behave in the same way, and are these social expectations accurate? No, not for everyone. However, many do take on at least some components of the role as they transition to grandparenthood (e.g., Bates et al., 2018; Pecchioni & Croghan, 2002).

The transition to grandparenthood can be both positive and negative, depending on perspective. How do we view ourselves being able to take on that role? Do we have reservations about being *old enough* or *wise enough*? Or do we have negative associations because the implication is that being a grandparent means that we are older and Western culture sees that as negative? These are reasonable concerns. However, overall, Condon et al. (2018) demonstrated that at least as it relates to mental health measures, individuals were positively impacted by the transition. Here, a large group of older adults' mental health was measured using a five-item self-report measure investigating anxiety (two measures) and depression (three measures). Measurements were taken during the pregnancy of the first grandchild, after one year, and after two years. Interestingly, neither grandmothers nor grandfathers showed change across time in these measures, indicating that these components of mental health were not negatively impacted through the transition to grandparenthood. There was some interaction with providing childcare for the grandchild, but that'll be discussed in the next section—spoiler alert, this interaction was mostly positive.

The role of a grandparent is often viewed positively (e.g., Pecchioni & Croghan, 2022; Stricker & Hillman, 1996), with individuals viewing their own grandparents most positively. This is different than views of older adults in general, who are viewed more negatively. This makes it clear that the role of a grandparent is something special, even in Western culture. The value here is found clearly in Erikson's (1950) stages of psychosocial development, particularly stage 7: **generativity** versus stagnation. In many instances, one of the roles of the grandparent is to engage with the next generation to preserve cultural traditions, build relationships, and develop a sense of worth in their grandchildren (Buchanan & Rotkirch, 2018). This stage of psychosocial development is important for progression through adulthood, but also provides benefits for the grandchildren (see the section later in this chapter on rewards and difficulties of grandparenting). Thiele and Whelan (2006) discuss the significance of the grandparent role in the structure of the family, indicating that expectations of the grandparents range from social and emotional support to engaging in and watching fun activities to providing regular childcare for their grandchildren. All these behaviors are valued, special, and important to the overall health and functioning of a family. And, because the role of grandparent is so multifaceted, it's important to recognize all the things a grandparent does. The first we'll discuss in detail next, and that is providing childcare for the grandchild.

Caregiving Grandparents

There are different ways that a grandparent can contribute to the caregiving of their grandchild, ranging from occasional babysitting all the way to full-time guardianship, and everything in between.

In the case of **custodial grandparenting**, a grandparent has taken full custody of their grandchild for full-time care, whether legally or informally (Hayslip & Kaminski, 2005). This happens in cases where the parent(s) are unable to care for their child due to illness (physical or mental), injury, substance abuse, incarceration, or death (e.g., Choi et al., 2016). Landry-Meyer and Newman (2004) tell us that custodial grandparents are often female, low income, and younger on the age spectrum of grandparents (average age between 53 and 59 in the United States). And, more recently, Choi et al. (2016) confirmed this living arrangement to be more common among those with lower incomes; 21% of custodial grandparents live below the poverty line. Moreover, Landry-Meyer and Newman (2004) suggest that the grandparents who take full guardianship/child-rearing are filling two roles at once: the grandparent role and the parent role. This is a difficult balance to strike because these roles involve different expectations and responsibilities and can lead to overwhelm and role overload (Hayslip & Kaminski, 2005). While a grandparent role is one expected to *visit* and *have fun*, the parent role is expected to discipline and provide life's essentials (food, shelter, clothing, etc.). The first difficulty in filling these two roles is the timeliness of the grandparenting/parenting roles. That is, these individuals expected that their parenting role was done when their children became adults and left home. But instead, they reentered the parent role. Age plays a part here in one's perception of timeliness (e.g., Burton & Bengston, 1985; Hayslip & Montoro-Rodriguez, 2023). Reentering the parenting role at the time one feels like they should be entering retirement or grandparenthood feels backwards from the typical flow of life stages. Participants in the Landry-Meyer and Newman (2004) study commented that they were "cheated of the time they were going to—a wonderful time" and "kinda like in limbo, or almost in a self-defined island, you know?" These comments clearly indicate that the costs of becoming a custodial grandparent are large. The grandparent sacrifices their retirement, and their traditional social clock and societal norms (including their friend groups), to take on the role of full-time caregiver (e.g., Backhouse, 2009). That is not to say that the grandparent doesn't feel the value in the role. They *do* feel the value, and know their role is important—a participant in the study by Landry-Meyer and Newman (2004) commented, "A tremendous relief when you know that they (the grandchildren) are all right. That they're safe. They're taken care of."

A second difficulty in custodial grandparenting is the ambiguity of the role—the individual flows between both parent and grandparent with no real clear line between the two. When do they fill which role? How do they transition from one to the other? The expectations here are not clear, and that makes it even more difficult. There's no guidebook or instruction manual for how to be a custodial grandparent, or a parent for that matter (imagine my surprise that I didn't get a handbook when I left the hospital after having my first child! Like, they just let me leave with him? Without any instructions?). Grandparents raising their grandchildren is not a typical arrangement (e.g., Hayslip & Kaminski, 2005; Hayslip & Montoro-Rodriguez, 2023), nor is it the idyllic picture of family we see portrayed in the media. Instead, it's complex, and finding a balance that works for each specific grandparent–grandchild pair may be the best strategy, because this dynamic is essentially norm-less.

Alternatively, a grandparent might occasionally babysit their grandchildren for a day, evening, or overnight, as my Neno and Mopsie did for me. These are still caregiving roles, but much reduced in time spent in that role. Here, grandparents can easily see their purpose, with no need to balance between two roles. It is clear that they aren't meant to provide day-to-day essentials or discipline (except as needed). Instead, grandparenthood in this regard is meant to be a time of joy and fun, where the relationship between grandparent and grandchild is established as a special type of intergenerational bond (e.g., Duflos & Giraudeau, 2022; Weber & Waldrop, 2000), instead of one filled with daily responsibilities.

In between these two extremes is the daycare situation. Since the 1980s and 1990s, when two-income households became the norm, there's been need for someone to care for the children while parents are at work. However, the prices of childcare/daycare centers and nannies have increased tremendously (Smith, 2002). In many cases, the cost for childcare, or for children to be at daycare for 40 hours per week while the parent is at work, is more than the cost for monthly rent (Child Care Aware of America, 2023). This is simply not financially feasible for many families, and so they turn to the grandparents to fill this need instead. The Annie E. Casey Foundation (2023) reports that more than half of working-aged adults have children, and 37% of those are in need of childcare for their young children. Of course, this poses an interesting problem in the United States, where we're delaying retirement age (or people need to work past age 65 for financial reasons—but more on retirement later in this chapter) and grandparents are unavailable to assist because they too are working. Additional complications arise when childcare is needed but grandparents do not live nearby. While this distance between family members isn't often the case in many European countries (e.g., Greece and the Netherlands), it is more common in the United States (e.g., Posadas & Vidal-Fernandez, 2004), yet the National Association of Child Care Resource and Referral Agencies (2008) reports that up to 40% of American grandparents provide extensive (i.e., more than occasional) care for their grandchildren (Fuller-Thomson & Minkler, 2001; see also Figure 6.1).

Culture and Grandparenthood

To be sure, culture also plays a role here, and expectations of a grandparent and grandparent as caregiver may be different between different cultures. Some grandparents may maintain a caregiver role as a way to uphold family traditions and cultural beliefs (e.g., Chan et al., 2022; Cox, 2018; Landry-Meyer & Newman, 2004). For instance, Geffen (2014) explored the role Jewish American grandparents play, and their perception of that role. Interviews revealed that Jewish American grandparents feel a responsibility to encourage a sense of Jewish identity in their

FIGURE 6.1 ■ Rates at Which Grandparents Provide Childcare Support for Their Grandchildren

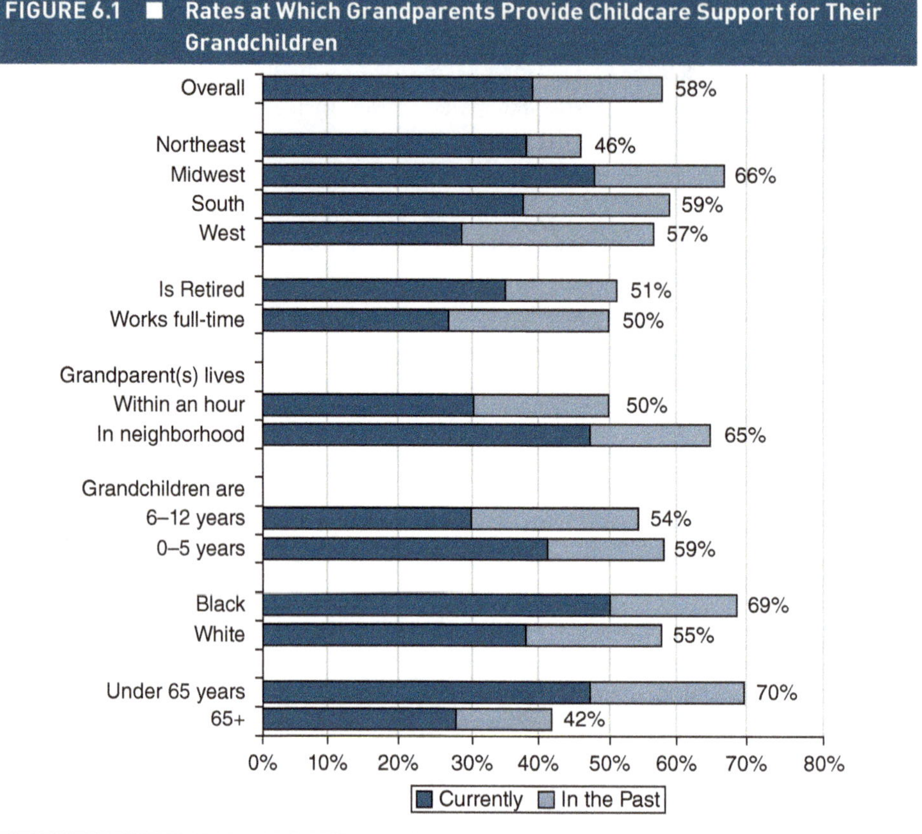

Source: National Association of Child Care Resource and Referral Agencies. (2008). *Grandparents: A critical child care safety net.* https://www.childcareaware.org/wp-content/uploads/2015/10/2008_grandparents_report-finalrept.pdf

grandchildren in the hopes that they carry on the traditions and *make Judaism timeless*. Personally, I felt this in how Neno encouraged Shabbat prayer on Friday nights and told my sister and me stories of our Jewish heritage and history. These expectations of responsibilities are not reserved for Jewish Americans but can be seen in other cultural exchanges through grandparent–grandchild interactions—among other role responsibilities (e.g., Mjelde-Mossey, 2007; Svensson-Dianellou et al., 2010). In a study conducted in Greece, Svensson-Dianellou et al. (2010) explored the role of the Greek grandparent. Here, Greek grandparents explain that they also see childcare as a normal, expected part of grandparenthood. Svensson-Dianellou et al. report that up to 80% of Greek mothers prefer to leave their children with their own mother over formal childcare, and at least 45% of Greek grandmothers provide that care as well as other household help like cooking and cleaning. This opportunity is seen as part of the role of a Greek grandmother, in addition to the expectation of passing on family and Greek traditions.

Similarly, Chinese elders are seen as a part of the child-rearing process (e.g., Mjelde-Mossey, 2007). Chinese cultural traditions revered the role of an older adult in the family structure, and as such, becoming and holding the position of a grandparent has always been highly anticipated and coveted. The grandparent is the object of **filial piety**, or the obligation to care for, honor, and obey. The grandparent in Chinese culture is the one who governs the family, is sought for wisdom and direction, and plays a significant role in the family's overall functioning. Additionally, Chinese elders demonstrate ***renqing***, or an obligation for the family to give, rather than receive (Mjelde-Mossey, 2007). In *renqing*, the older adult contributes to the family (similar to how we think of Erikson's [1950] generativity stage) and is successful when the family is successful. The Chinese family lives close by and contributes as a group to the well-being of one another, as you'd predict from a collectivist society (Chiu, 1990).

The role of child-rearing is not something to take lightly, and most grandparents don't. They are deep in Erikson's (1950) generativity stage of development and value their purpose in this role, which can contribute positively to their mental health (e.g., Condon et al., 2018). In measures of anxiety and depression, Condon et al. (2018) found that not only do grandparents show no declines in either of these measures (as described earlier), but those who spend time in the grandparent/caregiver role show an improvement in these mental health measures. However, improvements in mental health measures are not the only benefit. There are additional rewards to the grandparent role that we'll explore next.

Rewards and Difficulties of Grandparenting

The role of a grandparent can take many forms, and there are many rewards (but also some difficulties) that can come along with it. We've seen that as part of the grandparent-as-caregiver role, a grandparent can serve to provide a source of family and cultural reference (e.g., Chan et al., 2022; Cox, 2018; Geffen, 2014; Mjelde-Mossey, 2007). However, this isn't restricted to only those grandparents in a caregiving role. Robertson (1976) describes that grandchildren consistently view grandparents as sources of emotional support, generational wisdom, and keepers of family history (Robertson, 1976). Anecdotally, I can tell you that this is true. I always asked my grandmothers what was right/wrong/historically accurate as far as our heritage and family history was concerned. They always knew the answers.

Within these "historical" responsibilities, there's a reward of seeing younger generations take on cultural norms and traditions from your specific family heritage. For example, Geffen (2014) describes how one Jewish American grandparent hoped to "inspire my grandchildren to love being Jewish and be ***shomrei mitzvot*** (observers of the commandments)." Passing on these cultural values is important for the preservation of tradition, as generations move on, and contributes to the psychological and social development of the grandparent as well as the grandchild (Erikson, 1950). The grandparent in the generativity versus stagnation stage, as well as the subsequent ego integrity versus despair stage, develops by providing their knowledge in care and wisdom for the next generation. The grandchild moves through the earlier psychosocial stages, learning purpose, competence, fidelity, and love through the lessons and information shared from their grandparents.

Additionally, research has demonstrated that grandparenting can positively influence memory. Sounds crazy, right? Nope. You've heard the phrase *it keeps them young*, and in this instance, it's sort of true, though *young* isn't quite the right description. Interestingly, memory can be facilitated by the social context in which an individual finds themselves (e.g., Adams et al., 2002; Hartwick & Nagao, 1990; Meudell et al., 1992). In the context of a grandparent–grandchild relationship, this can mean that memory is better when their grandchild is the recipient of the information they are trying to remember. Adams et al. (2002) tested and found evidence to support this claim (see Figure 6.2). In their study, young and older adults were asked to read a passage and then retell the story to the adult researcher and to a child. Recall for older adults was comparable to that of the young adults when they were retelling to a child—but the same did not hold true for when they were retelling to the adult researcher. The explanation here is simple: The older adults were motivated to remember as much information as they could to "pass on" to the child whereas the adult researcher could, in theory, read and understand on their own. Passing on knowledge was valuable and contributed to the older adults' sense of generativity.

iStockPhoto/Drazen Zigic

While these rewards are significant, and certainly do outweigh the difficulties associated with grandparenthood, it is still important to recognize that difficulties do exist. First, the transition to the role of grandparent can be difficult if the transition is not timely. That is, negative reactions can occur if the transition happens earlier than expected (e.g., Burton & Bengston, 1985; Leopold & Skopek, 2015; Minkler & Roe, 1993). Specifically, researchers describe differences between adults entering grandparenthood at an early age (between ages 25 and 38) and those entering grandparenthood at the ages in a more normative age range (between 49 and 58), where the grandparent responses are more reactionary at an earlier age (e.g., Burton & Bengston, 1985). Those entering grandparenthood earlier have a harder time taking on the

FIGURE 6.2 ■ Average Complexity for Text Recalled

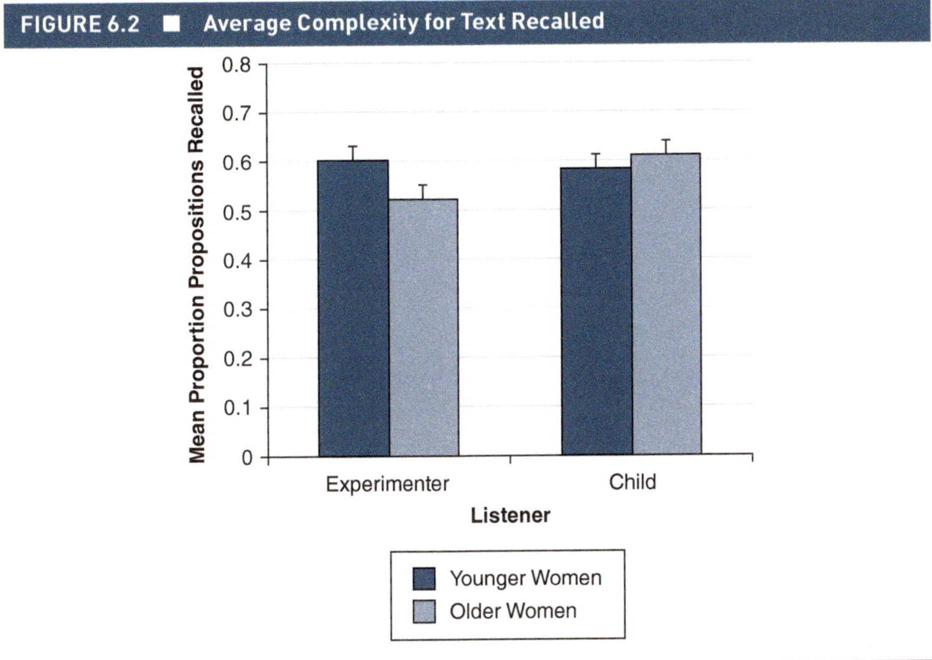

Source: Adams, C., Smith, M. C., Pasupathi, M., & Vitolo, L. (2002). Social context effects on story recall in older and younger women: Does the listener make a difference? *The Journals of Gerontology Series B: Psychological Sciences and Social Sciences, 57*(1), P28–P40.

responsibilities and expectations of the role. To be sure, some of these comparisons come within a context of other difficult life circumstances (e.g., adult child entrenched in drug use and drug culture; Minkler & Roe, 1993), so the move into grandparenthood is not coming from the same places as it would if the context were a more positive one. However, many of these confounds are often unavoidable.

Additionally, in the case of custodial grandparenting, difficulties arise when the individual takes on two roles at once: grandparent and parent. As we've already explored, this balance can be very difficult because there are no real norms associated with taking on these two roles at the same time, and therefore no real schema for guidance (Hayslip & Kaminski, 2005). Additionally, the research indicates that timeliness and loss of expected opportunities (like an expected retirement) can contribute to the difficulties associated with custodial grandparenthood (e.g., Backhouse, 2009; Landry-Meyer & Newman, 2004).

And, finally, difficulties can arise in the context of health concerns and the limitations associated with them. As discussed in the first chapter, there are some physical health issues that are common (not guaranteed) in older adulthood. For example, consider an older adult with arthritis. Activities like running, sports, and even small crafts such as stringing beads can be difficult to engage in—and these may be activities they'd like to do with their grandchild. However, this limitation can be viewed positively instead of negatively—perhaps instead of seeing what they can't do together, the grandparent and grandchild can learn something new together. Previous chapters have demonstrated that older adults can learn new things, so gaining a new skill with their grandchild would be a perfect way to enjoy something special together.

The grandparent–grandchild relationship is an important one for both involved but is not the only important relationship for an older adult, nor is it a role that all older adults take on. Just as in other life phases, friendships and romantic relationships are also important for the overall life satisfaction of an individual. We will discuss in the next sections the intricacies of those types of relationships and how late life, life experience, and some health concerns can impact those relationships.

INTIMATE RELATIONSHIPS IN LATE LIFE

In college, I worked in a pharmacy as a pharmacy technician. It was my job to assist the pharmacist and facilitate prescription fills and pickups, as well as keep the pharmacy organized. During that time was the launch of an innovative drug you probably all have heard of: Viagra. The intended use was for assistance in erectile dysfunction and was often associated with older adults. While the "new" drug seemed innovative and a fantastic solution to a "universal problem," this was far from the truth. First, Viagra was not the first drug to assist with erectile dysfunction—it was just the first that came in the form of a pill. Prior to this coming to market, there were creams, injections, and suppositories that served the same purpose. Second, erectile dysfunction is not universal, with rates reported at just under 40% of older adults assigned male at birth (Lindau et al., 2007). Rather, it is often the result of some other health or mental health concern, such as cardiovascular issues (Gandaglia et al., 2014) or depression (Liu et al., 2018). Regardless, the drug quickly became associated with old age because of assumptions about intimacy that are simply untrue. In this section, we'll discuss intimate relationships—and **intimacy** is not just sexual intimacy, but rather a closeness in relationship. Sometimes, it coincides with sexual relations, but it doesn't necessarily (e.g., Blieszner & De Vries, 2001; Connidis, 2013; Reis, 1990). Intimacy occurs in friendships and romantic partnerships as well as family relationships.

Like all other humans, older adults benefit from intimacy with romantic and nonromantic partners (e.g., Giddens, 2020). Familial relationships and friendships, as well as spouses and romantic partners, can provide this closeness and help support one's overall well-being (e.g., Walen & Lachman, 2000). This can be especially important in several instances, such as when social circles begin to shrink—as is normal in older adulthood (e.g., Cornwell et al., 2008)—and if the older adult moves toward assisted living, away from their familiar life arrangements. Assisted living, from the outside, can be viewed as lonely and isolating, but is far from it. (Keep in mind that assisted living is not needed or required for every older adult. See the discussion in Chapter 1 on physical aging and disability for more information here.) Fitzroy et al. (2022) describe how intimacy and support happens in assisted living. Here, there is a potential for intimacy of all different kinds among the many roles in the facility: intimacy between coresidents (married and unmarried), intimacy between friends, and intimacy with staff and volunteers as well. These close relationships and opportunities for trust help older adults continue with their overall well-being, even when some physical or mental health problems are present.

Within these intimate relationships, it is important to recognize that despite the stereotype of erectile dysfunction and the assumptions that older adults maintain only nonsexual relationships, this is not the case (Lindau et al., 2007). You could assume that if an older woman is no longer able to bear children, having passed menopause, she may no longer engage in sexual relations. This is untrue, and its belief contributes to a dramatic increase in sexually transmitted infections (STIs) in older adult age groups (Centers for Disease Control and Prevention, 2024). Here, condoms are not used frequently (or sometimes at all) because (1) the older woman cannot get pregnant, and (2) attention is not paid toward educating older adults about preventing STIs because of the assumption that older adults don't engage in sexual relations. And this only accounts for those in heterosexual relationships. Research on same-sex relationships also shows that older adults are engaging in sexual relations and are satisfied in those relationships, both generally and sexually (e.g., Fleishman et al., 2020).

Sexuality and Menopause

If we consider the one large physiological change in older adult biological females, marking the change from reproductively fertile to unable to bear children, we could see an impact on one's sexuality from many angles—only one of which is specific to reproduction. The others are more subtle but can still have a large impact. For example, there are hormone shifts associated with **menopause** (see Figure 6.3). These hormone shifts include changes to estrogen concentrations and production (e.g., Santoro & Randolph, 2011), which impacts one's ability to become pregnant, but can also impact mood and cognitive function (e.g., Rettberg et al., 2014). To the extent that mood is impacted, relationships can also be impacted.

The timing of menopause can be impactful as well (Graziottin, 2010). While typically the transition through menopause (it takes a few years for this to reach completion) takes place from an individual's mid-40s to mid-50s, the range means there are some individual differences.

FIGURE 6.3 ■ Hormonal Changes in the Menopause Transition

Final Menstrual Period (FMP)

Stages:	-5	-4	-3	-2	-1	0	+1	+2
Terminology:	**Reproductive**			**Menopausal Transition**			**Postmenopause**	
	Early	Peak	Late	Early	Late*		Early*	Late
				Perimenopause				
Duration of Stage:	variable			variable		ⓐ 1 yr	ⓑ 4 yrs	until demise
Menstrual Cycles:	variable to regular	regular		variable cycle length (*>7 days different from normal*)	≥2 skipped cycles and an interval of amenorrhea (*≥60 days*)	*Amen x 12 mos*	none	
Endocrine:	normal **FSH**		↑**FSH**	↑**FSH**			↑**FSH**	

**Stages most likely to be characterized by vasomotor symptoms* ↑ = *elevated*

Source: Soules, M.R., et al. (2001). Executive summary: stages of reproductive aging workshop (STRAW). Fertility and Sterility, 76(5), 874-878.

Graziottin (2010) describes that the younger a woman is during menopause, the less likely it is that they have progressed through their expected life events cycle (falling in love, having satisfying sexual relationships, marrying, having children, etc.). The implications of this can be felt on sexual desire, satisfying sexual relationships, and even sexual identity. Graziottin tells of some comments participants made surrounding menopause, including statements like "I do not have sexual interest for anybody; I feel sexually invisible" and "since I became menopausal, I have a worsening vaginal dryness; sex is no longer a pleasure." These can impact relationships in a serious way, making them devoid of sexual satisfaction and pleasure. However, Graziottin suggests that the individuals who experience menopause at a later/more typical age are less likely to be distressed by these physiological changes. Some of the reason for that is in one's expectation, and some is that changes in timely menopause are often gradual—as opposed to those that come in earlier menopause, which are sudden and often the result of **hysterectomy** (i.e., removal of some or all of the female reproductive organs, where removal of the ovaries results in premature menopause).

Additionally, culture plays a role in postmenopausal sexuality (Winterich, 2003). Rather than focus on the negative, Winterich (2003) found that both heterosexual and lesbian women tended to focus on the relationships they have rather than the biological changes (e.g., vaginal dryness) they are experiencing. This is positive. It tells us that while the biology changes, there is so much more that is important to the individual. Instead, women in this study described relationship quality, communications, willingness to change sexual activity as needed, and sexual history. While overall positive, this study did find that communication about difficulties with their partners differed between heterosexual and lesbian women. Here, difficulties for heterosexual women were exacerbated by cultural expectations of sex with their male partners, such as orgasm and their partner's complaints about their vaginal dryness. Alternatively, lesbian women reported being able to openly communicate with their partners and adjust sexual activities. These differences suggest a significant impact of sociocultural expectations for sex to change negatively with menopause, after the loss of reproductive viability. But the same-sex couples in Winterich's study show us that positivity and positive experiences in sexuality in menopause are possible, and a reality for many.

Marriage

One type of intimate relationship many individuals benefit from is marriage. While the hope is that marriage will last a lifetime, this isn't always the case. According to U.S. Census Bureau data (Mayol-Garcia et al., 2021), upwards of 43% of marriages through age 65 end in divorce. However, these rates do vary by ethnicity, with Hispanic American adults' rates of divorce hovering in the 14% range and rates for Asian American adults at just over 10%. Expectations of marriage, individuals growing apart, different lifestyle needs, and demeaning or abusive relationships are common reports of reasons for divorce (e.g., Gigy & Kelly, 1993; Hawkins et al., 2012; Scott et al., 2013).

The difficulties associated with divorce can be bountiful and may be different depending on the age of the individuals divorcing, the length of the marriage, whether there are children, and whether those children are still children or have become adults (Amato,

2000). That is, divorce in young adulthood and middle adulthood is much different from divorce in older adulthood. For example, some research has shown connections between divorce and physical health complications like chronic illness and mobility issues (e.g., Hughes & Waite, 2009) or cardiovascular disease (e.g., Zhang & Hayward, 2006) for adults in middle to late adulthood. This is not to say that divorce causes these health issues, but as we'll see in Chapter 10, there is a negative impact of stress (when internalized) on the physical and mental health of an individual. And if there is one thing I can be sure of, even without having experienced it, it is that divorce is stressful (Strizzi et al., 2021; I should also note that divorce is only one way that marriage ends. Widowhood is another, but that will be discussed in Chapter 11).

Still, over 50% of marriages last (a big positive), and within those—or even within the marriage before divorce—there has been much exploration into the satisfaction of the relationship (e.g., Bradbury et al., 2000; Tavakol et al., 2017). Research has shown a *U*-shaped trajectory, with the peaks of satisfaction at the beginning and end of a marriage and the lower ratings of marriage satisfaction during the years where the couple is rearing and raising children (e.g., Glenn, 1989; Twenge et al., 2003). This makes sense to the extent that time and energy that would be spent on the spouse and fostering that relationship is spent instead on the children, their well-being, and their activities. However, other research has demonstrated a similar pattern in marital satisfaction, even for couples who do not have children (e.g., Bradbury, 1998). And still other research has demonstrated a different trajectory with satisfaction declining in the early and later years (e.g., VanLaningham et al., 2001). All that's to say marital satisfaction is not static and changes depending on many factors, including timing, life circumstances, children, and many others. Importantly, Sears et al. (2016) have identified some specifics related to the daily difficulties in a marriage, such as daily overload, ignoring the spouse's needs, reduction in affection, and negative mood (Sears et al., 2016). When a relationship lasts and is successful, the partners in that relationship have found something beneficial in that relationship that is not minimized or dampened by these daily difficulties. We'll discuss that next.

Marital Success

A successful marriage is one whose benefits outweigh the costs and difficulties. Kaslow and Robison (1996) describe the factors that contribute to a successful marriage, including the ability to adapt, a commitment to the relationship and the family unit, a similar religious or spiritual orientation, appreciation for one another, clear roles and expectations, shared quality time together, and connection within their community as a couple. And, of course it makes sense that as a couple grows and ages together, so does their marriage. Kaslow and Robison also explored the factors that contribute to a long and successful marriage using the Dyadic Adjustment Scale (DAS; Spanier, 1976), as well as a questionnaire investigating their motivation for staying together and their personal perception of the components that contribute to their successful marriage (which on average were 22 years and still going). Results from these questions demonstrated that more than half of participants reported that they were still in love with their spouse. These participants also reported that they believed that marriage was for life and that they had a responsibility to stay committed to their spouse. Additionally, more than half of these couples suggested that the components for a good marriage were things like love, respect, trust, loyalty, fun and humor, and support of one another. As I wrote this paragraph, I giggled with my husband on some of this. I said, "I should just write that in order to have a long-lasting marriage, you should just marry a dork who tells bad jokes." He laughed and agreed. As part of a couple who has been married for almost 20 years, I can tell you that humor is a big contributor to marital success (and this is supported in research on marital success; Satici & Deniz, 2020). We laugh daily, and one of the things that I know keeps us going is the ability to laugh, even when things get hard. This choice is not always easy, but making a commitment to maneuver through the difficult times as well as share the burden with one another is well worth the effort. The success in a marriage isn't just all fun and games, though. It isn't just about making each other laugh either. Other factors that contribute to the success of a long-lasting marriage are respect, trust, financial security, sexual satisfaction, honesty, and listening (Asoodeh et al., 2010; Dey & Ghosh, 2016; Kaslow & Robison, 1996). These factors (along with the ability to laugh at life's curveballs) can allow individuals to remain in their chosen partnership well into their older years.

iStockPhoto/northlightimages

Interestingly, successful marriages have been linked to improved health and well-being in middle and older adulthood (e.g., Zhang et al., 2016), including physical, psychological, and economic well-being. And, while these positive implications have been established for heterosexual marriages, the next step in understanding relationship success is to examine whether these benefits hold true in same-sex marriages. Some research on long-term same-sex relationships (though not legal marriages, since those did not become legal in the United States until 2015) shows that long-term same-sex relationships have a significant positive impact on the sexual identity of the individuals and lowered levels of isolation from their community and concealment of their sexual orientations and identity (e.g., Riggle et al., 2017). Future research will give us more information on how legalizing same-sex marriage in the United States has impacted the longevity of these relationships as well.

FRIENDSHIPS

Marriage is not the only type of relationship that can be beneficial in older adulthood. Friendships are important as well. Friendships contribute to a social support system, companionship, outlets for hobbies and leisure activities, and so much more (Nussbaum, 1994). In fact, research supports a positive relationship between friend relationships and mental and physical health such that friendship is related to better physical health and higher survival rates (e.g., Holt-Lunstad, 2017; Holt-Lunstad et al., 2010). The contribution of friendship for well-being and happiness is significant as well (Helliwell et al., 2013; Holt-Lunstad, 2017).

When we are children, proximity to others our own age makes it relatively easy to make friends (e.g., Afshordi & Liberman, 2021). Kids are together in school classrooms and after-school activities and have opportunity to interact and find their buddies. In young adulthood and middle adulthood, the same could hold true for work. You are working in an environment with other adults and have opportunity to interact, albeit with often fewer people who are maybe focused more on work or other caregiving responsibilities that limit time to "hang out." However, in older adulthood, after retirement (and retirement will be addressed specifically in the next section), there is no forced opportunity to interact with others. An older adult, in theory, could stay at home by themselves for years at a time and never talk with another human being or form another friendship. This is not good for overall well-being, or rather our subjective well-being and overall perception of health is boosted when social interactions are included in our daily activities (Farriol-Baroni et al., 2021).

Friendships provide for us so much more than just human interaction. In fact, we choose our friendships based on what we need at that time in our lives (Blieszner & Adams, 1992). That is, what are our socioemotional goals? Are we seeking emotional support? Are we seeking help with finding information? Are we needing support in our self-concept? In this next section I'll discuss how friendships play a role in life satisfaction and the research that supports their role in the life of an older adult.

Functions of Friendships

A few years ago, when I was a dance fitness instructor, there were many older women in my classes. After our classes, many of the women (like groups of 8 and 10) would walk a few doors down in the shopping center to the local coffee shop, get a coffee, and sit and chitchat for hours. They told me time and again that they didn't go to the fitness classes just for fitness. They went because that was where their friends were. Over the years, I saw them support each other in so many different ways from birthday gifts to rides to the doctor to bringing dinner to one another when they lost a spouse. These are the things friends do, and what contribute to the strength of the relationship and each individual's satisfaction in life.

Research on friendships in older adulthood has shown just how much a friendship can impact someone's life (e.g., Blieszner & Adams, 1992; Farriol-Baroni et al., 2021; Powdthavee, 2008). For example, Powdthavee (2008) demonstrated that more than income or other material-based factors, a social network was significant in measures of life satisfaction. Other research has specifically examined the impact of the confidant role of a friendship (e.g., E. D. Hall et al., 2020)—that is, having one with whom you can be open about your deepest feelings and thoughts (though we'll discuss specific functions and different types of friendships in just a bit)—and has shown that having a rich network in which you can be open can positively impact both mental health and longevity (E. D. Hall et al., 2020). In fact, these relationships go beyond positively impacting risk for depression (E. D. Hall et al., 2020) and even show positive impacts in preserving memory function over time (e.g., Sharifian et al., 2020). Specifically, Sharifian et al. (2020) examined longitudinal data from the Health and Retirement Study (Sonnega & Weir, 2014), including information about individuals' social network, contact frequency, and episodic memory (i.e., memory for events). Data analysis showed that relationships with family differed in their impact on memory compared with friendship relationships, such that friendship relationships showed a positive relationship for memory preservation. Extensive social connections with family members did not. Sharifian et al. (2020) suggest that the reason for this difference is in the amount of cognitive work needed to maintain and continue with a friendship. That is, a friendship often connects two individuals with an activity, and it may require more effortful communication to maintain the relationship closeness that has not been there day in and day out for their entire lives, the way that family has. This makes sense, especially when we consider the different functions that a friendship may serve.

Friendships can be beneficial and can serve a variety of functions in our lives. Sometimes we have friendships that form from a shared activity. For example, my husband is a volunteer firefighter in our town, and the vast majority of his friends are also part of the fire department. They have bonded and experienced the same events, and the activity they share started their friendship. Alternatively, we may have a friend for emotional or affective needs. These are friends with whom you talk, ask advice, and communicate vulnerably. And, finally, we may have friends who are there simply for fun. These are ones with whom you laugh and enjoy your time without needing to have deep, personal conversation or a shared activity. Being with them is just fun. All of these friendships provide value and can fill a need in the life of an older adult (or a young adult, for that matter). However, research does show that the number of friendships we have tends to decline in our older years, leading to an increase in feelings of loneliness (e.g., Willroth & Hill, 2021), though those feelings diminish on days where older adults do spend time with their friends.

Gender differences in friendships are also apparent and can impact the way in which a friendship plays out (e.g., Felmlee & Muraco, 2009; J. A. Hall, 2011). For instance, Felmlee and Muraco (2009) asked participants to evaluate friend behavior (see Table 6.1).

TABLE 6.1 ■ Mean Ratings for Appropriate Friend Behaviors

	Male Respondent	Female Respondent
Told secret		
Male Friend	2.31	1.55
Female Friend	2.51	1.86
Cancels plans		
Male Friend	4.17	3.47
Female Friend	4.30	4.11
Asks to stay over		
Male Friend	4.62	4.55
Female Friend	5.18	4.97
Surprise visit		
Male Friend	3.79	3.17
Female Friend	3.70	3.16
Kiss on cheek		
Male Friend	3.93	4.85
Female Friend	5.03	5.08
Won't confide		
Male Friend	4.31	4.77
Female Friend	3.83	4.75
Didn't stand up		
Male Friend	3.48	3.30
Female Friend	3.60	2.94

Source: Felmlee, D., & Muraco, A. (2009). Gender and friendship norms among older adults. *Research on Aging, 31*(3), 318–344. https://www.doi.org/10.1177/0164027508330719

Participants read descriptions of men or women acting appropriately (e.g., helping a friend who needs help) or inappropriately (e.g., betraying trust) as per societal norms. Results showed that women rated violations of friendship norms as more negative than did men. The authors suggested that one reason for this gender difference was because women tend to have stronger, more intimate friendship bonds than men and have higher expectations for those friendships. (However, please note that this study, as well as many others, is limited in the definition of gender. Such studies do not include individuals who identify as nonbinary, nor do they include evaluations for individuals in the LGBTQIA+ community at all.) Interestingly, Felmlee and Muraco did not see age differences, demonstrating that both young and older adults have similar expectations for their friendship. Even friendships between young and older individuals (i.e., intergenerational friendships) can be beneficial.

Intergenerational Friendships

If there is one thing that older adults are motivated to do, it is "give back" to the next generation (e.g., Kruse & Schmitt, 2012; McAdams et al., 1993). It promotes a sense of generativity as we saw earlier in this chapter in discussing the grandparent role. However, being a grandparent isn't the only way an older adult can interact or have a relationship with a younger adult. Intergenerational friendships can be another, which can benefit both members of the relationship. A Dutch nursing home took advantage of this connection and began offering free housing for college students who spend at least 30 hours per week with their older adult residents (Reed, 2015). The students spend time with the older residents, offering company and being all-around good neighbors and citizens. One older adult says they "bring the outside world in." And this can prevent disconnectedness for the individuals who need the nursing home facility to maintain their physical health and provide an opportunity for seeing aging more positively for the young adults as well. This program has become so successful that it is being replicated in a variety of cities across the world, including Barcelona, Spain, and Cleveland, Ohio. Other research on intergenerational friendships has demonstrated similar positive outcomes (O'Dare et al., 2019) such as reduced feelings of loneliness (Andrews et al., 2003) and other "life-enhancing" benefits from even individuals with Alzheimer's disease, such as maintaining personal identity and coping skills (Ward et al., 2012), though research in this area needs substantial expansion.

RETIREMENT

Retirement can be thought of as social role change—like that of grandparenthood. The individual goes from the role of *worker* to the role of *retiree*, and as you would expect, there is a potential for mental health implications here. Specifically, when someone sees themselves and their role in their job as one and the same, it can be very difficult when that job is no longer there. For example, if you meet someone at a party and they say, "Hi, my name is Bob. I'm a lawyer," it is clear that Bob's job is very important to their identity. Now imagine how Bob's world and self-identity might change once they are no longer working as a lawyer. Additional complications, and possible negative feelings, can impact the new role as *retiree* when that role is given without warning or without the individual being willing to take it on. That's not to say that retirement is negative; it's not. However, it does indicate that the context in which one ends one role (worker) and begins the next (retiree) is important.

Context for Retirement

Retirement is largely a modern and Western construct. It used to be that we worked until we couldn't. But the modern interpretation of that is that we "can't" work if we're over 65. This is absolutely not true at all, especially in a society where we are not reliant on our physical bodies to do the labor, and we have machines to do a lot of that. However, we still hold on to the notion that once we reach age 65, we will no longer work in our chosen profession and will retire to spend the rest of our lives basking in leisure. But, with predicted average life spans getting longer and longer, the "rest of our lives" could be another 15, 20, or even 25 years. That's a long time to spend not working, which can have serious financial, social, and cognitive implications.

An added layer of complexity here is that the largest group of individuals ever born during a similar period of time, the **baby boomers**, are retiring/retired. This will mean that they are no longer in the workforce and the number of jobs that they held and the economy that they kept running will need to be maintained by fewer, younger workers (e.g., Collins, 2003). This is a large weight to bear, but is one made more personally relevant for an older individual when they also consider the family care and health care implications, as well as their personal feelings about their job, weighed against their desire to have time to pursue their leisure-time activities (but more on leisure in just a bit; Chevalier et al., 2013). That is, the decision to retire is a complicated matter, and one in which considerations should be made for how they will pay for life and how they will spend their time in the years postretirement. These considerations and the decisions we make regarding them can contribute to our decision of both when to retire and what to do with our time when we do.

In many instances, the transition to retirement isn't an abrupt change, where one day you are a worker and the next you are a retiree (though this is what most of us imagine it to be). Instead, some older adults choose to move to part-time work, per diem work, or consulting work, or leave the workforce entirely, only to return for a new/different job a short time later. This makes the transition to retirement a bit blurrier, but may work better for the individual in terms of financials, self-image, boredom, managing health conditions and expectations, and other factors.

When I was a teenager, I worked as a cashier at a grocery store. This particular grocery store had individuals who bagged up the groceries and carted them out to the shopper's car, free of charge. It was a great service and provided great customer care—and the vast majority of grocery baggers in the store in which I worked were part-time workers aged 65 or older. These older adults were retired and looking for something to do. This was the perfect thing. It was a job where they could get a bit of sunshine and meet lots of people with whom they could chat. Working this low-stress, high-social-payoff job was one way these individuals found to maintain happiness during retirement. They were no longer working in their previous career, but it didn't mean they needed to stay home by themselves to become bored and lonely. Instead, they took the opportunity of time to do something else. In fact, research shows that a blurrier transition to retirement like this may actually provide for better well-being and satisfaction because the individuals have time to adjust to the new lifestyle changes (e.g., de Vaus et al., 2007). But, no matter what retirement looks like for someone, there are some serious issues to consider. For instance, what happens if the decision to retire is forced on us?

iStockPhoto/JasonDoiy

Age Discrimination

It used to be the case that states, and some specific companies, made it law/company policy to retire at a certain age. That is, you *had* to retire at that age, even if you didn't want to. The reasoning behind this was twofold: They believed that (1) older workers were not capable of doing their job any longer (thanks, myths of aging! she says, dripping in sarcasm), and (2) they could hire someone younger to do the job and pay them less than the person who had been working there for many years. What was not being considered here was that older adults are perfectly capable of doing their job, and their experience in doing the job can provide valuable expertise to get that job done well (e.g., Cheung & Woo, 2021; McNaught & Barth, 1992). For example, McNaught and Barth (1992) examined a range of workers at the Days Inn motel chain in the reservations clerk position. These individuals were responsible for communicating with customers and securing reservations for motel rooms. In examining the age of workers, analyses showed that older workers obtained, secured, and retained more reservations than younger workers because of their age, life experience, and general willingness to communicate with the customer about their needs. The older adult was a better worker and made more sense to keep on for the company. That said, given the financial means, an older adult may want to take advantage of time to retire and engage in other activities, if given the autonomy to make the choice to do so. In the next section, we'll discuss ways an individual may maintain happiness (as well as cognitive well-being) when they are no longer working the way they once did.

Leisure in Retirement

Work is hard. Retirement is hard. Life is hard. But it doesn't always have to be. We can find joy in many things throughout our lives, even after we've said goodbye to a role that we've held for 30 or 40 years. In retirement, there is an opportunity to get back something that we may feel is lost a bit in our adult lives: time to and for ourselves. Research on activity in retirement supports this notion of finding joy in retirement (e.g., Borchard & Donohoe, 2008; Liechty et al., 2012). **Leisure activities** are those things that you do in your spare time, and the choices are endless and can provide ample opportunity to do something you once loved (and maybe couldn't do often while you were working) or learn something new. Gibson et al. (2002) interviewed retired women across Florida and found that they were doing all kinds of activities in their retired years (see Table 6.2). The most popular were reading and activities associated with their place of worship. Interestingly, they found only 4% of women fit the stereotype of knitting and sewing. Instead, women were gardening, swimming, and taking exercise classes. These activities held purpose for these retirees, but also helped them maintain physical and mental health (e.g., Kerstetter et al., 2008).

Not only does being physically active doing things like gardening and swimming maintain physical health (as we saw in Chapter 1 on physical aging), but they provide opportunity for social interaction and friendships, as described earlier in this chapter. Friendships bound by common activity are one example of friendships that serve purpose. Those activities need not be physical either. Reading is the most common leisure activity reported by Gibson et al. (2002), and my research shows that maintaining cognitive activity through frequent patronage to the public library can help an individual maintain memory function in their older years (Margolin, 2018). This may be particularly important in retirement, where work is no longer providing daily cognitive stimulation.

TABLE 6.2 ■ Different Types of Leisure Activities Among Older Adult Women

Educational/Cognitive	Reading, puzzles, card games, classes
Physical	Tennis, golf, gardening, exercise classes, tai chi, dance
Social	Church activities, family time, visiting friends, shopping/antiquing
Creative	Quilting, sewing, knitting, fine arts
Other	Cooking, travel, dining out, watching sports

Source: Gibson, H., Ashton-Shaeffer, C., Green, J., & Corbin, J. (2002). Leisure and retirement: Women's stories. *Loisir et Societe/Society and Leisure, 25*, 257–284.

AGING WELL: SOCIAL ROLES AND RETIREMENT

Aging well can mean a lot of things in the context of social roles and retirement, but the most important one is to remain open and adaptive. Allowing the shifting of roles to happen and adapting to them as they come is positive. Finding new ways to fill those roles in a productive and meaningful way can be beneficial as well. It is important to recognize that changing roles isn't the same as losing roles. Becoming a retiree doesn't mean you lost work or your purpose in a job, just as becoming a grandparent doesn't mean you lost purpose as a parent. Changing configurations of your friend group isn't loss; it's natural (though we've seen that maintaining friendships is good for overall well-being). All of this just means that now we can use our experiences in a new way, and we should revel in that, not fear it. It is positive to have those experiences and perspectives and, as the workers of Days Inn demonstrated, can be very effective and useful. Individuals can lean into using their strengths and their experiences in a generative way—fulfilling their own life's purpose and passing it on to the next generation.

KEY TERMS

baby boomers
custodial grandparenting
filial piety
generativity
hysterectomy
intimacy
leisure activity
menopause
renqing
shomrei mitzvot
social role

COMPREHENSION QUESTIONS

1. What expectations do we have from an individual in the grandparent role?
2. How can a grandparent play the role of a caregiver? What forms does this come in?
3. What are the mental health and cognitive benefits of grandparenthood?
4. Describe the cultural role of a grandparent.
5. Compare and contrast the rewards and difficulties of grandparenting.
6. What relationships are important for intimacy in older adulthood? And how do these benefit an older adult?
7. Describe how postmenopausal sexuality may change for an older adult.
8. How does divorce impact an individual in older adulthood? How does that compare to a long-term marriage?
9. Describe the factors that contribute to a long-term marriage.

10. How can friendships benefit an older adult? What are the functions of these friendships?

11. Describe the process of retirement and the role that leisure activities play in that stage of life.

ADDITIONAL READINGS

Antonucci, T. C., Lansford, J. E., & Akiyama, H. (2001). Impact of positive and negative aspects of marital relationships and friendships on well-being of older adults. *Applied Developmental Science, 5*(2), 68–75.

Chen Xugian, A., & Fung, H. (2020). Individualism increases the influence of perceived competence of older adults on attitudes toward them. *Innovation in Aging, 4*(1), 325–325.

Gibson, H. J. (2006). Leisure and later life: Past, present and future. *Leisure Studies, 25*(4), 397–401.

Jendrek, M. P. (1993). Grandparents who parent their grandchildren: Effects on lifestyle. *Journal of Marriage and the Family, 55*(3), 609–621.

Langer, N. (2009). Late life love and intimacy. *Educational Gerontology, 35*(8), 752–764.

Lind Seal, K., Doherty, W. J., & Harris, S. M. (2016). Confiding about problems in marriage and long-term committed relationships: A national study. *Journal of Marital and Family Therapy, 42*(3), 438–450.

O'Dare, C. E., Timonen, V., & Conlon, C. (2019). Escaping "the old fogey": Doing old age through intergenerational friendship. *Journal of Aging Studies, 48*, 67–75.

Ramirez Barranti, C. C. (1985). The grandparent/grandchild relationship: Family resource in an era of voluntary bonds. *Family Relations, 34*(3), 343–352.

Skopek, J., & Leopold, T. (2017). Who becomes a grandparent—and when? Educational differences in the chances and timing of grandparenthood. *Demographic Research, 37*, 917–928.

Stricker, G., & Hillman, J. L. (1996). Attitudes toward older adults: The perceived value of grandparent as a social role. *Journal of Adult Development, 3*(2), 71–79.

Walter, C. A. (2000). The psychosocial meaning of menopause: Women's experiences. *Journal of Women and Aging, 12*(3–4), 117–131.

iStockPhoto/gorodenkoff

7 SOCIAL COGNITION

LEARNING OBJECTIVES

7.1 Explain how dispositional and situational attributions contribute to our social judgments, as well as how accessibility of that information may influence impression formation.

7.2 Discuss stereotypes and how they influence our own and others' cognitive function, including processing capacity limitations.

7.3 Compare individual and collaborative cognition, as well as social motivations, to memory and comprehension.

In college, as noted in the previous chapter, I worked in a pharmacy as a pharmacy technician. I had a great time learning about our clients and taking care of them. My mom, however, couldn't understand why I liked working there so much. She just kept saying, "But those old people are so mean." Not only was her comment rude, but it also spurred me to wonder why she had that impression. It was clear to me that while she couldn't understand me, I couldn't understand her. As I furthered my study of psychology, however, it became clear what she was doing: She was assuming all older people were mean because of her limited interactions with them at the pharmacy. Truth be told, if I wasn't feeling well and had to pay a ton of money for my medicine, I'd be crabby too. However, my mom was failing to recognize this situation, which may actually have been the motivator behind the behavior she was encountering. Instead, she was attributing the negative interaction to the entire group of older adults, and not even the one or two individuals with whom she interacted. In this chapter, I'll discuss why this misattribution happened, but also why it was cognitively easier for my mom to think this way—even though she didn't intend it to be rude or malicious. Additionally, I'll discuss how these kinds of judgments form (and are maintained) in older adulthood, and how they can be internalized and impact the cognition and behavior of an individual in the stereotyped group.

In the area of cognition, we've come to realize that we don't often think in isolation, so studying cognition in isolation is only going to give us part of the picture. Humans are social creatures and, as such, are often influenced to think *about* and think *as* the result of other people's behaviors. It is important to recognize that there are interactions between our cognitive resources, the thoughts we have about others, the thoughts we have about ourselves, and the exchanges and motivations we have with others. It is a complex interaction that hasn't been completely teased apart, nor has its progression over older adulthood. However, there are some conclusions we have been able to draw about how older adults' social cognition progresses, how limitations in cognitive resources may be impacted, and how those limited resources may impact our thoughts about others as well. I'll explore those with you next.

SOCIAL JUDGMENTS

Social judgments are judgments made in a social or interactive situation. And, while the word *judgment* sounds negative, the judgments we make about others or about a situation are not necessarily negative. They are just a way to make sense of the incoming information and draw a conclusion so we can move on to the next thing. We use what we already know about the world, similar experiences, and previous interactions with people to understand the world around us as it currently exists. It's called **top-down processing**, and it guides our intake of all types of information, not just social. For example, you would use your experience to guide what to expect and what would be happening if you were to attend a baseball game. You have existing knowledge about the sport, have likely watched a game (or part of a game) before, and maybe have some experience with playing the game too. When you go, you can use what you have stored in your memory about baseball to guide what you are experiencing and understand why the umpire called a strike or why a player scored a home run. And, while every game is different, they are usually close enough to one another that you can use your previous knowledge to help you judge and interpret new incoming information.

The same can happen in instances of meeting new people. We all have experiences and knowledge about other people that we have accumulated across our lives—however limited those experiences may be. When we meet new people, we use those experiences and that knowledge to guide us on how to behave, speak, use manners, and so on. In some cases, our knowledge about a group of people may be very general or very limited (i.e., a stereotype)—and thus be entirely incorrect in guiding us when meeting a specific new person. This stereotype is typically used not in a malicious way, but rather in a cognitive way through top-down processing to guide our understanding of incoming information. For example, we have a stereotype of the information technology (IT) team at a company, and the individuals who make up that team. When we interact with the IT representative who comes to set up our printer, we are using what we know about the people who work in IT (whether it applies to this specific individual or not) to guide our expectations for conversation and our expectations for how they can help us. We may assume, correctly or incorrectly, that they can also help set up our email or firewalls if they are on the IT team. They may be able to help in that way, but they may just as easily not be able to help because their expertise is in networking printers, not firewall protection. Our top-down processing guides us, and as we experience more and more, our available knowledge can adjust our stereotypes as needed—if we remain open to that possibility and have the cognitive capacity to do so.

Attributional Biases

It was clear at the beginning of this chapter that something was happening in my mom's impression formation about older adults and how she used top-down processing to interpret the information she encountered. Something about how she thought about older adults in the pharmacy became pervasive in her perception of all older people. In this instance, she was creating **dispositional attributions** about these individuals (e.g., Funder, 1982; Hilton et al., 1995). That is, she assumed that the way they interacted with her (which she deemed very negative) said something about their disposition—or who they are as people. And then she applied that assumption to all older adults, in the same way we might assume all members of the IT team would be able to help with firewall protection. This is different than making **situational attributions**, where she would have accounted for situational factors that could have influenced their behavior (e.g., Funder, 1982; T. L. Stewart et al., 2010)—like an older adult not feeling well or having difficulties paying for expensive medication.

Another way of thinking about the differences between dispositional and situational attributions would be if you watched a person at the airport walking quickly and then tripping and falling. If you made a dispositional attribution, you might think "that person is clumsy." If you made a situational attribution, you might think "is the floor slippery?" or "they must be late for their flight." In one instance you are making an assumption about who they are, and in the other you are looking for something outside of the person to be a factor that influenced their behavior (see Table 7.1).

So, why would someone make dispositional attributions instead of situational attributions, if situational attributions may be more accurate? Unlike what you may think, it's not that they are mean or refuse to think of others instead of themselves. It's much simpler than that: limited cognitive resources (e.g., Galinsky & Moskowitz, 2007; Macrae et al., 1994). That is, it takes quite a lot of mental effort to process both the individual and the situation and then incorporate

TABLE 7.1 ■ Comparison of Situational and Dispositional Attributions

	Conclusion following watching a person trip and fall
Situational Attribution	They are in a rush.
Dispositional Attribution	They are clumsy.

that information together. If we then add in someone's own reasons for being in a particular place at a particular time (e.g., picking up their own medicine at the pharmacy), we're looking at a situation ripe for cognitive overload. Our discussion of limitations in attentional and working memory resources in previous chapters has told us that overload is not just possible, but likely, when too much information is available at once (see Chapters 3 and 4). When we reach that overload, or attempt to go beyond our available capacity, information gets "booted out of the system." In the case of my mom and her interpretation of older adults, it was the situational information.

In examining cognitive theory, we could think back to the inhibition deficit hypothesis (Hasher & Zacks, 1988), introduced in Chapter 3, which explained that an older adult's information processing system can be "clogged" because of limitations in inhibition and the resulting "extra" information held in the system. This inhibition deficit further limits the available resources for processing situational factors, leading an older adult to be more susceptible to making those dispositional attributions. Research in this area suggests that older adults' inhibitory deficits may lead them to rely on stereotypes (e.g., Radvansky et al., 2010), particularly when they are attempting to understand the perspective of another (e.g., Bailey & Henry, 2008). In one study, Bailey and Henry (2008) asked participants to view a series of videos that showed scenarios of an individual holding a false belief about the location of an item (see Figure 7.1). That is, the individual thought it was in one location, but it was in a different one. In one condition, older adults were told where the item was, though the person in the video didn't know. The difficulty here was that the older adult participant knew something that the video actor didn't. Did the older adult understand that their perspective was different, and what factors would influence their ability to differentiate the perspectives? And could the older adult predict what the actor would choose as the location of the item? Older adults made errors, and they did so more often in the condition where they were shown the real location of the object, suggesting that holding on to the information that the video actor knew something different from what the participant knew may have pushed the participant past their resource limitations. Statistical analyses showed that the primary factor influencing these errors was not an advanced thought process about the actor being deceived, but inhibition deficits (as measured by the Stroop test—as you may recall from Chapter 3 on attention). The conclusion here was that difficulties inhibiting the information about where the item was located interfered with the older adults' ability to take on the perspective of the other individual, and holding on to the conflicting perspectives was too much for their information processing system to handle.

FIGURE 7.1 ■ Accuracy Performance for Young and Older Adults With False Belief Knowledge

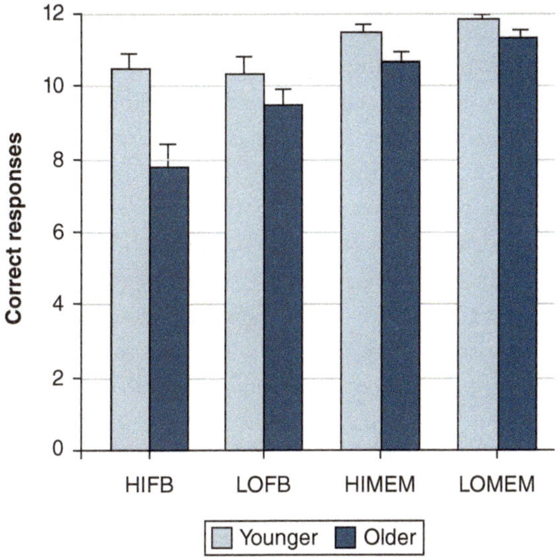

Note: HIFB = high-inhibition false belief, LOFB = low-inhibition false belief, HIMEM = high-inhibition memory control, and LOMEM = low-inhibition memory control.

Source: Bailey, P. E., & Henry, J. D. (2008). Growing less empathetic with age: Disinhibition of the self-perspective. *Journal of Gerontology: Psychological Sciences, 63B*(4), P219–P226.

However, other research in this area provides evidence that older adults can sift through information to hold on to reasonably important information (e.g., Hess & Smith, 2014). That is, while their capacity is limited—and therefore at risk of holding onto irrelevant information—an older adult can use social informational clues along with their experience to lighten the cognitive load and make correct judgments if given good context. In a series of two studies, Hess and Smith (2014) asked participants to make judgments about their general impression of a description of an individual as well as make judgments about the individual's fit for a particular occupation. Descriptions were short but contained six trait descriptors each (i.e., six bits of information about the person). Results showed similar judgments made for young and older adults. This is important because not all of the six traits included in the descriptions were relevant to the judgments being made. That is, some of the information was not needed and could have inhibited or been discarded from working memory. And, while we might have expected older adults to be poorer at this, the older adults in this study were able to sift through the information in a comparable way to their young adult counterparts. These results showed that within certain contexts, where there isn't an overload of information and the social outcomes are within normal boundaries (e.g., judging fit for a job), an older adult is not pushed beyond their cognitive limits and can continue to perform in the way they did when they were younger. Reliance on their knowledge about the world allows for their experience to help bolster performance—much in the same way we've seen how expertise can help support cognitive function (see Chapter 3; e.g., Salthouse, 1984).

Additional time may also be beneficial for older adults in drawing attributional conclusions. As discussed in previous chapters on information processing, inhibition deficit isn't the only age-related change that can impact incoming information. Processing speed also plays a role (e.g., Rey-Mermet & Gade, 2018; Salthouse, 1996). And, while processing speed doesn't always matter—real life doesn't necessarily mean you need to move and think quickly—there are some instances where limited time may impact judgments we make (e.g., Chen & Blanchard-Fields, 1997; Coats & Blanchard-Fields, 2013). In one study, Chen and Blanchard-Fields (1997) asked young and older adults to rate to what degree an individual's personal characteristics influenced the behavior described in short scenes (i.e., dispositional attributions). Results showed that older adults generally made higher dispositional attribution ratings than young adults, demonstrating that they are more likely to draw conclusions about people's behavior in terms of their personal characteristics, and not incorporate situational information—consistent with previous research in this area. Interestingly, in comparing ratings given immediately and ratings given after a 20-second delay, researchers demonstrated that older adults lowered their dispositional attribution ratings when given a delay before giving their rating. This decrease in rating suggests that the short delay allowed time for the older adults to incorporate more situational information about their judgments of the individuals described in the scenes, compensating for a slower processing time.

These conclusions are consistent with the ideas discussed in earlier chapters, where we understood that older adults may have some small limitations in inhibition and processing speed, clearly indicating that their information processing system works a bit differently than that of a young adult. Additionally, older adults' information processing systems influence social interaction and attributional judgments. However, given enough time and enough context to support their system, older adults can continue to perform well on day-to-day tasks, and typical patterns of cognitive change regarding social judgments are unlikely to interfere with daily functioning.

Impression Formation

In other instances, we may be curious to know how older adults fare when confronted with entirely new information and are asked to make a judgment quickly—as in a first impression upon meeting a new person. Moreover, if that first impression is weak and/or incorrect in any way, how well can an older adult adjust their judgment to make corrections later? Based on what we know about information processing, we may suspect that an older adult can make an accurate first impression, if the context is supportive and familiar (relieving some strain on resources) and if given sufficient time to make the judgment (as slower processing speeds would predict). Additional information may be incorporated later, again if time and processing resources allow. However, data from research in this area are mixed (e.g., Hess & Auman 2001; von Hippel et al., 2000).

iStockPhoto/Rawpixel

Research on impression formation has demonstrated that older adults may sometimes be able to come to a similar conclusion to that of young adults upon first impression, but by using different strategies to do so (e.g., Blanchard-Fields & Norris, 1994; Hess & Auman, 2001; Krendl et al., 2014). Other times less accurate judgments occur (e.g., Stewart et al., 2009; von Hippel et al., 2000). Krendl et al. (2014) suggested that older adults may have difficulties in impression formation because of limitations in emotion recognition and age-related changes in the frontal lobe (which may lead to difficulties in emotion recognition). So, they set out to determine the primary factor in influencing older adults' first impressions. In this study, participants made judgments about leadership abilities and political affiliations of various individuals, based on photos. They also made judgments of the individuals' emotions (e.g., joy, sadness, anger, fear) and completed a series of cognitive tests. As expected, and consistent with previous research in the area, young and older adults' emotion recognition accuracies were different. However, this difference was specific to anger and fear recognition. Moreover, results revealed no differences between young and older adults in their judgments on political affiliation. Further statistical analyses led Krendl et al. to conclude that not only can older adults form first impressions as accurately as young adults, but these first impressions may not be reliant on emotion recognition. Additionally, the cognitive measures taken (examining executive function, i.e., the higher-level function of resource allocation) did not seem to hinder older adults' impression formation here. The authors concluded that, at least generally speaking, older adults seem to preserve their ability to make social first impressions. However, the authors made sure to note that the judgments made here were judgments made about "generally respected" social groups, and not those that are commonly stigmatized or "undesirable" in some way. That is, negative impressions were not made here, nor were they measured. And, given the differences shown between young and older adults on recognizing fear and anger, there may be reason to investigate negative impressions.

B. D. Stewart et al. (2009) aimed to do just that. This study aimed to investigate negative social judgments and prejudices, and the factors that influence older adults to generally make more prejudiced judgments about stereotyped groups. One suggestion the authors made was the inhibition deficit, suggesting that unintentionally activating prejudices would become information that could not be inhibited in an older adult. Once in the information processing system, the stereotype would influence the impression they form, even if unintentionally. In a paradigm where participants categorized words (e.g., *happy, friend, joy, peace, terrible, evil, nasty*) and faces of Black and white individuals, results showed that older adults were slower to respond than young adults overall (we shouldn't be surprised here), but this slowdown was exaggerated when older adults needed to inhibit information—as in the case of pairings of negative words with white faces or positive words with Black faces, as these were not consistent with the negative (and wildly inaccurate) stereotypes many individuals hold. The slowdown allowed for more time and mental energy to be allocated to attempt to unpair the unintendedly activated stereotype, which was unfortunately ultimately unsuccessful. These results further suggest that older adults who make prejudicial judgments are not simply doing it to be mean or because they were "raised in a different time." Rather, if negative impressions are made, there is at least some influence of changes in cognitive resources leading to the impression. However, if these are inaccurate judgments, what can be done to change impressions once they are made? That'll be discussed next.

Correcting Social Judgments

Can negative, prejudiced judgments be changed? Can dispositional attributions be corrected? The short answer is, yes, judgments can be corrected. However, this takes significant mental energy (e.g., Chen & Blanchard-Fields, 2000) and may benefit from large amounts of contextual support (e.g., Wang & Chen, 2004). In one study, Wang and Chen (2004) aimed to determine the conditions under which older adults could or could not adjust their social judgments. That is, what context and level of contextual support was necessary to allow for older adults to be able to make the correction? In this experiment, participants were asked to rate their desire to spend a two-week vacation at a series of vacation spots. These vacation spots were either positive (e.g., Hawaii) or neutral (e.g., Indiana), creating context that was either positive or neutral. Next, participants were given another set of vacation spots to rate, and these were either similar to or different from the first set of vacation spots. Further, the messages at the top of the second set of vacation spots gave either additional contextual support (some subtle and some obvious) or no additional contextual support as a correction cue to this second set of judgment ratings. Results from analyses on ratings showed that when older adults were provided with obvious contextual support as a correction cue, they gave adjusted ratings similar to those of the young adults. And, older adults gave more positive ratings when provided an initial neutral context, rather than a positive one. These results show that when given enough support, older adults can adjust their impression. This makes sense if we consider it in terms of information processing resources (Atkinson & Shiffrin, 1968). When given contextual support, older adults were given a release from holding additional resources and information. That is, the context held the information, so they didn't need to. This allowed the older adult to process properly and perform at a level comparable to younger adults. However, subtle contextual support was not enough to provide that release, and the older adults were left needing to hold on to too much information and process it all at once. That is a situation ripe for cognitive overload.

This is positive, though, in our outlook of changing biases, interpretations, and judgments. Earlier, I discussed research that showed that older adults had difficulty unpairing negative, unintentionally activated stereotypes. However, it is clear from the research presented by Wang and Chen (2004) that we can help change that narrative by providing context to help relieve the limited and overloaded information processing system. And, while this research clearly showed the evidence in a controlled laboratory setting, that context may very well be available in typical day-to-day events and conversations. That is, under the right circumstances, we can support older adults in changing their impressions—and that's a very good thing.

Accessibility of Social Information and Processing Resources

In the context of interpretations, impression formation, and making judgments, there is an understanding (as discussed earlier) that we'll use top-down processing to assist. The complicated part here is that we need to (1) have the correct information available to us at the right time for it to be useful in the interpretation, and (2) be aware that the information that we've made available to help will also be taking up valuable real estate in the information processing system, which may leave fewer resources available for making the judgment or interpretation (e.g., Hasher & Zacks, 1988). Let's address each of these here.

We need supportive information accessible and available to us at the time we need to use it. For example, in the case of watching a baseball game, we will need to activate information stored in memory that relates to that baseball game. We'll access that information via the nodal network (remember node structure theory [see Figure 7.2]; MacKay, 1987), as long as we have strong enough connections to it. If we connect to incorrect or irrelevant information, like a football game, it won't help guide us in our interpretation of the incoming information. Moreover, we may see difficulty when connections are weakened due to infrequent use, nonrecent use, and age. The transmission deficit hypothesis (Burke et al., 2000) described that connections weaken generally as a typical age-related process, and this can impact the accessibility of the information needed for optimal top-down processing. Does this mean that top-down processing won't work in an older adult? Absolutely not. What it does mean is that additional context may be beneficial to use more connections (rather than relying on just one, which may be weak) and to strengthen those weakened connections.

Once that information has been accessed, information will move into working memory to use right now. That's where all information currently in use is held—like the desk at which we're working (hence the name *working memory*). The issue here is that working memory is limited (see Chapter 4 for more details on limitations and efficiency of working memory). For an older adult, who may be holding some additional information that's not needed because of an inhibition deficit, there may be even more limitations. The result here is that using the information from memory for top-down processing might be difficult, or at least limited. Moving that information out of working memory to reference, as in the example in the previous section about context (see Wang & Chen, 2004), may be a nice work-around. In this instance, providing

FIGURE 7.2 ■ Node Structure Theory

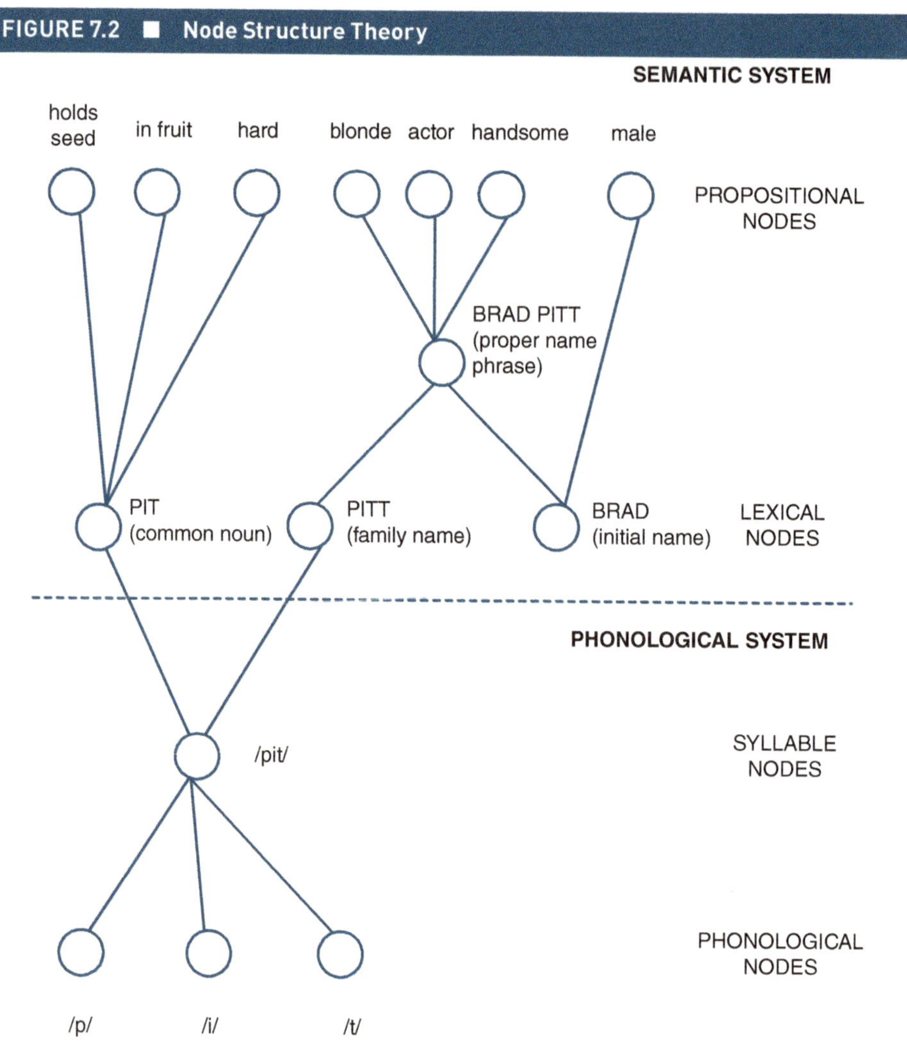

Source: Burke, D. M., Locantore, J. K., Austin, A. A., & Chae, B. (2004). Cherry pit primes Brad Pitt: Homophone priming effects on young and older adults' production of proper names. *Psychological Science, 15*(3), 164–170.

context (on paper for their second list of vacation spots to judge) allowed the older adult to use information without having to hold it along with everything else in their working memory buffer. Instead, limited resources were allocated to what was necessary, and better conclusions were drawn. The same could be true for my mom at the pharmacy. If we provided external context outside of her working memory to be used while encountering older adults at the pharmacy, she could relieve her overwhelmed working memory and draw a better conclusion. Perhaps a sign at the pharmacy reading "Please be kind; you never know what someone is going through" would be enough to provide context for situational variables outside of her knowledge and outside of her control that may be affecting others. Not having to hold that information and process it along with what she's already needing to handle may relieve overwhelmed working memory resources.

STEREOTYPES AND AGING

Even if we don't know it, we all hold stereotypes about aging. Me included. Remember, stereotypes are just conclusions drawn based on our knowledge to maximize cognitive efficiency and use our mental energy in the best way possible. We may have these stereotypes even if we know they are inaccurate; they may still exist because it is cognitively easier to think in terms of generalities than in terms of specifics. The stereotypes may be accurate in some instances and very far off in others. The trick is to recognize that you may be wrong in your conclusion and then adjust as needed. However, we aren't always able to do this because we aren't always aware that we are holding or using a stereotype in a given situation. We may draw a conclusion very quickly and not recognize that we've called up and applied information inaccurately through top-down processing. This can happen if we use the stereotype implicitly—that is, without conscious awareness.

Implicit Stereotypes

If you asked my mom, she would absolutely tell you that she does not hold stereotypes or false beliefs about older adults. However, our story from the beginning of the chapter tells us otherwise. Is she lying? No, probably not. Rather, the beliefs she holds and the assumptions she makes based on those beliefs are happening unconsciously. Remember, back in Chapter 4, we discussed implicit memory, or our ability to remember information without effortfully trying to think back and remember. Given that stereotypes are really just information stored in memory, they too can be recalled without conscious effort—**implicit stereotypes**. While this can be helpful in speed of activation and quickly making decisions, it can unfortunately work against us in that we may be unaware that we are using potentially inaccurate information to make a judgment or draw a conclusion. In many cases, we see implicit stereotypes being used to make those judgments negatively about a group that is different from us (e.g., a different race, gender identity, sexual orientation, or age; Nosek et al., 2007), and those stereotypes can be dangerous to the group dynamic/social interaction, to the person making the judgment, and to the person about which the judgment is being made (e.g., Blair, 2013). But, again, it is important to remember that while the implications of these judgments *can* be inaccurate and hurtful, they are not necessarily made with that intent; rather, they are made through unconscious activation of information that is intended to make information processing easier. With that in mind, let us consider the implicit stereotypes that may exist about our group of focus—older adults—and how others may judge the group and how the group judges itself.

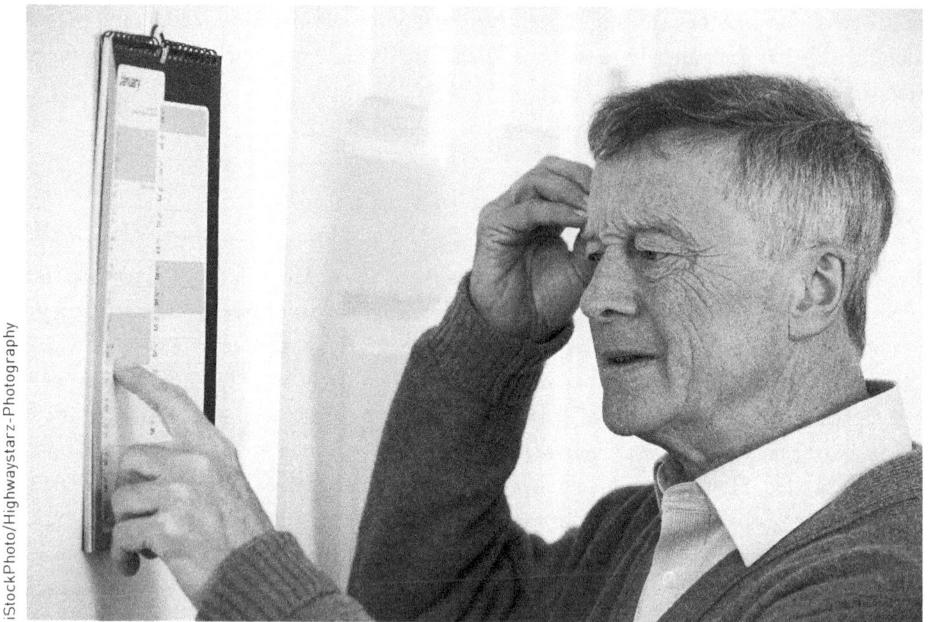

iStockPhoto/Highwaystarz-Photography

Implicit stereotypes are strong beliefs and associations that are activated quickly because the connection is quite strong. One of the strongest and most pervasive stereotypes surrounding the aged (at least in the United States) is that about memory (e.g., Levy et al., 2014). While we have addressed much of the difficulties surrounding memory and aging in this book, your ideas about older adults' poor memory have existed for a long time and are likely very strong. So, while you now know that older adults don't just forget *everything*, you maybe just learned that, and most people don't know that at all. This is common in our ideas about how older adults shift and change. And as such, it becomes an automatically retrieved piece of information used to create a judgment about how an older adult is remembering or will remember a given bit of information. This can lead to unnecessary concerns about an older adult. For instance, imagine your grandmother has forgotten where she put her keys. Immediately, and unconsciously, you may conclude that her memory is failing because she is older. Or, worse, you may become concerned that she is beginning to develop Alzheimer's disease. An implicit stereotype has been activated and used here, and it creates both false conclusions and misplaced worry. Moreover, it also reflects an **age-based double standard** we have regarding memory (e.g., Erber et al., 1990). That is, if a young adult did the same thing, your conclusion would be different. If you misplaced your keys, your conclusion wouldn't be Alzheimer's disease. It would be that you weren't paying attention, that you always misplace things, or something of the like. Why couldn't those same things be true for your grandmother? They likely are. But our implicit stereotype of poor memory and aging can lead us to draw conclusions through top-down processing that are just inaccurate. But rather than use additional cognitive resources to process more about the situation (i.e., maybe your grandmother was distracted when she came in the house and was holding so many items that she just tossed her keys wherever), we take the easier way out and draw the conclusion based on automatic processes instead. The reality is that both young and older adults can have memory failures (e.g., Burke et al., 1991). It is part of being human, and the double standard only fuels the fire of our incorrect ideas about aging. Instead, we should consider situational variables and individual differences, as well as age, when we draw conclusions about someone's behavior.

Research on implicit stereotypes confirms how pervasive this automatic activation can be (e.g., Chasteen et al., 2002), and these stereotypes cover more than just memory (e.g., Fiske et al., 2002; Hummert et al., 1994). Stereotypes about older adults are a mixed bag, involving negative ideas about aging such as memory, physical impairments, and slow speed, as well as positive ideas such as warmth, love, and wisdom. This makes summarizing stereotypes about aging difficult. There is no one theme, nor is there one tone (negative or positive). However, Chasteen and colleagues (2002) attempted to gain some understanding of the implicit activation of these stereotypes and how they influence judgments.

In their study, Chasteen et al. (2002) aimed to determine whether young and older adults held the same stereotypes and whether those stereotypes were more positive toward one's own group (see Table 7.2). Participants here were presented very quickly with a prime aimed to activate the stereotypes of an age group (the word *old*, the word *young*, or the symbols XXX), and then presented with a word or a nonword for a lexical decision task. The words presented for lexical decision were varied in their applicability to a stereotype of young and older adults. In a lexical decision task, a participant is asked to verify whether a word is real or not. The speed of response is measured, where a slow speed indicates longer processing time to figure out whether a word is real, and a faster speed indicates that the information needed little processing because it was easily accessible (presumably when easily cued/primed and connected in their nodal network). Results from the lexical decision task indicated that young and older adults responded similarly to older adult stereotypes and both age groups also responded more quickly to older

TABLE 7.2 ■ Reaction Times for Young and Older Adults in Responding to Age-Related Stereotypes

	Trait Stereotypicality		Trait Valence	
Prime	Young	Old	Positive	Negative
Young Adults				
Young	716	712	710	718
Old	742	693	703	731
Older Adults				
Young	887	855	868	874
Old	894	839	850	884

Source: Chasteen, A. L., Schwarz, N., & Park, D. C. (2002). The activation of aging stereotypes in young and older adults. *Journal of Gerontology Psychological Sciences, 57B*(6), P540–P547.

adult stereotypes than young adult stereotypes. These patterns indicate that these beliefs are pervasive for both age groups, and that the stereotypes we hold for older adults tend to be strong. Additionally, the responses toward positive stereotypes were faster than those for negative ones, and this was especially true for older adult stereotypes. This pattern supports the idea that older adults are not necessarily perceived poorly, and people do have a lot of positive associations with older adults (even if my mother isn't one of them), and confirms previous research that indicated that there are many different types of stereotypes that we hold about older adults. However, it remains unclear under what circumstances a positive stereotype would be automatically activated compared to a negative one.

Other research on implicit stereotypes suggests that not only do we automatically activate the stereotypes that we hold for others, but we also can internalize those stereotypes. Internalizing those stereotypes about a group to which we belong can impact our own behavior and performance.

Stereotype Threat

The beliefs we hold about groups of people don't just influence our opinion of the group, but the beliefs become part of our internal belief system—automatically activated and automatically impacting our performance. This internalization of stereotypes to the extent that they have this type of power over our behavior is called **stereotype threat**. It would work like this: If my mom thoroughly believes that older people are just mean, she too will also become mean as she moves into that age range. The research supports the existence of stereotype threat in many social groups, including older adults (e.g., Hertzog & Hultsch, 2000; Hess et al., 2003; Hess et al., 2004; Levy & Langer, 1994; Yoon et al., 2000). Here, evidence shows clear social impacts on cognitive performance, including things like memory. Internalizing stereotypes that older adults' memory performance is poor sets the stage for actual poor memory performance (e.g., Hertzog & Hultsch, 2000; Hess et al., 2003; Rahhal et al., 2001). And, while one may argue that you cannot necessarily tease apart difficulties stemming from real age-related cognitive changes from those stemming from age-related stereotypes, Levy and Langer (1994) demonstrate support for the influence of social constructs over cognitive performance.

In American culture, it is obvious that we hold and maintain negative stereotypes around aging and memory and that these negative stereotypes feed a fear of aging (e.g., Levy et al., 2014). Moreover, they feed discouraging ideas about aging. In comparing memory performance between individuals raised in American culture and those raised in Chinese culture (a culture that holds the aged in high esteem), Levy and Langer (1994) demonstrated better memory performance for those from Chinese culture. The researchers suspected that the difference in memory was not due to age, because all participants were older. Rather, the researchers suggested that the difference in beliefs about aging from the different cultures was internalized, and the individuals allowed these beliefs to influence performance via the amount of effort expended and the strategies used—even if unconsciously. It was as if the individuals who deeply believed in the ideas that aging equals poor memory simply gave up and didn't put in the effort because *it didn't matter*. And, while there are certainly other cultural factors at play here, the distinct surrender that older adults gave to their internalized stereotypes is supported in other research as well (e.g., Yoon et al., 2000).

Lest we conclude that the impact of stereotypes on aging is all doom and gloom, it is not. The extent to which one is influenced by stereotype threat does vary (e.g., Hess et al., 2003); it is not a universally defeating phenomenon—not everyone in every culture succumbs to the negative beliefs about aging. Hess et al. (2003) argue that the impact that stereotype threat has on an older adult's memory performance is at least partially dependent on the situational factors surrounding it and how much of the stereotype threat an individual feels while performing a specific task. In their study, they manipulated the level of threat participants would experience by allowing participants to read about positive or negative relationships between memory and aging. Then, they completed a free recall measure of memory, where they studied a list of words for two minutes and then retrieved as many as they could from memory. Results demonstrated that when older adults were exposed to descriptions of negatively stereotyped explanations regarding older adults' memory, their recall was lower than when they were exposed to positively stereotyped explanations. This means that the context in which an older adult exists, and whether that context is supportive of the positive aspects of aging or the negative aspects of aging, can differentially impact how older adults' memory functions. This is consistent with the idea that other cultures (e.g., China) whose older members are not implicitly associated with poor memory and poor cognitive functioning do not experience the same stereotype threat outcomes that we do in the United States. In countries like China, the context and support are positive, and that positivity is internalized to improve and maintain solid memory performance.

iStockPhoto/nano

Other research in this area has further demonstrated positivity in the realm of stereotypes of old age (e.g., Levy, 1996; Rahhal et al., 2001; Weiss et al., 2013), where older adults can combat the internalization of stereotypes on their own, even in situations where the culture they live in doesn't provide it for them. Levy (1996) was able to alter the impact of stereotype threat on participants' memory performance and memory self-efficacy by providing descriptions of stereotypes that were positive. As long as the stereotyped information was something important to the individual's self-image, positive descriptions moved the needle and made a positive impact on memory performance. Instructions and presentation can matter as well, as demonstrated in a study by Rahhal et al. (2001). Here, older adults' memory performance was impacted negatively when they were told they were to remember information, but no negative impact was demonstrated when they were told they were going to "learn something new." Both studies demonstrate that older adults can have some control over what impact stereotype threat has if they can alter their perception of that incoming information. If they can turn it around to be positive, it'll be positive. To be sure, changing our cultural beliefs surrounding aging is important. This book is the first step to breaking down the negative and understanding that not all of aging is a negative experience. However, until we can change things more broadly, we can start small with the older adults in our lives and making sure they know that they have this power.

SOCIAL CONTEXT AND COGNITIVE SKILL

As discussed throughout this chapter, our human thought does not happen in isolation. And in some cases, we can see improvements and support in our thought processes (specifically memory) through social interactions, social motivation, and relationship (e.g., Haghighi & Oremus, 2023; Kelly et al., 2017; Oremus et al., 2020). We do not have to, nor do we, handle this life alone. There's no reason why memory should be any different. Even a loner (ahem, hermit) like myself can appreciate and benefit from the social components that contribute to our cognitive function. Let's explore how these benefits can play out.

Socially Facilitated Memory

One component of cognition that is supported by social interaction, motivation, and relationship is memory. Consider an older adult who may exhibit the hallmark age-related attention, processing, and memory changes. We have seen that context and external memory aids can help in relieving some of the limitations and result in performance comparable to young adults. However, another factor that can also bolster performance for an older adult is increased motivation (e.g., Castel, 2007), and one very valuable source of motivation for older adults is their grandchildren. In one study, young and older adults read passages and were asked to retell the stories to either a child or an adult researcher (Adams et al., 2002; see also Figure 7.3). In analyzing the results, they found that the older adults retold just as much of the story with comparable accuracy to young adults when retelling the story to a child. The motivation was clear here: The older adults were retelling a story to pass on to another generation, and they saw value in that. The same cannot be said for retelling to the adult researcher, who could theoretically read and handle the story on their own. This is a tale as old as humankind: one generation working to

FIGURE 7.3 ■ Recall Proportions for Older and Younger Women Differ Depending on the Listener

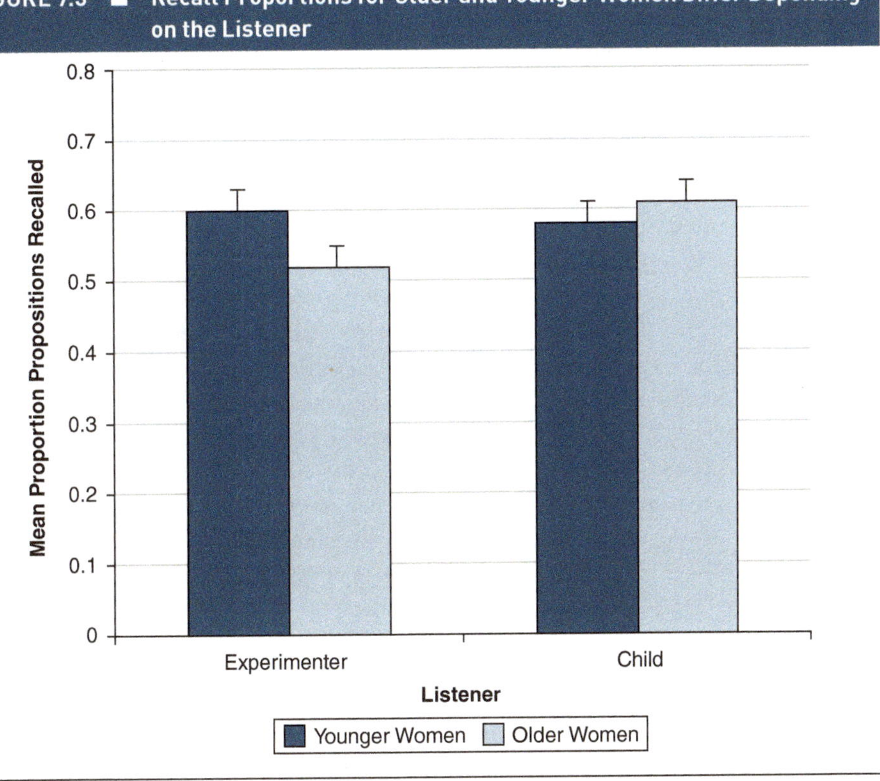

Source: Adams, C., Smith, M. C., Pasupathi, M., & Vitolo, L. (2002). Social context effects on story recall in older and younger women: Does the listener make a difference? *Journal of Gerontology: Psychological Sciences, 57B,* P28–P40.

pass information on to the next through verbal communication. We are clearly equipped to do that, even through older adulthood.

Collaborative Retrieval

We know that working together as a team is also a tale as old as humankind. The phrase *it takes a village* is truer than we could imagine. It isn't just that teamwork provides benefits when rearing and raising children, but we also benefit from teamwork throughout our adulthood as well. We can see that collaborating with another individual can provide supportive context and retrieval cues. I'm sure you've seen this happen. You start to recall a memory of an event that happened with your family, and halfway through recalling the story, your sister chimes in with "yeah, I remember that" and then continues telling the second half of the story. Your initial retrieval provided a cue for her to retrieve her memory, and the retrieval becomes a collaborative effort until, together, you've pieced together a memory for the entire event.

The idea here is that when pressed to remember, the collaborator provides context and an external memory aid to help in retrieval. Research in this area supports the idea that individuals, both young and older, can benefit from collaborative retrieval (e.g., Barnier & Sutton, 2008; Henkel & Rajaram, 2011). Henkel and Rajaram (2011) demonstrated that older adults recalled more information with a collaborator than without and performed much like their young counterparts. To be sure, there are downsides to collaborative remembering, such as poorer memory when an individual tries to remember on their own after collaboration is over. Some research has exclusively aimed to point out these limitations (e.g., Andersson & Rönnberg, 1996; Weldon, 2001), but these negatives are usually reserved for newly formed memories rather than those formed long ago. Moreover, much of this research examined memory for word lists—stimuli that are just not what is typical for an older individual to want or need to remember (except for maybe what they need to pick up at the grocery store).

A more practical look at collaborative remembering examines the positive perspective and demonstrates that benefits can outweigh the costs in collaboration (e.g., Blumen et al., 2013). Specifically, Blumen et al. (2013) suggested that when collaborating during retrieval, each individual in the team/group is reexposed to the memory, strengthening the connections to that memory. Not only do the collaborators fill the gaps during the collaboration, but they also help strengthen the connections for later. Additionally, the relationship each individual has with their collaborators matters. The closer the relationship, the better. So, benefits are higher when collaborating with spouses, children, and close friends, compared to strangers or acquaintances. The "village" an older adult has on a regular basis in their life is the one that will contribute most beneficially to their retrieval of meaningful memories.

AGING WELL: SOCIAL SUPPORT, STEREOTYPES, AND SOCIAL PERCEPTION

When we consider cognition in aging, we have traditionally only thought about the way an individual thinks. As an individual. However, what we've come to realize is that human interaction, social connections, motivations, and influences play an important role in what and how we think. Aging well can happen when social supports provide context, support, and motivation. More widely, though, how we think about older adults as a group needs to change (at least in American culture). Aging is not the enemy. However, as we have seen in this chapter, negative stereotyping can be internalized. And, while individual older adults can combat this stereotype threat through positive self-stereotyping, the problem is larger and more societal. Social support is beneficial all the way around. Aging well can happen on this larger scale when we learn more about aging (in places like this textbook) to alleviate fears and correct the myths surrounding the aging process. When we know the truth, more positivity will come to light, and the impact on older adults' cognition will be positive as well.

KEY TERMS

age-based double standard
dispositional attributions
implicit stereotypes
situational attributions
social judgments
stereotype threat
top-down processing

COMPREHENSION QUESTIONS

1. What types of attributional errors does an older adult tend toward? What is the cognitive explanation for these?
2. How do social judgments relieve a strain on cognitive resources?
3. Explain the influence of top-down processing on impression formation.
4. Under what circumstances would social judgments be corrected or adjusted? Why and how does this play out in terms of cognitive resources and contextual support?
5. What are the theoretical explanations of the limitations in the accessibility of social information? How do these impact the judgments an older adult makes?
6. How do implicit stereotypes impact older adults?
7. How does stereotype threat impact older adults? Is there an alternative to this impact?
8. Describe the influences of social context and support on memory.

ADDITIONAL READINGS

Blanchard-Fields, F., Hertzog, C., & Horhota, M. (2012). Violate my beliefs? Then you're to blame! Belief content as an explanation for causal attribution biases. *Psychology and Aging, 27*(2), 324–337. https://www.doi.org/10.1037/a0024423

Coats, A. H., & Blanchard-Fields, F. (2013). Making judgments about other people: Impression formation and attributional processing in older adults. *International Journal of Ageing and Later Life, 8*(1), 970–110.

Hess, T. M., McGee, K. A., Woodburn, S. M., & Bolstad, C. A. (1998). Age-related priming effects in social judgments. *Psychology and Aging, 13*(1), 127–137. https://www.doi.org/10.1037/0882-7974.13.1.127

Hess, T. M., & Pullen, S. M. (1994). Adult age differences in impression change processes. *Psychology and Aging, 9*(2), 237–250.

Hummert, M. L. (1999). A social cognitive perspective on age stereotypes. In T. M. Hess & F. Blanchard-Fields (Eds.), *Social cognition and aging* (pp. 175–196). Academic Press.

Kite, M. E., & Johnson, B. T. (1988). Attitudes toward older and younger adults: A meta-analysis. *Psychology and Aging, 3*, 233–244.

Levy, B. R., & Banaji, M. R. (2002). Implicit ageism. In T. D. Nelson (Ed.), *Ageism: Stereotyping and prejudice against older persons* (pp. 49–75). MIT Press.

Radvansky, G. A., Copeland, D. E., & vonHippel, W. (2010). Stereotype activation, inhibition, and aging. *Journal of Experimental Social Psychology, 46*(1), 51–60. https://doi.org/10.1016/j.jesp.2009.09.010

Stanley, J. T., & Blanchard-Fields, F. (2011). Beliefs about behavior account for age differences in the correspondence bias. *Journals of Gerontology, Series B: Psychological Sciences and Social Sciences, 66B*, 169–176. https://www.doi.org/10.1093/geronb/gbq078

von Hippel, W., & Dunlop, S. M. (2005). Aging, inhibition, and social inappropriateness. *Psychology and Aging, 20*(3), 519–523.

Zebrowitz, L. A., Franklin, R. G., Jr., Hillman, S., & Boc, H. (2013). Older and younger adults' first impressions from faces: Similar in agreement but different in positivity. *Psychology and Aging, 28*(1), 202–212. https://www.doi.org/10.1037/a0030927

UNIT

IV

MYTH: MENTAL ILLNESS AND DEMENTIA RUN RAMPANT IN OLDER POPULATIONS

This unit will discuss how mental health does and does not change with age (spoiler alert: it mostly does not change, at least not in the way we think it does), including the differences in the presentation of symptoms, assessment, biases, and rate of occurrence of mental health issues. Additional discussion of those changes that occur with the different types of dementias is provided, demonstrating the differences between typical and atypical aging processes.

This unit will also discuss the development of identity and personality throughout the life span, stress and stressors, and several different perspectives on coping. Physiological impacts of stress on the body, including at the cellular level and on the immune system, will be addressed. The positive impacts of adaptation, a change of perspective, and social support will be included as well.

iStockPhoto/greenleaf123

8 MENTAL HEALTH AND DEMENTIA

LEARNING OBJECTIVES

8.1 Identify the key factors that influence mental health in older adults.

8.2 Discuss types of mental health assessments and the external factors that might affect their use.

8.3 Identify the mental health disorders found in older adults including anxiety and mood disorders.

8.4 Describe different types of dementia and highlight the differences between them.

Years ago, I was having a conversation with a neighbor while taking my dog outside for a walk. She told me that she was going to the doctor because she wasn't feeling like herself. I was concerned, because I knew she had some health problems like diabetes and high blood pressure—nothing too serious when treated properly—and she was great about taking her medication, exercising, and sleeping well. When she came home from her appointment, I happened to be outside and see her arrive. So, I asked her how her appointment went. Her response sent me through the roof. Like steam coming out of my ears. Mad. She said, "The doctor said that my blood pressure and diabetes were stable, but he gave me some antidepressants. He said that because I'm older, I just need to deal with this kind of feeling. It is something that everyone goes through when they reach a certain age." What!? There are so many things wrong with what happened at that appointment: things that perpetuate our negative views on and fears about aging, both societally and from practitioners like her doctor (they are human too and aren't immune to influence from biases). I felt terrible that my neighbor's difficulties had been dismissed, but unfortunately this is not uncommon. Her doctor made an assumption (not just about my neighbor, but about all older adults)—assuming that not only do people experience significant mood changes universally when they get older, but they also need to be medicated for it without proper psychological assessment. This is not how mental health and mental health concerns display in older adulthood, nor is the treatment in this manner appropriate without more information (that's to say that medication is fine and helpful for many, but more discussion, assessment, and other mental health treatments should be considered).

While change in mood can be a sign of a mental health disorder, it isn't necessarily. Many other things can contribute to mood changes, including life circumstances, nutrition, changes in relationships, physical changes/illness, and more . . . and it isn't always a sign of a mental health disorder. Importantly, a hallmark of something being classified as a mental health disorder is if it is **maladaptive**—that it interferes with everyday life. Mental health disorders are not something anyone should simply "deal with" or dismiss. Mental health disorders are not an inevitable part of aging and don't affect everyone. Finally, experiencing a mental health disorder such as depression or anxiety is not an expected part of the aging process. Do some of the symptoms of mental health disorders change as we get older? Yes. Do older adults respond differently to medication or to being approached about medication? Certainly. Do assessments need to be adjusted or be sensitive to someone's age and any physical changes they've experienced? Absolutely. But what you'll learn in this chapter is that mental health disorders are not universal in older adulthood, nor should they be addressed as such.

Moreover, not everyone who struggles with a mood disorder or anxiety disorder needs medication. Unfortunately, many general practitioners think about aging in the same way most Americans do—that aging is negative and sad, and everything goes wrong, including our mental health. As a result, too many people are just given medication when they reach their older years, without actually having a mental health condition warranting it. In this chapter, we'll distinguish different symptoms that older adults may experience, and when it may or may not be considered something of concern. We'll also discuss different assessments of those disorders and recognize the contributing factors and real rates of occurrence. Finally, this chapter will present a discussion of dementia, how it differs from other mental health disorders, and how it can occur as the result of illnesses other than Alzheimer's disease.

FACTORS INFLUENCING MENTAL HEALTH

To be sure, there isn't one specific trigger or path to a mental health disorder. Nor is there one specific way to maintain good mental health. However, research over the years has told us a great deal about what kinds of factors influence mental health and mental health disorders. Some of these factors include genetics, stress, trauma, access to and use of alcohol and drugs, limited social networks, nutrition, comorbidities, ethnicity, and more (e.g., Barry et al., 2014; Donovan et al., 2007; Harbottle, 2019; Hudson & Hudson, 2021; Webb & Chen, 2022). Most likely, there is some combination of these factors in motion at any one given time. Depending on the disorder, we'll see more of one factor, less of another, and so on. But importantly, we know that there are multiple factors. And so, a comprehensive bio-psycho-social perspective is the best way to examine, assess, learn, and treat. Let's examine some specific risk factors here—though we will see more details on these when we address specific disorders later in the chapter.

Research has identified that comorbidities of physical health disorders are linked to development of mental health disorders (e.g., Geerlings et al., 2000; Luo et al., 2020; Wang & Kim, 2020). The influence could be physiological, social (through lack of support in dealing with those physical health issues), or perspective-based (through catastrophizing thought processes). Regardless, the link of physical health and mental health is real and should be addressed by medical practitioners. Always.

In a longitudinal survey of over 16,000 older adults, Luo et al. (2020) examined physical and mental health, and the relation between the two (see Figure 8.1). They took measures of chronic illness, competence in instrumental activities of daily living (IADLs), and functional limitations (e.g., walking a few blocks' distance). Additionally, they measured mental health through the Center for Epidemiological Studies Depression Scale (CES-D; Radloff, 1977)—as they used depression as their marker for mental health. Over the course of their 20 years of measurements, the researchers found a reciprocal relationship between physical and mental health, such that physical health influences mental health and mental health influences physical health. Interestingly, the patterns of change across the 20 years were different for individuals who were male versus female (nonbinary individuals were not included in the sample), and for individuals who were white versus nonwhite (no distinctions were made among the nonwhite). These variables mediated the relationship between physical and mental health such that younger (closer to 50 years of age) white men reported better health, both physical and mental, at the beginning of the 20 years. However, this changed more quickly compared to those who were nonwhite. These findings are important in our examination of health on a larger scale, because we now know that one piece can impact many others, and that the pieces are influenced by factors outside of just health (gender, ethnicity, age, etc.).

Another factor that influences our mental health is trauma. While we may readily recognize that trauma may result in post-traumatic stress disorder (PTSD) after some large event like fighting in a war or experiencing sexual assault, there are other traumas and other impacts of those traumas. Some research suggests that trauma early in life can impact us in our later years, both in our physical health (e.g., Krause et al., 2004; Lanius et al., 2010; Maschi et al., 2013) and in our mental health (e.g., Carr et al., 2013; Grainger et al., 2020; Hovens et al., 2010). And, ultimately,

FIGURE 8.1 ■ Changes in Older Adults' Physical and Mental Health

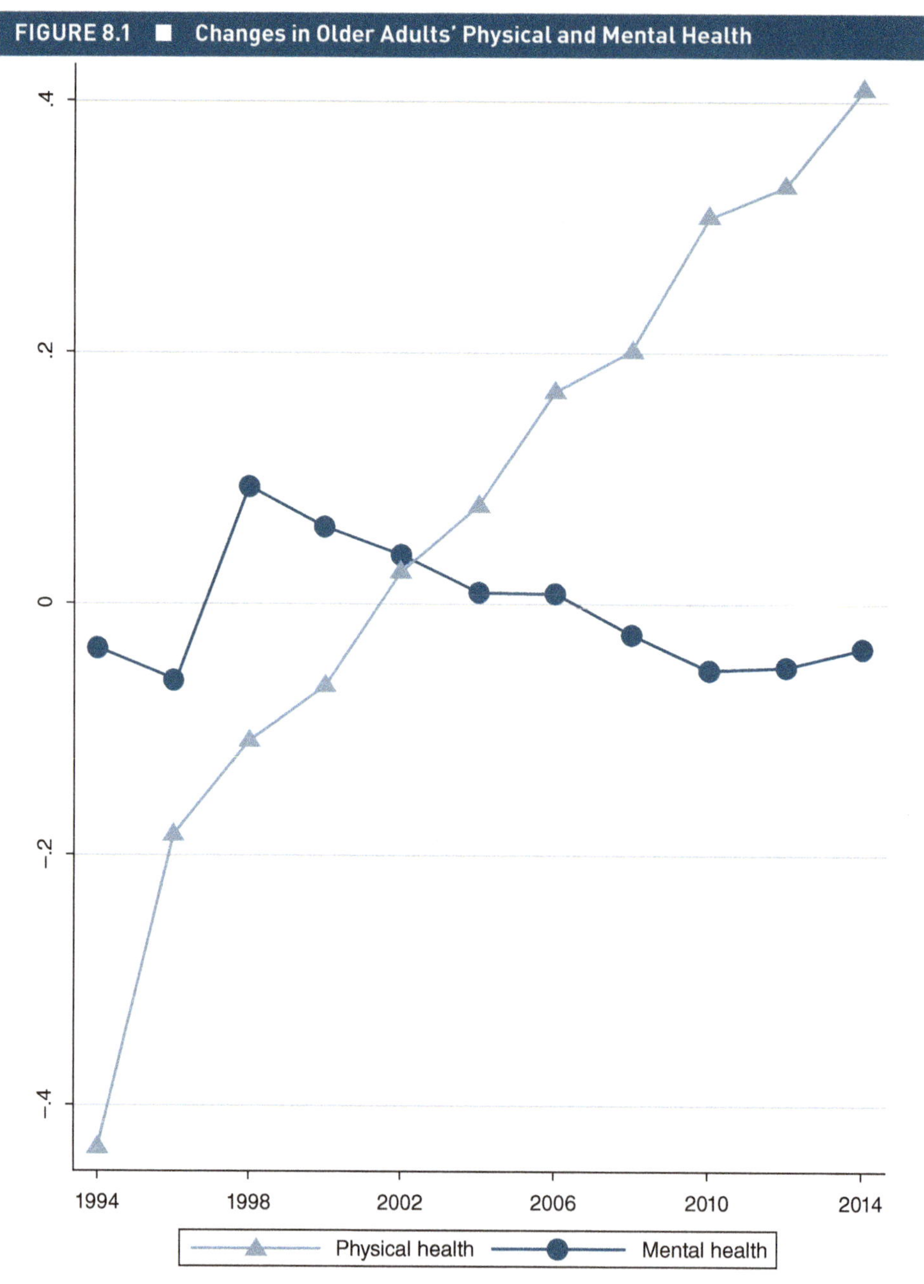

Source: Luo, M. S., Chui, E. W. T., & Li, L. W. (2020). The longitudinal associations between physical health and mental health among older adults. *Aging and Mental Health, 24*(12), 1990–1998.

those impacts on physical health can contribute to further difficulties with mental health (see discussions on stress and on grief in Chapters 10 and 11 of this text). In one study, Grainger and colleagues (2020) measured early life stress using a childhood trauma questionnaire, where they determined how many types of stress and trauma individuals experienced early in their life (if any). Additionally, researchers measured several components of cognitive function, including attention, processing speed, memory, language, reasoning, and social cognition. Results from the analysis of these data showed that individuals who experienced childhood neglect were more likely to experience significant cognitive declines in older adulthood, across all measures except social cognition. This is important in that it demonstrates the importance of care throughout our lifetime, not just during adulthood or just during childhood.

Lifelong care is important in other areas that can impact mental health in older adulthood, like nutrition. Good nutrition throughout our lives is important for physical development, emotional development, and—especially for our purposes—brain development (e.g., DeLong, 1993; Prado & Dewey, 2014; Uauy & Dangour, 2006). Have you ever heard that mother's milk (and similarly formulated man-made baby formula) is very high in fat? Why all the fat? Other than the opinion (ahem, fact) that chubby babies are cute, there is physiological evidence to suggest that the fat is necessary for brain development (e.g., Guesnet & Alessandri, 2011). Neurons are growing and forming connections rapidly in infancy and need to be myelinated. **Myelin** is the lipid (i.e., fat) layer coating our neurons to support their structure, provide channels through which ions pass to generate the action potential, help insulate, and propel signals along the axon. To be sure, our brain is developing not only in childhood, but throughout our lives, and so maintaining good nutrition (not always through intake of breastmilk, obviously) becomes important to support development and maintain what has developed (e.g., Dauncy, 2009; Monti et al., 2015). Moreover, healthy brain development can protect against the effects of disease by buffering the impact and damage they produce (e.g., Melzer et al., 2021).

Good nutrition includes some crucial nutrients for brain function: omega-3 fatty acids and B vitamins (e.g., Rathod et al., 2016). Omega-3 fatty acids are found in foods such as fish, soybeans, and flaxseed (National Institutes of Health [NIH], 2022), and B vitamins (specifically B12) are found in foods such as fish, meat, poultry, milk, and eggs (NIH, 2023). These foods can, and should, be part of a solid nutritious diet. When my family and I have salmon for dinner (the only fish my 10-year-old will eat), we call it "brain food." Even from a young age, my kids have known that food can fuel their bodies and their brains. However, understandably, this is a diet that could be hard to access for folks with lower incomes. Soybeans and eggs, though, are less expensive than others on this list and can still provide the necessary nutrition for brain health. Research on nutrition for brain health demonstrates the Mediterranean diet—a diet rich in foods containing omega-3 fatty acids, vitamin B12, and fresh fruits and vegetables—is associated with a lower risk of cognitive impairment and Alzheimer's disease in later life (e.g., Féart et al., 2010; Huhn et al., 2015; Maggi et al., 2023; Pelletier et al., 2015). In their study, Féart et al. (2010) followed a set of older adults for four years, assessing their dietary habits and cognitive function. Across time, some individuals were diagnosed with Alzheimer's disease, but this percentage remained low (only 12%). Moreover, the individuals who closely adhered to a Mediterranean-style diet were 40% less likely to be diagnosed with Alzheimer's disease. This was a striking difference and was maintained even when accounting for genetic components (i.e., the APOE genotype that we'll discuss in more detail later in this chapter).

iStockPhoto/fcafotodigital

Further support for maintaining mental health involves creating and maintaining social connections. Social networks provide several things for older adults, including continued opportunities to use cognitive skills through shared activities and conversations (e.g., Gow et al., 2013), opportunities to diffuse and buffer the impacts of stress (e.g., Krause, 1986; we'll discuss more on that in Chapter 10), and affection (e.g., Bunt et al., 2017). Research in this area has suggested that social engagement may be particularly impactful for older adults who are at risk for Alzheimer's disease (e.g., Pillemer & Holtzer, 2016). Pillemer and Holtzer (2016) even go so far as to suggest that social interactions may be an important component of interventions for those individuals.

Other research has also suggested that social relationships can buffer the impact of physical illness on declines in mental health (e.g., Newsom & Schulz, 1996). Specifically, Newsom and Schulz (1996) argue that in many instances, when individuals develop illnesses resulting in functional impairments—for example, arthritis limiting their ability to cook meals for themselves—their mental health suffers. Sometimes, these instances are linked with increases in depressive symptoms, sometimes these instances are linked with lower life satisfaction, and sometimes these instances are linked with thoughts of suicide. But what if there was something that could reduce this link and lower the risk of poor mental health outcomes for people who are already suffering with physical health issues? According to Newsom and Schulz, there is: social support. In their study, they measured older adults' function limitations (through completion of IADLs) and diagnoses of chronic illnesses that lead to physical impairment, as well as measures of social networks (through the Lubben Social Network Scale [LSNS]; Lubben, 1988), perceived support, depressive symptoms, and ratings of life satisfaction. Through a series of regression analyses and structural equation modeling, the researchers determined that these variables are intertwined and related through many different relationships. The most important of these relationships is that decreased functional capabilities are related to more depressive symptoms. More depressive symptoms are then related to fewer social relationships and subsequently even poorer mental health outcomes and a reduction in life satisfaction. So, if we could intervene in the middle of this net of variables to improve mental health outcomes, we might do so with the one variable that seems most likely to impact and be impacted: social support. If functional limitations are reducing the access to or willingness to engage in those interactions with others, but those limited interactions have negative effects on mental health, let's support those social interactions.

With internet access in most homes across the United States, social experiences become easier than ever before. They can come in the form of Zoom dinners with family and friends, support groups for those with the same physically limiting conditions (e.g., a support group for older adults with diabetes), online book clubs through public libraries and bookstore websites, and so many more. These options are accessible and helpful for even those whose limitations may preclude them from driving or leaving their house without the help of another, but still provide support and social interaction that is meaningful and impactful for older adults' mental health. Other options for social interactions are more obvious and traditional, including walking and fitness groups, church or other religious organizations, community service activities, part-time work, and book clubs.

MENTAL HEALTH ASSESSMENTS

At some point, we need to discern what changes in someone's mood, social relationships, interactions, and perceptions are natural reactions to normative age-related changes or are atypical and have crossed the line into being maladaptive for the individual. This is an important distinction. Some broad guidelines in distinguishing mental health from mental pathology are that a mentally healthy individual will have a positive self-image, will be independent and capable of ADLs and IADLs (as their physical health allows), will accurately understand reality, and will have balance in their personality (e.g., Bhugra et al., 2013; Fusar-Poli et al., 2020; Sartorius, 2002). Signs of mental pathology will look like behaviors or thoughts that are harmful to oneself or others, a negative self-image, a lack of balance in personality, and/or a false perception of reality. Importantly, for these to be considered mental pathology, they need to disturb or impair day-to-day life for the individual. We must keep in mind, though, that what is maladaptive for one individual may be adaptive for another—and this may differ by age and life circumstances (e.g., Zarit & Zarit, 2011).

For example, consider a woman who uses extreme caution with every item that enters her home, wiping it down with disinfectant. She washes her hands before and after every activity and refuses to allow anyone to wear shoes in her home. It sounds disruptive and maladaptive, right? Maybe for someone, but not for everyone. What if this person has a child with an impaired immune system because they are being treated with chemotherapy for cancer? Her behavior isn't harmful in this instance, but rather it is adaptive for the health and safety of her child. Alternatively, consider individuals with shrinking social circles. If the individual is a young college student and was once thriving in social groups, a change to smaller, less frequent, and fewer social relationships may be indicative of something negative happening to their mental health. However, if the individual is 85 years old, their spouse has passed away, and many of their friends have too, it is normal that they will have fewer social relationships and their social circles will shrink. Therefore, it is crucial that a clinician take note not of just the symptoms, but also how those symptoms fit within the life context of the individual.

Usually, a doctor or clinician will perform at least one set of assessments for the individual (a primary care provider is a great place to start for these assessments, but a psychiatrist or a mental health provider working in conjunction with an internal medicine doctor would be great too). This is important to get a sense (hopefully) of all biological, psychological, and social contributors, and rule out any physiological illness that could display as a mental health disorder. For example, deficits in vitamin B12 can display as memory loss (e.g., Borelli et al., 2020; Iqtidar & Chaudary, 2012; Lewis et al., 2005), and other nutritional deficits (e.g., in folic acid and omega-3 fatty acids) are linked to increased rates of depression (e.g., Alpert & Fava, 1997; German et al., 2011; Payne, 2010). These nutritional deficits may only be compounded by difficulties discussed in other chapters of this text, such as changes in taste and smell, physical limitations in preparing meals, or even the loss of a loved one with whom they used to share meals. These factors will only fuel the deficit and further increase the likelihood or occurrence of depression (or other mental health difficulties) in an older adult. Therefore, physiological assessments are a necessary add-on to the cognitive, mood, and functional assessments.

Types of Assessment

One of the first types of assessment a doctor may (and in my opinion *should*) conduct is a physiological assessment. They may perform blood tests to check for nutritional deficiencies, they may perform a brain scan (fMRI, PET, or CAT) to determine whether there has been a stroke; and they may check for infection or viral illness (some of these can cause inflammation and changes to the brain itself, even if that wasn't the original place of infection). Once physiological assessments give reason to rule in or rule out a physiological cause for symptoms, a doctor can move on to other explanations for the symptoms an individual has been experiencing. When they move on to other assessments, they can perform a variety of or a combination of interviews, performative tasks, observations, tests, and clinical examinations. The reason for using a combination here is to get information from several perspectives—the individual experiencing the symptoms, their family, their spouse, and others—and for the doctor to see the symptoms play out in action before them, when possible or when informative.

For an interview, a clinician may ask the patient and/or a family member a variety of questions surrounding their symptoms. When did they start? How are they impacting day-to-day life? Are they limiting the patient in some way? Has the patient had any changes to life circumstances? Et cetera. These are important, because clinicians need to get a good idea of not only what the symptoms are, but also how they may interfere with functioning (i.e., are they maladaptive for the individual?) and how they may or may not be the natural result of a significant life change. For example, if someone is feeling sad or withdrawn and it is impacting their daily functioning, that may be a sign of depression. However, if their spouse has just passed away, then it may be a natural reaction to a life event. Understanding the context surrounding the individual can help put the symptoms in appropriate perspective and help the clinician draw the correct conclusion.

In addition to an interview, a clinician may utilize diaries or checklists—again for the individual and for the family. These checklists should be used during daily life at home (see Figure 8.2 for an example). They can help to identify what is happening as it happens. Sometimes it

FIGURE 8.2 ■ The Katz Index (a useful tool to report at-home functioning to one's health care provider)

Katz Index of Independence in Activities of Daily Living

Name:		Date:
Activities Points (1 or 0)	**Independence** (1 Point) **NO** supervision, direction or personal assistance.	**Dependence** (0 Points) **WITH** supervision, direction, personal assistance or total care.
BATHING Points: ________	**(1 POINT)** Bathes self completely or needs help in bathing only a single part of the body such as the back, genital area or disabled extremity.	**(0 POINTS)** Need help with bathing more than one part of the body, getting in or out of the tub or shower. Requires total bathing.
DRESSING Points: ________	**(1 POINT)** Get clothes from closets and drawers and puts on clothes and outer garments complete with fasteners. May have help tying shoes.	**(0 POINTS)** Needs help with dressing self or needs to be completely dressed.
TOILETING Points: ________	**(1 POINT)** Goes to toilet, gets on and off, arranges clothes, cleans genital area without help.	**(0 POINTS)** Needs help transferring to the toilet, cleaning self or uses bedpan or commode.
TRANSFERRING Points: ________	**(1 POINT)** Moves in and out of bed or chair unassisted. Mechanical transfer aids are acceptable.	**(0 POINTS)** Needs help in moving from bed to chair or requires a complete transfer.
CONTINENCE Points: ________	**(1 POINT)** Exercises complete self-control over urination and defecation.	**(0 POINTS)** Is partially or totally incontinent of bowel or bladder.
FEEDING Points: ________	**(1 POINT)** Gets food from plate into mouth without help. Preparation of food may be done by another person.	**(0 POINTS)** Needs partial or total help with feeding or requires parenteral feeding.
Total points: ____________	**Scoring** **6** = High (patient independent) **4** = Moderate (patient is moderately functioning) **0-2** = Low (patient very dependent)	
Additional Notes:		

https://Carepatron.com

Source: SHELKEY, M and WALLACE, M. Katz Index of Independence in Activities of Daily Living. Home Healthcare Nurse 19(5):p 323-324, May 2001. Originally adapted from Katz S., Down, TD, Cash,HR et al. (1970) Progress in the development of the index of ADL. Gerontologist 10:20-30.

can be difficult to remember all the ways something can impact your life when you're on the spot in a doctor's appointment. I know I often feel blank when I'm in a doctor's appointment and forget what to ask or what to tell them. This can be problematic when symptoms are interfering with daily life functions. The doctor needs to know. Using a checklist to check off what happens as it happens (forgot to turn the stove off, broke down crying with no trigger, etc.), and then bringing the list to the appointment, gives a real window into what happens at home. This is particularly useful when memory is something of concern. Someone who is forgetting, and is seeking help with a possible dementia diagnosis, really may not remember all that goes on day-to-day. Relying on their retrieval of that information in an appointment isn't going to give the most accurate information. Getting the perspective from them as events occur—or as a report from a family member—is better.

Sometimes, a clinician may choose to ask an individual to complete activities on the spot so they may observe the individual as the activity occurs. For example, the clinician may give a list of items to remember or ask one to carry out a laundry-sorting task. These simulate daily activities but happen right before the clinician's eyes so they do not have to rely on self-report, which may succumb to memory failures, or completion of a diary, which may fall by the wayside as life gets busy. A direct observation allows for precise identification of where difficulties fall. To be sure, these are not without their faults. For instance, if a laundry-sorting task is carried out in a laboratory or medical office, this is not where the individual normally does this sort of task, so the context can be unsettling or add to the confusion or disorientation. And so, adding observation or performative tasks to a checklist or diary can be helpful in gaining multiple perspectives.

Clinicians may also perform standardized assessments for specific disorders. These can help to determine whether further testing is needed or if the individual meets the criterion for a specific diagnosis. Standardized assessments exist for many things, including cognitive impairments and depression, and can even be specified for the older adult age group. Sometimes a quick screening is all you need, and in other cases they can give some information that more testing is necessary. In both instances, the screening tools are useful and important.

One baseline screening used often for evaluation of cognitive impairments is the **Mini–Mental State Examination** (MMSE; Folstein et al., 1975). This screening goes through a series of questions and tasks asking about orientation to time and space, short-term memory, the ability to follow simple instructions, and spatial representation. The screening is a good "first pass" screening that can signal to a clinician that more testing is needed. On close examination, the MMSE has been demonstrated to closely align with IADLs, and shows high sensitivity to detect moderate and large cognitive impairments (e.g., Tombaugh & McIntyre, 1992). Its ability to detect mild cognitive impairments is less sensitive, which is one reason why the MMSE alone may not be enough for diagnosis. However, it is a great quick way to get a sense of cognitive impairments in a primary care office or emergency room without a lot of muss or fuss and is an assessment that can be used for anyone at any age. Other versions, translations, and similar assessments to the MMSE (e.g., Choi et al., 2001; Jiang et al., 2020; Shapiro et al., 1999) are also useful for basic screening of cognitive impairments.

When screening or assessing for depression, things can get a little trickier. Here, an assessment should be tailored to the older adult population, rather than using a uniform, one-size-fits-all assessment, because there are often differences in how an older adult experiences depression (but more on that later). Two common depression assessments that clinicians might use are the **Beck Depression Inventory** (Beck et al., 1961) and the **Geriatric Depression Scale** (Yesavage et al., 1983). Both of these assessments show validity and reliability for adults over the age of 60 (Gallagher et al., 1992) and so are appropriate to use to screen for depression. These evaluations ask questions about fatigue and activity level, feelings of sadness and hopelessness, and feelings of happiness or emptiness. These feelings and their intensity, duration, and frequency are also important for identifying depression as disordered (rather than a passing mood). Moreover, it is crucial that assessments of depression include questions about physical symptoms (e.g., fatigue) because it is more common for older adults experiencing depression to demonstrate physical symptoms than for young adults (e.g., Fiske et al., 2009).

Importantly, knowing which assessments to conduct is part of the process. This may be influenced by positive or negative biases surrounding aging—which I hope to minimize with this book by shedding light on the facts about the aging process. **Positive biases** are those that project positive assumptions on an older adult, such as they would never abuse illicit drugs or alcohol. This is not necessarily true, as drug and alcohol abuse impacts individuals of all ages (e.g., Zilberman, 2009). This positive bias can impact an individual because a clinician may never look for it in an assessment—and the patient misses out on proper treatment. Alternatively, **negative bias** can pigeonhole an older adult into a clinician looking for only the bad things that are supposed to happen in old age. For example, a clinician may look for and assess for Alzheimer's disease and not anxiety. When they don't come up with evidence supporting an Alzheimer's diagnosis, they may say the individual is fine, and completely miss the anxiety—leaving them untreated. Neither type of bias is OK or helpful in treatment. Instead, a comprehensive assessment should be performed in an unbiased way (I know, easier said than done). Considerations for the individual as an older adult should be taken, as they may display symptoms differently and may be impacted by some difficulties not associated with the issue being addressed at all. These external issues will be discussed next.

External Impacts on Assessment

When a doctor or clinician is assessing an individual for the presence of mental illness, the obvious focus is the symptoms and the questions, interview, checklist, or other assessment being performed. However, there are factors outside of the symptoms that may play a role in how an individual can answer those questions or perform the tasks on the assessment that may have absolutely nothing to do with the illness being investigated. Most of these will seem familiar to you and will likely make sense in the context of mental health assessment.

First are the sensory capabilities of the individual. That is, are they able to hear well? If an individual's hearing is impaired (you learned in Chapter 2 that this is common, but not inevitable), so will be their answers to the questions the clinician is asking—even if the question is something they are able to answer. Considerations for hearing are also important in the context they are being assessed in. For instance, is the evaluation occurring in the emergency room? It is likely very loud and busy in there. Additional stimuli can not only hinder hearing in this instance but also clog the working memory system—as we learned in Chapters 3 and 4. These can interfere with assessments on cognitive function, making it look like the individual has difficulties with their memory, when they may not. And finally, we also need to understand that, at least in the instances of performative tasks or direct observations, we are removing the older adult from their familiar context (where was Nana baking those muffins in Chapter 4?). As we have learned already in this book, context is particularly helpful for relieving strained attentional and working memory resources. Removing context and then asking one to complete a task that can be straining may also make the individual appear to have deficits where none exist. Understanding these nuances of older adults' cognitive functioning can help a clinician make appropriate judgments on when/how assessments should be conducted, but also on the conclusions they draw from them.

SPECIFIC DISORDERS

Because a discussion of mental health is not complete without addressing the specific disorders one may encounter and/or experience, this section will examine specific disorders as they occur generally and how those experiences may or may not differ in an adult over 60 years of age (spoiler alert: older adults are *not* more prone to mental health disorders than young adults).

Anxiety Disorders

Anxiety disorders encompass a group of disorders where an individual primarily experiences a nervous, panicky feeling. This feeling can come in response to a stimulus or situation or without any provocation at all. These disorders include generalized anxiety disorder, social anxiety disorder, panic disorder, specific phobias, and obsessive-compulsive disorder. The common theme here is based in a natural, human experience meant to keep us alive. That is, our nervous system is designed to enter a state of fight, flight, or freeze at signs of danger (e.g., Donahue, 2020). It is adaptive when we are fleeing from a predator. The problem arises, and functioning in a state of heightened arousal becomes maladaptive, when we enter this state of "I must survive" when not facing any danger at all. The individual may rearrange their life to avoid a specific stimulus (e.g., a specific phobia of fire may preclude them from using birthday candles or lighting a menorah) or may be unable to complete daily tasks if the anxiety is all encompassing (e.g., generalized anxiety disorder may keep someone from getting out of bed and going to work).

Knowing this, we may ask: Do older adults experience anxiety disorders in the same way as a younger adult? Does it happen more often or less often? Are the symptoms similar? The general answer to these questions is that, yes, the experience is similar. Symptoms are similar, and treatment is similar, but older adults may often experience anxiety disorders as "add-ons" to other things like physical health conditions or depression (Brown et al., 2001; Wolitzky-Taylor et al., 2010; we'll discuss more on depression and mood disorders in the next section). And it may surprise you to know that the rate of occurrence of anxiety disorders in the older adult population is the same as, if not lower than, it is in the general population (e.g., Bower et al., 2015; Wolitzky-Taylor et al., 2010). The Anxiety and Depression Association of America (2024) documents that just over 18% of adults over the age of 18 experience an anxiety disorder. The American Association for Geriatric Psychiatry (2022) documents the rate to be somewhere between 10% and 20% of older adults. These rates of occurrence alone should dispel any fear that advancing age brings with it disordered, anxious thoughts and feelings. To be sure, everyone experiences anxiety as a passing feeling at any time throughout their life. However, the maladaptive, life-altering version of an anxiety disorder is not a universal experience at any age.

Genetics play a role in risk levels for the development of an anxiety disorder, and these risks carry throughout the life span. Genetics alone are not responsible for the development of an anxiety disorder, and other factors such as environment and life circumstances (e.g., physical health conditions) play a part as well. Current research in this area has suggested that these genetic influences become stronger as one moves through their lifetime (e.g., Hettema et al., 2005; Petkus et al., 2016), though not to the extent that they become all-defining. Moreover, the specifics of genetic mapping have identified at least four genes associated with anxiety disorders: MAO-A, COMT, CCK-B, NPSR1, and more (see Domschke & Maron, 2013, for a summary of these). These genes seem to interact with one another and with environmental influences to create the perfect storm for the development of an anxiety disorder, and these are not isolated to any particular age group.

iStockPhoto/PixelsEffect

For an older adult, anxiety can be just as difficult to manage as it is for a younger adult. That's to say it interferes with life in the same way, even if day-to-day tasks are somewhat different in a retired adult compared to a working young adult. Treatment is often effective and can include a variety of approaches (e.g., Bower et al., 2015), such as medication like **selective serotonin reuptake inhibitors** (SSRIs; e.g., Zoloft) or benzodiazepines (e.g., Xanax), **cognitive behavioral therapy** (CBT), exposure and response prevention (ERP), and stress reduction techniques (e.g., meditation). Importantly, we should recognize some precautions when dealing with treatment for anxiety disorders in an older adult. The first of these is that an older adult's body does not metabolize and break down medication in the same way that a younger body does. So, when treating with medication, dosage needs to start low and then increase slowly as needed. Moreover, the medication could interact with others the individual is taking for other health conditions, so checking with a pharmacist for interactions is helpful. Another issue to consider with older generations is their willingness to seek out help with mental health conditions at all. While research has demonstrated that older adults do see mental health support as positive, they are significantly less likely to seek it out than their young counterparts (e.g., Mackenzie et al., 2012; Mackenzie et al., 2008).

Getting older adults to get the help they need is important, but it may be limited by the overlap between symptoms of an anxiety disorder and physical health problems that many people associate with old age (e.g., Al-Ani & Winchester, 2015; Carleton et al., 2014). For example, some symptoms of a panic attack are tightness in the chest and increases in heart rate. These symptoms may seem like a heart attack. So, an older adult may seek help for a heart attack, and when they are told they haven't had one, they are sent on their way with no assistance for the anxiety. Awareness of this overlap for a health care provider is important, but reception on the part of the older adult is also important.

Mood Disorders

Another category of psychological disorders to be considered is mood disorders. Mood disorders affect the mood of the individual over long periods of time, as opposed to short-term fleeting feelings about a temporary situation. Mood disorders like major depressive disorder, bipolar disorder, dysthymia, mood disorder related to other health conditions, and substance abuse–induced mood disorders can affect anyone at any age (Brown et al., 2001). Like anxiety disorders, they are not universal in old age, even though my neighbor's doctor might have thought that to be true. Instead, consider that there are risk factors that contribute to the development of mood disorders at any age (e.g., Merikangas & Low, 2004): genetics, a medical condition, lack of social support systems, inactive lifestyles, and even external stressors like the COVID-19 pandemic. To be sure, some of these risk factors like dwindling social support systems can occur naturally in older age as life circumstances change. However, these are not a guarantee, nor are mood disorders.

The NIH reports rates of occurrence of major depressive disorder are only 8.4% of adults over the age of 18 in the United States, with the largest portion of these between the ages of 18 and 25 (National Institute of Mental Health, 2023), not over the age of 60. Interestingly, depression can display differently in an older adult than in a younger adult (e.g., Gallo et al., 1994; see also Table 8.1). For example, an older adult experiencing depression is more likely to struggle with physical symptoms like fatigue, body aches, and general feelings of malaise (unwellness). This difference in symptoms can make it less likely for an older adult to seek help and then for health care providers to diagnose. Therefore, it is important for assessments, like those discussed earlier, to rule out physiological reasons not only for feeling unwell but also for depression, specifically to assess physical symptoms as well as mental/emotional ones. Additionally, there is evidence of gender differences between men and women (transgender and nonbinary individuals not included), where women experience depression at a higher rate than men, even in older adulthood (Girgus et al., 2017). This also could contribute to difficulties in assessment, diagnosis, and treatment through biases on the part of the clinician.

Like anxiety disorders, mood disorders are treatable with methods like medication such as SSRIs (Zoloft, Prozac, Lexapro, etc.) and CBT. Additional treatment methods can include interpersonal psychotherapy (IPT), repetitive transcranial magnetic stimulation (rTMS), and even electroconvulsive therapy (ECT; though usually this is reserved for when other treatments don't work). And, like all treatments, some work better than others. The most common, and

TABLE 8.1 ■ Young and Older Adults' Symptoms of Depression

Young Adults	Sadness, loss of interest in activities, irritability, changes in appetite, changes in sleep
Older Adults	Sadness, hopelessness, anger, irritability, pain, fatigue, changes in memory/attention, malaise

Source: Gallo, J. J., Anthony, J. C., & Muthén, B. O. (1994). Age differences in the symptoms of depression: A latent trait analysis. *Journal of Gerontology, 49*(6), P251–P264.

often most effective, treatment for mood disorders is a combination of medications (like SSRIs) and therapy (like CBT). This combination allows neurotransmitters, as well as thoughts and behaviors, to change over time. These adjustments are slow and gradual, but as the tortoise taught us, slow and steady wins the race. And, in some instances, an individual may need medication before even attempting therapy because they need to get to a place where they are able to do the work required in something like CBT (e.g., Wetherell et al., 2013).

Additional considerations can be made for prevention and maintenance of a healthy mind and brain, including an active lifestyle, good nutrition, and social support. Research on nutrition has demonstrated that a low-sodium DASH diet—that is, dietary approaches to stop hypertension—can be effective in prevention of depression (e.g., Perez-Comago et al. 2017; Torres & Nowson, 2012). In their study, Perez-Comago and colleagues (2017) measured depression symptoms initially and again after 8 years of moderately following a diet designed to minimize hypertension (i.e., high blood pressure) and found lower risk of depression, even at the 8-year mark. However, Perez-Comago et al. did not consider the genetic influences of depression.

Research on genetics not only has demonstrated a larger risk of developing depression if a family member has been diagnosed, but has possibly narrowed down some genetic markers as well (e.g., Ku et al., 2017; Skoog et al., 2015). In their study, Skoog and colleagues (2015) were able to predict the incidence of depression by the genetic marker most know to be associated with the development of dementia: the APOE*E4 allele (more on this relationship in the next section). However, this gene may be responsible for more. Even after removing participants who later developed Alzheimer's disease, Skoog et al. found that the APOE*E4 allele predicted development of severe depression, minor depression, and incidental depressive episodes (see Table 8.2).

This is not to say that individuals with the APOE*E4 allele will automatically develop depression, dementia, or both. There are many other factors at play. External stressors are an important one (e.g., Cramer et al., 2016; Trifu et al., 2020). External stressors can include things like losing a loved one, financial difficulties, medical conditions, and loss of social support systems. All of these can make conditions for developing depression more likely and were combined to create what I like to call a "mega-stressor" (à la Johnny Depp's mega-pint) during

TABLE 8.2 ■ Relationship of Depression Occurrence at a Five-Year Follow-Up for Those With and Without the APOE*E4 Allele

	Without APOE*E4	With APOE*E4
Any Depression	15%	23%
Minor Depression	13%	21%
Major Depression	3%	2%

Source: Skoog, I., Waern, M., Duberstein, P., Blennow, K., Zetterberg, H., Börjesson-Hanson, A., Östling, S., Guo, X., Kern, J., Gustafson, D., Gudmundsson, P., Marlow, T., & Kern, S. (2015). A 9-year prospective population-based study on the association between the APOE*E4 allele and late-life depression in Sweden. *Biological Psychiatry, 78*(10), 730–736.

the recent COVID-19 pandemic. Here, people were isolating away from loved ones and social support systems, losing their loved ones to the disease, contracting the illness themselves, and often confronted with financial difficulties resulting from the economic closures. Add to that the time during the beginning of the pandemic where food was difficult to get, and nutrition became part of the mega-stressor as well. Research on COVID-19 and depression in older adults has supported this combination of factors in the examination of the development of mental health issues during the duration of the pandemic and afterward (e.g., García-Portilla et al., 2021; Krendl & Perry, 2021; Vahia et al., 2020). García-Portilla et al. (2021) reported that depression was the second-highest psychological response following the COVID-19 lockdown for adults over the age of 60, while Krendl and Perry (2021) showed increases in loneliness and depression and decreases in strength of relationships with others. This research is clear in that the mental health implications surrounding the circumstances of the COVID-19 pandemic were large. And this research is just beginning. When we can examine physiological outcomes, long-term outcomes, and recovery effects postpandemic, we may see differences in how older adults return to normal and/or create their new normal compared to young and middle-aged adults. But this research hasn't yet been completed.

DEMENTIAS

Perhaps to your surprise, the section here discussing dementia is not titled *Alzheimer's Disease*, and that's because *dementia* is a broad term, while Alzheimer's disease is a type of dementia. And, while some people use these terms interchangeably, they are not interchangeable. That is, one can have a type of dementia that is not Alzheimer's. There are several ways one could develop dementia. However, all types of dementia do show similar symptoms, including loss of memory, confusion, disorientation, aggression, sleep difficulties, wandering, mood changes (e.g., depression), and the inability to recognize people and things. This all sounds scary and is one of the top fears of individuals when they discuss their fears about the aging process. Hopefully, this section will alleviate some of these fears, as we learn about the rates of occurrence, genetic influences, and interventions for the dementias.

Alzheimer's Disease

The most well-known type of dementia is **Alzheimer's disease** (AD). And while there are others, AD is the most common type, accounting for almost 70% of all cases of dementia (World Health Organization, 2023). While that number might seem high, recognize that the instances of AD overall are not that high. The Alzheimer's Association (2023) estimates that approximately 10% of adults over age 65 are affected by AD. This number is certainly not insignificant, but it is far from universal. With that in mind, we can begin to piece together the distinction between normative aging (as was discussed in Chapters 2–4) and the cognitive changes that come with the impairments of AD. Normative changes are not the same as the changes seen as the result of the physiological brain changes occurring in AD.

Symptoms

Like all dementias, AD results in symptoms that affect cognitive function, including memory, orientation to time and space, impaired reasoning, and object/person recognition; later stages may also include language difficulties as well as problems performing daily tasks like dressing and bathing, changes to personality, and inappropriate social behavior and wandering. The progression of the illness results in more and more deficits in cognitive function. What starts as mild cognitive impairment and forgetting the name of a familiar object becomes confusion, disorientation, and the inability to care for oneself over time. The reason for the advancement in the magnitude of the symptoms is the direct result of changes occurring in the brain: the development of **neuritic plaques** and **neurofibrillary tangles.** Neuritic plaques are buildups of beta-amyloid proteins in clogs around the brain, while neurofibrillary tangles are masses of tangled, dying neurons. Together, these create roadblocks in sending signals throughout the brain. Moreover, while the disease progresses and these two physiological changes occur, the brain matter is also atrophying and becoming less dense overall (see Figure 8.3; e.g., Pini et al., 2016; Poulakis et al., 2018). All together, these neurological changes reduce brain function for the individual, eventually leading to a point where the brain itself can no longer sustain life. This is the tragic end for most AD patients, and we hope that research can get us to a place where treatment cannot just prolong life but can stop progression of the disease early, before too much

FIGURE 8.3 ■ Comparison of a Healthy Brain and a Brain With Alzheimer's Disease

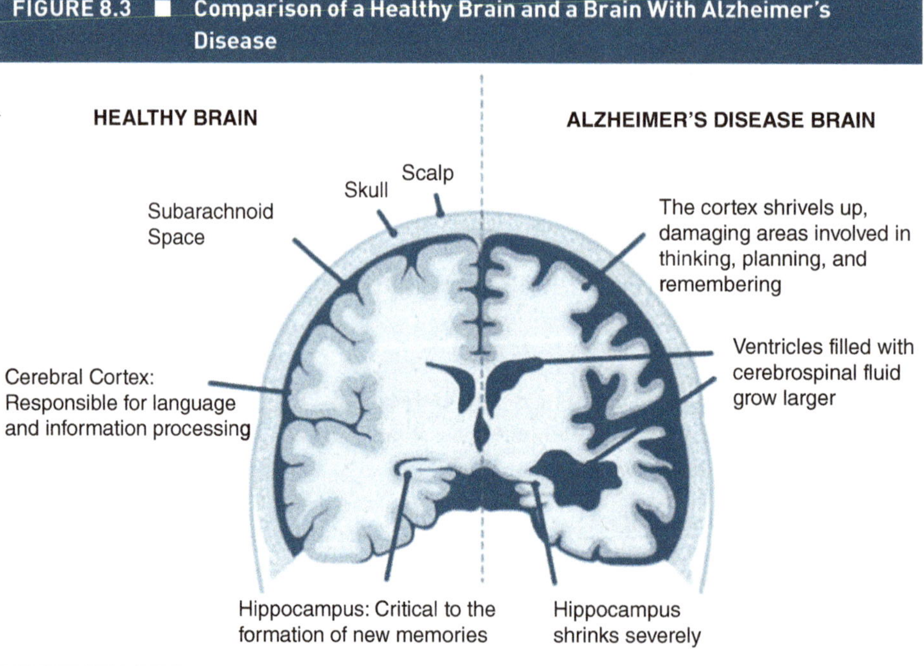

Source: Dan, S., Sharma, D., Rastogi, K., Shaloo, Ojha, H., Pathak, M., & Singhal, R. (2022). Therapeutic and diagnostic applications of nanocomposites in the treatment Alzheimer's disease studies. *Biointerface Research in Applied Chemistry, 12*(1), 940–960.

damage is done and function is lost. One way to get there is to find the source of the problem, which research has shown to be at least partially influenced by genetics.

Genetic Link

The genetic influence of AD has been the source of a variety of research studies and has shown a significant genetic link (e.g., Bagyinszky et al., 2014; Bellenguez et al., 2020; Bertram & Tanzi, 2012), though this link has been demonstrated to vary from ethnicity to ethnicity (e.g., Green et al., 2002). And, while there is variability in risk, there is one commonality among many individuals who develop AD: the APEO genotype (e.g., Bagyinszky et al., 2014). The APEO*E4 allele represents significant heritability for individuals, and its presence increases the risk of developing AD. To be sure, other factors play a role, including old age, ethnicity (where African Americans show almost double the heritability compared to whites), higher cholesterol, standard American diet, low levels of physical activity, and social disengagement (e.g., Qiu et al., 2022). However, the genetic link is undeniable. Moreover, research has also shown that early-onset AD has additional genetic influences, including autosomal mutations of the amyloid precursor protein and the presenilin genes (e.g., Blennow et al., 2006), though these cases only account for a small percentage of all AD cases. The predominant link is through the APEO*E4 allele.

Diagnosis and Intervention Strategies

With the potential implications for the progression of AD, it is important to assess and diagnose early to achieve the greatest chance of quality life and intervention if possible. These assessments should include reports from the individual (as discussed earlier, this is more beneficial in the early stages of disease) and family members regarding what symptoms and concerning changes have happened and over what period they have occurred (i.e., was it a subtle, slow change or a sudden one?). Additionally, physiological measures to rule out biological reasons for the symptoms occurring, such as nutritional deficits, stroke, and medication side effects, should be conducted. Cognitive measures like the MMSE (described earlier in this chapter) and performative/behavioral tasks, alongside a brain scan (e.g., fMRI, PET, or CAT), can help make a final determination and diagnosis of AD. And this in and of itself is progress—it used to be the case that diagnoses only came postmortem.

Truth be told, this illness and its progression is difficult—not only for the patient, but also for the family and the caregivers (e.g., Iavarone et al., 2014; Richardson et al., 2013; Vellone et al., 2008). At first, the confusion and memory loss can be frustrating and unsettling. Later, the personality changes and difficulties to function can push people to denial and anger. The family may try to resist and correct, providing the "right information." Unfortunately, this usually backfires. Instead, the patient remains confused, because all the information is unfamiliar, and arguments can ensue involving "who is right." The reality is that the argument won't undo the changes that are occurring in their brain, and frustration and anger just pile more on to the patient. Instead, redirecting to a different topic of conversation, emphasizing the positive and familiar, is more comfortable for all involved. Often, cognitive-directed treatment for these kinds of cognitive changes isn't effective because thought processes are disrupted by the deteriorating brain. Instead, focusing on the behavioral is more useful. Reinforcing desired behavior without arguing, but with engaging and attention, while ignoring to extinguish difficult or undesired behavior, is effective. It's called **differential reinforcement** of incompatible behavior, and it works even beyond the early stages of AD (Boucher, 1999). In later stages, when aggression or personality changes are presenting, differential reinforcement can be extremely useful to extinguish difficult, stubborn, or violent behaviors too.

Other interventions to treat the disease itself (as opposed to the resulting cognitive loss and behavior change) have shown positive effects of exercise (e.g., Yu et al., 2006), music (e.g., Leggieri et al., 2019), and spaced memory retrieval training (e.g., McKitrick et al., 1992). Qiu et al. (2022) discuss a multitude of different strategies for intervention, including altering blood pressure (blood pressure too low in older adulthood has been linked to increased risk of AD), eliminating smoking, lowering cholesterol, and implementing a Mediterranean diet, as well as increased social interactions and support systems, cognitive activities, and exercise. According to Qiu et al., the most support has been shown for Mediterranean diet, exercise, social interactions, and cognitive activities. This all makes sense, though, right? A Mediterranean diet is high in B12 and omega-3 fatty acids, which we have seen to be protective in creating a healthy brain (e.g., Féart et al., 2010). Exercise, cognitive exercise, and leisure activities do the same thing (e.g., Crowe et al., 2003). A healthy brain is more resistant to the damage that AD can cause. And, while there are medications that doctors can use to mitigate and adjust acetylcholine levels (donepezil, galantamine, etc.), these only remain effective if deterioration doesn't progress too far. Therefore, a multifactorial approach is likely our best strategy, targeting diet, exercise, social, and cognitive factors as well. Newer research is currently investigating other pathways for treatment, including the role of mitochondria (Reiss et al., 2022), regulation in the gut microbiome (Varesi et al., 2022), and chemically bound treatments directed at both cell biology and cognitive difficulties (Kumar et al., 2022).

Vascular Dementia

However, AD is only one type of dementia. There are other ways that an individual can develop the cognitive decline of dementia. One of these is **vascular dementia** (VaD) and is the second most common type of dementia after AD (Alzheimer's Disease International, n.d.). VaD is a dementia that develops because of stroke, blood vessel deterioration, or other vascular changes in the brain where blood flow is reduced or hindered. Often, VaD is the result of multiple strokes impacting brain health. Risk of this increases when an individual is obese or has diabetes (Korczyn et al., 2012). Different from AD, VaD patients often show more difficulties with executive function, attention, planning, and speed of processing, as opposed to memory difficulties. And, because VaD is the result of stroke or brain vasculature difficulties anywhere in the brain, physical impairments may coexist. Therefore, diagnosis should separate functional limitations resulting from physical impairments from those resulting from cognitive/executive function impairments (Kalaria, 2002). AD and VaD can occur together, and this happens more often than you'd think. A study on nuns with dementia demonstrated that nuns who displayed with AD also had cerebrovascular disease and evidence of multiple strokes (Snowden et al., 1997), suggesting that their cognitive impairments may have been the result of AD, VaD, or a combination of both. Importantly, treatment by medication that can alter acetylcholine levels (donepezil, galantamine, etc.) seems to help in VaD as well (see Figure 8.4). Moreover, increasing activity of acetylcholine may trigger further neurotransmitter release for serotonin, GABA, and glutamine, all of which are implicated in contributing to cognitive function (Kalaria, 2002).

FIGURE 8.4 ■ Impact of Anticholinesterase Drugs

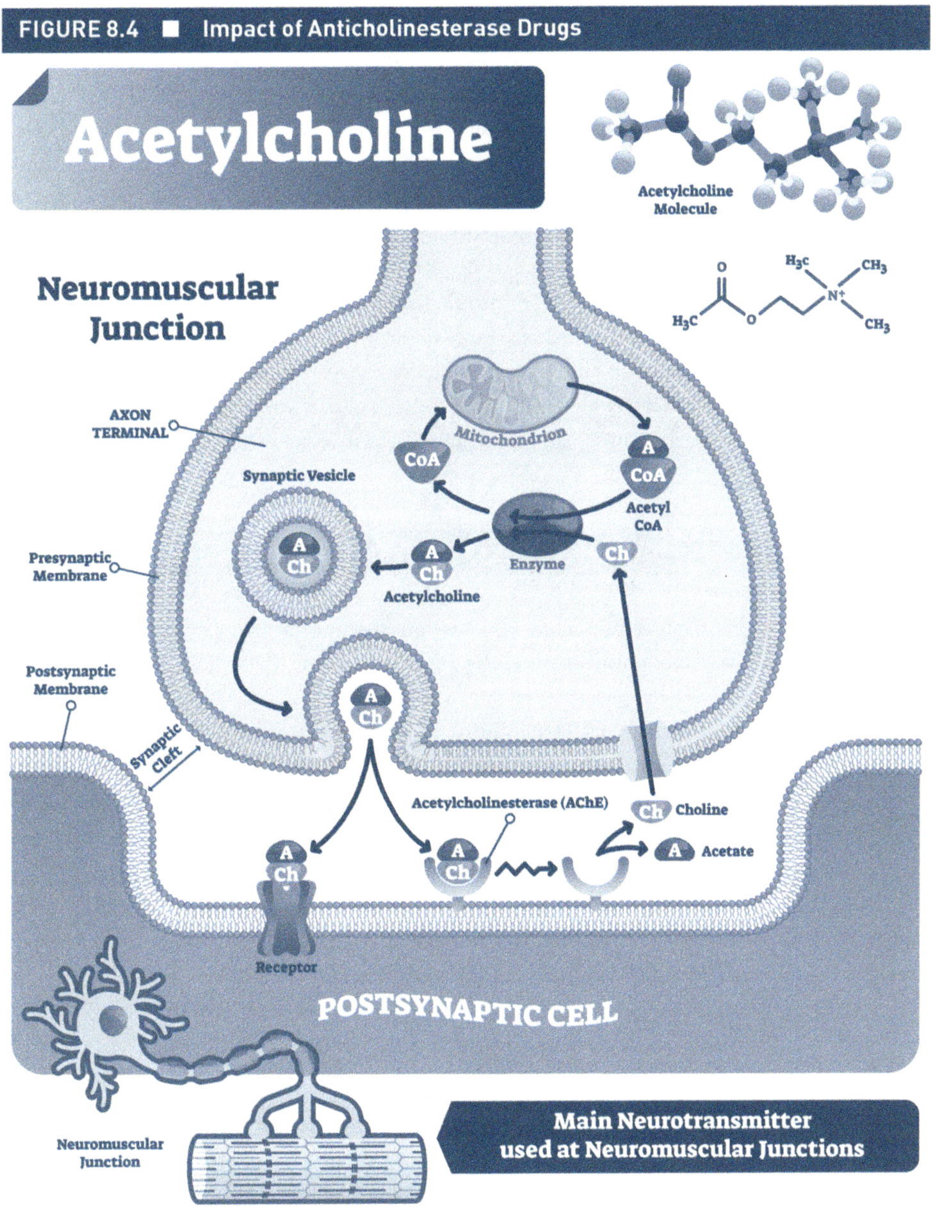

Source: iStockPhoto/VectorMine

Dementia Associated With Parkinson's Disease

An even smaller number of individuals with dementia develop it because of Parkinson's disease (e.g, Goetz et al., 2008). Parkinson's disease primarily begins in the basal ganglia area and substantia nigra areas of the brain and occurs when too little dopamine is produced and/or received by the neurons initiating and coordinating movement. However, as the disease progresses, some individuals will experience changes to cognitive function as well. **Parkinson's disease dementia** (PDD) then develops as recognition difficulties and attention and perceptual difficulties. Unfortunately, much remains unknown about the mechanisms underlying PDD, as it seems to reflect several physiological components: plaques and tangles as well as cerebrovascular changes (Gratwicke et al., 2015). These variations have made understanding the root cause difficult; however, Gratwicke and colleagues (2015) pointed out that there may be some network communication issues in the neural networks that may at least contribute to the dysfunction seen in PDD. They also add that adjustments to dopamine levels, via treatment by levodopa (as is common for the motor symptoms of Parkinson's disease), does not seem to be enough to combat some of the cognitive deficits in this type of dementia. Additional attention to changes in activity in the frontal lobes, which are responsible for executive function, remains important. However, for now, Gratwicke et al. explain that some of the treatments used for other types of dementia (donepezil, galantamine, etc.) do seem to help in some of the attentional difficulties in PDD.

AGING WELL: MENTAL HEALTH

While much of this chapter presented information about what can go wrong with mental health and cognitive function in older adults, it should be clear that what goes wrong is far from universal, does not happen to everyone, and is just not that common. This realization is positive and should put the myths of "losing one's mental faculties" to rest. This becomes particularly clear when we compare this chapter with previous chapters on attention, memory, and cognitive processing. We can shift our focus on what we can do to age well mentally and cognitively. Evidence in this chapter showed that having a nourishing diet is important—and by diet, I mean what we eat, but also what we consume mentally, socially, and emotionally. Checking in with how we care for ourselves by the food we eat (getting in B12 and omega-3 fatty acids), challenging ourselves with mental exercise (reading is a great one), engaging in social relationships and support systems (lunch with friends), and moving our bodies (walking is great exercise) can mitigate many of the risk factors that can contribute to mental illnesses, dementias, and the associated functional limitations.

KEY TERMS

Alzheimer's disease
Beck Depression Inventory
cognitive behavioral therapy
differential reinforcement
Geriatric Depression Scale
maladaptive

Mini–Mental Status Examination (MMSE)
myelin
neuritic plaques
neurofibrillary tangles
Parkinson's disease dementia
positive biases
selective serotonin reuptake inhibitors
vascular dementia

COMPREHENSION QUESTIONS

1. How can one determine whether changes in mental status are indicative of possible mental illness?
2. What type of assessments might a clinician perform? And what is the rationale for each?
3. How could a clinician go about assessing for depression?
4. How do symptoms of depression differ between young and older adults?
5. Describe negative and positive biases in assessment of mental health conditions as they pertain to older adults.
6. How can external conditions impact assessment?
7. How do young and older adults differ in their experience of anxiety disorders?
8. How do genetics impact anxiety disorders? Depression? Alzheimer's disease?
9. What are some treatment options for anxiety disorders? Depression? Dementias?
10. How can nutrition impact mental health?

ADDITIONAL READINGS

Beaudreau, S. A., & O'Hara, R. (2008). Late-life anxiety and cognitive impairment: A review. *American Journal of Geriatric Psychiatry, 16*, 790–803.

Cukrowicz, K. C., Franzese, A. T., Thorp, S. R., Cheavens, J. S., & Lynch, T. R. (2008). Personality traits and perceived social support among depressed older adults. *Aging and Mental Health, 12*(5), 662–669.

de Mendonça Lima, C. A., & Ivbijaro, G. (2013). Mental health and wellbeing of older people: Opportunities and challenges. *Mental Health in Family Medicine, 10*(3), 125–127.

Gehlich, K. H., Beller, J., Lange-Asschenfeldt, B., Köcher, W., Meinke, M. C., & Lademann, J. (2019). Fruit and vegetable consumption is associated with improved mental and cognitive health in older adults from non-Western developing countries. *Public Health Nutrition, 22*(4), 689–696.

Mener, D. J., Betz, J., Genther, D. J., Chen, D., & Lin, F. R. (2013). Hearing loss and depression in older adults. *Journal of the American Geriatrics Society, 61*(9), 1627–1629.

Phillips, M. A., & Murrell, S. A. (1994). Impact of psychological and physical health, stressful events, and social support on subsequent mental health help seeking among older adults. *Journal of Consulting and Clinical Psychology, 62*(2), 270–275. https://doi.org/10.1037/0022-006X.62.2.270

Robb, C., Haley, W. E., Becker, M. A., Polivka, L. A., & Chwa, H. J. (2003). Attitudes towards mental health care in younger and older adults: Similarities and differences. *Aging and Mental Health, 7*(2), 142–152.

Tu, H., Zhang, Z. W., Qiu, L., Lin, Y., Jiang, M., Chia, S.Y., Wie, Y., Ng, A. S. L., Reynolds, R., Tan, E.-K., & Zeng, L. (2022). Increased expression of pathological markers in Parkinson's disease dementia post-mortem brains compared to dementia with Lewy bodies. *BMC Neuroscience, 23*(1), 1–13.

Wilcox, S., Sharkey, J. R., Mathews, A. E., Laditka, J. N., Laditka, S. B., Logsdon, R. G., Sahyoun, N., Robare, J. F., & Liu, R. (2009). Perceptions and beliefs about the role of physical activity and nutrition on brain health in older adults. *The Gerontologist, 49*(S1), S61–S71.

iStockPhoto/FG Trade Latin

9 PERSONALITY

LEARNING OBJECTIVES

9.1 Describe dispositional personality traits including those in the five-factor model and the three-level system of personality.

9.2 Explain how personality changes and remains the same over the course of a lifetime.

9.3 Identify gender differences in personality development and self-image.

9.4 Describe midlife crisis and the research that supports the concept of a correction versus a crisis-based change.

9.5 Explain the impact of various life factors on aging and well-being.

I remember my grandma (not my maternal grandmother, who you read about in Chapter 6, but my paternal grandmother, the one to whom this book is dedicated) telling me a story about when she got married to my grandpa at just 17 years old. Grandpa was raised in a home that kept kosher. For his family, that meant that many of his dishes were separated, and often during meals different parts of the meal were served on different plates. As you can imagine, this made for lots of cleanup after dinner. However, Grandma did no such thing. When she served dinner, all components of the meal were on one plate. Grandpa balked at it. She told him that if he wanted multiple plates, then he could wash them himself. If she was going to cook and clean, then this was the way it was going to be. And that is the way it was—for over 50 years. This feisty nature was in my grandmother for her whole life. Until she passed at the age of 94, you could find her telling it like it was, answering to nobody, and doing as she pleased whether other people liked it or not. Was this her personality? Was it just who she was? Did it ever waiver? And is this typical for personality development across the life span, or does one's personality change as their age climbs? In this chapter, we'll discuss stability and change in personality—and, spoiler alert, some things change, and some stay the same.

DISPOSITIONAL TRAITS AND PERSONALITY FACTORS

Dispositional traits are those characteristics about a person that remain consistent in influencing their choices and behavior across time and across contexts (e.g., McAdams & Olson, 2010). For example, the way that Grandma behaved at age 17 in her decision to only use one dish at dinner showed a dispositional trait about her that showed up time and again when she refused to do things just because other people wanted her to—such as bake cookies like a "typical" grandmother. To be sure, if I asked for cookies, I got cookies, but more than likely they came from the bakery or the grocery store instead of her oven. That just wasn't something she wanted to spend her time doing, just as washing extra dinner dishes wasn't something she wanted to spend her time doing. Some personality researchers suggest that these dispositional traits are born out of early temperament in infancy (e.g., Cloninger, 1994; Rothbart, 2007; Saucier & Simonds, 2006). That is, as soon as an individual can interact with their social world, their personality begins to develop—first through temperament (cheerful, relaxed, tense, etc.), then through dispositional traits and other factors we'll discuss in just a bit (personal life narrative, human nature, social and cultural context, etc.).

Measurement of dispositional traits tends to rely on self-report, at least in the case of adults (examining children and temperament may rely on observation and parent/guardian report). These reports can be given by survey, interview, or a combination of the two. One of the most well-known personality assessments is the **NEO Personality Inventory** (NEO-PI; Costa & McCrae, 1985). Here, respondents rate applicability of statements referring to various aspects of traits known as facets. For example, participants might respond to statements like "I am a worrier" or "I keep a cool head in emergencies." Responses are scored, and scores are calculated to give an overview of an individual's traits. Other times, a researcher may choose to use a narrative or storytelling technique. McAdams et al. (2004), for example, elicited story responses to what they called "key life-narrative scenes" from their participants. These narratives were then analyzed for content and tone in terms of agreeableness, openness, contentiousness, and extraversion (four of the Big Five personality factors described in the next section; see also Table 9.1).

However, regardless of the measurement technique, personality researchers by and large agree that there are several larger categories or factors of personality. While originally thought of as having only three factors—neuroticism, extraversion, and openness (NEO)—researchers have come to support a five-factor model developed by Costa and McCrae (1985, 1988; McCrae & Costa, 1989). This model describes five factors of personality as assessed by the NEO-PI, including the three originals—neuroticism, extraversion, and openness—as well as agreeableness and conscientiousness. These **factors**, along with their underlying concepts (called **facets**), are described next.

Five-Factor Model

In the most widely accepted model of personality, McCrae and Costa (1989) describe the five large headers or groupings of personality: openness to experience, conscientiousness, extraversion, agreeableness, and neuroticism (it's easy to remember these with the acronym OCEAN). Each of these factors describes an overarching theme of the smaller components underneath, which McCrae and Costa call facets. Each factor is made up of several facets that help to encompass the larger personality construct. These facets help in determining whether an individual is high or low in a particular factor. I'll discuss each of the factors and their corresponding facets here.

Openness to experience is a personality factor indicating that one remains willing to try new things and understand new ideas. This can be in mindset, in word, or in action—or all three. Signs or facets that contribute to one being high in openness to experience are imagination, depth of emotions, willingness to experiment, tolerance for diversity, and appreciation for art and beauty (i.e., aesthetics). Individuals high in openness to experience also have broad, diverse ideas and actions and are often attracted to careers that call for creative, hypothetical, or philosophical thinking (e.g., J. M. George & Zhou, 2001).

The **conscientiousness** trait marks one's work ethic, ambitions, energy, and fortitude for persevering in the face of challenge. Facets of conscientiousness are sense of competence,

TABLE 9.1 ■ The Big Five Personality Factors and Corresponding Facets

Openness to experience	imagination, depth of emotions, willingness to experiment, tolerance for diversity, aesthetics
Conscientiousness	competence, orderliness, responsibility, self-discipline, deliberateness
Extraversion	warmth, excitement-seeking, gregariousness, assertiveness, positive emotions, activity
Agreeableness	modest, altruistic, trust in others, dislikes confrontation, sincere, sympathetic
Neuroticism	anxious, tense, hostile/prone to anger, self-conscious, impulsive, vulnerable

Source: Costa, P. T., Jr., & McCrae, R. R. (1985). *The NEO Personality Inventory manual.* Psychological Assessment Resources.

orderliness, responsibility, self-discipline, and deliberateness. When someone is high in conscientiousness, they are often detail oriented, work well on project-type tasks (e.g., Zia et al., 2019) with less structure (because they impose the structure on themselves), and work hard to achieve their goals and hit the expectations they have of themselves (e.g., Colquitt & Simmering, 1998; "and if that doesn't describe me perfectly, I don't know what does," she says as she takes on a large project like writing this textbook and works on a strict timeline with organized outlines).

The third of the five factors is **extraversion**. The facets of extraversion are warmth, excitement-seeking, gregariousness, assertiveness, positive emotions, and activity. These facets can be grouped into subsets of **interpersonal traits** and **temperamental traits**. Interpersonal traits describe how someone high in extraversion would interact with others (e.g., with warmth, gregariousness, and assertiveness), while temperamental traits describe how they would behave in a variety of circumstances (e.g., looking for activity and excitement, with positive emotions). Extraversion is maybe one of the most well known of the Big Five and is often used colloquially to describe how one interacts in social situations. That is, saying someone is "extraverted" may mean that they are outgoing, enjoy spending time in social gatherings, and speak their mind (just like Grandma). However, this is only one component of that factor.

The last two of the five factors are **agreeableness** and **neuroticism**. Someone high in agreeableness is modest, is altruistic, has trust in others, dislikes confrontation (i.e., is compliant), and is sincere and sympathetic. One who is high in neuroticism is anxious or tense, hostile or prone to anger, self-conscious, and impulsive or vulnerable (although these last two facets are often displayed as behaviors, rather than emotions).

No one of these five dispositional traits excludes the others, nor does being high on the levels of one indicate that an individual will necessarily be high on others. However, together these traits are a great first step in describing personality for a variety of purposes. Researchers and employers alike have been able to use personality assessments to examine fit for a job (e.g., Chiu & Francesco, 2003) and attitudes toward cheating (e.g., Saulsbury et al., 2011), as well as emotional regulation and social interactions (e.g., Cumberland-Li et al., 2003). These predictions can help determine the risk of negative behavior and relationships, as well as negative life satisfaction. However, some considerations have been left out of this conceptualization of personality (e.g., McAdams, 1996, 2006).

Critique of the Five-Factor Model

To be sure, the five-factor model describes a good lot of how humans consistently maneuver through a variety of life situations, acknowledging that individual differences reign supreme in how they summarize an individual's thoughts, feelings, and actions (Costa & McCrae, 2006). And, specifically, Costa and McCrae (2006) suggest that the traits we see in individuals are the result of them carrying out their biological programming as it was always meant to be. Moreover, they go so far as to say that any changes we see in our traits as we progress through the life span are simply due to our genetic code and were always meant to happen. For example, Costa and McCrae describe that when one's traits of agreeableness and conscientiousness increase, it is simply the result of a biological and developmental need to take on, care for, and provide for the next generation (much like Erikson's [1959] generativity discussion) and the responsibilities associated with that, rather than based on life experience, context, or situation.

However, McAdams (1996, 2006) suggests that if we only consider the dispositional traits described in the five-factor model, we are missing some very important considerations in describing and understanding personality. That is, dispositional traits are important, but they are only one piece of the personality puzzle. McAdams (1996) made it clear that some very important variables are missing from this earlier conceptualization of personality. Specifically, McAdams understood that humans do not live in isolation, and our personality needs to be explored and measured within our own cultural context, which had not been done previously with the five-factor model. Additionally, McAdams argued that our sense of self develops over time, and with time passing comes life experiences and an ability to develop a personal life narrative about who we are and who we view ourselves to be. As you can imagine, this occurs at peak development in our older adult years after so many years of life experience.

To sure, there is consensus on the role of personality traits and their implications for predicting mental health, job success, life and marital satisfaction, and so on (e.g., Hosseinkhanzadeh & Taher, 2013; Kotov et al., 2007; McAdams, 2006; Rostami et al., 2022), but there is also an argument to be made for the influence of the life narrative in one's personality and personality development (e.g., McAdams, 2006; Wrzus & Roberts, 2017). Specifically, narratives can help us understand how individuals use those traits in making life decisions, create change in their lives, and maneuver through adversity (because that hits us all at one time or another), as well as create depth in our understanding of personality. To encompass all of this, McAdams (2006) suggests that there is a three-level system of personality (see Table 9.2). The first level is the dispositional traits (i.e., what is described in the five-factor model). These traits are broad, two-ended (e.g., introversion vs. extraversion), and interpreted without sociocultural context. The second level is that of **characteristic adaptations**. Here, details can fill in how individuals differ from one another, even when they share some similar dispositional traits. Time, place, individual contexts, and personal goals are included at this second level to describe the nuances of how different people are motivated to do different things and how those may vary from situation to situation. The third, and final, level is **integrative life stories**. At this level, we can begin to understand the whole individual, integrating their culture, class, gender, and other social contexts in which they fit. Integrative life stories allow for us to understand that people live in social worlds, and their personality reflects their social experiences and the context that they have been a part of for their whole lives. And, unlike dispositional traits, these social contexts change with time (Campbell et al., 2003; Lang et al., 1998; Webster & Ward, 2011)—and so their life story gets written and revised over and over again. This distinction between what stays the same and what can change about personality will be addressed next.

TABLE 9.2 ■ Levels of Personality

Dispositional Traits	Broad traits interpreted independent of any context (e.g., introversion vs. extraversion)
Characteristic Adaptations	Incorporates individual differences in time, space, and context
Integrative Life Stories	Fills in with stories that interact with others in one's social space

Source: McAdams, D. P. (2006). The role of narrative in personality psychology today. *Narrative Inquiry, 16*(1), 11–18.

CHANGE AND STABILITY IN PERSONALITY DEVELOPMENT

Consider yourself at age 10, then again at 15, and at perhaps 20 or 25. Do you feel like you're the exact same? Probably not. A lot of time, experience, and development occurs over the course of those years. According to Costa and McCrae (1994), our dispositional traits continue to develop from temperament as infants through personality development into our 20s. But what about after that? Are we the same? I'd argue that in the way that we experience so much life between ages 10 and 20, we experience so much more between the ages of 20 and 65. Why wouldn't we change?

Dispositional traits (i.e., the five factors) have been demonstrated to link quite clearly to our genetics (e.g., Bouchard et al., 1990)—I'm reminded of this when I tell my children to do something and realize that I sound just like my mother. I must react (generally speaking) similarly to how she does across circumstances. However, it should be noted that dispositional traits are just that: general. Nevertheless, general as they are, Bouchard et al. (1990) did demonstrate that there is considerable heritability in these traits. Here, over 100 sets of identical and fraternal twins who had been reared apart since infancy were assessed on several measures of personality and temperament (as well as other assessments on occupational interest and mental abilities). Those assessments were compared to assessments of twins reared together. Data showed very little influence of environment on personality traits. That is, identical twins reared together were as similar to one another as identical twins reared apart, suggesting that traits were largely genetic. These are the levels of personality that may remain stable across the life span. And any changes we see in traits such as decreases in openness or in extraversion may simply be the unfolding of an already genetically predetermined set of traits that were set to change at a specific time as per their genetic programming, independent of life circumstances (Costa & McCrae, 2006).

However, characteristic adaptations and integrative life stories are much more dependent on the life situations and social environments that individuals find themselves in (e.g., McAdams, 2006), which inevitably change over the course of a lifetime. Caspi and Roberts (2001) describe how personality develops across the life course and argue that there is no set time for personality to stop developing. It's not a light switch we can turn off in an instant. Rather, experiences we have help to shape these components of our personality as we learn and grow. However, the more we learn and grow from our experiences, the more consistency we have in how we interact with our environment. We develop patterns over time, and these patterns become more and more consistent in middle and later adulthood—as if we've figured ourselves out.

Moreover, we see these changes occur but then become more and more consistent over time as an individual gains life experiences and perspective (Caspi & Roberts, 2001). These experiences serve to help us develop our **cognitive schema**, or guide, by which we interpret and subsequently respond in specific circumstances (e.g., Caspi & Moffitt, 1993). In terms of characteristic adaptations, we see how goals and motivations change as we enter adulthood, but then level out to be something more consistent with how we choose to manage our later adult years. For example, choosing an occupation may be ever changing as we grow up thinking we'll be a teacher or a police officer or a nurse—and may continue to change into young adulthood. But, soon those ideas settle down and are tweaked rather than widely varied, where we choose to be a kindergarten teacher or a middle school teacher or a pediatric nurse or an orthopedic nurse. These ideas further develop, and we write and then revise our integrative life story as well, which also goes through smaller and smaller revisions as life goes on (Roberts & DelVecchio, 2000). Early adulthood changes become later adulthood tweaks, not dramatic shifts in the revision of our self-perception.

Personality theorists support this pattern (e.g., Arnett, 2000; McAdams, 2006; Roberts & Jackson, 2008), showing that changes in characteristics and life stories happen more often in young adulthood than in older adulthood (though there is some argument for change at midlife, but we'll discuss that in just a bit). Here, Arnett (2000) describes emerging adults as those who have not yet connected or committed to their identity long-term. That is, they're still figuring it out. Alternatively, research on older adults has demonstrated consistency in emotional stability, which may be a reflection of stronger commitment (psychological, social, and neurological) to their personality and identity, developed over time (e.g., Donnellan & Lucas, 2008). Others have also shown this to be an indicator of maturity (Roberts & Wood, 2006). Regardless, these changes aren't dramatic, and as we get older, we tend more toward stability than change (e.g., Specht, 2017).

GENDER DIFFERENCES IN PERSONALITY DEVELOPMENT

While we examine the individual differences in dispositional traits, characteristic adaptations, and integrative life stories among humans, it may be worthwhile to investigate individual differences in gender as well as gender norms for these pieces of personality as well. That is, do men and women experience personality development in the same way? And what influences do social expectations and norms have on the three levels of personality? I should note that research, to date, has not examined the context of nonbinary individuals (though I hope that we are heading in that direction) but has examined self-identity development for those identifying as transgender or nonbinary (e.g., Tate, 2014). And, while Tate (2014) does argue that we could consider self-identity development part of personality development, this will not be the focus here for this aging perspective.

Across cultures, we can see different norms and perspectives on expectations from different genders (Costa et al., 2001; Triandis & Suh, 2002; Weisberg et al., 2011). These cultural influences play an important role in how our personality develops from infancy through adulthood and into older adulthood. Specifically, Costa et al. (2001) demonstrated that gender differences between individuals were more pronounced in Western cultures (e.g., Europe and America) where traditional social roles do not have as heavy an influence over day-to-day life. Here, differences between men and women on the components of personality traits were such that women were higher in neuroticism, agreeableness, openness to feelings, and warmth. Alternatively, men showed higher measures of assertiveness and openness to ideas. These are consistent with traditional gender roles of men and women and may hold the key to why these differences are greater in Western cultures. Costa et al. suggested that in Western cultures, where individualism is valued, behavior that is consistent with a gender role is interpreted as an individual's choice and therefore reflective of the person's personality traits. Alternatively, in Eastern cultures, where collectivism is valued, these same behaviors may be interpreted as their expected social role rather than having anything to do with one's personality (i.e., these gender-role behaviors are not a choice).

iStockPhoto/Marcus Chung

This is one level of personality that may retain stability in older age (e.g., Chapman et al., 2007). Chapman et al. (2007) demonstrate these same gender differences between older men and older women: Women are higher in neuroticism and agreeableness. However, if we consider the other levels, characteristic adaptions and integrative life stories, we may see other patterns. These parts of our personality adjust as we gain life experiences and refine our identity (and, as such, may be the place where we see differences for transgender and nonbinary individuals as well, though we are waiting on data to show what's happening here—see earlier note). McAdams (2003) describes how our identity develops from late adolescence through adulthood as a construction of our autobiographical memories from our distant and recent past. As you may recall from Chapter 4, the changes associated with informational types of memory—including autobiographical memory—are positive. Recalling information about ourselves is just that: information. Therefore, our ability to do so readily to integrate the meaning of it to create a cohesive vision of who we are will only build with time. And our ability to update that representation is also positive and, as such, can be adjusted as experiences shape us. But the question remains: What happens to these changes as we age? And do we ever experience abrupt, negative change? That'll be addressed next, in the context of the midlife crisis.

MIDLIFE CRISIS

Common in pop culture and in movies is the portrayal of the midlife crisis. One I remember quite clearly occurs in the 1990s film *Father of the Bride Part II* (Shyer & Meyers, 1995), where George Banks finds out he is going to be a grandfather. In the subsequent scenes, you see him dyeing his gray hair brown and purchasing a red convertible. Then he sells his house without consulting his wife. It is meant to portray the idea that once we reach a certain age, we go through a stage of denial of our own aging process, pause in the activity of working toward our life goals, and take stock in what we really want—and it's referred to as the **midlife crisis**. It is often shown as a problem that occurs for men in Western culture, resulting in dramatic and "out-of-character" behaviors. But our stories about these life transitions are *so* dramatic that it makes me wonder—and should make you wonder as well—is this really what happens, and is this a midlife crisis? Do our personalities interact with our reflection and ideas about aging? And how does personality impact our development at the end of life?

iStock/Getty Images Plus/Getty Images

Theories of life transition tell us that changes that happen in middle—and late—life are likely the result of a combination of social roles and expectations, the relationship between location and individual well-being, and the individual differences of social context (e.g., L. K. George, 1993). That's to say there is a lot of variability in how one will transition into middle and later adulthood. Additionally, when we reach middle adulthood and are looking down the barrel of older adulthood, some may feel a sense of loss (e.g., Ebaugh, 1988). Specifically, we are leaving a role—maybe parenting, work, or something else. The idea of role loss can signify a change that can be difficult. Ebaugh (1988) suggests that becoming an "ex," or leaving a role, can be particularly difficult if the change is sudden, off-time, or not voluntary. Aging (or losing your role as a "young adult") is not voluntary and, as such, may cause some challenges in adaptation and taking on a new role. This may be where the midlife crisis comes into play.

Carl Jung was the first to examine the midlife crisis as a transitional role in adult development. Here, based on personal observations of his own life, Jung theorized that there's a turning point during which an adult reevaluates what they've done and explores who they are more deeply—resulting, often, in a change based on balancing and accepting that they're growing older. However, the midlife crisis is, unless triggered by a negative event, often a less dramatic turn of events than it is depicted as in the media. What I mean is that, yes, we do hit a point where we are confronted with the realization that we are getting older. And, yes, we do have to eventually come to terms with that. However, this realization and adjustment comes over time, rather than suddenly, and the process comes as we resolve the conflicts associated with Erikson's (1959) last two stages: generativity versus stagnation and ego versus despair (see Table 9.3).

Reflection during these last two stages involves considering the changes and the progression of one's own life. In resolving generativity versus stagnation, an adult works through how they are contributing to society and the next generation. Being generative, here, is having a positive influence toward those who come after. Interestingly, adults demonstrating generativity measure high on extraversion and openness (Cox et al., 2010). However, Cox et al. (2010) also

TABLE 9.3 ■ Erikson's Stages of Psychosocial Development

Trust vs. Mistrust	Infancy (ages 0–1)
Autonomy vs. Shame and Doubt	Early childhood (ages 1–3)
Initiative vs. Guilt	Play age (ages 3–6)
Industry vs. Inferiority	School age (ages 7–11)
Identity vs. Role Confusion	Adolescence (ages 12–18)
Intimacy vs. Isolation	Early adulthood (ages 19–29)
Generativity vs. Stagnation	Middle adulthood (ages 30–64)
Ego Integrity vs. Despair	Older adulthood (ages 65+)

Source: Erikson, E. (1959). *Identity and the life cycle.* International Universities Press.

found that generativity was more strongly associated with societal involvement and community attachments.

While the changes we see in midlife are considered by Jung and Jungian theorists to be a midlife crisis, further research on this change has demonstrated that it isn't so much a midlife crisis as it is a **midlife correction** (Stewart & Ostrove, 1998; Stewart & Vandewater, 1999). That's to say that the changes are not dramatic (unless coming off the heels of a traumatic event), but rather the result of cognitive growth and reassessment that comes from life experience, adjustment of cognitive schemas, and tweaks in our personal life narrative. This is consistent with Erikson's theory of development as we discussed earlier, where midlife and late life stages focus on generativity and reflection. And, if there is life left to live, adjustments can be made if the reflection is not what we hoped it would be. Torges et al. (2008) examined individuals who made these life assessments, and tried to determine what that did for their development and life satisfaction later in life. This study surveyed women born in the 1940s (before the women's movement, and before women in the workforce became the norm) on their reflection of life. Questions assessed personality, life regrets, spiritual beliefs, and more. Results showed that those who had resolved their regrets at an earlier age had moved toward higher levels of ego integrity (i.e., being happy with how their life was ending). Additionally, results showed that those who experienced generativity in middle adulthood reached higher levels of ego integrity earlier in their older adult years (closer to age 60 than to 70 or 80). These results suggest not only that we are happier and more satisfied in life if we are able to do what we hope to do in our time on this earth, but also that the things that we hope to do are more satisfying if they contribute to the next generation. Though it may not feel that way when we're young adults, the perspective can change as we move through middle and older adult years. Other research on adjustments and generativity in late life confirms the influence of generativity (e.g., Versey et al., 2013). Versey et al. (2013) found that increased generativity was associated with higher levels of successful aging and lower levels of concerns about aging.

When considering resolving regret and midlife corrections, research shows that the implications of those tweaks can be beneficial even much later in life when adapting to the loss of a spouse (Torges et al., 2008; see Figure 9.1). Specifically, Torges et al. (2008) examined individuals who were caregivers of terminally ill patients both before and after the loss. Interview questions focused on a regret measure (i.e., looking back on your life, is there something that you wish you had done?), as well as measures of well-being, anxiety, and rumination. Results showed that older adults were more likely to resolve their regrets than young adults, presumably because they had lived more life to know what to value and what was important to them. Additionally, results showed that those who did make strides to resolve those regrets declined in depressive symptoms and levels of depression over time, especially postloss (though there'll be much more discussion about bereavement in the last chapter of this book). Torges et al. concluded, consistent with the other research on midlife corrections, that regret resolution is important for overall well-being, success, and satisfaction in late life. And, importantly, the correction isn't dramatic as depicted by our conceptualization of the midlife crisis—just a little adjustment can do so much.

FIGURE 9.1 ■ Mean Level of Depressive Symptoms Compared to Regret Resolution

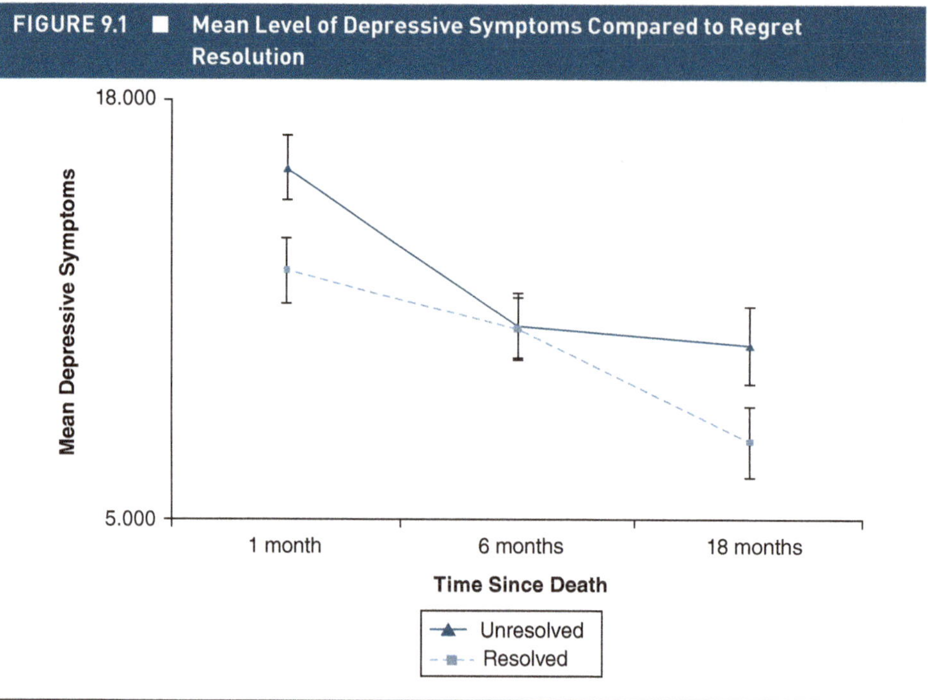

Source: Torges, C. M., Stewart, A. J., & Nolen-Hoeksema, S. (2008). Regret resolution, aging, and adapting to loss. *Psychology and Aging, 23*(1), 169–180. https://doi.org/10.1037/0882-7974.23.1.169.

IMPACT ON LIFE FACTORS AND WELL-BEING

Our personality can impact a variety of life factors as well, and it doesn't have to be just in reflection at middle and late life. It makes sense that since personality is a long-term construct, it will have implications beyond individual moments. That's to say personality traits are not the same as mood and do not change from moment to moment. Instead, they develop over time and over a lifetime, and will have long-lasting effects on various life situations and how we live our life in larger chunks of time. In this section, you'll see how personality variables impact life satisfaction (Tauber et al., 2016), health-promoting behaviors (e.g., Friedman et al., 2013; Herero & Extremera, 2010), financial behaviors (e.g., Asebedo et al., 2019), future planning (e.g., Sörensen et al., 2008), and even executive function (e.g., Williams et al., 2010). These variables range widely and reflect the notion that one's personality touches on every corner of life.

Life satisfaction is one variable that can be significantly influenced by personality factors. The idea here is that when our personality matches our living environment, it is easier to be content with the way things are going (Roberts & Jackson, 2008). Finding a fit, long-term, as adjustments, changes, and developments occur, can be difficult. As you can imagine, as life ebbs and flows and life circumstances change, there isn't always going to be perfect alignment. However, when successful fit between these two variables does occur, there is a better likelihood of higher levels of life satisfaction. Research in this area suggests the same (e.g., Tauber et al., 2016). Tauber et al. (2016) examined the relationships between life satisfaction and both neuroticism and extraversion in middle-aged and older adults. Results showed that these two personality traits significantly predicted life satisfaction for both age groups, but life satisfaction did not predict the personality factors. That's to say that personality works to help us produce a satisfying life, but not necessarily the other way around. A satisfying life isn't going to encourage personality to present itself in one particular way or another. (Importantly, Tauber et al. statistically removed the influence of health factors, as we know that health can impact life on so many different levels. Personality can even impact health behaviors, which you'll see in just a bit.) The authors also suggested that these results can have specific implications in life satisfaction, such that neuroticism could impact life variables like social isolation or health behaviors, whereas extraversion could impact life satisfaction through social activities and participation.

Research has also investigated how personality can impact health-promoting behaviors, like the use of health care in older adults for both acute and long-term care (e.g., Friedman et al., 2013; Herero & Extremera, 2010). These studies have shown that personality has some significant influence over older adults' access to and use of the health care system available to them, as measured in the Big Five personality traits in the five-factor model. Specifically, Friedman et al. (2013) measured these personality factors as well as the use of a variety of health care functions, including emergency department visits, skilled nursing facilities, hospital stays, home health care, and more general custodial nursing home care. An analysis of these measures showed significant relationships between several items. Individuals higher in neuroticism were more apt to use the emergency department, and those who were high in conscientiousness were less likely to use the emergency department. Individuals who scored high in openness were more likely to access general custodial nursing home care, as were those higher in agreeableness. Additionally, analyses showed that those high in neuroticism showed higher use of skilled nursing facilities, but fewer hospital stays. And those high in openness had fewer visits to the emergency department and fewer days accessing a skilled nursing facility.

These findings are interpreted in the context of how older adults handle their health and take responsibility for their own treatment regimen on a regular basis. Styles differ as personality traits differ. For example, those who are high in neuroticism may be more sensitive to bodily sensations and more likely to have worries about their health, both of which could lead them to use the emergency department more than those who are lower in neuroticism. Alternatively, those who are high in openness might be more apt to keep up with their self-care and home management regimens for their health and then may be less likely to need to visit the emergency department and may also be more open to alternatives like home health care. Clearly, having options for accessing the needed health care is important for all individuals, whose personalities vary as widely as their behaviors and health conditions.

The relationship between personality and health is further examined in other research, exploring overall well-being (e.g., Herero & Extremera, 2010). Here, Herero and Extremera (2010) examined the interplay between other personality variables like self-esteem and optimism and how they influence participation in daily activities that can (as you've seen in previous chapters in this book) positively impact the psychological, cognitive, and social development of an older adult. And, while the relationship between personality and happiness is not a direct one

(Tkach & Lyubomirsky, 2006), there is some evidence that both lead to behaviors that are positive and give a positive life experience. And, ultimately, that's what we all want. Isn't it? Herero and Extremera (2010) measured positive and negative affect, optimism, and engagement in 28 activities ranging from community service to solitary card games to building knowledge or communication. Data showed that higher levels of optimism and self-esteem were related to higher ratings of life satisfaction and overall well-being. Additionally, results showed a positive relationship between engaging in "outside activities," such as social interactions and mass communication (e.g., newspapers), and older adults' subjective ratings of well-being. This was contrasted by those who preferred solitary activities, like playing cards by themselves, who showed lower levels of well-being. These results suggest that well-being is influenced by not just physical factors, but social and emotional ones as well. The interplay between these factors comes in their personality, where those who have certain behavioral tendencies may positively influence their own well-being. However, more research is needed on what types of behaviors are more likely for which individuals and to what degree those behaviors may be limited by physical health constraints.

iStockPhoto/Cecilie_Arcurs

Physical and mental health is not the only place where personality may have large influence. Financial health is also significantly affected by individuals' personality traits and overall tendencies toward financially oriented behaviors (e.g., Asebedo et al., 2019; Gillen & Kim, 2014). If you've ever considered yourself a "saver" or a "spender" (in case you are wondering [you probably aren't], I'm a saver), you may wonder how your personality plays a role, and we can also consider how this may play out in our older years. As you can imagine, saving for retirement and/or not spending all you have already saved is crucial as we live longer than ever before—and therefore spend more years in retirement than ever before (see Chapter 6 for more information on retirement). Running out of money, when rent and medical bills need paying, is definitely not ideal. However, knowing your tendencies and how they relate to your personality traits can allow for you to make accommodations as needed. For example, if you are a spender, you may set an allowance for what you can spend without consequence, leaving other saved money alone. Asebedo et al. (2019) examined this relationship between personality and saving. Here, researchers examined personality traits such as introversion/extraversion, openness, neuroticism, agreeableness, and conscientiousness along with motivation and saving behaviors. A complex relationship emerged such that extraversion and conscientiousness contributed positively to saving behavior, while openness and neuroticism negatively influenced saving. The reason for saving was also important. Were participants saving to have emergency money on hand? Or were they saving for luxuries/extra spending? Data showed that while motivation and even an individual's net worth were important in determining how they were saving, those factors were less influential than the impact of personality traits. And even those impacts of personality traits were indirect—influenced by positive or negative affect. Negative affect was fed by neuroticism and agreeableness, which undermined the saving behavior pattern, but positive affect was related to extraversion and conscientiousness and bolstered saving behaviors through confidence and higher self-efficacy. As one comes up on their retirement, any fears and negative emotions can come to the surface and negatively impact saving behaviors through fear and loss of motivating factors. The intricacies between these factors can put the older adult on a steady financial road or on shaky ground.

In instances where finances are tight, such as when someone needs medication and groceries and does not have the money for both purchases, personality also plays a role in how one will reach out to and/or accept help from others (Chatterjee & Fan; 2021; Gillen & Kim, 2014; though, as a side note, some large American pharmaceutical companies now have financial assistance programs for this very reason, and therefore can be considered another alternative for help). It is not uncommon for older adults to be in a position where they aren't able to make ends meet. For instance, only 40% of older adults have benefits from a traditional pension or 401(k) (U.S. Government Accountability Office, 2011), and I suspect this number is not going up any time soon. So, it may be important to know under what conditions, and by what methods, an older adult may reach out for help.

In an examination of older adults' personality traits based on the five-factor model, Gillen and Kim (2014) measured levels of neuroticism, openness, agreeableness, extraversion, and conscientiousness along with a questionnaire that addressed financial help factors (did they receive help, did they apply for a loan or credit card, etc.) and economic characteristics (e.g., income, employment, and wealth). Data analyses showed that older adults who were higher in neuroticism and agreeableness were more likely to need financial assistance, but those who were high in neuroticism were more likely to handle those situations independently through credit cards or loans. Those high in agreeableness instead were more likely to reach out to family for that assistance. Alternatively, older adults higher in conscientiousness were less likely to find themselves in financial hardships. These patterns with traits clarify how we may choose different, potentially damaging behaviors (e.g., using credit cards or home equity loans) over other, safer alternatives (e.g., financial planning, food stamps, or asking for help from loved ones). The choices we make day-to-day based on our personality can have implications far beyond the day we make the decision.

The future of our lives is significantly impacted by our personality and the decisions we make. Even though the future is shorter when we are older than when we are younger, we are still making decisions for the days, weeks, months, and years ahead of us. Preparing for our future and setting up for potential health care needs, such as costs, medical proxy, the possibility of nursing home care, and so on, can be daunting to say the least. Many people will avoid making these plans and early decisions and leave the choices and decisions to their spouse and family. This can put undue pressure on them as well. The avoidance of the need to make these plans has been associated with our personality traits (e.g., Sörenson et al., 2008). In one study, Sörenson et al. (2008) examined the Big Five personality traits along with measures of depression, beliefs about planning, and planning behaviors themselves. For example, participants were asked about their awareness of the need to make those decisions and/or their avoidance of doing so, as well as about what kinds of planning, decision making, and information gathering they engaged in. Data analyses revealed that individuals who were high in neuroticism, openness, and agreeableness were more aware of future care planning, but those high in extraversion and conscientiousness (surprisingly!) showed no relationship with future care decisions. Actual steps toward planning were also related not to those personality variables but rather to just the thoughts about needing to take these steps. The researchers suggested that these personality variables contributed to more open-minded and thorough thinking processes about all parts of life—even those that aren't as fun. Additionally, research (including this study by Sörenson et al.) has shown that personality factors, such as low levels of extraversion, contribute to additional negative perceptions of health as we age (e.g., Chapman et al., 2006). These results underline the importance of communication about facts about aging, especially about health and mental health, and even primary care doctors can contribute to education and support in assessing patients' personality and helping them plan for reality rather than myth. You can help here too, by sharing the knowledge you learn from this book with your friends and loved ones.

These planning functions, and the thoughts surrounding them, can be impacted by our cognitive capabilities as well. As discussed in earlier chapters, there are some components of memory and processing that change (not necessarily for the negative) in our older years. One such component that is influenced significantly is our executive functioning (e.g., Williams et al., 2010). Specifically, the executive function refers to the mental flexibility, allocation of mental resources, planning, and inhibitory control that we have as part of our information processing system. It can help to maintain information in working memory, as well as decide when to let go of that information or when to send it to long-term storage (flip back to Chapter 4 for more information on the flow through the information processing system; Atkinson & Shiffrin, 1968). Along with personality, executive functioning can influence our decisions and behaviors. Williams et al. (2010) showed that executive function was significantly related to neuroticism, openness, and agreeableness (but not extraversion or openness). These relationships show that some components of our personality can influence our cognitive function—for example, neuroticism was related to error monitoring as part of executive function, and openness was related to experimentation/trying out new tasks. Interestingly, the authors suggest that these relationships show that the connection between personality and cognitive processes details how the neuropsychological pathways can influence our mental and physical health. It is all connected.

AGING WELL: PERSONALITY

To age well in our personality development is to understand how it is all a process that ebbs and flows with time and with experience. At the same time, there is an innate temperament in us that develops into our personality traits (from the temperament your parents said you had as a young child to the personality traits you have now). The experiences we have early in life largely influence our personality—which then tweaks in adjustment in our older adult years. These years are not the ones where we dramatically change and become "different people," but rather we adjust more subtly and step into our individual differences more fully. Importantly, aging well is also recognizing that different people do things in different ways, and that is OK. Your development won't look like someone else's, and someone else's won't look like yours.

KEY TERMS

agreeableness
characteristic adaptations
cognitive schema
conscientiousness
dispositional traits
extraversion
facets
factors
integrative life stories
interpersonal traits
midlife correction
midlife crisis
NEO Personality Inventory
neuroticism
openness to experience
temperamental traits

COMPREHENSION QUESTIONS

1. Describe the NEO-PI.
2. What does an assessment of personality entail? What information does it give us?
3. What are the Big Five personality factors? How do personality factors relate to facets of personality, to temperament, and to one another?
4. What is missing from the conceptualization of personality with just five personality factors? How do theorists redefine or expand the conceptualization?
5. Describe the relationship between dispositional traits, genetics, and environment. How do life experiences influence personality?
6. How do gender norms across and between cultures influence personality?

7. Describe the midlife crisis from the Jungian perspective and from the Eriksonian perspective. Which is more consistent with current research?
8. How does personality influence health behavior and health planning?
9. Explain the relationship between life satisfaction and personality.
10. How do personality and cognition relate to one another?

ADDITIONAL READINGS

Burns, K. M., Burns, N. R., & Ward, L. (2016). Confidence—More a personality or ability trait? It depends on how it is measured: A comparison of young and older adults. *Frontiers in Psychology, 7,* 518.

Graham, E. K., James, B. D., Jackson, K. L., Willroth, E. C., Boyle, P., Wilson, R., Bennett, D. A., & Mroczek, D. K. (2021). Associations between personality traits and cognitive resilience in older adults. *The Journals of Gerontology: Series B, 76*(1), 6–19.

Hooker, K., Choun, S., Mejía, S., Pham, T., & Metoyer, R. (2013). A microlongitudinal study of the linkages among personality traits, self-regulation, and stress in older adults. *Research in Human Development, 10*(1), 26–46.

Judges, R. A., Gallant, S. N., Yang, L., & Lee, K. (2017). The role of cognition, personality, and trust in fraud victimization in older adults. *Frontiers in Psychology, 8,* 588.

McClendon, J., Bogdan, R., Jackson, J. J., & Oltmanns, T. F. (2021). Mechanisms of Black–white disparities in health among older adults: Examining discrimination and personality. *Journal of Health Psychology, 26*(7), 995–1011.

Oddone, C. G., Hybels, C. F., McQuoid, D. R., & Steffens, D. C. (2011). Social support modifies the relationship between personality and depressive symptoms in older adults. *The American Journal of Geriatric Psychiatry, 19*(2), 123–131.

Snitz, B. E., Weissfeld, L. A., Cohen, A. D., Lopez, O. L., Nebes, R. D., Aizenstein, H. J., McDade, E., Price, J. C., Mathis, C. A., & Klunk, W. E. (2015). Subjective cognitive complaints, personality and brain amyloid-beta in cognitively normal older adults. *The American Journal of Geriatric Psychiatry, 23*(9), 985–993.

Weston, S. J., Edmonds, G. W., & Hill, P. L. (2020). Personality traits predict dietary habits in middle-to-older adults. *Psychology, Health & Medicine, 25*(3), 379–387.

iStockPhoto/Jelena Stanojkovic

10 STRESS

LEARNING OBJECTIVES

10.1 Discuss the effects of stress on physical and mental health.

10.2 Identify the perspectives older adults can have in adapting to stress, including different types of coping strategies.

10.3 Explain gender differences in coping with stress.

10.4 Explain age differences in coping with stress.

10.5 Discuss the positive outcomes associated with post-traumatic growth.

"You're making me turn gray and go bald."
"You're giving me wrinkles."
"You're stressing me out."

I hear these phrases all the time. I heard them from my parents and grandparents as a child, I hear them from friends, and occasionally, I hear them from my husband (though he is usually joking, and then lovingly tells me that his baldness is my fault and the gray in his beard is from the kids). The thing about it is these phrases have an underlying connotation that whatever happens to us physically is the result of something outside of us that makes it so. That's not really how it works, though. Do we naturally lose our hair or turn gray with age? Sometimes, yes. Does our skin naturally wrinkle? Also yes. And the implication here is that someone or something else is causing us stress, and that is what makes our bodies do these things. That's simply not true. And, while it might feel better to us to push blame for these processes outside of ourselves, there is really a different process at play here. This chapter will discuss how we can internalize the external, and how coping strategies and adaptations to the stressors can work for us or against us in the aging process.

EFFECTS OF STRESS ON PHYSICAL AND MENTAL HEALTH

Stress is a reaction to an external stressor. Let's repeat that: Stress is a *reaction* to an external stressor. **Stress** is the mental and physiological response to an external event and depends on the individual and the individual's interpretation of the event (e.g., Teichner, 1968). So, it is not the fault of something outside of us making our internal changes occur, but rather the response to it that is responsible. And in many cases, what is stressful to one person may not be stressful to another. For example, sitting in traffic could lead to a stress reaction in one person, but another person in that same traffic jam may react by enjoying their extra time in the car with their favorite music. The external event is separate from our reaction to it, and while our reaction may cause some negative effects to our physical and mental health—and this may change over time and with age—there is nothing inherent in the stressor that will make your hair gray, your skin wrinkle, or your body age. Our interpretation and subsequent reaction to it can, however, have physiological effects (e.g., McEwen, 2017, 2022; Reisman, 1997; Teichner, 1968).

These stress reactions can (and should) come as the result of appropriate appraisal of a stressor. Initial contact with the stressor should first lead to a **primary appraisal**. In this primary appraisal, an individual first assesses whether the stressor is applicable to them at all (e.g., Peacock & Wong, 1990). It almost acts like a filter, where irrelevant things get filtered out. For example, consider an instance where you hear about an earthquake that happens on the other side of the world. While scary and sad, this may not apply to you. This stressor can be appraised and deemed irrelevant or benign with relation to you at this time, and you can move on. Alternatively, this primary appraisal may filter *in* the relevant stressor. That is, if the earthquake happened on the other side of the world, but it happened near where your parents were vacationing, you may deem it relevant to you at this time. In this instance, you would further evaluate the stressor and perform a **secondary appraisal**. In a secondary appraisal, an individual determines what the stressor is, and what kind of reaction and/or coping is appropriate (e.g.,

Lazarus & Folkman, 1984; Peacock & Wong, 1990). This additional processing of the stressor is important and is a clue toward how the stress reaction can impact our physical and psychological health.

The effects a stressor has on our physical and mental health can be significant and can impact our body and our mind on many different levels in a variety of ways. In some cases, the impact can be quite large—especially if the stress reaction is also large. Some research has shown the power of this stress reaction can have implications down to the cellular level (e.g., Epel et al., 2004; Epel et al., 2006; O'Donovan et al., 2012). Within a cell, the DNA holds some power in how old a cell can get and how many times it can divide and replicate. Specifically, structures within the DNA, called **telomeres**, shorten each time a cell divides (see Figure 10.1). The ends of the telomeres get thinner as well, ultimately ending with the cell aging out and dying without being able to replicate again once it has hit its replication limit (i.e., **Hayflick limit**; Hayflick, 1965). That is, the telomere can only get so short before it cannot divide anymore. This process is a normal part of cellular aging (e.g., Blackburn, 2000) but can be accelerated when an individual experiences significant psychological or physical stress (e.g., Epel et al., 2004; Epel et al., 2006). This acceleration of cellular aging has been linked to a variety of illnesses including cardiovascular disease, neurodegenerative diseases, and autoimmune diseases (e.g., Epel et al., 2006; O'Donovan et al. 2012).

O'Donovan et al. (2012) demonstrated that the impacts of stress are dependent on the interpretation and appraisal of the stressor. That is, many of us are exposed to stressors all day, every day. But our interpretation of the stressor as something negative and stress*ful* is necessary for the telomeres to shorten the way they do in cellular aging. According to O'Donovan and colleagues, this stress appraisal can happen prior to the stressor, during the stressor, or after it occurs. If prior, the stress appraisal is called an **anticipatory appraisal**. If it happens during the event, it is called a **challenge**. And if appraisal occurs after, it is **retrospective appraisal**. In the O'Donovan et al. study, individuals with higher levels of anticipatory stress appraisals showed shortened telomere length, indicative of a stress response mimicking cellular aging. This type of stress

FIGURE 10.1 ■ DNA With Telomeres

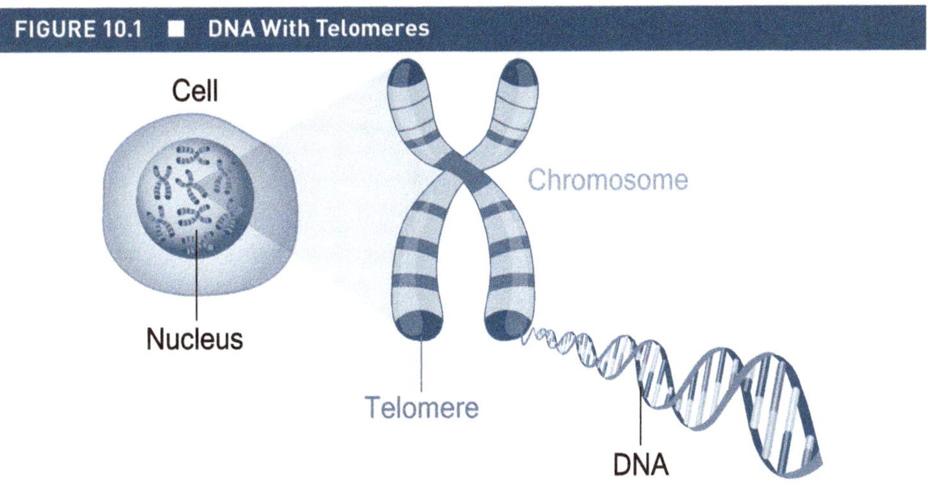

Source: iStockPhoto/FancyTapis

response—determining the event is stressful before it even happens—may be a modulating mechanism for the relationship between stressor, psychological stress, and cellular aging, and may be the impetus for the remarks about "stress making us old, wrinkly, and gray."

Moreover, if the stressors keep coming over and over again, it makes sense that one will be on their toes, so to speak, to expect that more are on the way. This type of "impending doom" worry or expectation is also impactful in how our cells hit their limits earlier than necessary. It's perpetual anticipatory stress. In one study, Epel et al. (2004) compared mothers of children with chronic illnesses (who played the role of caregiver) to mothers of children who were healthy. Presumably, the mothers whose children had chronic illnesses were exposed to more psychological stress than those whose children did not have chronic illness. As you can imagine, mothers caring for chronically ill children are always on alert for symptoms, keeping to medication schedules, doctors' appointments, and more. The life of someone in this role is filled with stressors left, right, and sideways. In this study, researchers examined DNA and telomere length and recorded other data including how long the mothers had been caring for their chronically ill children. Interestingly, researchers found shorter telomere lengths for mothers who were caregivers for sick children longer (upwards of 12 years), compared to mothers of healthy children. However, they did not see a difference in telomere length when mothers were playing that caregiver role for less time. This indicates that the amount of stress extended over time is what makes significant impact. I can tell you, from personal experience, this is absolutely true. As the mother of a child with a chronic illness, I know all too well that watching for symptoms, managing medications and doctors' appointments, and other stressors can be difficult and can be exhausting emotionally and physically (though I haven't looked at my own DNA to see how it compares to others). So even if the DNA doesn't show it, the stress response is there and impacts us deeply.

But, is there a way to mitigate the effects of stress on cellular aging and maybe limit the likelihood of its contributing to physiological illness? The answer is yes, and research has demonstrated efficacy of several strategies, including exercise (e.g., Puterman et al., 2010) and meditation (e.g., Epel et al., 2009). We will discuss these more fully later in the chapter, but this makes sense in that these activities can help us change the perception of the stressor and/or change the focus of our attention away from the stressor.

Immune System

Have you ever noticed that you often get a cold at the end of finals week? Yes, finals in December are smack dab in the middle of cold and flu season, but there is something else at play here too. Stress. Stress reactions can have a significant impact on the way our immune system functions. In some ways this impact is positive (e.g., for survival against pathology), and in other ways it is negative (e.g., leading to reduced immune response to illness or vaccination). For instance, consider that the underlying reason for having a stress reaction at all is for survival. That is, in the case of predatory danger, we should recognize the stress inherent in that situation and react accordingly. Our biology follows that logic as well, and our immune response can amp up for a short time following this short-term stressor–stress reaction scenario (i.e., **acute stress**; Pruett, 2003). This is beneficial in a case where maybe the predator didn't get us, but we were injured and need our immune system to help prevent infection so that we aren't weakened enough to allow the predator to get us later.

However, in an instance where the stressor–stress reaction scenario is longer (i.e., **chronic stress**), we can see a different impact on our immune system. We saw the impact of chronic stress earlier in the case of mothers caring for their children with chronic illness (Epel et al., 2004). Mothers' telomeres shortened significantly over the course of a decade of stress inherent in the caregiving role. More than that, the stress can begin to break down the efficacy of the immune system, leaving us vulnerable to illness, infection, or even cancer (e.g., Dhabhar, 2009, 2014) . . . or maybe just a cold after a week of unending stressors (aka exams).

In taking a closer look at acute stress compared to chronic stress, we see some major differences in impact (Dhabhar, 2009). Acute stress may last for a couple minutes or a couple hours and allows us heightened protection and time to remove ourselves from a dangerous situation. Survival at its finest. Here, research shows a spike in CD8 lymphocytes following a short, 20-minute laboratory stressor (Manuck et al., 1991; see Table 10.1). However, Manuck et al. (1991) showed that this immune response depended on the response from the sympathetic nervous system. That is, individuals whose sympathetic nervous system showed heightened arousal during the stressor (increased heart rate, increased blood pressure, etc.) were the ones who also showed increased lymphocytes in their blood draw. Their immune system ramped up as part of their fight, flight, or freeze response. The opposite was also true: Individuals who showed very little sympathetic nervous system response did not show a heightened immune response. Clearly, individual differences abound when acute stress is involved. However, research on chronic stress shows more consistency in the physiological responses, such that decreased immune response and dysregulation are the norm when stress is more long-lasting (e.g., Godbout & Glaser, 2006; Rozlog et al., 1999), and this impact is similar to what can happen with aging alone (e.g., Fali et al., 2018). Compound the two, and larger difficulties can occur.

TABLE 10.1 ■ Comparison of Lymphocyte Activity for Low and High Reactors to Stress

	CD4 Lymphocytes	CD8 Lymphocytes	CD19 Lymphocytes
High Reactors Baseline Experimental Period	740 715	**545** **684**	207 199
Low Reactors Baseline Experimental Period	662 625	540 541	248 226
Control Subjects Baseline Experimental Period	711 707	566 596	311 285

Note: CD4 lymphocytes work to activate the immune system, including macrophages, and are known as helper T-cells; they work to kill infections. CD8 lymphocytes activate to ward off cancer cells and other invaders (like viruses), while CD19 lymphocytes are primarily identified in cancers such as leukemia.

Source: Manuck, S. B., Cohen, S., Rabin, B. S., Muldoon, M. F., & Bachen, E. A. (1991). Individual differences in cellular immune response to stress. *Psychological Science, 2*(2), 111–115.

Fali et al. (2018) describe that typical aging impacts all the cells in the immune system: T-cells, B-cells, lymphocytes, neutrophils, monocytes, macrophages, and others. These cells change in distribution, production, and concentration throughout the body. Sometimes, as in the case of monocytes and macrophages, the amount of cells remains the same, but the distribution changes in a way that is more indicative of inflammatory processes. Commonly, older adults demonstrate higher-than-normal levels of pro-inflammatory cytokines (e.g., tumor necrosis factor [TNF] or c-reactive protein [CRP]; Franceschi & Campisi, 2014)—sometimes referred to as **inflammaging**. This process is only exaggerated with stress, leading to a cascade of hormone and neurotransmitter changes that alter the immune response (e.g., Butcher & Lord, 2004; Marketon & Glaser, 2008). Specifically, Butcher and Lord (2004) explain that stress—whether physical or psychological—impacts the hypothalamic-pituitary-adrenal connection as well as the sympathetic-adrenal-medullary connection (see Figure 10.2). In both of

FIGURE 10.2 ■ The Effects of Stress on the Nervous and Endocrine Systems

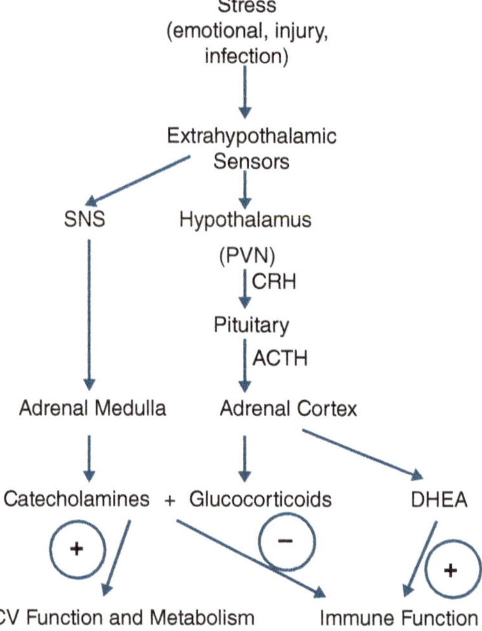

SNS = sympathetic nervous system

CV = cardiovascular

PVN = paraventricular nucleus

CRH = corticotropin-releasing hormone

ACTH = adrenocorticotropin hormone

DHEA = dehydroepiandrosterone sulfate (also known as androstenolone sulfate)

Source: Butcher, S. K., & Lord, J. M. (2004). Stress responses and innate immunity: Aging as a contributory factor. *Aging Cell, 3*(4), 151–160.

these pathways, changes in the production of hormones like cortisol and neurotransmitters like catecholamines contribute to our fight, flight, or freeze response and can suppress our immune function (e.g., Marketon & Glaser, 2008). Combine normative changes to our immune system that occur with age with these additional changes that occur with the response to stress, and we open ourselves up to increased risk of a variety of negative outcomes, including skin cancer (e.g., Saul et al., 2005), cardiovascular disease, and autoimmune diseases (e.g., Epel et al., 2006; O'Donovan et al. 2012).

To be sure, not every stressor is avoidable or can be interpreted in a positive way, nor is the natural aging process avoidable. Perhaps you have heard stories where a longtime married couple dies in rapid succession—first one from a long illness and then the other a few months later. Is this real? Yes, it can and does happen. Let us consider this situation in the context of cellular aging and stress-impacted immune function. Consider the scenario where an older adult is managing their own aging process along with the chronic stress of caring for their spouse at the end of a long illness like cancer. The individual playing the role of caregiver is likely under tremendous stress—worrying about the pain their spouse is experiencing, anticipating the changes that are about to occur, experiencing the loss itself, considering life without their long-term partner, and so on. In this situation, the caregiver is already experiencing cellular aging. Chronic stress, probably occurring over the course of years, makes that process occur more quickly (e.g., Epel et al., 2004; Epel et al., 2006). Then, the changes in the immune function in response to the stress likely implicate more inflammation in their body as well, leaving the caregiver more susceptible to illnesses and immune dysfunction (e.g., Dhabhar, 2009). A compilation of these physiological effects as well as the psychological impact of grief (that'll be discussed in more detail in Chapter 11) can create the perfect storm for the caregiver to pass away a short time later. A spiritual or religious person may see this as natural for the two partners to be together again in the afterlife. And I can't confirm or deny that to be the case—my heart says it's romantic, but science isn't spiritual or romantic. However, the physiological effect on the Earth-side of life is clear: Stress can have significant impact.

Depression and Anxiety

Stressors and stress reactions don't just impact the DNA or the immune system. They impact the individual on many different levels. In the previous section, we saw that stress can cause a cascade of reactions impacting hormones and neurotransmitters. Impacting neurotransmitter balance is a situation ripe for mental health implications, including depression and anxiety (e.g., McEwen, 2017). Research on stress and mental health has examined these two quite closely and showed that early-life adversity and late-life stressors are linked to the development of depression and anxiety (e.g., Inoue et al., 2022; Irwin et al., 1990; Nakamura et al., 2022). Specifically, these studies demonstrated that both stressful events in childhood and those that occur late in life can increase the likelihood of developing depressive symptoms. These events do not have to co-occur either. Inoue et al. (2022) showed that encountering stressors early in life (parental divorce, loss of a parent, family financial trouble, witnessing abuse, etc.) can impact how an individual manages stressors later in life (see Figure 10.3). Additionally, they showed that if individuals did not encounter childhood adversities but dealt with late-life stress, their likelihood of developing depression was similar. This effect was different than in instances where participants dealt with childhood adversity *and*

FIGURE 10.3 ■ Incidence Rates of Childhood Adversity and Stressors in Late Life

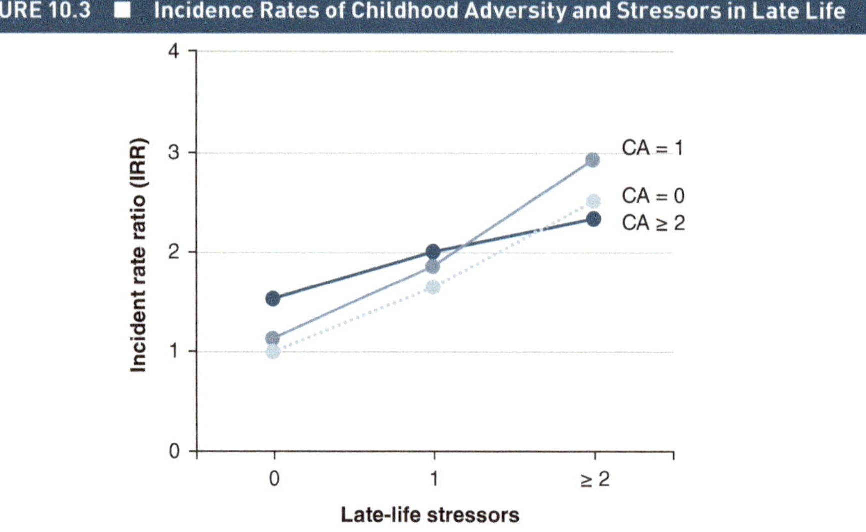

Source: Inoue, Y., Stickely, A., Yazawa, A., Aida, J., Koyanagi, A., & Kondo, N. (2022). Childhood adversities, late-life stressors and the onset of depressive symptoms in community dwelling older adults. *Aging and Mental Health, 26*(4), 828–833.

late-life stressors. These individuals had a lower likelihood of developing depressive symptoms. Inoue et al. attributed this effect to stress inoculation, like stimulus adaptation. It's positive in that there wasn't an additive effect of the stressors, though for me it's difficult to consider how awful it is that those individuals endured a lifetime of stressful situations.

Additional research showed changes in the immune system as the result of chronic stress and depression (Irwin et al., 1990). In this study, researchers compared older individuals who were hospitalized with major depressive disorder with those who were not depressed. An examination of both groups' cytotoxicity (a measure of natural killer, related to T-cells) showed a change by half. This decrease in immune response from chronic stress was discussed earlier, but this study demonstrated that a similar reduction in response occurs in the context of depression. This is not unlike the impact of anxiety. Research on stress and anxiety has also shown negative impacts on the immune system. In one study on animal models, Dhabhar et al. (2012) demonstrated anxiety increased the stress burden on the neurophysiology and immune system of rats, resulting in decreases in immune response and increased response of cancer cells.

The question here becomes can treatment of depression and anxiety lessen the stress burden and moderate the physical health implications of these mental health concerns? The answer is yes. In one study, researchers examined the factors most associated with depression, anxiety, and stress along with factors that mitigate them (Thapa et al., 2020). Here, results showed that although depression and anxiety can be concerning when stress reactions are abundant, factors such as social support, physical exercise, and financial stability were helpful in mitigating these effects (but you'll see more strategies for coping later in this chapter). Elsewhere, Norris and Murrell (1988) demonstrated that prior experience with a stressor can lessen its impact and lessen the associated anxiety. This is similar to the stress inoculation described by Inoue et al. (2022), suggesting that "getting used to" stressors can make the reaction easier to manage and ultimately lessen the negative effects it can have on one's physical and mental health. To be sure, stress and mental health can always be a concern, but when we mange stressors well, our experience can give us a better foundation for when we encounter new stressors.

Post-Traumatic Stress Disorder

In some cases, extreme stressors (i.e., trauma) can lead to prolonged stress reaction. That is the case with **post-traumatic stress disorder** (PTSD; e.g., Averill & Beck, 2000). While we typically think about PTSD in relation to soldiers in wartime (e.g., Pless Kaiser et al., 2019), there are many other stressors that can create this experience where an individual continues to react in a fight, flight, or freeze response even when the stressor is no longer present. For example, a sexual assault, a sudden loss of a spouse, or even a difficult medical procedure can all create a scenario where PTSD can occur. In fact, sexual assault is the most common trigger for PTSD in women (e.g, Tihonen Möller et al., 2004). These stressors are above and beyond day-to-day work stressors, stress about being late to an appointment, or stress about forgetting your homework, and as such the stress reaction will naturally be larger. However, when the stress reaction lingers, becomes fear, and impinges on daily functioning, it is no longer a necessary or reasonable response to a stressor and is a signal that something bigger is happening.

iStockPhoto/NoSystem images

Of course, not everyone who experiences an extreme stressor will develop PTSD. Those more likely to develop PTSD are those who experienced early-childhood adversity, such as neglect, parental divorce, or a parent's mental illness; already suffer from depression or anxiety; or have a history of at least one other trauma (e.g., Raabe & Spengler, 2013; Tiihonen Möller et al., 2004). However, the good news is that older adults are less likely to succumb to PTSD than their young or middle-aged counterparts (e.g., Cook & Simiola, 2017). Unfortunately, research in this area is often focused on male veterans who experienced trauma earlier in life, or it is focused on those who experienced the trauma of a natural disaster later in life. Research on women and people from traditionally marginalized groups is very limited (e.g., Thorp et al., 2011), and the low rates of occurrence overall (and small samples sizes in the research that does exist) make it difficult to draw real conclusions on the progression and treatment of PTSD in older adults. Despite these limitations, some research has demonstrated that older adults who experience trauma may bounce back better than their young adult and middle-aged adult counterparts (e.g., Acierno et al., 2006), showing tremendous resiliency in the wake of trauma.

In one study, Acierno et al. (2006) examined the mental health of young and older adults who had experienced the 2004 Florida hurricanes—which, if you've ever experienced a hurricane, you know can be quite scary. The subsequent power outages and displacement from home could only add to the stressors involved and extend the length of time in which an individual was exposed to those stressors. In this study, a sample of Florida residents answered questions about previous trauma (including natural disasters like hurricanes), social supports, the impact of the hurricanes, and health status, as well as about symptoms of PTSD, generalized anxiety disorder, and depression. Data showed that younger adults showed more symptoms of PTSD, generalized anxiety disorder, and depression than did older adults after the 2004 hurricane season (which I personally endured, and I can tell you it was quite something, with *four* hurricanes in just a month and a half). Moreover, higher rates of those symptoms were related to Hispanic ethnicity, specifically in the young adult group. For older adults, postevent psychopathology was significantly related to health status and how long the individual would be displaced from their home in the aftermath of the storm. These data showed that older adults do not struggle with traumatic events in the same way that young adults do. There are different perspectives, different priorities, and different outcomes—and older adults may be more resilient after the trauma, at least as it is prompted by something like these natural disaster events.

iStockPhoto/CHUYN

A similar positive outcome was demonstrated in the aftereffects of military experiences (e.g., Jennings et al., 2006). Here, older adults who had served in the military reported feelings of generativity and contribution in cases of what was termed "low combat." (As someone not in the military, I can't fathom what is *low* about any kind of combat, but I suppose you can adapt to it, like any stimulus. Insert shoulder-shrugging emoji here.) Moreover, these individuals reported benefits of these military experiences upon retrospective evaluations of that experience. Additionally, more than 10 years later, these individuals had evaluated their time in the military as beneficial and showed higher levels of wisdom compared to those with no combat experience or those with high combat experiences (turn back to Chapter 5 for more on wisdom). These results suggest that the interpretation that individuals have about trauma experiences can impact how that trauma affects them later in their life. Remember that stress reactions are different from stressors, and our reaction plays an important role. In the next sections, you'll see how we react to and interpret stressors and how those perspectives can help in handling stressors throughout our life.

PERSPECTIVES ON ADAPTING TO STRESS

Obviously, negative effects of stress occur—and those can accelerate aging as well as leave us vulnerable to disease and mental health disorders. However, coping strategies and perspective shifts can also occur, and when they do, they can change our stress reactions and ultimately the impact that stress has on our body, our mind, and our aging process.

Types of Coping Behaviors

Different types of coping behaviors can apply in different scenarios (see Table 10.2). That is, depending on the stressor, we can have different interpretations and different responses to the event. For example, one of the things I have discovered to bring me to the pinnacle of convenience is grocery delivery service. Like, I am not sure how I ever lived without it (yes, I realize this is dramatic and I am absolutely spoiled). Occasionally, in my grocery order a shopper will substitute an item for something that I wouldn't have chosen myself. When this happens, my appraisal of the substitution and subsequent reaction to it may vary from one extreme of ranting at a customer service agent and demanding a refund to the other end of the spectrum and simply adjusting what's for dinner that night. My ability to adapt what I make for dinner makes my stress reaction positive and my internalization of the stress virtually none. This is an example of **problem-focused coping**. I assess the situation and realize that it's a problem that I can do something about. Rather than complain, make myself nuts, and upset my day, I fix the problem and move on. While this situation is benign (and, really, a first-world problem if I've ever heard of one), more serious stressors can also benefit from problem-focused coping. For example, a medical diagnosis could prompt problem-focused coping. In an instance where a diagnosis is something easily treatable, like appendicitis, problem-focused coping would concentrate on the surgery to remove the appendix and the steps toward recovery. This strategy would minimize the internalization of the stressor and allow for a solution, and then for the individual to move

TABLE 10.2 ■ Types of Coping

Problem-Focused Coping	Finding a solution to the stressful event, and implementing the solution effectively	Treating an infection with an antibiotic
Emotion-Focused Coping	Shifting one's emotions surrounding an event/stressor	Shifting from frustration to relief when a meeting is canceled
Meaning-Focused Coping	Finding meaning as a result of the stressor	Understanding the meaning and power in a relationship with a spouse, when a terminal diagnosis is given

Sources: Ben-Zur, H. (2020). Emotion-focused coping. In V. Zeigler-Hill & T. K. Shakelford (Eds.), *Encyclopedia of personality and individual differences* (pp. 1343–1345). Springer; Folkman, S., & Moskowitz, J. T. (2007). Positive affect and meaning-focused coping during significant psychological stress. *The Scope of Social Psychology: Theory and Applications, 10*, 193–208.

on with minimal long-term impact on their physical or mental health. Other types of coping can also be used in other situations.

Emotion-focused coping does what it sounds like. It focuses on the emotions surrounding a stressor, rather than fixing a problem or finding a solution (e.g., Ben-Zur, 2020). A stressor lends itself toward emotion-focused coping when there is not an easy solution. Rather than finding a solution, an individual would do better to change their emotions surrounding the stressor, rather than do something about the stressor itself. For example, suppose you find that you have an appointment that was canceled, and you are frustrated. You can't do anything to solve the problem of the canceled appointment, but you can change how you feel about it. Rather than being frustrated, you can shift your emotion to be grateful and be happy to spend your newly found free time doing something you enjoy—like reading a book or watching a movie.

Some stressors don't call for either problem-focused or emotion-focused coping. If there is no problem to fix, or the emotion you feel is the emotion you feel (e.g., sad), you may shift to **meaning-focused coping**. This type of coping allows us the opportunity to find the meaning in the stressor, and in that meaning we can learn a lesson or change the way we think about some of the aspects of our lives (e.g., Folkman & Moskowitz, 2007). For instance, if your spouse is diagnosed with cancer, and they are given a poor prognosis, you are unlikely to turn to problem-focused or emotion-focused coping. You can't fix the cancer, and you can't change that you feel sad—there is no "bright side" here. However, you can find meaning in this stressor. That is, you can find the time now left with your spouse as a valuable gift and find the moments together more meaningful than the drudgery of the day-to-day life you were living before the diagnosis.

Beyond these types of coping, you may wonder what you can actively do to cope with stressors as they come. Research shows that exercise, meditation, and religious activities can be impactful (e.g., Epel et al., 2009; Puterman et al., 2010; Whitehead & Bergeman, 2020). For instance, Puterman et al. (2010) demonstrated that exercise can be beneficial in buffering the effects of stress and cellular aging. In comparing the telomeres of sedentary and active older adult women in addition to measures of perceived stress, they found shortened telomeres in only the sedentary individuals. For those who were physically active, not only did the telomeres measure longer, but they also showed lower measures of perceived stress. I saw this in action several years ago when I was teaching group fitness classes. Many of the individuals in the classes were older and often talked about how they were grateful they had those classes to help them through their stressful times. Not only did the class itself bring physical activity, but it also brought friendship and social support (more on social support and stress in just a bit). I know of one woman who took my classes who managed to continue as she moved through treatment for breast cancer. The class brought her health and joy, and no doubt mitigated some of the stress of that time in her life. These older adults certainly were aging well and used exercise to help themselves do it.

Other research has examined mindfulness meditation in its impact on stress and coping (e.g., Conklin et al., 2019; Epel et al., 2009; Kurth et al., 2017; Tolahunase et al., 2017). Here, too, researchers found positive influences all the way down to the telomeres (Epel et al., 2009). Now before you get skeptical here, let's first discuss what meditation is and what it isn't. At least as it pertains to our discussion here, you don't need to clear your mind and achieve a higher level of existence to be meditating. It isn't about vibrations and levels of energy, or anything woo-woo. Rather, mindfulness meditation is ongoing practice where you allow yourself to release the thoughts you have and come back to them later. You don't need to forget, nor do you need to effortfully ignore. And you definitely don't need to "clear your mind." Instead, the practice is to stop ruminating and just let thoughts be. This takes practice, and can't happen successfully after one meditation session, as it takes time to change the neural pathways in your brain. However, many who use this practice regularly find that it can impact their ability to let go of stressors. (Perhaps Elsa would have found letting it go easier if she had been practicing meditation.) Hoppes et al. (2012) describe mindfulness meditation as a shift in focus from actively doing to mindfully being, and I think that's a great way to conceptualize it.

Researchers who've examined mindfulness meditation have demonstrated neurological changes throughout the practice of meditation—creating new connections and new pathways with which we think (e.g., Treadway & Lazar, 2010). These new pathways allow us to stop ruminating and deal with stressors in a different way; they can ultimately decrease the arousal and reactivity with which we respond to stressors (i.e., lessen the fight, flight, or freeze reaction; Epel et al., 2009). Conklin et al. (2019) argue that the more one practices meditation, the less severe the reactions to stressors become. This is incredibly useful over time and can mitigate the impact of stress on the mind and body. Through the practice of meditation, individuals can learn to shift their appraisal of an event from "stressor" to "just another event," and avoid mind-wandering toward the negative. For older adults, research has shown that meditation can be influential as an intervention for difficulties surrounding the aging process (should they occur), including loneliness and chronic pain, and it can be impactful for caregivers of the older adult as well (e.g., Sorrell, 2015). Importantly, these findings demonstrate that when stressors come up, there is a mechanism to help, and that mechanism is free, accessible, and doable by everyone. Is it a cure-all? No. But it can be very powerful in reducing stress reactions that can negatively affect physical and mental health.

However, meditation is not the only ancient practice that has been explored in coping with stressors. Religious activities have also shown some benefits regarding managing stress and stress reactions (e.g., Whitehead & Bergeman, 2020). One could argue that meditation and religion are related, and they wouldn't be wrong, so it would make sense that they could both be beneficial for coping. Lazarus and Folkman (1984) suggest that religion provides a way of thinking that allows for a shift in the appraisal of the stressor from a threat to a challenge, and it can serve as a method of coping with a stressor that they initially appraise as more negative. Religion can provide opportunities for coping through meaning-focused coping and emotion-focused coping, as described earlier in this chapter (e.g., Koenig, 2012; Park, 2005). These are important ways we can cope with stressors that can allow for positive change in our perception of stress, as well as our physical and mental health. Whitehead and Bergeman (2020) asked older adult participants to keep a daily diary, recording religious coping (e.g., finding strength and/or comfort in religion), perceived stress, and negative affect ratings. They also recorded measures of metabolic health through body composition measures, waist-to-hip ratio, and hemoglobin A1c—a long-term measure of blood sugar levels. Analysis of these data demonstrated a buffering effect of religious coping on perceived stress ratings and negative reactions to stressors. Additionally, religious coping was related to metabolic health, where those who engaged in more religious activities were more likely to have better health measures than those who engaged in fewer. This is impactful to say the least: Regular use of religious coping was supportive of older adults' physical health and supported more positivity overall.

Social Support

Many individuals find help through **social coping**. As social beings, humans benefit from interactions with others, and in some cases, those social interactions can provide a moderating effect on the stress reactions endured. Social support can provide room to express one's emotions, affirmation, and help when appropriate or desired. These opportunities can be helpful for specific stressors, such as bereavement or crime (e.g., Krause, 1986; Stroebe et al., 2005). However, Krause (1986) clarifies that social support is not the be-all and end-all for *all* types of stressors an older adult can experience. Specifically, he compared four types of social support—informational support, tangible help, emotional support, and integration—on four different stressors: bereavement, crime, financial stressors, and social network crises. In measuring older adults' social support using the Inventory of Socially Supportive Behaviors (ISSB; Barrera et al., 1981; Stokes & Wilson, 1984), as well as the occurrence of stressors and depressive symptoms, Krause (1986) demonstrated that some types of support work better for some types of stressors. For example, while none of the types of social support examined helped buffer the effects of financial stressors, there was a significant impact for individuals experiencing bereavement. For bereaved older adults, all the types of social support were impactful and helpful. Moreover, only integration was helpful in supporting older adults experiencing social network crises. The conclusion here is that social coping is helpful when provided for individuals in specific ways under specific circumstances.

Recently, we saw older adults (well, really everyone) struggling with an extreme stressor: the COVID-19 pandemic. Not only was the pandemic a health stressor, but layered upon that was the lack of social interaction during the early days—when social isolation was our primary method to stave off the illness. In this situation, with forced social isolation, social support and social coping were difficult. However, researchers have shown that older adults were able to adapt to the stressor and learn new technologies to regain control over their social interactions (e.g., Sin et al., 2021). Sin et al. (2021) interviewed older adults about their social interactions during the early days of the pandemic. These interviews specifically asked older adults to reflect on the differences in their technology use during the pandemic compared to before, as well as their motivation to learn and comfort levels with communication through technology. Results of the interviews demonstrated that the pandemic was a motivator in older adults' acquisition of technology skills. While difficult, and made even more difficult with a lack of face-to-face technology support and the lack of desire to bother their friends and family with "tutoring" on technology, older adults still learned new skills—using Zoom, FaceTime, email, and so on. Does this mean that older adults are just as tech-savvy as their grandchildren? Not necessarily. But, the pandemic did motivate many to move past their preexisting beliefs that older adults can't learn new things, especially when it comes to technology. They recognized the importance of social interactions during times of stress and took steps to engage in social coping. Moreover, Vannini et al. (2021) demonstrated that while older adults felt the impact of the stress associated with the pandemic, those who used appropriate coping behaviors showed greater resiliency as they moved through it.

iStockPhoto/monkeybusinessimages

To be sure, not everyone benefits the same way from the same types of coping behaviors. There are differences specific to gender, age, and social group. Let's examine these differences next.

STRESS, COPING, AND GENDER

Traditionally, we've observed gender differences between men and women in their tendency toward how they cope with stressors. In those observations, we've seen a tendency of men to "fight or flight" and women to "tend and befriend." This is consistent with our hunter/protector and nurturer evolutionary roles. That is, the role of a man to protect their family and offspring would lead to fighting predators or gathering their family and fleeing, whereas the role of the woman to rear and raise offspring would lend itself toward tending toward the care of others during stressful times. While we no longer live in the times where these roles are the norm, some gender differences do still exist in coping with stress throughout the life span (e.g., Melendez et al., 2012; Navarro & Bueno, 2005). Navarro and Bueno (2005) showed that even in the oldest old, differences in coping strategies between men and women showed active, problem-focused coping in the men and emotion-focused coping in the women—retaining the traditional roles and coping patterns.

Research further examined these gender differences regarding different types of stressors. That is, health-related stressors may be different from everyday life problems, which may be different from financial stressors or even family problems. Navarro and Bueno (2005) also found differences here. In assessing older adults in Spain, using a standardized coping styles and strategies measure, researchers found that men tended to cope with everyday life stressors and family problems using emotion-focused coping (just like women). However, Moos et al. (2006) showed gender differences in coping with health-related stressors. Here, men tended toward problem-focused coping, which makes sense from an evolutionary perspective. For the "protector," attempting to change the threat and keep your bloodline (including yourself) alive is vital. But, when family relationships or interpersonal stressors occur, men tend to avoid the stressor altogether, rather than approach with problem-solving or emotion-focused coping. This is different from the traditional tend-and-befriend approach of women in the face of those types of stressors. Overall, though, it's clear that different genders—at least traditionally—often approach and handle stressors differently.

But this distinction on gender is very binary and based in comparing men and women. So, this begs the question: What types of coping style patterns appear for gender-nonconforming, transgender, or nonbinary individuals? To note, these individuals not only manage life with all the stressors that others endure, but also have added layers of minority stress, prejudice, discrimination, reduced or difficult access to health care (especially mental health and reproductive health), and many more stressors that binary individuals may never be able to fully understand. Research in this area is new, and very incomplete. However, there *is* some research that speaks to the impact of minority stress as it relates to transgender individuals. In one study, McLemore (2018) examined the relationship between transgender individuals being misgendered and subsequent feelings of anxiety, depression, stress, and transgender felt stigma (see Figure 10.4). The survey also examined feelings of social support and stigmatization. Results showed that higher levels of stress were felt among those who also felt stigmatized and depressed. But more research is needed. Even these data show a window into something very real: additional stressors that

FIGURE 10.4 ■ Felt Stigma and Gender Identity and Their Effects on Depression and Anxiety

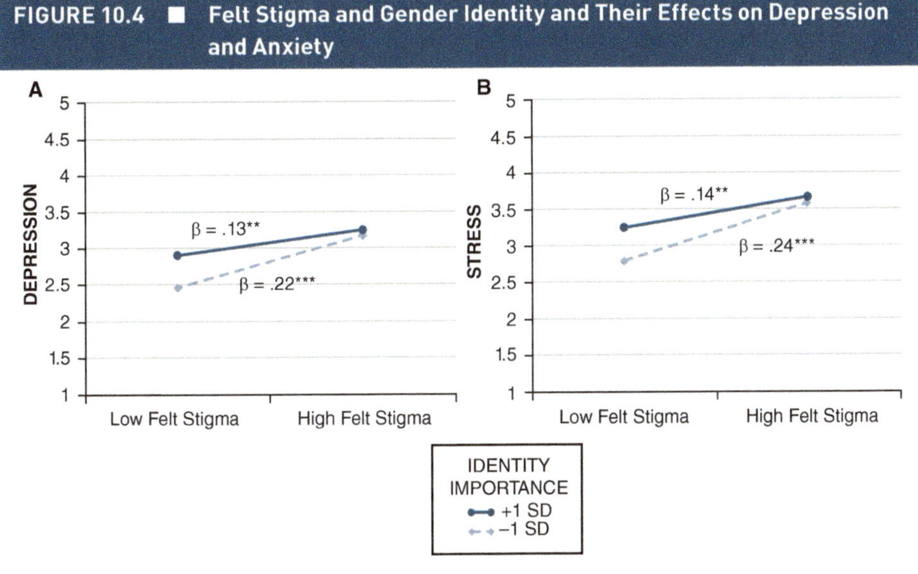

Note: ***$p < .001$, **$p < .01$.

Source: McLemore, K. A. (2018). A minority stress perspective on transgender individuals' experiences with misgendering. *Stigma and Health, 3*(1), 53–64. https://doi.org/10.1037/sah0000070

need coping and support, individuals who feel the negative impact of minority stress, and outcomes that are detrimental to mental health. Coping skills, social support, and gender inclusivity can hopefully minimize the psychological and physical impact—time and more research will help us make that determination. We do not yet know what coping mechanisms would work best for these circumstances and stressors, but I am looking forward to a day when we have that information.

STRESS, COPING, AND AGE

It's clear that older adults have a different perspective on life, because of their vast experience. This is helpful in gaining perspective and appraising incoming stressors. Knowing how to react can help in approaching a stressor with the right coping strategy, and then adapting to it. It is important to recognize, however, that interpreting stressors and managing to cope and/or adapt to them involves cognitive resources. In this section, we'll explore how older adults differ from their young counterparts in their approach to coping, and how potential cognitive limitations may impact their ability to cope (e.g., executive function and working memory limitations).

Because of their lifetime of experience, some research has demonstrated that older adults are better able to avoid significant stressors when possible (e.g., Folkman et al., 1987; Nieto et al., 2020; Schryer & Ross, 2012). As you can imagine, this strategy can be well played and can allow for older adults to encounter stressors only when they cannot be avoided. This is not to say that older adults avoid stressors as they come (i.e., avoidance behavior); rather, they are choosy about the situations and circumstances they find themselves in. Folkman et al. (1987) argued that the life circumstances between young and older adults are sufficiently different to present fewer life stressors to the older adult. Additionally, they presented data that showed that when those stressors occurred, older adults' perspective was markedly different. When older adults found themselves experiencing these events, they retrospectively appraised them more positively. This positive perspective allowed for better coping as well as less time spent ruminating on the stressor. The types of coping demonstrated in these data were significantly different by age as well. Young adults showed problem-focused coping, confrontation, and actively seeking social support, whereas older adults showed emotion-focused coping, positive reappraisal, and distancing themselves from the stressor. It's important to recognize, though, that using any of these coping strategies involves additional cognitive resources. This may lead us to question how older adults are accomplishing these coping strategies within the context of their changing availability of cognitive resources and speed of processing.

Nieto et al. (2020) examined the impact of executive function on older adults' coping strategies. Executive function is our ability to plan, inhibit, and allocate cognitive resources to the appropriate stimulus or task. We know this function to be different in older adults, compared to their younger counterparts (see our earlier chapters on attention and memory for more information here), and so it makes sense to examine it in the context of different types of coping strategies too. In their study, Nieto et al. examined older adults' working memory, inhibitory function, and general coping strategies (using the Coping Responses Inventory [CRI]; Moos, 1993). Interestingly, none of the examined variables showed to be significant predictors of older adults' coping strategies. That is, inhibitory function and working memory did not seem to predict ineffective/different types of coping. This may suggest that experience trumps cognitive limitations. We've seen this before in the context of driving—slower processing speed didn't lead to more car crashes in older adults. They've driven long enough to know what kinds of circumstances to avoid and how to react when driving. Clearly, the same holds true for coping. Older adults have lived long enough to know what kinds of coping works for them (often emotion-focused coping and positive reappraisal), and they employ those strategies.

STRESS AND POST-TRAUMATIC GROWTH

As we've seen, stressors aren't always tied to a negative outcome. Interpretation upon approach of a stressor is helpful in coping, and interpretation poststressor is helpful in recovery and resiliency (e.g., Crane et al., 2020; Crane & Searle, 2016). Earlier in this chapter, we discussed reflections of war veterans on their experiences in low and high levels of combat and showed that those who had experienced lower levels of combat (though still combat) found the experience valuable and generative toward their growth and productivity as an adult (Jennings et al., 2006). That combat experience played a role in their wisdom as well. Tedeschi and Calhoun (2004) termed this positive experience following stress and trauma **post-traumatic growth**. In post-traumatic growth, an individual moves through the trauma, gaining new coping skills, new perspectives, and in some cases even a new self-perception. Or, as Kelly Clarkson (2012) sang, "what doesn't kill you makes you stronger."

While it seems obvious that a combat veteran could experience post-traumatic growth, war is not the only situation out of which positive experiences bloom. Post-traumatic growth can come after many types of trauma including cancer, loss of a spouse, or a large shift in social network (e.g., a move across the country or into a nursing home) and can happen for anyone at any age. Older adults are more at risk for finding themselves in some of these difficult scenarios, like losing a spouse or a difficult medical diagnosis, but can come out the other side of the struggle having new perspective and increased positivity (e.g., Kadri et al., 2022). Kadri et al. (2022) presented evidence to suggest that not only is post-traumatic growth possible, but there are some factors that make it more likely to occur following significant trauma. These factors include social support (especially from children and family members), religious beliefs (to help find meaning), a positive outcome from the trauma (e.g., surviving cancer), female gender (especially in the case of bereavement), physical health, and time since trauma (more time for increased post-traumatic growth).

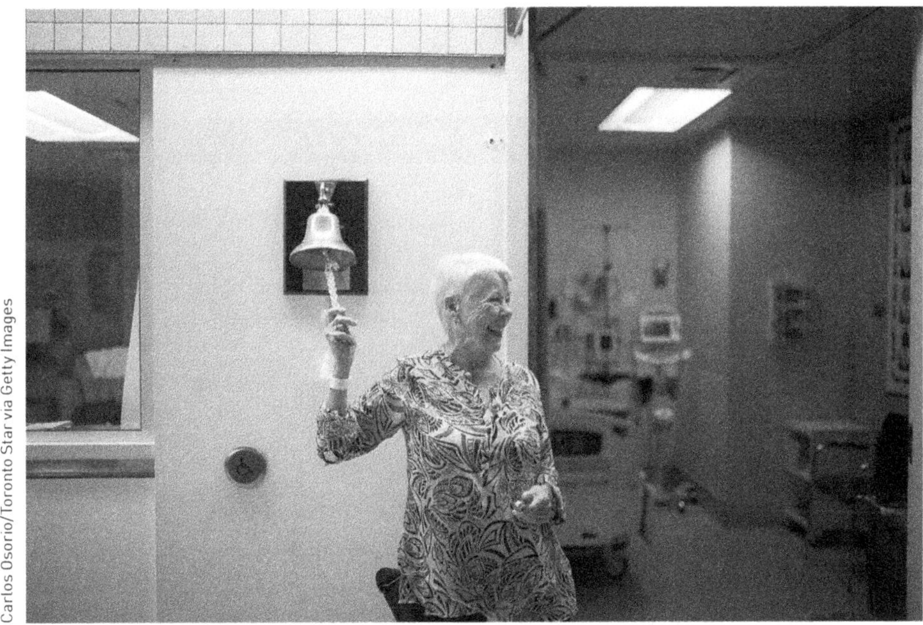

Carlos Osorio/Toronto Star via Getty Images

Specifically examining widowhood, researchers have been able to isolate one factor that contributes quite strongly to the development of post-traumatic growth: religion and spirituality (e.g., Koenig, 2009)—and not one specific religion, but the practice itself. In one study examining widowhood in African American women, Harrison et al. (2004) showed women reporting feelings of support through their religious beliefs—even for those who'd been widowed more than once. That's not to say they didn't suffer and struggle through the trauma of losing their spouse; they did. However, as they moved through the struggle, they were able to find meaning and strength—that is, meaning-focused coping. And in some cases, participants reported increased feelings of independence and freedom as well. This is a positive light after a struggle through darkness.

AGING WELL: STRESS

Aging well with stressors means managing them, coping with them, and possibly growing from those experiences. Easier said than done? Possibly. But remember that older adults have a whole lifetime of experience. With that experience comes data and knowledge—a "been there, done that" kind of perspective. Aging well can mean many things: appropriate appraisal of a stressor (and subsequent positive reappraisal), useful coping strategies (e.g., emotion-focused coping), healthy perspective, and social support (your friends and family are invaluable). Each of these can and should be specific to the stressor and to the individual, and it is important to remember that stressors are different from the stress reaction. We often cannot control the stressor—life happens—but we can control our reaction to it. Older adults seem to have this well figured out. In many instances, the way an older adult situates their life, along with a combination of emotion-focused coping, social supports, and positive reappraisals, allows for not a stress-free life, but a stress-manageable one. Nobody is turning gray from just negative life events, but many are gaining knowledge and personal growth.

KEY TERMS

acute stress
anticipatory appraisal
challenge
chronic stress
emotion-focused coping
Hayflick limit
inflammaging
meaning-focused coping
post-traumatic growth
post-traumatic stress disorder
primary appraisal
problem-focused coping
retrospective appraisal
secondary appraisal
social coping
stress
telomeres

COMPREHENSION QUESTIONS

1. What is the difference between a stressor and a stress reaction?
2. Why is an appraisal of a stressor necessary?
3. What impact does stress have on our cellular aging process?

4. How can stress impact our immune system both in the short term and in the long term?
5. What are the similarities between anxiety/depression and stress on our physical and mental health?
6. How is post-traumatic stress disorder different from a typical stress reaction?
7. How do older adults differ in their stress reactions, compared to their young adult counterparts?
8. What types of coping behaviors are best for an older adult?
9. How can social support impact our stress reactions?
10. How can an older adult benefit from post-traumatic growth?

ADDITIONAL READINGS

Acierno, R., Brady, K., Gray, M., Kilpatrick, D. G., Resnick, H., & Best, C. L. (2002). Psychopathology following interpersonal violence: A comparison of risk factors in older and younger adults. *Journal of Clinical Geropsychology, 8*(1), 13–23.

Ben-Zur, H. (2002). Coping, affect, and aging: The roles of mastery and self-esteem. *Personality and Individual Differences, 32*(2), 357–372.

Blanchard-Fields, F., Sulsky, L., & Robinson-Whelen, S. (1991). Moderating effects of age and context on the relationship between gender, sex role differences, and coping. *Sex Roles, 25*(11), 645–660.

Breslau, N., Davis, G.C., & Andreski, P. (1995). Risk factors for PTSD-related traumatic events: A prospective analysis. *The American Journal of Psychiatry, 152*(4), 529–535.

Emerson, K., Mois, G., Kim, D., & Beer, J. (2023). Gender differences in coping with long-term COVID-19 impacts among older adults. *Journal of Women and Aging, 35*(3), 259–267.

Helgeson, V. S. (2011). Gender, stress, and coping. In S. Folkman (Ed.), *The Oxford handbook of stress, health, and coping* (pp. 63–85). Oxford University Press.

Irie, M., Asami, S., Nagata, S., Miyata, M., & Kasai, H. (2001). Relationships between perceived workload, stress and oxidative DNA damage. *International Archives of Occupational and Environmental Health, 74*(2), 153–157.

Kneavel, M. (2021). Relationship between gender, stress, and quality of social support. *Psychological Reports, 124*(4), 1481–1501.

Lin, J., Epel, E., & Blackburn, E. (2012). Telomeres and lifestyle factors: Roles in cellular aging. *Mutation Research/Fundamental and Molecular Mechanisms of Mutagenesis, 730*(1–2), 85–89.

Marciniak, R., Sheardova, K., Čermáková, P., Hudeček, D., Šumec, R., & Hort, J. (2014). Effect of meditation on cognitive functions in context of aging and neurodegenerative diseases. *Frontiers in Behavioral Neuroscience, 8*, 17.

Preston, D. B. (1995). Marital status, gender roles, stress, and health in the elderly. *Health Care for Women International, 16*(2), 149–165.

Redwine, L., Mills, P. J., Sada, M., Dimsdale, J., Patterson, T., & Grant, I. (2004). Differential immune cell chemotaxis responses to acute psychological stress in Alzheimer caregivers compared to non-caregiver controls. *Psychosomatic Medicine, 66*, 770–775.

UNIT

V

MYTH: OLDER ADULTS FEAR DEATH AND CANNOT COPE WITH LOSS

This unit will discuss the process of loss and grief, how religion can help us cope with death, and making end-of-life decisions. Understandably, death can be anxiety-provoking. Nobody has died and then come back to tell us what happens, and so we all go into it without knowing what's to come. Certainly, if you are faith-driven, you may have an idea based on your religious teachings, but there's no real way to know what's true. Of course, research does support religion as a method for coping (more detail on this ahead) because it provides some comfort and some way of knowing what to expect. However, there are still things that need addressing on the Earth side of the dying process: grief, coping, treatment and care, symptom management, and more.

Death isn't an easy topic to broach, as many people are fearful or avoidant of death and related topics. However, I know that many of my previous students have found solace and relief in learning more about the process and have told me that after learning about it they are no longer afraid. I hope the same for you.

Jacek Boczarski/Anadolu Agency via Getty Images

11 DEATH AND DYING

LEARNING OBJECTIVES

11.1 Explain the process and stages of grief and how bereavement can differ from person to person.

11.2 Discuss how cultural and religious differences support coping from a loss.

11.3 Explain end-of-life care decisions, including palliative care and hospice care, as well as advance directives and physician-assisted suicide.

A few years ago, my husband and I lost a friend to pancreatic cancer. He was an incredibly generous, warm, loving, community-oriented man we became friends with about 15 years ago when my husband joined our local volunteer fire department. As members of the fire department, men and women put their lives on the line to help others every single day and, in turn, develop a tremendous amount of trust in their fellow firefighters. This man was one we trusted with our whole beings. When he passed, my husband asked if we were available and/or had babysitting coverage to attend the funeral, the wake, or the "Code F." While I knew what Code F meant from many years of being a firefighter's wife (it's a fire department honoring of the individual they lost by standing vigil for them), I was unsure of the difference between the wake and the funeral. Weren't they the same thing? The reason I didn't know is because I am Jewish, and so my schema of events that occur after someone dies is different from what happens when that individual is of another religion (in this case, Catholicism). For me, protocol following death is a quick burial service, to take place before the Friday sunset (aka Sabbath), then seven days of mourning with immediate family (Shiva), followed by a full year of remembrance culminating in placement of the headstone and a ceremony for the end of the year of mourning. This is very different from a funeral, a viewing, and a wake. As such, I was introduced to new cultural norms and traditions—all of which were beautiful ways to remember our friend. We miss him dearly but know that he is no longer suffering. This helps bring meaning to his death, but we know that there was tremendous meaning to his life as well. He contributed more than anyone I've ever known to the well-being of others, and I could not be more grateful to have known him.

GRIEF

The process of grief following a loss can be a complicated journey. There are many levels and stages that we go through, and none of them are easy. A traditional view of grief includes the Kübler-Ross (1973) model, which explains **five stages of grief** in order as denial, anger, bargaining, depression, and acceptance (see Figure 11.1). According to this model, an individual moves through these stages in order following the loss. The original conceptualization was that we can move very quickly through the stages (in sequential order) to adjust to, and find some personal protection in, our new reality (either with a diagnosis or to the life we are now living without the loved individual). In the first stage, someone may deny that the death has happened at all. This can present as avoidance, procrastination, forgetting, mindless behaviors, or keeping busy all the time. Then, they may get angry about the loss, and this can play out in all the many ways that people express their anger, such as crying, yelling, snapping at others, engaging in violence,

FIGURE 11.1 ■ Kübler-Ross Model of Grief

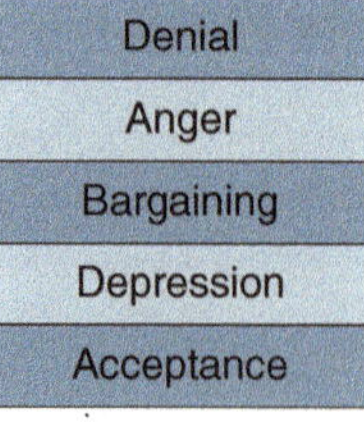

or even increased substance use (Cerney & Buskirk, 1991; and as some would argue, anger is a secondary emotion, which fits here as a second process through which the grieving are going). Following anger, the person may attempt to bargain about things surrounding the death, suggesting "If only I had _____" or ruminating in the past or future. Depression comes next, where feelings of sadness come on strong. Depression can display as changes in sleep and appetite, lowered levels of motivation, crying, hopelessness, and increased substance use. Finally, the individual can accept the loss as permanent, and can continue in their new reality without the person they've lost (or accept their personal fate as in the case of a personal diagnosis). Here, an individual can be present in the moment, using coping skills, tolerating the emotions that come, and existing as they are now, rather than how it was. Importantly, acceptance is not "getting over it," but rather dealing with the loss as the current reality and coping with the loss in appropriate and healthy ways (e.g., Shear, 2012). Acceptance also doesn't mean that sadness or distress isn't still present. Rather, reaching acceptance shows that we understand the emotions, stop fighting against them, and become grounded in the present moment with the current reality. These feelings are hard, and allowing them to be hard makes us vulnerable and keeps us from staying stuck in the past or in the loss.

Obviously, there is a long process and a lot of feelings that come with grief. As more research was conducted on the topic, a slightly different story from one Kübler-Ross told many years ago was revealed (e.g., Hays & Hendrix, 2008; Rosenblatt, 1988; Shear, 2012). Instead, researchers have found that the stages happen differently from person to person, last different amounts of time, can happen in different sequences, and can happen over and over, with the individual bouncing back to and from stages as they move through grief (e.g., Shucter & Zisook, 1993). That is, the process is more complex than originally thought (e.g., Jacobs, 1993), and every individual experiences grief in their own way (Friedman & James, 2008). Grief is not clean, neat, or orderly, and the implications of following such a model are that people may believe that they are expected to process their loss in a certain time in a certain way and may feel they are grieving incorrectly if they fail to do so (Silver & Wortman, 2007)—their social support system may confirm this and provide support that isn't helpful as a result. So, then, how *does* grief happen? And what do we do about it?

More recent research on grief processing has demonstrated an even less linear pattern in grief, and definitely no "end" to the grieving process (e.g., Arizmendi & O'Connor, 2015). That's to say that not only do we not cleanly maneuver our way through the five stages described earlier (Maciejewski et al., 2007), but we also don't just eventually "get over it" or even "reach acceptance." What an outsider may perceive as someone getting past a loss is really just the resolution of the acute grief experience (e.g., Shear, 2012; see also Figure 11.2). There isn't a way to move on, get past it, or get over it. The loss is an event. And, just like any other event in our life that changes us, the loss that leads to grief also changes us. We can't undo it, and we can't get over it. Instead, we process it and hopefully integrate the event into our life story and move forward, functioning with a new context that includes that loss. Our mental representation shifts. To be sure, this takes time and doesn't happen the same way for everyone. We all experience the loss differently, under different circumstances, with different perspectives, so it makes sense that our adjustment to that loss also happens differently.

FIGURE 11.2 ■ Updated Model of Grief

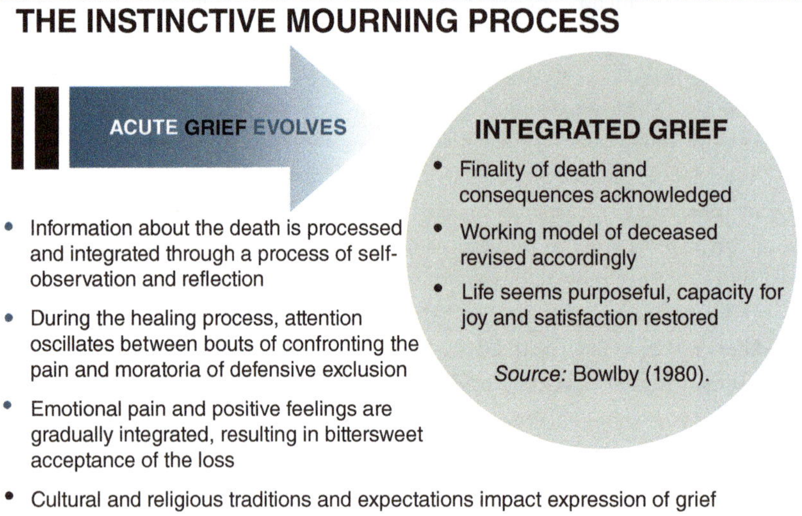

Source: Shear, M. K. (2012). Getting straight about grief. *Depression and Anxiety, 29*(6), 461–464.

Galatzer-Levy and Bonanno (2012) explain that these different patterns of grief can be grouped into four different pathways: resilient, chronic grief, distress-improved, and chronic depression. Individuals experiencing grief via the **resilient pathway** don't outwardly display much sadness, distress, or grief. You could see them as being somewhat "normal" after the loss. While this display may seem detached or maladaptive, researchers have demonstrated that these individuals are often well off mentally and emotionally, and are not detached at all (e.g., Bonanno, 2005). Instead, research both immediately after loss and after up to 18 months post-loss has shown that individuals demonstrating resilience are low on measures of depression (e.g., Bonanno et al., 2002). And, interestingly, this resilient type of grief processing seems to be the most common pathway through grief. To be sure, these individuals aren't always happy, and they do express feelings of sadness surrounding their loss. However, those symptoms don't tend to interfere with their daily living.

Another, less common, pathway through grief is the **chronic grief pathway**. Here, individuals experience much higher levels of sadness and emotional distress postloss and tend to take much longer to process their loss and integrate their new normal into their life story schema. Research shows that reconciliation of the loss and successful settling of their mental representation/schema can take up to four years (e.g., Bonanno, 2005) and is most often experienced in situations where one spouse is highly dependent on the other before the loss (e.g., Bonanno et al., 2002), and therefore many additional life skills, behaviors, and circumstances need adjustment (paying bills, socialization, meal planning, etc.).

Different from these more sadness-based grief scenarios, some individuals experience relief or depression improvement after a loss (e.g., Anderson, 2010; Elison & McGonigle, 2003). For instance, for individuals who showed distress before a loss because of a difficult relationship situation, because the loved one was in tremendous pain (e.g., cancer), or because of the strain surrounding caregiving duties, the loss could be a relief. That's not to say that they aren't sad about losing their loved one, but individuals' relief in these scenarios allows for a **distress-improved pathway** of grief. These individuals are able to find meaning in the loss, solace in the knowledge that their loved one is no longer in pain, or even a release from the round-the-clock need to be there to do everything for another person. Those experiencing chronic depression are similar in their grief pathway here because they are also in distress before the loss. However, rather than relief after the loss, these individuals continue feeling distress, often in the form of depression. And this depression seems to remain ongoing for years after the loss (e.g., Bonanno, 2005), though given the length of time this depression lasts and that it existed before the loss (usually), this pathway of grief may be more intertwined with the individual's mental health struggles than with the loss itself.

These pathways through grief are indicative of the individual differences surrounding grief processing, and the limitations of previous conceptualizations of grief (à la Kübler-Ross). And, as there are different ways in which people process loss, there are different ways to help with this as well. Different methods of grief therapy (e.g., Allumbaugh & Hoyt, 1999), mindfulness (e.g., Huang et al., 2021), and even internet resources (e.g., Dominick et al., 2010) or social and cultural support (e.g., Rosenblatt, 1988) can be helpful in moving through the grieving process. If you've ever heard of someone doing "grief work," they may be referring to grief therapy. Allumbaugh and Hoyt (1999) analyzed data on a large range of different types of grief therapy to determine characteristics of effective treatment for grief. The types of therapy that showed larger efficacy were therapy conducted by trained professionals (as compared to those in training), therapy conducted individually (as compared to in a group setting), and therapy received by middle-aged clients (as compared to those younger or older). Additionally, therapy that was ongoing for longer periods of time resulted in better outcomes than therapy that went for fewer sessions. And, interestingly, they showed that there was no difference for the closeness of the relationship to the departed. That is, those who were closer in relationship would have been at higher risk for negative grief outcomes but didn't benefit any more or less from therapy than those who were at lower risk. All that's to say there are benefits to using therapy as part of the coping strategies to move through grief.

Some of those strategies were examined more specifically in other research (e.g., Dominick et al., 2010; Huang et al., 2021; Neimeyer, 1999). For example, Huang et al. (2021) examined how mindfulness could benefit those experiencing anxiety after the loss of a loved one. Here, they aimed to adjust the neural response that happens when someone experiences loss. That is, an individual's resting state changes globally across their brain, often leading to unintentional mind wandering and increased activity in the frontoparietal cortices. Using mindfulness-based cognitive therapy, Huang et al. trained individuals experiencing grief for emotional regulation over the course of eight weeks. The training was effective in allowing individuals' resting state to adjust and their neural connections to facilitate inhibition of unwanted mind wandering. This is positive in showing that mindfulness practices (which, let's face it, we could all benefit from) are especially beneficial for those experiencing grief.

Mindfulness isn't the only intervention that's shown promise. In our increasingly technological world, it might behoove us to use that technology to our advantage. Dominick et al. (2010)

attempted to do just that. The internet has been able to connect people across the country and the world—and in this instance has allowed for those maneuvering through grief to see that they aren't the only ones, and that the feeling they are experiencing is normal. Dominick et al. launched and tested an online self-help tool that included video modules that showed several individuals describe their experiences in the grieving process, asked users to consider any positive changes that may have occurred since their loss, showed examples of typical symptoms of grief, and offered additional education and referrals. For those who'd lost a parent or another relative in the last six months, the findings were that this programming resulted in positive improvements in emotions, self-efficacy, and reductions in feelings of anxiety surrounding the loss. However, this couldn't be a replacement for other types of social interactions, nor could it replace grief therapy if that also could be beneficial. More than anything, this tool showed users that all humans struggle with settling into a new reality after a loss. This is a natural reaction when you lose someone you love. And it's OK. The social construct of being human allows for us to connect and begin to adjust within our adjusted social network (Rosenblatt, 1988). There are instances, however, when the relationship between an individual and the deceased was complex or the grief reaction is outside of what we'd typically expect as per one of the four pathways of grief described earlier. In these instances, additional exploration for understanding is necessary. It's these examples of complicated grief that will be discussed next.

iStockPhoto/SDI Productions

Complicated Grief

In some instances, the feelings of grief can be so intense, can be so overwhelming, and can last for so long that the individual may feel trapped in them, with no escape. As described in the previous section, it is obvious that people experience grief in different ways. However, Shear et al. (2013) suggest that there is a small percentage of people (just under 10%, though Newson et al. [2011] suggest it's closer to 5%, and yet others report the range is upwards of 30%–40% in clinic populations) who have difficulty integrating the loss into their life schema and ultimately reforming their new reality without that loved one. In this group of people, the acute or immediate experience of grief does not wane or change, and people continue to feel hard loss and cannot engage in their regular life activities. This condition is labeled **complicated grief**, and it is maladaptive and requires treatment to return to baseline and adjust to life again. For individuals with complicated grief, this can be difficult, but once identified, they can be helped. Interestingly, complicated grief symptoms overlap with other mental health conditions such as anxiety and depression. And, while diagnostic criteria have been developed, it is not currently recognized in the *Diagnostic and Statistical Manual of Mental Disorders* (DSM-5-TR; American Psychiatric Association, 2022). Nonetheless, it is a hindrance for those struggling and, as such, requires some attention.

Newson et al. (2011) explored the diagnosis using the 17-item Inventory of Complicated Grief (ICG; Prigerson et al. 1995; see also Table 11.1) after a self-report of grief. Additionally, participants here were assessed on anxiety and depression measures, as per the DSM-IV criteria (American Psychiatric Association, 1994). Analyses showed as many as 20% of individuals who scored high in their measure of complicated grief also met criteria for major depressive disorder and an anxiety disorder (and this makes sense, since some of those symptoms do overlap). Additionally, the risk of complicated grief was significantly higher in the older adults in the sample compared to the younger adults. Other research has identified additional risk factors of complicated grief as losing a partner/spouse and already having a diagnosed mood disorder, like depression (e.g., Bruinsma et al., 2015). When losing the person with whom the individual has shared their whole life, in the context of depression, it makes sense that someone would have an even more difficult time reformulating their schema of how life is supposed to go. It is these losses—of a loved one with whom we have a very close relationship—that can hit the hardest.

Bereavement

Grief can be the result of loss of anyone or anything, such as the loss of a friend, the loss of a coworker, or even the loss of a social role. Some even experience grief when diagnosed with a chronic illness, like rheumatoid arthritis. These individuals are grieving a loss of the life they had before the diagnosis. But grief reaches a different level, and really just hits differently, when the loss is more specific to the loss of a loved one. This type of grief is **bereavement** (Shear, 2012). Bereavement is experienced when we lose the people closest to us—our spouses, partners, and children. And, while loss is loss (and all are difficult), there are differences in how we respond to a death that is expected or unexpected. That is, is the person struggling with an illness that stretches on for years? In this instance, there is some expectation for the impending loss, and the spouse/partner can prepare and even begin the grieving process before the loss. Alternatively, something sudden can feel harder in some ways because it's unexpected, and there's no time to prepare.

TABLE 11.1 ■ Complicated Grief

Question	All grievers		Normal grievers		Complicated grievers		Test for difference
	Mean	(SD)	Mean	(SD)	Mean	(SD)	*F*-value[a]
I feel stunned or dazed over what happened	0.91	(1.21)	0.51	(0.91)	2.06	(1.24)	487.09
I find that life is empty without the person who died	1.74	(1.47)	1.28	(1.29)	3.10	(1.01)	436.67
I have pain in the same area of my body or have some of the same symptoms as the person who died	0.59	(1.16)	0.27	(0.77)	1.56	(1.56)	377.40
I feel anger over this person's death	0.79	(1.23)	0.45	(0.92)	1.82	(1.43)	350.59
I cannot accept the death of this person	1.35	(1.51)	0.92	(1.28)	2.60	(1.46)	328.58
I feel it is unfair I should live when this person has died	1.17	(1.38)	0.76	(1.12)	2.38	(1.37)	305.74
I think about the person so much that it is hard for me to do the things I normally do	0.74	(1.14)	0.44	(0.84)	1.64	(1.39)	293.75

TABLE 11.1 ■ Complicated Grief *(Continued)*

Question	All grievers		Normal grievers		Complicated grievers		Test for difference
	Mean	(SD)	Mean	(SD)	Mean	(SD)	*F*-value[a]
I feel disbelief over what happened	1.27	(1.56)	0.85	(1.33)	2.51	(1.53)	293.07
Memories of the person who died upset me	1.89	(1.26)	1.57	(1.18)	2.82	(1.01)	257.42
I feel myself longing for the person who died	2.75	(1.13)	2.48	(1.12)	3.53	(0.73)	205.35
I feel drawn to places and things associated with the person who died	1.51	(1.42)	1.18	(1.27)	2.47	(1.38)	197.24
Ever since the person died, it is hard for me to trust people	0.25	(0.77)	0.08	(0.41)	0.74	(1.22)	180.94
I hear the voice of the person who died speak to me	0.93	(1.22)	0.67	(1.06)	1.70	(1.34)	166.88
I feel envious of others who have not lost someone	0.45	(0.95)	0.24	(0.68)	1.05	(1.32)	166.59
I feel distant from people I care about	0.22	(0.71)	0.10	(0.47)	0.58	(1.07)	110.93

(Continued)

TABLE 11.1 ■ Complicated Grief *(Continued)*

Question	All grievers		Normal grievers		Complicated grievers		Test for difference
	Mean	(SD)	Mean	(SD)	Mean	(SD)	*F*-value[a]
I go out of the way to avoid reminders of the person who died	0.29	(0.86)	0.17	(0.67)	0.61	(1.22)	57.41
I have felt lonely a great deal of the time since the person died	0.14	(0.56)	0.10	(0.47)	0.24	(0.74)	14.74

Note. Scores ranged from 0 (*never*) to 4 (*always*) and are presented in descending order of significance for test of difference.

a. An age- and sex-adjusted analysis of covariance (ANCOVA) was conducted to detect group differences; all group difference tests were significant at $p < 0.001$.

Source: Newson, R. S., Boelen, P. A., Hek, K., Hofman, A., & Tiemeier, H. (2011). The prevalence and characteristics of complicated grief in older adults. *Journal of Affective Disorders, 132*(1–2), 231–238.

Other factors that can influence the reaction are whether the death is on-time or off-time. That is, is the individual older or younger? Losing a loved one at age 80 is much different than losing them at age 30. We know to begin to expect that death will come when someone is an older adult, so it isn't nearly as surprising as a loss of a younger adult. And, in some ways, the off-time loss feels more tragic, or the bereaved experience more symptoms of the loss (e.g., Kitson, 2000). We hear comments like "they didn't get to live their full life" when there is an off-time loss but hear comments like "at least they lived a good long life" when it is on-time. These comments translate to how one copes with and responds to the loss of their loved one as well and can contribute to how they adjust after the loss and during bereavement. Remember that we adjust and create new schemas of what our life looks like. We don't *move on* or *get over it*. And, if the loss is a spouse or partner, you can imagine how difficult the redefining of that life schema could be. This difficulty impacts the individual on many levels—these losses can impact us physically (e.g., Arizmendi & O'Connor, 2015; Stroebe et al., 2007) as well as emotionally (e.g., Gerra et al., 2003).

Research on bereavement has identified a pattern among widows and widowers, where there is a significant increase in the likelihood of one's passing within the first six months of widowhood (e.g., Moon et al., 2014). Moon et al. (2014) have demonstrated that this increase is larger for men than for women in heterosexual relationships (whether some similar effect holds on same-sex relationships remains to be demonstrated). The reasons for this increase were not shown to be related to anything socioeconomic or behavioral (e.g., Arizmendi & O'Connor, 2015). Rather, the bereaved has entered a severe stress response. And, if you think back to Chapter 10, you should remember the tremendous physiological toll that stress reactions can have on the body. In the context of bereavement, researchers have demonstrated increases in epinephrine and blood pressure, leading to increased risk of stroke (e.g., Buckley et al., 2011). Additional research has shown changes in immune function, with decreases in T- and B-cell response (Bartrop et al., 1977), increases in cortisol levels (Gerra et al., 2003), and decreases in natural immunity (Irwin et al., 1987). This research suggests that the physiological response to the severe stress reaction of bereavement is to reduce the ability to fight off infection and increase the work of the cardiovascular system, possibly to the point of breakdown. This is a recipe for increased mortality risk and makes it clear that although there is considerable emotional impact of bereavement (e.g., increased depressive symptoms and anxiety; Gerra et al., 2003; Irwin et al., 1987), the impact is systemic.

Knowing the extent to which bereavement affects our physical and mental health, what may assist in this specific type of grief? Stroebe et al. (2005) demonstrated that social supports may be beneficial for mental health. Here, researchers examined a group of older adult women who had lost their older adult male spouses, and obtained a variety of measures of psychological well-being, including measures of depression and perceived social support. In this investigation, the authors found an initial increase of depressive symptoms immediately, six months, and one year after a loss. However, those symptoms seemed to dissipate after approximately four years. Interestingly, the role of social support was important for improvements after the loss but did not work to prevent these depressive symptoms. Other research further supports interventions for the bereaved (e.g., Nseir & Larkey, 2013; Yoo & Kang, 2006) and suggests that there may be some merit to mind–body interventions. In this type of intervention, Yoo and Kang (2006) showed that the practice of *Dan-jeon* breathing (a Korean mindfulness breathing technique where an individual takes slow, deep abdominal breaths coupled with stretching exercises), over the course of 10 sessions, decreased measures of depression and increased measures of life satisfaction. My two cents? It doesn't hurt to try. Even if the outcome of these interventions was similar to the outcome without them, why wouldn't you seek the support? If nothing else, you expand relationships, redefine how you interact with others, and create mindfulness practices that can help in other stressful situations you may encounter in the future. For others, seeking support through religion can help as well. This context for coping through loss can be traditional and comforting.

RELIGIOSITY AND COPING

Religion can play a large role in death for many reasons. It can help in preparing for it, finding meaning from it, and coping with it after it happens (e.g., Anderson, 2010). Religion provides context and tradition for these adjustments as well. We won't address all the different specific religions or religious traditions surrounding death here—that's not the focus. However, it's obvious from the story at the beginning of this chapter that, at the very least, religion provides a context for which we can orient ourselves during the loss. This is a human experience that is quite possibly woven into our biology. Neuroscientist V. S. Ramachandran discovered how the temporal lobe and its connection to the amygdala, combined with the wonder and awe people experience in the world each day, can be interpreted as the presence of God (Ramachandran et al., 1998). The neural activity, simply put, lends itself to religion and the belief in something bigger than the world we live in (e.g., Azari et al., 2001; see also Figure 11.3). And, as meaning-seeking beings, we often find that meaning in religion.

To the extent that one's religion (and sometimes their cultural or ethnic identity) is part of how they make sense of their life and their world, their religion will also make sense of a loss (e.g., Cruz-Ortega et al., 2015). Research on religion and grief/bereavement has shown a significant impact of religion helping in accepting and adjusting to the loss (e.g., Hays & Hendrix, 2008). Research also shows how individuals use their relationship with God to help create meaning from their loss (e.g., Kelley & Chan, 2012; Lichtenthal et al., 2011). This research has demonstrated that people often use religion to cope (both positively and negatively) with stressful events (e.g., Pargament et al., 1998). Dealing with death can *absolutely* be classified as one of those. In their study, Pargament et al. (1998) showed that individuals who have a secure relationship with God, often rely on spiritual explanations, and engage in religious forgiveness had positive religious coping and ultimately fewer symptoms of depression and less negative quality of life. Here **positive religious coping** was demonstrated

FIGURE 11.3 ■ Neural Activation of Religious Recitation

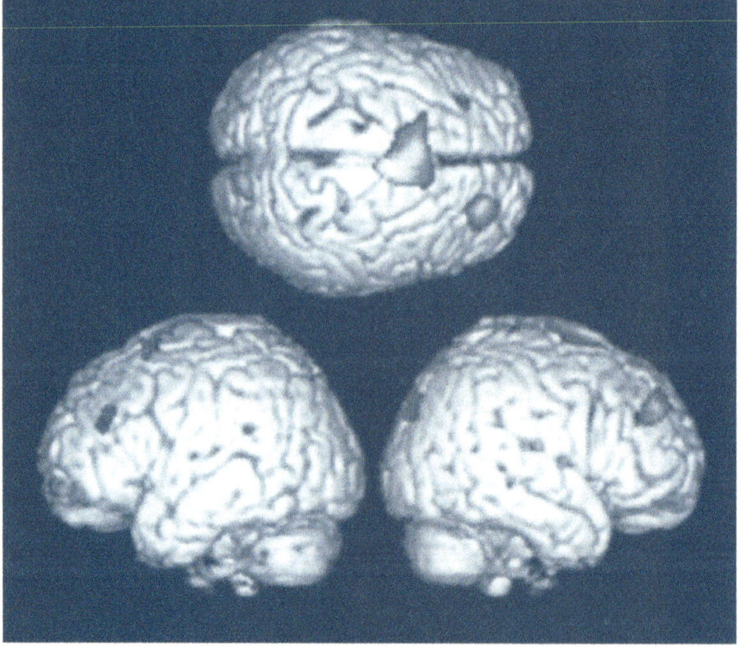

Source: Azari, N. P., Nickel, J., Wunderlich, G., Niedeggen, M., Hefter, H., Tellmann, L., Herzog, H., Stoerig, P., Birnbacher, D., & Seitz, R. J. (2001). Neural correlates of religious experience. *European Journal of Neuroscience, 13*(8), 1649–1652.

through things like asking God to help find purpose in living, looking for support at church, and thinking about how life (and loss) is part of a larger spiritual story. Alternatively, those who showed derailment of spirituality, entertained ideas of discontent with God, and fought against finding meaning through religion showed higher levels of psychological distress and symptoms of depression in the face of severe stress. These individuals questioned the existence of God, expressed anger at God for letting the loss happen, and tried to make sense of the loss on their own without guidance or support from God or their church.

These patterns of observation are not isolated, either. Other research has demonstrated similar impact of religion during bereavement (e.g. Lichtenthal et al., 2011). Here, Lichtenthal et al. (2011) measured meaning-making through the Integration of Stressful Life Experiences Scale (ISLES; Holland et al., 2010), as well as religious coping and symptoms of prolonged grief disorder. Data analysis showed that individuals who used negative religious coping were less able to engage in meaning-making surrounding their loss. That is, they had trouble finding the value in and understanding why the loss occurred—explanations that are often found in religion. Additionally, they showed that people who struggled to find meaning and used negative religious coping were more likely to display prolonged grief disorder symptoms like anxiety and depression postloss. Those who were successful in meaning-making regarding their loved one's death were less likely to demonstrate those symptoms. This is important for the human experience. As *The Lion King* (Allers et al., 1994) showed us, death is involved in the circle of life (I sing as if I think I'm Elton John. I'm definitely not. You don't want to hear me sing. I'm serious). Learning to accept the loss, adapt to the change, and find meaning in it are helpful in finding our way back to center and moving forward with life satisfaction, positivity, and good mental health. Rafiki was quite a wise character in that movie and very clearly told us: "The past can hurt. But you can either run from it or learn from it." To learn from it is to make meaning and create a new schema for your life circumstances. And sometimes, religion can be the facilitator for this lesson.

END-OF-LIFE CARE

In previous generations, death was something that happened in the home, with family and friends, and it wasn't uncommon to have one's dead relative in the front room of the house for a few days while people came by to say goodbye. However, more often in modern times, death happens behind closed doors, away from others, and often in an unfamiliar environment like a hospital. Try as they might (and nurses are utterly fantastic at providing warmth and comfort), it is simply not the same as at home. That's not to say that there is anything wrong with a hospital, but it does contribute to the mystery surrounding death as well as the fear associated with it because it happens away from where we live. Without seeing death happen, we can make up stories in our mind and build it up to be something that it isn't. The reality is that in many cases, death is a relief or a release from pain and suffering. In this section, we'll pull back the curtain on the end of life, discussing how palliative care works and how hospice can assist both the patient and their loved ones in the last stages of death. Additionally, this section will examine physician-assisted suicide or physician-assisted death and how we may have some control over when and how we die.

Palliative Care and Hospice

When death isn't sudden, as in the case of cancer or some other drawn-out sickness, there is often tremendous pain and discomfort. This creates not just physical strain on the individual, but emotional and mental strain as well. To combat the impact of the illness on the individual's well-being, a patient and their care team may turn to a **palliative care** plan. Here, a multidisciplinary team works to enhance the quality of life for the individual, maintain function, and reduce excessive pain and stress (e.g., Buss et al., 2017). This team often consists of nurses and doctors but also social workers, therapists, and members of clergy, all of whom play a role in reducing the negative impacts of illness and increasing the positive experiences of life. It's important to note that palliative care isn't just for the end of life. Many individuals who live with chronic illness or chronic pain (e.g., multiple sclerosis) also benefit from palliative care programs to improve their quality of life and ability to function (e.g., Effiong & Effiong, 2012).

Buss et al. (2017) explain that there are three pillars of palliative care: symptom management, psychospiritual care, and medical decision making. Within these categories, different parts of the care team work to assist the patient and their family. Often, the first point of contact for beginning a palliative care plan is the primary care physician. And for many, this is enough. Other times, they may bring in therapists, social workers, medical specialists, and others, depending on what the patient's needs are. Unfortunately, some research suggests that while almost all primary care physicians agree that discussing palliative care (and subsequent end-of-life planning) is important, they only engage in these conversations approximately 45% of the time (Snyder et al., 2013). Snyder et al. (2013) also reported that 20% of doctors believed that they didn't need to discuss these care plans unless the patient had less than six months to live. As indicated earlier, this is absolutely not true. Anyone with any chronic *or* terminal illness can benefit from at least some aspects of palliative care. Hospice, however, is a different story—but more on that in just a bit.

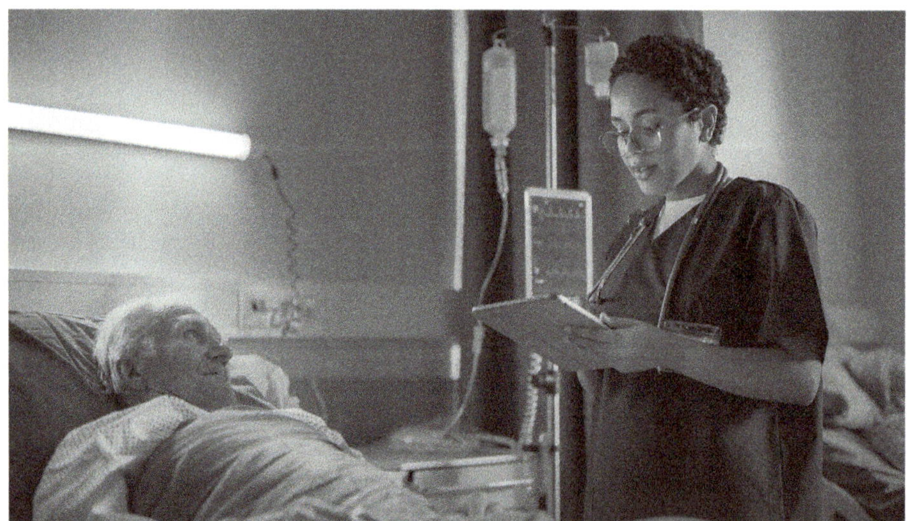

iStockPhoto/gorodenkoff

Palliative care is compassionate care, and research has shown positive impacts on patients' symptoms and pain management, life functioning, medical costs, end-of-life treatment, and overall quality of life (e.g., Meier & Brawley, 2011; Schlick & Bentrem, 2019). And, because the benefits are so great with implementing palliative care, making sure to either offer (if you're a medical provider) or ask for (if you're a patient, family member, or caregiver) it is important. Schlick and Bentrem (2019) suggest that the timing of palliative care is important, and the earlier during the course of disease one can access this care, the better. And this makes sense—illness of any kind is difficult, and the more support we can have as a patient, the better. Other research on palliative care outcomes is consistent with the idea that increased support early on in the disease process leads to better personal ratings of quality of life and even a small effect of lessened symptom intensity over time (e.g., Fliedner et al., 2019; Haun et al., 2017). Psychologically speaking, the confrontation of the illness may be hard, but acknowledging it head-on can be beneficial for ultimately accepting the diagnosis and reformulating one's schema of their life (e.g., Fliedner et al., 2019). Once they accept the reality, a patient can begin to address other issues concerned with the end of life, such as future care planning, advance directives, and wishes for future health care interventions.

Anecdotally, I have watched the benefits of palliative care in a friend with several chronic illnesses, including Crohn's disease, connective tissue disease, and diabetes (among others yet to be diagnosed). For her, palliative care means pain management, physical mobility supports, and therapy to help with the emotional repercussions of these diagnoses. The result for her was not a cure for any of her illnesses, but instead support in managing them and a new view of how to live a purposeful, valuable, positive life with them. She is now able to continue to work in her chosen field (academia), can manage pain levels and blood sugar, and has a schema of herself that reflects who she is, rather than who she can't be. Can these diagnoses be life-threatening? Yes. Are they life-threatening in the near future? Not for her at this time. But, for someone who is looking at the end of life, palliative care can include ***hospice***, a term that may sometimes (incorrectly) be used interchangeably with the term *palliative care*.

Instead of helping with disease management, hospice care specifically functions for a patient at the end of their life only, and only after other disease-altering treatments have ceased (Morris & Christie, 1995), either because they no longer work or because the patient has chosen to no longer seek treatment. Therefore, the primary focus of hospice is comfort—for the patient and for the family. Hospice care is palliative in the sense that it helps the patient feel comfort in a situation that is inherently uncomfortable (or outright painful).

Patients can benefit from hospice care in a variety of contexts, including in their home, in the hospital, in a nursing home, or in a hospice care facility. Providing hospice care means providing care physically, psychologically, socially, and spiritually (e.g., Carlson et al., 2007). In all these instances, though, the focus is improved patient care, without attempts to cure or treat the illness. Rather, the attempt is to treat the person and to make their last stages of life as enjoyable and whole as possible. And the research supports the effectiveness in providing this for patients (e.g., Kleinpell et al., 2019). Kleinpell et al. (2019) examined the relationship between hospice and health care outcomes and health care variables during patients' last six months of life, finding that hospice was positively correlated with patient experience and pain management and negatively correlated with intensive care unit admissions. These relationships suggest that patients felt better on hospice and the supportive care provided by hospice reduced the time and likelihood they'd be admitted to intensive care. That is, the benefits were not just in the patient's perception, but also in the objective, physical manifestation of their illness progression.

Importantly, hospice care isn't just found in the United States, and it isn't just Western cultures whose patients benefit. Cross-cultural research shows that individuals think highly of hospice care both when they use it and when they think about the benefits it provides for others (e.g., Bosma et al., 2010; Yun et al., 2004). The benefits they cite aren't really that different from culture to culture. For example, in their review of 15 studies, Bosma et al. (2010) suggest that most participants report receiving a multifaceted approach to care in hospice, and that their experience was holistic in nature and focused on many components of well-being. And, since the care was provided within a culture, it was adjusted based on the patients' needs—such as differed spiritual guidance for those of different religions. These spiritual practices weren't just for the patient's need to cope with their own illness, pain, or imminent passing; patients' family members benefited from these practices as well. As discussed earlier, using religion to cope with death is often helpful. Bosma et al. described how Catholic patients reported regular visits from their priest as being helpful, and Jewish patients viewed positively the opportunity to bring family together (as would be the practice of a Jewish family upon the death of a loved one). The consensus, cross-culturally, is that hospice care provides a means for individuals to die with dignity and strength and can remove some of the burden from family members as well (e.g., Yun et al., 2004). That is, having health care professionals, counselors, and religious figures assist with the comfort of the ill can allow the family the freedom to spend time with their loved one, make their last bit of time together meaningful, and begin to cope with their loss.

Advance Directives

Anticipating death from a long illness can be scary. There may not be a lot we can control about what is happening, and we need to leave the process up to our body, our medical care team, and the illness itself (and God/Gods/the Universe/etc. for those who are religious). However, there are some things that we can control and make decisions about before they even become an issue—so we are prepared, and so our loved ones are prepared. These types of decisions can be made ahead of time in an **advance directive** (see Table 11.2). In this legal document, you can specify what type of medical care you'd prefer and who you'd like to designate to make those decisions for you in the event that you are not able to make them on your own (i.e., **durable power of attorney** or **medical power of attorney**), as in the case of brain injury, long-term unconsciousness, or similar. You can decide what types of life-saving interventions you would like to or not like to receive, such as feeding tubes, ventilators, or dialysis. In this document, you can be very specific about your wishes for end-of-life care, including how you'd like to be treated for pain and/or how and under what circumstances you'd like your care team to begin palliative care. These wishes are respected and followed when needed (except in the case where the doctor does not think they are medically appropriate—though this is usually not the case, since medical consultation is needed for an advance directive), suggesting their use far outweighs the effort in creating one (Silveira et al., 2010).

TABLE 11.2 ■ Information to Include in an Advance Directive

Medical Power of Attorney	Health care agent Not your doctor/health care provider Trusted advocate
Living Will	Specify which treatments you do or do not want, including ● CPR ● Mechanical ventilation ● Tube feeding ● Dialysis ● Antibioitics/antivirals ● Comfort/palliative care ● Organ/tissue/full body donations ● Do not resuscitate orders ● Do not intubate orders
Physician Orders (legal in some states)	Like a prescription for what life-sustaining treatments your doctor has pre-approved, including ● Resuscitation ● Mechanical ventilation ● Antibiotics/antivirals ● Tube feeding ● Hospital admissions/emergency room visit ● Pain management

Source: Mayo Clinic Staff. (2022, August 2). *Living wills and advance directives for medical decisions.* www.mayoclinic.org/healthy-lifestyle/consumer-health/in-depth/living-wills/art-20046303

Having a terminal diagnosis isn't a prerequisite for creating an advance directive; anyone can (and should) create one. It is estimated that almost three quarters of older adults have prepared one (Teno et al., 2007). However, a survey of American adults shows that those who have created an advance directive are more likely to be older, have a higher income, and have more education (Rao et al., 2014). And, while their younger-aged, nonwhite counterparts are less likely to have created one, it doesn't stop being important in executing the treatment desired by the patient. In fact, it's arguably more important to educate patients about the need for this document, which, according to research, significantly overshadows the durable power of attorney (Ditto et al., 2001). In their study, Ditto et al. (2001) compared the judgments made on care plans from loved ones (who would presumably be the medical proxy in the case of the patient being unable to make decisions about their own care) and found that while the partners were confident that they made the judgment "correctly" in terms of what their spouse/parent would want, they were only accurate 30% of the time. That means that 70% of the time, they would have made a decision to engage in medical intervention that the patient did not want. We can conclude that, even when our partner/durable power of attorney knows us well, they may not always make the same choice we would. Therefore, a more direct way of making sure that our wishes are honored is to have an advance directive.

The advance directive provides some security for the family as well. Knowing that the plans are already made leaves less for the family to handle, and research comparing the stress levels of families whose loved ones have created an advance directive to those whose loved ones haven't created one confirms this claim (e.g., Davis et al., 2005; Tilden et al., 2001). Not only have Davis et al. (2005) demonstrated that stress levels were lower (as measured by the Horowitz et al. [1979] Impact of Event Scale), but other research has shown that presence of an advance directive also allowed the family to focus on the patient and the last moments they had together, and they were less likely to draw out the end of life (to increase both emotional and financial costs to the individual and the family; Tilden et al., 2001). That's not to say that death with an advance directive in place is without stress, under any circumstances. However, we know from Chapter 10 that when we can deem something as irrelevant or not applicable, it can dispel us from feeling the impact of that particular stressor (e.g., Peacock & Wong, 1990). This may be the case (at least to some degree) with an advance directive. If the decisions for medical interventions have already been made, then those stressors are not applicable for the family. This piece is not a stimulus for which they would have a stress reaction, and the family can instead use their energy for the other processes needed at the end of life—coping, grief, saying goodbye, prayer, and so on. Making the decisions early can remove the burden for both the patient and the family and provide some relief in knowing that one step of the process is complete.

Physician-Assisted Suicide and Euthanasia

If you've ever experienced having to put a pet dog or cat to sleep, you've experienced **euthanasia**. This happens when a doctor (in this case a veterinarian) helps end the life of the animal. The reason I bring up pets (because humans are definitely *not* the same) is just that we clearly hold a different standard for pets than we do for our beloved humans. Our rationale for ending the life of our dog is often that we don't want them to suffer anymore. But couldn't we say the same for our grandmother, friend, uncle, or spouse? Wouldn't we want the same mercy and relief for them that we gave to our pet? It's this argument that some countries around the world, and some states within the United States, have used to allow for legalizing **physician-assisted death (PAD)**. While not the same thing as euthanasia, because PAD allows for the doctor to prescribe the life-ending medications but does not allow for the administration of it (the individual needs to do that on their own), this act of mercy is becoming more and more common.

As of the writing of this text, PAD is legal in countries such as Belgium, the Netherlands, Switzerland, and Canada (though this varies by country and location within each country; see https://compassionandchoices.org), as well as locations within the United States such as California, Colorado, Hawaii, Maine, New Jersey, New Mexico, Oregon, Vermont, and Washington (ProCon.org, 2023). The first of these states to establish the legalization of PAD was Oregon, with the Death with Dignity Act in 1997 (see Table 11.3). This established guidelines by which physicians can evaluate a patient's case to see if they are eligible, and of sound

TABLE 11.3 ■ Requirements to Be Eligible for Physician-Assisted Death

1	Two verbal requests, at least 15 days apart
2	Written request to the doctor, signed by two witnesses
3	Two doctors must confirm patient's diagnosis and prognosis (i.e., terminal illness)
4	Doctor must determine that the patient is capable of making health care decisions
5	Referral to psychiatric/psychological evaluation as determined by the doctor
6	Patient must be aware of alternatives, including palliative care, hospice care, and pain management
7	Patient is advised that their family should know of their request for PAD

Source: Oregon Health Authority. (n.d.). *Death with Dignity Act.* https://www.oregon.gov/oha/ph/providerpartnerresources/evaluationresearch/deathwithdignityact/pages/index.aspx

mind, to make the decision to terminate their own life. Importantly, the individual needs to make the decision and carry out the act themselves. Nobody, not even a medical proxy, can make the decision for them. Other guidelines are that the individual needs to be cognitively and emotionally able to make the decision, have been medically diagnosed with a terminal illness with less than six months left to live (as determined by both the prescribing physician and a consulting physician), and be aware of other alternative options like palliative care, hospice, and pain control. Smith et al. (2015) have demonstrated that the individuals who are most likely to ask for and follow through with PAD are those who have higher levels of depression, have higher ratings of self-reliance and independence, and are less spiritually oriented (consistent with the previous discussion on religion as a coping mechanism). Other researchers have added that individuals requesting PAD were largely male in gender, were college educated, were diagnosed with some form of cancer, were experiencing severe pain, had a life expectancy of less than one month, and were cognitively sound (Meier et al., 2003). These characteristics suggest that individuals who wish to end their lives in this way are aware of what they are doing; they know that it will provide relief of their symptoms and will happen in an independent way on their own terms. By using this method to end their life, they are taking matters into their own hands and are able to control the way in which they die.

Of course, there are ethical considerations to the idea of physician-assisted suicide, and many people understand the difficulties in legislating this personal decision. How can one know that they are doing the right thing, and that they aren't crossing the line into unethical territory? Landry et al. (2015) discussed these ethical issues as they pertained to the legalization of PAD in Canada, including the considerations of autonomy, cognitive capacity for making decisions, and access to these life-ending treatments. Specifically, ethical considerations (as well as regulations) should be made so that individuals cannot exert power over others and make decisions where they shouldn't. Cognitive autonomy is extremely important here. The patient and their doctor should know exactly what it means to make this decision. This can provide protection against abuse and misuse and can leave little room for coercion. For instance, the regulations in

Oregon are that an individual must have opinions of two doctors, they must be cognitively able to make the decision, and time between request for and prescription of medication must be less than 15 days. The expeditious nature of PAD here allows for wishes to be granted without time for others to intervene and coerce the patient out of their decision to end their life.

This leaves to question whether some illnesses are on the "ethical side" of allowing for PAD and maybe others aren't. That's to say are physical illnesses the limiting factor, or are psychiatric illnesses also included in relevant, terminal illness? One could argue that desire to end one's life could be a symptom of some psychological illness, and therefore make these individuals incapable of making sound decisions concerning the end of life (Appelbaum, 2017). Alternatively, the argument could be that once all treatments have been exhausted (and deemed ineffective), continuing to suffer from psychological illness would be as painful as suffering from any physical illness. In the 1990s, doctors in the Netherlands were questioned regarding this issue (e.g., Groenewoud et al., 1997), and while most psychiatrists reported that they had received requests for PAD from their patients, the requests are rarely granted. However, in 1997, the Dutch Supreme Court ruled this a justified circumstance. Of course, arguments can be made for both sides of this ethical coin (Kim & Lemmens, 2016; Shaffer et al., 2016). Regardless, our understanding of individuals wishing to take control over the way they die is expanding, as is our compassion for our fellow humans. And that is a beautiful thing.

AGING WELL: END OF LIFE

Aging well in the end stages of life, on the surface, may seem counterintuitive. That is, what's the point in "doing it well" if we're already dying? But that's just it. Making that last bit count. Making that last bit peaceful, meaningful, and as pain-free as possible. Removing the burden from your loved ones and making sure they know you love them. Aging well means knowing that death doesn't have to be scary or painful, and leaning into your faith can be powerful. I think because no human has experienced death and come back to tell the tale of what happens, we all go into it with a bit of the fear of the unknown. We don't know what's to come. But this chapter may help in preparing us on how to handle it—whether it's ours or someone else's. When we have a plan, some of the mystery goes away, and the sense of control we have can make it so the fear does too. Having access to palliative care and hospice care, physician-assisted death, advance directives, and spiritual guidance can help give us some control over the uncontrollable.

KEY TERMS

advance directive
bereavement
chronic grief pathway
complicated grief
distress-improved pathway
durable power of attorney
euthanasia
five stages of grief
hospice
medical power of attorney

palliative care
physician-assisted death (PAD)
positive religious coping
resilient pathway

COMPREHENSION QUESTIONS

1. What are the stages of grief as originally conceptualized? How do we now know these play out through three pathways of grief?
2. Explain strategies for coping through grief.
3. Under what circumstances does grief become complicated or maladaptive?
4. How does death create a negative stress response? What are the implications of this?
5. What role does religion play in our grief?
6. Explain the benefits of palliative care.
7. How is hospice care palliative care but palliative care is not hospice care?
8. What kinds of end-of-life care options are there? What are the strengths and weaknesses of these?
9. How can an advance directive relieve stress and increase patient outcomes?
10. Why would someone choose physician-assisted death? What are the issues to consider when addressing this end to life?

ADDITIONAL READINGS

Corden, A., & Hirst, M. (2013). Economic components of grief. *Death Studies, 37*(8), 725–749.

Eisma, M. C., Tamminga, A., Smid, G. E., & Boelen, P. A. (2021). Acute grief after deaths due to COVID-19, natural causes and unnatural causes: An empirical comparison. *Journal of Affective Disorders, 278*, 54–56.

Ersek, M., Kagawa-Singer, M., Barnes, D., Blackhall, L., & Koenig, B. A. (1998, November). Multicultural considerations in the use of advance directives. *Oncology Nursing Forum*, *25*(10), 1683–1690.

Goveas, J. S., & Shear, M. K. (2021). Grief and the COVID-19 pandemic in older adults. *Focus, 19*(3), 374–378.

Houwen, K. V. D., Stroebe, M., Stroebe, W., Schut, H., Bout, J. V. D., & Meij, L. W. D. (2010). Risk factors for bereavement outcome: A multivariate approach. *Death Studies, 34*(3), 195–220.

Kosminsky, P. S. (2022). This is your brain on grief. *Death Studies, 46*(8), 2031–2033.

Landry, J. T., Foreman, T., & Kekewich, M. (2015). Ethical considerations in the regulation of euthanasia and physician-assisted death in Canada. *Health Policy, 119*(11), 1490–1498.

Martin, K., & Elder, S. (2020). Pathways through grief: A model of the process. In J. Morgan (Ed.), *Personal care in an impersonal world: A multidimensional look at bereavement* (pp. 73–86). Routledge.

O'Connor, M. F. (2019). Grief: A brief history of research on how body, mind, and brain adapt. *Psychosomatic Medicine, 81*(8), 731–738.

Oldham, R. L., Dobscha, S. K., Goy, E. R., & Ganzini, L. (2011). Attachment styles of Oregonians who request physician-assisted death. *Palliative and Supportive Care, 9*(2), 123–128.

Ott, C. H., Lueger, R. J., Kelber, S. T., & Prigerson, H. G. (2007). Spousal bereavement in older adults: Common, resilient, and chronic grief with defining characteristics. *The Journal of Nervous and Mental Disease, 195*(4), 332–341.

Park, C. L., & Halifax, R. G. (2021). Religion and spirituality in adjusting to bereavement: Grief as burden, grief as gift. In R. A. Neimeyer, D. L. Harris, H. R. Winokuer, & G. Thornton (Eds.), *Grief and bereavement in contemporary society* (pp. 355–363). Routledge.

Root, B. L., & Exline, J. J. (2014). The role of continuing bonds in coping with grief: Overview and future directions. *Death Studies, 38*(1), 1–8.

Steinbock, B. (2017). Physician-assisted death and severe, treatment-resistant depression. *Hastings Center Report, 47*(5), 30–42.

Stroebe, M., Schut, H., & Boerner, K. (2017a). Cautioning health-care professionals: Bereaved persons are misguided through the stages of grief. *OMEGA—Journal of Death and Dying, 74*(4), 455–473.

Stroebe, M. S., Schut, H., & Boerner, K. (2017b). Models of coping with bereavement: An updated overview. *Studies in Psychology, 38*(3). https://doi.org/10.1080/02109395.2017.1340055

Zerzan, J., Stearns, S., & Hanson, L. (2000). Access to palliative care and hospice in nursing homes. *JAMA, 284*(19), 2489–2494.

GLOSSARY

accommodation: adjustment of the lens shape to focus the light properly onto the back of the eye

activities of daily living (ADLs): daily functions that address basic needs, including feeding oneself, dressing, bathing, and toileting

acute stress: a short-term stressor–stress reaction situation

advance directive: a legal document specifying the type of medical treatment you would prefer (or not prefer) as well as who you would like to make those decisions for you in the instance where you are unable to decide

age-based double standard: holding different age groups to different expectations, simply because of the age that they are

ageism: discrimination and/or judgment based on age, rather than skill or ability

agreeableness: a personality factor that describes how compliant an individual may be when trusting others, handling confrontation, and expressing modesty

Alzheimer's disease: the most common type of dementia characterized by neuritic plaques and neurofibrillary tangles

anticipatory appraisal: stress reaction happening before the stressor occurs/is encountered

antioxidants: chemical molecules that can interrupt the oxidation process by intercepting the free radicals before they take electrons from healthy cells

apoptosis: programmed cell death

auditory nerve: a bundle of nerves responsible for sending information from the inner ear to the brain

auditory threshold: the quietest sound an individual can detect

automatic processes: mental processing that occurs without conscious effort or attentional resources

baby boomers: a generation of individuals born between 1946 and 1964

Beck Depression Inventory: a common depression assessment showing both validity and reliability in adults over 60

bereavement: a specific type of grief resulting from the loss of the people with whom we have a close relationship, such as spouses, partners, and children

buffer: a memory storage bucket

challenge: stress reaction happening during the stressful event

characteristic adaptations: a second level of personality, which fills in details about individual differences, how individuals are motivated to do different things, and how context plays a role in the display of our dispositional traits

choice reaction time: a measure of response time for making a choice between two different stimuli, usually responding one way to one stimulus and a different way to another stimulus

chronic grief pathway: a pathway through grief where individuals show high levels of sadness and distress and take longer than most to adjust to life after loss

chronic stress: longer and/or repeated encounters to a stressor

cochlea: structure in the inner ear, which contains receptors responsible for transduction

cognitive behavioral therapy: a type of psychotherapy consisting of challenging beliefs and thought patterns, as well as behaviors that result from those thoughts, to rewire patterns of maladaptive thought and behavior

cognitive schema: an internal guide by which we interpret (and subsequently respond to) specific circumstances

cognitive structural approaches: methods for measuring intelligence where the focus is on why or how an individual came up with their response

complex reaction time: a measure of response time after several decisions or choices are made

complicated grief: a maladaptive grief pathway that signals difficulty adjusting to life after loss; symptoms overlap with depression and anxiety

compression of morbidity: the decrease in time spent with illness or disability before the end of life

conscientiousness: a personality factor that shows one's fortitude in work ethic, ambitions, and deliberate pursuit of a goal

cornea: the clear outer coating of the eye, responsible for balancing moisture and focusing light

creativity: developing novel ideas, useful propositions, and unique solutions to problems using originality, fluency, and mental flexibility

cross-sectional study: a research method that compares different age groups to measure age differences

crystallized intelligence: intelligence marked by an accumulation of knowledge

custodial grandparenting: an instance where a grandparent has taken on full custody of their grandchild for full-time care

differential reinforcement: a behavioral technique often used in dementia patients, where desired behaviors are rewarded with attention and engaging interaction and undesired behaviors are extinguished by ignoring the individual

disability: substantial limitation in at least one major life activity

dispositional attributions: concluding that behaviors of an individual are the result of their personality traits and personal characteristics, rather than situational factors

dispositional traits: characteristics about a person that remain consistent in influencing their choices and behavior across time and across contexts

distress-improved pathway: a pathway of grief where individuals experience relief or improved depressive symptoms following a loss

divided attention: splitting attentional resources between two or more tasks or stimuli (i.e., multitasking)

dual task paradigm: an experimental condition in which a participant is asked to complete two tasks at once

durable power of attorney: the individual designated to make medical decisions in the instance you are unable to make those decisions yourself (see also *medical power of attorney*)

elderspeak: condescending, simplified language used with older adults; sounds a bit like baby talk and is characterized by simple sentences, a higher register, and closed-ended questions

emotional intelligence: a type of intelligence focused on emotions, facilitating thought, and understanding and managing emotions

emotion-focused coping: a coping strategy where an individual adjusts their emotions surrounding the stressor, rather than doing something about the stressor itself

episodic memory: memory for an event or episode

euthanasia: the practice of a doctor peacefully ending the life of an animal or human; the human practice of euthanasia is illegal in most countries

explicit memory: memory for information that is purposefully encoded and purposefully retrieved

extraversion: a personality factor characterized by warmth, excitement-seeking, gregariousness, and positive emotions

eye-tracker device: a device that uses infrared lights and computer software to track the time, distance, and location of eye movements during tasks such as reading

facets: underlying concepts of each factor/component of personality

factors: components of personality (e.g., neuroticism, extraversion, openness, agreeableness, and conscientiousness)

filial piety: the expectation to provide care, honor, and respect to one's elders in Chinese tradition

five stages of grief: also known as the Kübler-Ross (1973) model of grief, where an individual moves through denial, anger, bargaining, depression, and acceptance while they process their loss

flavor: the joint experience of smell and taste

fluid intelligence: intelligence using mental flexibility, problem solving, creative thinking, and hypothetical reasoning

free radicals: chemical molecules missing electrons in their outer atomic layer; have ability to bond to any available electron (as could be taken from a healthy cell)

general intelligence: a traditional concept of intelligence, including knowledge and skills associated with that knowledge

generativity: engaging with and providing guidance to the next generation to pass on wisdom and cultural traditions, build relationships, and develop a sense of worth in the generations to come

Geriatric Depression Scale: a common depression assessment showing both validity and reliability in adults over 60

Hayflick limit: the maximum number of times a cell can divide

hospice: a type of palliative care specific to the end of life that allows for comfort during an individual's last days; the focus is improved quality of life without medical interventions to attempt to treat or cure the illness

hysterectomy: surgical removal of some or all of the female reproductive organs

implicit memory: memory that is automatic or not effortfully encoded or retrieved

implicit stereotypes: conclusions applied to a whole group in order to maximize cognitive efficiency; these are applied automatically and without conscious effort

inflammaging: when older adults show higher-than-normal levels of pro-inflammatory cytokines, influencing their immune response and mimicking inflammatory processes

information processing system: a system through which environmental stimuli get attended to, perceived, processed, used, remembered, and stored for later

inhibition deficit hypothesis: older adults are less able to discard unnecessary information from their information processing system

instrumental activities of daily living (IADLs): daily functions that allow for an individual to live independently, such as paying bills or doing laundry

integrative life stories: how we understand a whole individual, combining their culture, class, gender, and other social contexts into our understanding of their personality

interpersonal traits: traits that indicate how an individual will interact with others

intimacy: closeness in relationship, sexual or not

leisure activities: activities done in one's spare time, outside of work and other obligatory responsibilities

lens bruescence: a process in which, as a result of exposure to UV rays, the lens allows for longer wavelengths to pass through, while absorbing shorter wavelengths of light

lens: located directly behind the pupil, serving to finish focusing the light as it enters the eye

longitudinal study: a research method where the same individuals are followed over time to gain insight into age changes

long-term memory: a memory storage buffer used to hold large amounts of information for an indefinitely long period of time

macula: center of visual focus

maladaptive: describing something that interferes with daily functioning and everyday life

meaning-focused coping: a coping strategy where an individual finds meaning in the stressor, where they can learn a lesson or change the way they think about some aspect of their lives

mechanoreceptors: receptors located in the skin, which function to transduce touch, temperature, and pain stimuli to neural signal

medical power of attorney: the individual designated to make medical decisions in the instance you are unable to make those decisions yourself

(see also *durable power of attorney*)

menopause: period of time where individuals assigned female at birth experience changes in hormones shifting them from reproductively fertile to unable to reproduce

midlife correction: a gentler realization and adaptation toward the middle of life (as compared to the midlife crisis), resulting from cognitive growth, where we adjust our goals, schemas, and identity to resolve generativity and ego conflicts

midlife crisis: an abrupt change in course toward the middle of life, when an individual shifts to "out-of-character" behaviors to reassess their identity as they transition toward their older years

Mini-Mental State Examination (MMSE): a primary screening assessment to address cognitive impairment; asks a series of questions about orientation to time and space, short-term memory, following instructions, and spatial representation

moral intelligence: an understanding of how values and universal human truths are put into action

moving window technique: a research protocol used to reveal portions of text to a reader as a "window" (usually) around a point of eye fixation

myelin: the fatty coating of a neuron that helps to support its structure, facilitate the action potential, and provide insulation

negative biases: assumptions made about an individual that are negative in nature (e.g., assumptions about the bad things that happen in old age)

NEO Personality Inventory: a personality inventory that scores an overview of an individual's traits based on responses about statements that the respondent indicates apply (or don't apply) to them

neural plasticity: adjustment and change to neural networks over time

neuritic plaques: the buildup of beta-amyloid proteins in the brain, which inhibit normal neural communication

neurofibrillary tangles: masses of tangled, dying neurons, which do not communicate normally

neuroticism: a personality factor that shows levels of anxiety or tension, impulsivity, self-consciousness, and/or a hostile nature of an individual

nodal network theories: a set of theories describing that information is stored and interconnected as a network within the long-term memory buffer

openness to experience: a personality factor indicating that one remains willing to try new things and understand new ideas

operationalize: to define a construct in measurable terms

osteoarthritis: a common arthritic condition, resulting from overuse/injury and breakdown in the cartilage around a joint

osteoporosis: large loss in bone density, resulting in brittle bones prone to fracture

oxidation: cellular damage resulting from the loss of electrons

palliative care: comfort care that may come before the end of life or at the end of life; the intention is to make the individual as comfortable as possible, reduce excessive pain and/or stress, and increase function and quality of life

Parkinson's disease dementia: a type of dementia that results in progressed Parkinson's disease, characterized by both plaques and tangles and cerebrovascular changes

physician-assisted death (PAD): a doctor prescribes life-ending medication intended for their patient to self-administer to end their own life; different from euthanasia, where the doctor administers the medication

positive biases: assumptions made about an individual that are positive in nature (e.g., assuming that older adults would never abuse alcohol)

positive religious coping: managing adjustment after loss through religious or spiritual explanations, leading to a more positive experience, fewer depressive symptoms, and an easier time redefining one's life schema

postformal thought: thinking with understanding and tolerance in ambiguity, and using these to think about a problem or make a decision within the context in which it's presented

post-traumatic growth: personal growth resulting from stress and trauma, where an individual gains new coping skills, new perspectives, and a new self-perception

post-traumatic stress disorder: a psychological disorder characterized by prolonged, maladaptive stress reactions

presbycusis: loss of hearing for high-frequency sounds

presbyopia: age-related hardening of the lens

primary appraisal: the first assessment of a stressor to determine whether the stressor is applicable to the individual at all

problem-focused coping: a coping strategy where the response to the stressor is to find a way to solve the problem and take action toward the solution

procedural memory: memory for how to execute a task

prospective memory: memory for future intended actions

pruning: reduction in neural connections, eliminating those that are no longer used or necessary

psychometric: a method of measuring intelligence where the focus is on accuracy of answers to the questions, rather than the thought processes behind those answers

pupil: the entry point for light into the eye; dilates or contracts to control the amount of light that enters the eye

quality of life (QoL): ability to live a life full of health, joy, and well-being; prioritizing positive over negative experiences, functioning, and perspective

reliability: consistency across measures of the same construct

renqing: an obligation for a Chinese family to give, rather than receive

resilient pathway: a pathway through grief where an individual does not show much sadness or distress.

retina: the back of the eye, containing receptors called rods and cones

retrospective appraisal: assessment of a stress reaction after the stressor has been experienced

rheumatoid arthritis: an autoimmune, inflammatory arthritis where an inappropriate immune response attacks the joints, resulting in damage to the bone within the joint

rods and cones: receptors located in the back of the eye (i.e., retina) that serve to change light information to neural signal

sarcopenia: loss of skeletal muscle mass and strength

secondary appraisal: an assessment of a stressor to determine what the stressor is and what kind of reaction and/or coping is appropriate

selective attention: filtering incoming information to select what is needed and ignore everything else

selective serotonin reuptake inhibitors: medications that disrupt the reuptake process, allowing for more serotonin to remain in the synapse to be used by the receiving neuron

semantic memory: memory for knowledge and information

sensory memory: an extremely short-term landing zone for raw, unprocessed sensory information; here, information can be attended to for entrance into the information processing system

sequential design: a research method that combines longitudinal design and cross-sectional design to see comparison and change across age ranges

shomrei mitzvot: the role of Jewish individuals to be observers of the commandments

short-term memory: memory storage buffer for information being held for immediate retrieval

simple reaction time: time between the presentation of a stimulus and the response to the stimulus

situational attributions: concluding that behaviors of an individual are driven by events and conditions outside of themselves

social coping: a coping strategy where an individual seeks interactions with others to provide opportunities to express emotions, receive affirmations, and garner comfort or help when appropriate or desired

social judgments: forming an opinion, making a decision, or drawing a conclusion about or in a social/interactive situation

social role: societal expectations of attitudes and behaviors

source memory: memory for where information came from

span of anticipation: a window ahead of what's to come to plan moves or strategies for performance

speed-accuracy trade-off: a slowing of response time purposefully to increase accuracy of response

stereotype threat: internalizing a stereotype so that it influences our own behavior

stress: the mental and physiological response to an external event, which depends on the individual and the individual's interpretation of the event

telomeres: ends of DNA strands, which are required for cell division

temperamental traits: personality traits that describe how an individual will behave in a variety of circumstances and situations

tip-of-the-tongue phenomenon: failure to retrieve and use the word you want when you want

top-down processing: using previous knowledge and experiences to make sense of incoming information and understand the world around us

transduction: transforming an environmental stimulus (light, sound, etc.) to neural signal

tympanic membrane: also called the *ear drum*; vibrates to transmit sound waves into the ear

useful field of view: a measure of how much visual information can be taken in and attended to with a single glance

valid: a measure that is measuring the intended construct

vascular dementia: a type of dementia that develops as the result of a stroke, blood vessel deterioration, or other vascular changes in the brain where blood flow is reduced or hindered

vertigo: a condition where one experiences extreme dizziness and poor balance

vestibular system: a multi-organ system responsible for maintaining balance in the body

working memory: memory storage buffer for information being held for use right now and may include manipulation of this information while holding it in storage

REFERENCES

CHAPTER 1

Affleck, G., Tennen, H., Keefe, F. J., Lefebvre, J. C., Kashikar-Zuck, S., Wright, K., Starr, K., & Caldwell, D. S. (1999). Everyday life with osteoarthritis or rheumatoid arthritis: Independent effects of disease and gender on daily pain, mood, and coping. *PAIN®*, *83*(3), 601–609.

Amarya, S., Singh, K., & Sabharwal, M. (2018). Ageing process and physiological changes. In G. D'Onofrio, A. Greco, & D. Sancario (Eds.), *Gerontology* (pp. 3–24). IntechOpen.

Archer, J. (1996). Sex differences in social behavior: Are the social role and evolutionary explanations compatible? *American Psychologist*, *51*(9), 909–917.

Bachmann, A. G. (1994). The changes before "the change": Strategies for the transition to the menopause. *Postgraduate Medicine*, *95*(4), 113–124.

Bagshaw, D., Wendt, S., Zannettino, L., & Adams, V. (2013). Financial abuse of older people by family members: Views and experiences of older Australians and their family members. *Australian Social Work*, *66*(1), 86–103.

Balasubramanian, A. B., Kawas, C. H., Peltz, C. B., Brookmeyer, R., & Corrada, M. M. (2012). Alzheimer disease pathology and longitudinal cognitive performance in the oldest-old with no dementia. *Neurology*, *79*(9), 915–921.

Baltes, P. B., Smith, J. (2003). New frontiers in the future of aging: From successful aging of the young old to the dilemmas of the fourth age. *Gerontology*, *49*, 123–135.

Bax, M., van Heemst, J., Huizinga, T. W., & Toes, R. E. (2011). Genetics of rheumatoid arthritis: What have we learned?. *Immunogenetics*, *63*(8), 459–466.

Beard, H., & Payne, B. K. (2005). The portrayal of elder abuse in the national media. *American Journal of Criminal Justice*, *29*(2), 269–284.

Beard, J. R., & Bloom, D. E. (2015). Towards a comprehensive public health response to population ageing. *The Lancet*, *385*(9968), 658–661.

Becker, C. B., Diedrichs, P. C., Jankowski, G., & Werchan, C. (2013). I'm not just fat, I'm old: Has the study of body image overlooked "old talk"? *Journal of Eating Disorders*, *1*(1), 1–12.

Beckman, K. B., & Ames, B. N. (1998). The free radical theory of aging matures. *Physiological Reviews*, *78*(2), 547–581.

Bedin, M. G., Droz-Mendelzweig, M., & Chappuis, M. (2013). Caring for elders: The role of registered nurses in nursing homes. *Nursing Inquiry*, *20*(2), 111–120.

Birkhead, T. (2000). *Promiscuity: An evolutionary history of sperm competition*. Harvard University Press.

Brach, J. S., VanSwearingen, J. M., Newman, A. B., & Kriska, A. M. (2002). Identifying early decline of physical function in community-dwelling older women: Performance-based and self-report measures. *Physical Therapy*, *82*(4), 320–328.

Burke, S. N., & Barnes, C. A. (2006). Neural plasticity in the ageing brain. *Nature Reviews Neuroscience*, *7*(1), 30–40.

Burnet, S. F. M. (1974). *Intrinsic mutagenesis: A genetic approach to ageing*. MTP.

Busetto, L., Romanato, G., Zambon, S., Calò, E., Zanoni, S., Corti, M. C., Baggio, G., Enzi, G., Crepaldi, G., & Manzato, E. (2009). The effects of weight changes after middle age on the rate of disability in an elderly population sample. *Journal of the American Geriatrics Society*, *57*(6), 1015–1021.

Carlsen, M. H., Halvorsen, B. L., Holte, K., Bøhn, S. K., Dragland, S., Sampson, L., Willey, C., Senoo, H., Umezono, Y., Sanada, C., Barikmo, I., Berhe, N., Willett, W. C., Phillips, K. M., Jacobs, D. R., Jr., & Blomhoff, R. (2010). The total antioxidant content of more than 3100 foods, beverages, spices, herbs and supplements used worldwide. *Nutrition Journal*, *9*(3), 1-11.

Cawley, J., Maclean, J. C., & Kessler, A. S. (2017). Reporting error in weight and height among older adults: Implications for estimating healthcare costs. *The Journal of the Economics of Ageing*, *9*, 122–144.

Chatterji, S., Byles, J., Cutler, D., Seeman, T., & Verdes, E. (2015). Health, functioning, and disability in older adults—present status and future implications. *The Lancet*, *385*(9967), 563–575.

Colón-Emeric, C. S., Whitson, H. E., Pavon, J., & Hoenig, H. (2013). Functional decline in older adults. *American Family Physician*, *88*(6), 388–394.

Cooney, J. K., Law, R. J., Matschke, V., Lemmey, A. B., Moore, J. P., Ahmad, Y., Jones, J. G., Maddison, P., & Thom, J. M. (2011). Benefits of exercise in rheumatoid arthritis. *Journal of Aging Research*, *2011*: 681640.

Cooper, C. (1995). Occupational activity and the risk of osteoarthritis. *The Journal of Rheumatology Supplements*, *43*, 10–12.

Craik, F. I., & Bialystok, E. (2006). Cognition through the lifespan: Mechanisms of change. *Trends in Cognitive Sciences*, *10*(3), 131–138.

Cutler, R. G., & Rodriguez, H. (2003). *Critical reviews of oxidative stress and aging: Advances in basic science, diagnostics and intervention* (Vol. 2). World Scientific.

Deane, K. D., Demoruelle, M. K., Kelmenson, L. B., Kuhn, K. A., Norris, J. M., & Holers, V. M. (2017). Genetic and environmental risk factors for rheumatoid arthritis. *Best Practice and Research: Clinical Rheumatology*, *31*(1), 3–18.

Di Pietro, L., Dziura, J., & Blair, S. N. (2004). Estimated change in physical activity level (PAL) and prediction of 5-year weight change in men: The Aerobics Center Longitudinal Study. *International Journal of Obesity*, *28*(12), 1541–1547.

Disterhoft, J. F., & Oh, M. M. (2006). Learning, aging and intrinsic neuronal plasticity. *Trends in Neurosciences*, *29*(10), 587–599.

Dunson, D. B., Colombo, B., & Baird, D. D. (2002). Changes with age in the level and duration of fertility in the menstrual cycle. *Human Reproduction*, *17*(5), 1399–1403.

Drewnowski, A., & Evans, W. J. (2001). Nutrition, physical activity, and quality of life in older adults: Summary. *The Journals of Gerontology Series A: Biological Sciences and Medical Sciences*, *56*(Suppl. 2), 89–94.

Edmonds, E. V., Mammen, K., & Miller, D. L. (2005). Rearranging the family? Income support and elderly living arrangements in a low-income country. *Journal of Human Resources*, *40*(1), 186–207.

Edwards, R. R., Bingham, C. O., III, Bathon, J., & Haythornthwaite, J. A. (2006). Catastrophizing and pain in arthritis, fibromyalgia, and other rheumatic diseases. *Arthritis Care and Research: Official Journal of the American College of Rheumatology*, *55*(2), 325–332.

Elsawy, B., & Higgins, K. E. (2011). The geriatric assessment. *American Family Physician*, *83*(1), 48–56.

England, P., & McClintock, E. A. (2009). The gendered double standard of aging in US marriage markets. *Population and Development Review*, *35*(4), 797–816.

Epel, E. S., Blackburn, E. H., Lin, J., Dhabhar, F. S., Adler, N. E., Morrow, J. D., & Cawthon, R. M. (2004). Accelerated telomere shortening in response to life stress. *Proceedings of the National Academy of Sciences*, *101*(49), 17312–17315.

Evans, M., Lewis, E. D., Zakaria, N., Pelipyagina, T., & Guthrie, N. (2021). A randomized, triple-blind, placebo-controlled, parallel study to evaluate the efficacy of a freshwater marine collagen on skin wrinkles and elasticity. *Journal of Cosmetic Dermatology*, *20*, 825–834.

Fali, T., Vallet, H., & Sauce, D. (2018). Impact of stress on aged immune system compartments: Overview from fundamental to clinical data. *Experimental Gerontology*, *105*, 19–26.

Farage, M. A., Miller, K. W., Berardesca, E., & Maibach, H. I. (2010). Psychological and social implications of aging skin: Normal aging and the effects of cutaneous disease. In M. A. Farage, K. W. Miller, & H. I. Maibach (Eds.), *Textbook of aging skin* (pp. 949–957). Springer Berlin Heidelberg.

Fernihough, A., & McGovern, M. E. (2015). Physical stature decline and the health status of the elderly population in England. *Economics and Human Biology*, *16*, 30–44.

Franceschi, C., & Campisi, J. (2014). Chronic inflammation (inflammaging) and its potential contribution to age-associated diseases. *Journals of Gerontology Series A: Biomedical Sciences and Medical Sciences*, *69*(Suppl. 1), S4–S9.

Fransen, M., McConnell, S., Harmer, A. R., Van der Esch, M., Simic, M., & Bennell, K. L. (2015). Exercise for osteoarthritis of the knee: A Cochrane systematic review. *British Journal of Sports Medicine*, *49*(24), 1554–1557.

Fries, J. F. (2003). Measuring and monitoring success in compressing morbidity. *Annals of Internal Medicine*, *139*(5, Part 2), 455–459.

Frost, H. M. (1999). On the estrogen–bone relationship and postmenopausal bone loss: A new model. *Journal of Bone and Mineral Research*, *14*(9), 1473–1477.

Gill, T. M., Allore, H. G., Hardy, S. E., & Guo, Z. (2006). The dynamic nature of mobility disability in older persons. *Journal of the American Geriatrics Society*, *54*(2), 248–254.

Glaser, K. (1997). The living arrangements of elderly people. *Reviews in Clinical Gerontology*, *7*(1), 63–72.

Graham, J. A., & Kligman, A. M. (1985). Physical attractiveness, cosmetic use and self-perception in the elderly. *International Journal of Cosmetic Science*, *7*(2), 85–97.

Gupta, M. A., & Gilchrest, B. A. (2005). Psychosocial aspects of aging skin. *Dermatologic Clinics*, *23*(4), 643–648.

Gupta, M. A., & Gupta, A. K. (2003). Psychological impact of aging and the skin. In J. Y. M. Koo & C. S. Lee (Eds.), *Psychocutaneous medicine* (pp. 381–390). CRC Press.

Halter, J. B., Musi, N., McFarland Horne, F., Crandall, J. P., Goldberg, A., Harkless, L., Hazzard, W. R., Huang, E. S., Kirkman, M. S., Plutzky, J., Schmader, K. E., Zieman, S., & High, K. P. (2014). Diabetes and cardiovascular disease in older adults: Current status and future directions. *Diabetes*, *63*(8), 2578–2589.

Harris, S., Witt, P. J., & Thomas, T. (Executive Producers). (1985–1992). *The golden girls* [TV series]. Witt/Thomas/Harris Productions; Touchstone Television.

Hayflick, L. (1968). Human cells and aging. *Scientific American*, *218*(3), 32–37.

Horiuchi, A. C., Pereira, L. H. C., Kahlow, B. S., Silva, M. B., & Skare, T. L. (2017). Rheumatoid arthritis in elderly and young patients. *Revista Brasileira de Reumatologia*, *57*, 491–494.

Horstman, A. M., Dillon, E. L., Urban, R. J., & Sheffield-Moore, M. (2012). The role of androgens and estrogens on healthy aging and longevity. *Journals of Gerontology Series A: Biomedical Sciences and Medical Sciences*, *67*(11), 1140–1152.

Hutfless, S., Maruthur, N. M., Wilson, R. F., Gudzune, K. A., Brown, R., Lau, B., Fawole, O. A., Chaudhry, Z. W., Anderson, C. A. M., & Segal, J. B. (2013). Strategies to prevent weight gain among adults (Report No.: 13-EHC029-EF). *Comparative Effectiveness Reviews*, *7*. Agency for Healthcare Research and Quality (US).

Johannesen, M., & LoGiudice, D. (2013). Elder abuse: A systematic review of risk factors in community-dwelling elders. *Age and Ageing*, *42*(3), 292–298.

Joosten, M., Vrantsidis, F., & Dow, B. (2017). *Understanding elder abuse: A scoping study.* Melbourne Social Equity Institute, National Ageing Research Institute.

Junqueira, V. B., Barros, S. B., Chan, S. S., Rodrigues, L., Giavarotti, L., Abud, R. L., & Deucher, G. P. (2004). Aging and oxidative stress. *Molecular Aspects of Medicine*, *25*(1–2), 5–16.

Kamo, Y., & Zhou, M. (1994). Living arrangements of elderly Chinese and Japanese in the United States. *Journal of Marriage and the Family*, *56*(3), 544–558.

Kelly, B. O. (2011). Menopause as a social and cultural construction. *XULAneXUS*, *8*(2), 4.

Kimura, S., Steinbach, G. C., Watenpaugh, D. E., & Hargens, A. R. (2001). Lumbar spine disc height and curvature responses to an axial load generated by a compression device compatible with magnetic resonance imaging. *Spine*, *26*(23), 2596–2600.

Kligman, A. M., & Koblenzer, C. (1997). Demographics and psychological implications for the aging population. *Dermatologic Clinics*, *15*(4), 549–553.

Koblenzer, C. (1996). Psychological aspects of ageing and the skin. *Clinical Dermatology*, *14*(2), 171–177.

Kuznik, B. I., Linkova, N. S., & Ivko, O. M. (2022). Oxidative stress, aging, and short peptides. *Neuroscience and Behavioral Physiology*, *52*(1), 183–189.

Lachs, M., & Berman, J. (2011, May). *Under the radar: New York State Elder Abuse Prevalence Study: Self-reported relevance and documented case surveys*. https://ocfs.ny.gov/reports/aps/Under-the-Radar-2011May12.pdf

Lane, N. E., Michel, B., Bjorkengren, A., Oehlert, J., Shi, H. O. N. G., Bloch, D. A., & Fries, J. F. (1993). The risk of osteoarthritis with running and aging: A 5-year longitudinal study. *The Journal of Rheumatology*, *20*(3), 461–468.

Lauzen, M. M., & Dozier, D. M. (2005). Maintaining the double standard: Portrayals of age and gender in popular films. *Sex Roles*, *52*(7), 437–446.

Liguori, I., Russo, G., Curcio, F., Bulli, G., Aran, L., Della-Morte, D., Gargiulo, G., Testa, G., Cacciatore, F., Bonaduce, D., & Abete, P. (2018). Oxidative stress, aging, and diseases. *Clinical Interventions in Aging*, *13*, 757–772.

Lin, J., Epel, E., & Blackburn, E. (2012). Telomeres and lifestyle factors: Roles in cellular aging. *Mutation Research/Fundamental and Molecular Mechanisms of Mutagenesis*, *730*(1–2), 85–89.

Majithia, V., & Geraci, S. A. (2007). Rheumatoid arthritis: Diagnosis and management. *American Journal of Medicine*, *120*, 936–939.

Masunari, N., Fujiwara, S., Kasagi, F., Takahashi, I., Yamada, M., & Nakamura, T. (2012). Height loss starting in middle age predicts increased mortality in the elderly. *Journal of Bone and Mineral Research*, *27*(1), 138–145.

McConatha, J. T., Schnell, F., Volkwein, K., Riley, L., & Leach, E. (2003). Attitudes toward aging: A comparative analysis of young adults from the United States and Germany. *The International Journal of Aging and Human Development*, *57*(3), 203–215.

McCrory, M. A., Suen, V. M., & Roberts, S. B. (2002). Biobehavioral influences on energy intake and adult weight gain. *The Journal of Nutrition*, *132*(12), 3830S–3834S.

Michalaki, M. A., Vagenakis, A. G., Leonardou, A. S., Argentou, M. N., Habeos, I. G., Makri, M. G., Psyrogiannis, A. I., Kalfarentzos, F. E., & Kyriazopoulou, V. E. (2006). Thyroid function in humans with morbid obesity. *Thyroid*, *16*(1), 73–78.

Morano, C., & Berical, E. (2022). *Final report: Elder abuse interventions and Enhanced Multidisciplinary Teams (E-MDTs)*. School of Social Welfare and Center for Human Services Research, State University of New York at Albany.

Mosca, L., Barrett-Connor, E., & Wenger, N. K. (2011). Sex/gender differences in cardiovascular disease prevention: What a difference a decade makes. *Circulation*, *124*(19), 2145–2154. https://doi.org/10.1161/CIRCULATIONAHA.110.968792

Murphy, K., Cooney, A., Shea, E. O., & Casey, D. (2009). Determinants of quality of life for older people living with a disability in the community. *Journal of Advanced Nursing*, *65*(3), 606–615.

Olovnikov, A. M. (1996). Telomeres, telomerase, and aging: Origin of the theory. *Experimental Gerontology*, *31*(4), 443–448.

Pillemer, K., Burnes, D., Riffin, C., & Lachs, M. S. (2016). Elder abuse: Global situation, risk factors, and prevention strategies. *The Gerontologist*, *56*(Suppl. 2), S194–S205.

Plath, D. (2008). Independence in old age: The route to social exclusion? *British Journal of Social Work*, *38*(7), 1353–1369.

Power, M., Bullinger, M., & Harper, A. (1999). The World Health Organization WHOQOL-100: Tests of the universality of quality of life in 15 different cultural groups worldwide. *Health Psychology*, 18, 495–505.

Pradhan, A. D., Manson, J. E., Rossouw, J. E., Siscovick, D. S., Mouton, C. P., Rifai, N., Wallace, R. B., Jackson, R. D., Pettinger, M. B., & Ridker, P. M. (2002). Inflammatory biomarkers, hormone replacement therapy, and incident coronary heart disease: Prospective analysis from the Women's Health Initiative observational study. *JAMA, 288*(8), 980–987.

Quine, S., & Morrell, S. (2007). Fear of loss of independence and nursing home admission in older Australians. *Health and Social Care in the Community, 15*(3), 212–220.

Quiñones, A. R., Markwardt, S., & Botoseneanu, A. (2016). Multimorbidity combinations and disability in older adults. *Journals of Gerontology Series A: Biomedical Sciences and Medical Sciences, 71*(6), 823–830.

Schmeidel, A. N., Daly, J. M., Rosenbaum, M. E., Schmuch, G. A., & Jogerst, G. J. (2012). Health care professionals' perspectives on barriers to elder abuse detection and reporting in primary care settings. *Journal of Elder Abuse and Neglect, 24*(1), 17–36.

Schmiege, S. J., Aiken, L. S., Sander, J. L., & Gerend, M. A. (2007). Osteoporosis prevention among young women: Psychosocial models of calcium consumption and weight-bearing exercise. *Health Psychology, 26*(5), 577–587.

Shanb, A. A., & Youssef, E. F. (2014). The impact of adding weight-bearing exercise versus nonweight bearing programs to the medical treatment of elderly patients with osteoporosis. *Jounral of Family and Community Medicine, 21*(3), 176–181.

Sherwin, S., & Winsby, M. (2011). A relational perspective on autonomy for older adults residing in nursing homes. *Health Expectations, 14*(2), 182–190.

Silverman, S. L. (2005). Quality-of-life issues in osteoporosis. *Current Rheumatology Reports, 7*(1), 39–45.

Solomon, D. H., Avorn, J., Katz, J. N., Finkelstein, J. S., Arnold, M., Polinski, J. M., & Brookhart, M. A. (2005). Compliance with osteoporosis medications. *Archives of Internal Medicine, 165*(20), 2414–2419.

Soshi, T., Andersson, M., Kawagoe, T., Nishiguchi, S., Yamada, M., Otsuka, Y., Nakai, R., Abe, N., Aslah, A., Igasaki, T., & Sekiyama, K. (2021). Prefrontal plasticity after a 3-month exercise intervention in older adults relates to enhanced cognitive performance. *Cerebral Cortex, 31*(10), 4501–4517.

Sözen, T., Özışık, L., & Başaran, N. Ç. (2017). An overview and management of osteoporosis. *European Journal of Rheumatology, 4*(1), 46–56. https://doi.org/10.5152/eurjrheum.2016.048

Stark, S. (2012). Elder abuse: Screening, intervention, and prevention. *Nursing2021, 42*(10), 24–29.

Stewart, A. L., & King, A. C. (1991). Evaluating the efficacy of physical activity for influencing quality of life outcomes in older adults. *Annals of Behavioral Medicine, 13*, 108–116.

Timmerman, K. L., Dhanani, S., Glynn, E. L., Fry, C. S., Drummond, M. J., Jennings, K., Rasmussen, B. B., & Volpi, E. (2012). A moderate acute increase in physical activity enhances nutritive flow and the muscle protein anabolic response to mixed nutrient intake in older adults. *The American Journal of Clinical Nutrition, 95*(6), 1403–1412.

Tomassini, C., Glaser, K., Wolf, D., Broese van Groenou, M., & Grundy, E. (2004). Living arrangements among older people: An overview of trends in Europe and the USA. *Population Trends, 115*, 24–34.

van Thiel, G. J., & van Delden, J. J. (2001). The principle of respect for autonomy in the care of nursing home residents. *Nursing Ethics, 8*(5), 419–431.

von Bernhardi, R., Eugenín-von Bernhardi, L., & Eugenín, J. (2017). What is neural plasticity? *The Plastic Brain, 2017*(1015), 1–15.

Walston, J. D. (2012). Sarcopenia in older adults. *Current Opinion in Rheumatology, 24*(6), 623–627.

Wang, X., & Stocco, D. M. (2005). The decline in testosterone biosynthesis during male aging: A consequence of multiple alterations. *Molecular and Cellular Endocrinology, 238*(1–2), 1–7.

Whitborne, S. K. (2002). *The aging individual: Physical and psychological perspectives*. Springer.

Wilson, D. J., Mitchell, J. M., Kemp, B. J., Adkins, R. H., & Mann, W. (2009). Effects of assistive technology on functional decline in people aging with a disability. *Assistive Technology, 21*(4), 208–217.

World Health Organization. (2015). *World report on ageing and health*. World Health Organization.

Zilio, B. (2022, June 1). Kim Kardashian says she'd "eat poop" daily if it made her look younger. *Page Six*. https://pagesix.com/2022/06/01/kim-kardashian-would-eat-poop-if-it-made-her-look-younger/

CHAPTER 2

Adams, C., Smith, M. C., Pasupathi, M., & Vitolo, L. (2002). Social context effects on story recall in older and younger women: Does the listener make a difference? *Journal of Gerontology: Psychological Sciences, 57B*, P28–P40.

Barker, F., Mackenzie, E., Elliott, L., Jones, S., & de Lusignan, S. (2016). Interventions to improve hearing aid use in adult auditory rehabilitation. *Cochrane Database of Systematic Reviews, 2016*(8), CD010342.

Barrenetxea, J., Yang, Y., Pan, A., Feng, Q., & Koh, W. P. (2022). Social disconnection and living arrangements among older adults: The Singapore Chinese Health Study. *Gerontology, 68*(3), 330–338.

Bitsios, P., Prettyman, R., & Szabadi, E. (1996). Changes in autonomic function with age: A study of pupillary kinetics in healthy young and old people. *Age Ageing, 25*, 432–438.

Blatteis, C. M. (2012). Age-dependent changes in temperature regulation–a mini review. *Gerontology, 58*(4), 289–295.

Borda, M. G., Reyes-Ortiz, C. A., Heredia, R. A., Castellanos-Perilla, N., Copete, A. M. A., Soennesyn, H., Cano-Gutierrez, C. A., & Perez-Zepeda, M. U. (2019). Association between self-reported hearing impairment, use of hearing aid and performance of instrumental activities of daily living. *Archives of Gerontology and Geriatrics, 83*, 101–105.

Burmedi, D., Becker, S., Heyl, V., Wahl, H. W., & Himmelsbach, I. (2002). Emotional and social consequences of age-related low vision. *Visual Impairment Research, 4*(1), 47–71.

Calleja-Agius, J., Muscat-Baron, Y., & Brincat, M. P. (2007). Skin ageing. *Menopause International, 13*(2), 60–64.

Ciorba, A., Bianchini, C., Pelucchi, S., & Pastore, A. (2012). The impact of hearing loss on the quality of life of elderly adults. *Clinical Interventions in Aging*, 159–163.

Cornwell, E. Y., & Waite, L. J. (2009). Social disconnectedness, perceived isolation, and health among older adults. *Journal of Health and Social Behavior, 50*(1), 31–48.

Cruickshanks, K. J., Nondahl, D. M., & Tweed, T. S. (2010). Education, occupation, noise exposure history and the 10-yr cumulative incidence of hearing impairment in older adults. *Hearing Research, 264*(1–2), 3–9.

Daneault, V., Vandewalle, G., Hébert, M., Teikari, P., Mure, L. S., Doyon, J., Gronfier, C., Cooper, H. M., Dumont, M., & Carrier, J. (2012). Does pupil constriction under blue and green monochromatic light exposure change with age? *Journal of Biological Rhythms, 27*(3), 257–264.

David, D., & Werner, P. (2016). Stigma regarding hearing loss and hearing aids: A scoping review. *Stigma and Health, 1*(2), 59–71.

Dintica, C. S., Marseglia, A., Rizzuto, D., Wang, R., Seubert, J., Arfanakis, K., Bennett, D. A., & Xu, W. (2019). Impaired olfaction is associated with cognitive decline and neurodegeneration in the brain. *Neurology, 92*(7), e700–e709. https://doi-org.brockport.idm.oclc.org/10.1212/WNL.0000000000006919

Doty, R. L. (2018). Age-related deficits in taste and smell. *Otolaryngologic Clinics of North America, 51*(4), 815–825.

Dubno, J. R. (2013). Benefits of auditory training for aided listening by older adults. *American Journal of Audiology, 22*(2), 335–338.

Eckert, M. A., Vaden, K. I., Jr., & Dubno, J. R. (2019). Age-related hearing loss associations with changes in brain morphology. *Trends in Hearing, 23*, 2331216519857267.

Elsawy, B., & Higgins, K. E. (2011). The geriatric assessment. *American Family Physician, 83*(1), 48–56.

Farage, M. A., Miller, K. W., Elsner, P., & Maibach, H. I. (2008). Intrinsic and extrinsic factors in skin ageing: A review. *International Journal of Cosmetic Science, 30*(2), 87–95.

Farage, M. A., Miller, K. W., Elsner, P., & Maibach, H. I. (2013). Characteristics of the aging skin. *Advances in Wound Care, 2*(1), 5–10.

Farrell, A. K., Stanton, S. C., & Marshall, E. M. (2022). Social network structure and combating social disconnection: Implications for physical health. *Current Opinion in Psychology*, 101313.

Fransen, M., McConnell, S., Harmer, A. R., Van der Esch, M., Simic, M., & Bennell, K. L. (2015). Exercise for osteoarthritis of the knee: A Cochrane systematic review. *British Journal of Sports Medicine*, 49(24), 1554–1557.

Freund, P. R., Watson, J., Gilmour, G. S., Gaillard, F., & Sauve, Y. (2011). Differential changes in retina function with normal aging in humans. *Doc Ophthalmology*, *122*, 177–190.

García-Piqueras, J., García-Mesa, Y., Cárcaba, L., Feito, J., Torres-Parejo, I., Martín-Biedma, B., Cobo, J., García-Suárez, O., & Vega, J. A. (2019). Ageing of the somatosensory system at the periphery: Age-related changes in cutaneous mechanoreceptors. *Journal of Anatomy*, *234*(6), 839–852.

Gates, G. A., Feeney, M. P., & Mills, D. (2008). Cross-sectional age-changes of hearing in the elderly. *Ear and Hearing*, *29*(6), 865–874.

Gates, G. A., & Mills, J. H. (2005). Presbycusis. *The Lancet*, *366*, 1111–1120.

Gibson, J. J. (1962). Observations on active touch. *Psychological Review*, *69*, 477–491.

Glennon, E., Svirsky, M. A., & Froemke, R. C. (2020). Auditory cortical plasticity in cochlear implant users. *Current Opinion in Neurobiology*, *60*, 108–114.

Goertz, A. D., Stewart, W. C., Burns, W. R., Stewart, J. A., & Nelson, L. A. (2014). Review of the impact of presbyopia on quality of life in the developing and developed world. *Acta Ophthalmologica*, *92*(6), 497–500.

Goette, W., Schmitt, A., & Clark, A. (2019). Relationship between smell identification testing and the neuropsychological assessment of dementia in community-dwelling adults. *Applied Neuropsychology: Adult*, *26*(3), 201–214. https://doi-org.brockport.idm.oclc.org/10.1080/23279095.2017.1392303

Golub, J. S. (2017). Brain changes associated with age-related hearing loss. *Current Opinion in Otolaryngology and Head and Neck Surgery*, *25*(5), 347–352.

Gottlieb, B. H., & Gillespie, A. A. (2008). Volunteerism, health, and civic engagement among older adults. *Canadian Journal on Aging/La Revue Canadienne du Vieillissement*, *27*(4), 399–406.

Gross, C. R., Lindquist, R. D., Woolley, A. C., Granieri, R., Allard, K., & Webster, B. (1992). Clinical indicators of dehydration severity in elderly patients. *The Journal of Emergency Medicine*, *10*(3), 267–274.

Gruber, N., Mosimann, U. P., Müri, R. M., & Nef, T. (2013). Vision and night driving abilities of elderly drivers. *Traffic Injury Prevention*, *14*(5), 477–485.

Hall, C. D., & Meldrum, D. (2016). The aging vestibular system: Implications for rehabilitation. In G. P. Jacobson & N. T. Shepard (Eds.), *Balance function assessment and management* (pp. 793–808). Plural Publishing.

Hanratty, B., Lawlor, D. A. (2000). Effective management of the elderly hearing impaired: A review. *Journal of Public Health Medicine*, *22*, 512–517.

Hao, J., Bonnet, C., Amsalem, M., Ruel, J., & Delmas, P. (2015). Transduction and encoding sensory information by skin mechanoreceptors. *Pflügers Archiv–European Journal of Physiology*, *467*, 109–119.

Hayashi, K., Hayashi, H., & Hayashi, F. (1995). Topographic analysis of the changes in corneal shape due to aging. *Cornea*, *14*(5), 527–532.

Hear.com. (n.d.). *Hearing aid technology*. https://www.hear.com/hearing-aids/technology/

Heller, M. A., & Myers, D. S. (1983). Active and passive tactual recognition of form. *Journal of General Psychology*, *108*, 225–229.

Herdman, S. J., Blatt, P., Schubert, M., & Tusa, R. (2000). Falls in patients with vestibular deficits. *American Journal of Otology*, *21*, 847–851.

Hiel, A. L., Gerard, J. M., Decat, M., & Deggouj, N. (2016). Is age a limiting factor for adaptation to cochlear implant? *European Archives of Oto-Rhino-Laryngology*, *273*, 2495–2502.

Holt-Lunstad, J. (2017). The potential public health relevance of social isolation and loneliness: Prevalence, epidemiology, and risk factors. *Public Policy and Aging Report*, *27*(4), 127–130.

Icahn School of Medicine at Mount Sinai. (2024). *Tonometry*. https://www.mountsinai

.org/health-library/tests/tonometry#

Jones, A. Y., Dean, E., & Scudds, R. J. (2005). Effectiveness of a community-based Tai Chi program and implications for public health initiatives. *Archives of Physical Medicine and Rehabilitation, 86*(4), 619–625.

Joo, Y., Cruickshanks, K. J., Klein, B. E., Klein, R., Hong, O., & Wallhagen, M. I. (2020). The contribution of ototoxic medications to hearing loss among older adults. *The Journals of Gerontology: Series A, 75*(3), 561–566.

Keller, B. K., Morton, J. L., Thomas, V. S., & Potter, J. F. (1999). The effect of visual and hearing impairments on functional status. *Journal of the American Geriatrics Society, 47*(11), 1319–1325.

Kemper, S. (1994). Elderspeak: Speech accommodations to older adults. *Aging and Cognition, 1*(1), 17–28.

Kenney, W. L., & Munce, T. A. (2003). Invited review: Aging and human temperature regulation. *Journal of Applied Physiology, 95*(6), 2598–2603.

Kessel, L., Lundeman, J. H., Herbst, K., Andersen, T. V., & Larsen, M. (2010) Age-related changes in the transmission properties of the human lens and their relevance to circadian entrainment. *Journal of Cataract Refractive Surgery, 36*, 308–312.

Komagata, S., & Newton, R. (2003). The effectiveness of Tai Chi on improving balance in older adults: An evidence-based review. *Journal of Geriatric Physical Therapy, 26*(2), 9–16.

Krause, N. (1986). Social support, stress, and well-being among older adults. *Journal of Gerontology, 41*(4), 512–519.

Kreisl, W. C., Jin, P., Lee, S., Dayan, E. R., Vallabhajosula, S., Pelton, G., Luchsinger, J. A., Pradhaban, G., & Devanand, D. P. (2018). Odor identification ability predicts PET amyloid status and memory decline in older adults. *Journal of Alzheimer's Disease, 62*(4), 1759–1766. https://doi-org.brockport.idm.oclc.org/10.3233/JAD-170960

Kuo, C. L., Shiao, A. S., Wang, S. J., Chang, W. P., & Lin, Y. Y. (2016). Risk of sudden sensorineural hearing loss in stroke patients: A 5-year nationwide investigation of 44,460 patients. *Medicine, 95*(36), e4841. https://www.doi.org/10.1097/MD.0000000000004841

Lavizzo-Mourey, R. J. (1987). Dehydration in the elderly: A short review. *Journal of the National Medical Association, 79*(10), 1033–1038.

Legge, G. E., Granquist, C., Lubet, A., Gage, R., & Xiong, Y. (2019). Preserved tactile acuity in older pianists. *Attention, Perception, & Psychophysics, 81*, 2619–2625.

Leung, D. P., Chan, C. K., Tsang, H. W., Tsang, W. W., & Jones, A. Y. (2011). Tai chi as an intervention to improve balance and reduce falls in older adults: A systematic and meta-analytical review. *Alternative Therapies in Health and Medicine, 17*(1), 40–48.

Lin, F. R., Chien, W. W., Li, L., Niparko, J. K., & Francis, H. W. (2012). Cochlear implantation in older adults. *Medicine, 91*(5), 229–241.

Lin, F. R., Niparko, J. K., & Ferrucci. L. (2011). Hearing loss prevalence in the United States. *Archives of Internal Medicine, 171*, 1851–1853.

Lin, M. R., Hwang, H. F., Wang, Y. W., Chang, S. H., & Wolf, S. F. (2006). Community-based tai chi and its effect on injurious falls, balance, gait, and fear of falling in older people. *Physical Therapy, 86*(9), 1189–1201. https://doi.org/10.2522/ptj.20040408

Lindell, E., Kollén, L., Johansson, M., Karlsson, T., Rydén, L., Falk Erhag, H., Wetterberg, H., Zettergren, A., Skoog, I., & Finizia, C. (2021). Benign paroxysmal positional vertigo, dizziness, and health-related quality of life among older adults in a population-based setting. *European Archives of Otorhinolaryngology, 278*, 1637–1644. https://doi.org/10.1007/s00405-020-06357-1

Lindsey, D. T., & Brown, A. M. (2002). Color naming and the phototoxic effects of sunlight on the eye. *Psychological Science, 13*(6), 506–512. https://doi10.1111/1467-9280.00489

Lombardo, M., Pucci, G., Barberi, R., & Lombardo, G. (2015). Interaction of ultraviolet light with the cornea: Clinical implications for corneal crosslinking. *Journal of Cataract and Refractive Surgery, 41*(2), 446–459.

Lord, S. R. (2006). Visual risk factors for falls in older people. *Age and Ageing, 35*(Suppl. 2), ii42–ii45.

Maciaszek, J., & Osiński, W. (2010). The effects of Tai Chi on body balance in elderly people—a review of studies from the early 21st century. *The American Journal of Chinese Medicine*, *38*(02), 219–229.

Maharani, A., Pendleton, N., & Leroi, I. (2019). Hearing impairment, loneliness, social isolation, and cognitive function: Longitudinal analysis using English longitudinal study on ageing. *American Journal of Geriatric Psychiatry*, *27*(12), 1348–1356.

McMurdo, M. E., & Gaskell, A. (1991). Dark adaptation and falls in the elderly. *Gerontology*, *37*(4), 221–224.

Mercer, R. N., Milliken, C. M., Waring, G. O., IV, & Rocha, K. M. (2021). Future trends in presbyopia correction. *Journal of Refractive Surgery*, *37*(S1), S28–S34.

Mick, P., Kawachi, I., & Lin, F. R. (2014). The association between hearing loss and social isolation in older adults. *Otolaryngology–Head and Neck Surgery*, *150*(3), 378–384.

Mick, P., & Pichora-Fuller, M. K. (2016). Is hearing loss associated with poorer health in older adults who might benefit from hearing screening? *Ear and Hearing*, *37*(3), e194–e201.

Moser, S., Luxenberger, W., & Freidl, W. (2017). The influence of social support and coping on quality of life among elderly with age-related hearing loss. *American Journal of Audiology*, *26*(2), 170–179.

Mosnier, I., Bebear, J., Marx, M., Fraysse, B., Truy, E., Lina-Granade, G., Mondain, M., Sterkers-Artières, F., Bordure, P., Robier, A., Godey, B., Meyer, B., Frachet, B., Poncet-Wallet, C., Bouccara, D., & Sterkers, O. (2015). Improvement of cognitive function after cochlear implantation in elderly patients. *JAMA Otolaryngology–Head and Neck Surgery*, *141*(5), 442–450. https://www.doi.org/10.1001/jamaoto.2015.129

National Institutes of Health, National Eye Institute. (2010a). *Age-related macular degeneration (AMD) tables*. https://www.nei.nih.gov/learn-about-eye-health/outreach-campaigns-and-resources/eye-health-data-and-statistics/age-related-macular-degeneration-amd-data-and-statistics/age-related-macular-degeneration-amd-tables

National Institutes of Health, National Eye Institute. (2010b). *Glaucoma data and statistics*. https://www.nei.nih.gov/learn-about-eye-health/outreach-campaigns-and-resources/eye-health-data-and-statistics/glaucoma-data-and-statistics

Norman, J. F., Kappers, A. M. L., Cheeseman, J. R., Ronning, C., Thomason, K. E., Baxter, M. W., Calloway, A. B., & Lamirande, D. N. (2013). Aging and curvature discrimination from static and dynamic touch. *PLoS ONE*, *8*(7), e68577.

Oleszkiewicz, A., Abriat, A., Doelz, G., Azema, E., & Hummel, T. (2021). Beyond olfaction: Beneficial effects of olfactory training extend to aging-related cognitive decline. *Behavioral Neuroscience*, *135*(6), 732–740. https://doi.org/10.1037/bne0000478

Park, S.-J., Lee, J.-E., Lee, K.-S., & Kim, J.-S. (2018). Comparison of odor identification among amnestic and non-amnestic mild cognitive impairment, subjective cognitive decline, and early Alzheimer's dementia. *Neurological Sciences*, *39*(3), 557–564. https://www.doi.org/10.1007/s10072-018-3261-1

Patel, I., & West, S. K. (2007). Presbyopia: Prevalence, impact, and interventions. *Community Eye Health*, *20*(63), 40–41.

Peelle, J. E., Troiani, V., Grossman, M., & Wingfield A. (2011). Hearing loss in older adults affects neural systems supporting speech comprehension. *Journal of Neuroscience*, 31(35), 12638–12643.

Peters, R. M., McKeown, M. D., Carpenter, M. G., & Inglis, J. T. (2016). Losing touch: Age-related changes in plantar skin sensitivity, lower limb cutaneous reflex strength, and postural stability. *Journal of Neurophysiology*, *116*, 1848–1858.

Pokorny, J., Smith, V. C., & Lutze, M. (1987). Aging of the human lens. *Applied Optics*, *26*(8), 1437–1440. https://www.doi.org/10.1364/AO.26.001437

Purdy, J. (2001, March 12). Hearing loss associated with aging. *Audiology Online*. https://www.audiologyonline.com/articles/hearing-loss-associated-with-aging-1259

Saito, H., Nishiwaki, Y., Michikawa, T., Kikuchi, Y., Mizutari, K., Takebayashi, T., & Ogawa, K. (2010). Hearing handicap predicts the development of depressive symptoms after 3 years in older community-dwelling

Japanese. *Journal of the American Geriatrics Society, 58*(1), 93–97.

Salvi, S. M., Akhtar, S., & Currie, Z. (2006). Ageing changes in the eye. *Postgraduate Medical Journal, 82*, 581–587.

Schwartz, B. L., & Krantz, J. H. (2023). *Sensation and perception.* SAGE.

Shaffer, S. W., & Harrison, A. L. (2007). Aging of the somatosensory system: A translational perspective. *Physical Therapy, 87*, 193–207.

Shukla, A., Harper, M., Pedersen, E., Goman, A., Suen, J. J., Price, C., Applebaum, J., Hoyer, M., Lin, F. R., & Reed, N. S. (2020). Hearing loss, loneliness, and social isolation: A systematic review. *Otolaryngology–Head and Neck Surgery, 162*(5), 622–633.

Silsupadol, P., Siu, K. C., Shumway-Cook, A., & Woollacott, M. H. (2006). Training of balance under single-and dual-task conditions in older adults with balance impairment. *Physical Therapy, 86*(2), 269–281.

Smith, S. K., & House, M. (2006). Snowbirds, sunbirds, and stayers: Seasonal migration of elderly adults in Florida. *The Journals of Genrontology: Series B, 61*(5), S232–S239. https://doi.org/10.1093/geronb/61.5.S232

Solé-Auró, A., & Crimmins, E. M. (2013). The oldest old: Health in Europe and the United States. In J.-M. Robine, C. Jagger, & E. Crimmins (Eds.), *Annual review of gerontology and geriatrics: Healthy longevity, a global approach* (Vol. 33, chap. 1). Springer.

Sponsel, W. E., Paris, G., Trigo, Y., & Pena, M. (2002). Comparative effects of latanoprost (Xalatan) and unoprostone (Rescula) in patients with open-angle glaucoma and suspected glaucoma. *American Journal of Ophthalmology, 134*(4), 552–559.

Stamps, J. J., Bartoshuk, L. M., & Heilman, K. M. (2013). A brief olfactory test for Alzheimer's disease. *Journal of the Neurological Sciences, 333(1–2)*, 19–24. https://doi.org/10.1016/j.jns.2013.06.033

Steinman, B. A., Pynoos, J., & Nguyen, A. Q. (2009). Fall risk in older adults: Roles of self-rated vision, home modifications, and limb function. *Journal of Aging and Health, 21*(5), 655–676.

Stuen, C., & Faye, E. E. (2003). Vision loss: Normal and not normal changes among older adults. *Generations, 27*(1), 8–14.

Sturr, J. F., Zhang, L., Taub, H. A., Hannon, D. J., & Jackowski, M. M. (1997). Psychophysical evidence for losses in rod sensitivity in the aging visual system. *Vision Research, 37*, 475–481.

Swan, G. E., & Carmelli, D. (2002). Impaired olfaction predicts cognitive decline in nondemented older adults. *Neuroepidemiology, 21*(2), 58–67. https://doi-org.brockport.idm.oclc.org/10.1159/000048618

Tambs, K. (2004). Moderate effects of hearing loss on mental health and subjective well-being: Results from the Nord-Trondelag hearing loss study. *Psychosomatic Medicine, 66*, 776–82.

Taylor, D., Hale, L., Schluter, P., Waters, D. L., Binns, E. E., McCracken, H., McPherson, K., & Wolf, S. L. (2012). Effectiveness of tai chi as a community-based falls prevention intervention: A randomized controlled trial. *Journal of the American Geriatrics Society, 60*(5), 841–848.

Tu, R., Wang, S., He, H., Ding, J., Zeng, Q., Guo, L., Li, Y., Xu, T., & Lu, G. (2022). Association between subjective cognitive complaints, balance impairment and disability among middle-aged and older adults: Evidence from a population-based cohort study. *Geriatrics and Gerontology International, 22*(12), 1025–1031.

Tuorila, H., Niskanen, T., & Maunuksela, E. (2001). Perception and pleasantness of a food with varying odor and flavor among the elderly and young. *Journal of Nutrition, Health and Aging, 5*(4), 266–268.

University of Michigan Kellogg Eye Center. (n.d.). *Cataract.* https://www.umkelloggeye.org/conditions-treatments/cataract

Vallbo, A. B., & Johansson, R. S. (1984). Properties of cutaneous mechanoreceptors in the human hand related to touch sensation. *Human Neurobiology, 3*(1), 3–14.

van Kuijk, F. J. (1991). Effects of ultraviolet light on the eye: Role of protective glasses. *Environmental Health Perspectives, 96*, 177–184.

Von Faber, M., Bootsma-van der Wiel, A., van Exel, E., Gussekloo, J., Lagaay, A. M., van Dongen, E., Knook, D. L., van der Geest, S., &

Westendorp, R. G. (2001). Successful aging in the oldest old: Who can be characterized as successfully aged? *Archives of Internal Medicine*, *161*(22), 2694–2700.

Walden, T. C., & Walden, B. E. (2004). Predicting success with hearing aids in everyday living. *Journal of the American Academy of Audiology*, *15*(05), 342–352.

Wallhagen, M. I. (2010). The stigma of hearing loss. *Gerontologist*, *50*, 66–75.

Walling, A., & Dickson, G. (2012). Hearing loss in older adults. *American Family Physician*, *85*(12), 1150–1156.

Walsh, N. P., Fortes, M. B., Raymond-Barker, P., Bishop, C., Owen, J., Tye, E., Esmaeelpour, M., Purslow, C., & Elghenzai, S. (2012). Is whole-body hydration an important consideration in dry eye?. *Investigative Ophthalmology and Visual Science*, *53*(10), 6622–6627.

Watson, G. R. (2001). Low vision in the geriatric population: Rehabilitation and management. *Journal of the American Geriatrics Society*, *49*(3), 317–330.

Weinstein, B. E., Sirow, L. W., & Moser, S. (2015). Relating hearing aid use to social and emotional loneliness in older adults. *American Journal of Audiology*, *25*, 54–61.

West, C. G., Gildengorin, G., Haegerstrom-Portnoy, G., Lott, L. A., Schneck, M. E., & Brabyn, J. A. (2003). Vision and driving self-restriction in older adults. *Journal of the American Geriatrics Society*, *51*(10), 1348–1355.

Whiteside, M. M., Wallhagen, M. I., & Pettengill, E. (2006). Sensory impairment in older adults: Part 2: Vision loss. *AJN The American Journal of Nursing*, *106*(11), 52–61.

Wiley, T. L., Chappell, R., Carmichael, L., Nondahl, D. M., & Cruickshanks, K. J. (2008). Changes in hearing thresholds over 10 years in older adults. *Journal of the American Academy of Audiology*, *19*(04), 281–292.

Williams, K., Kemper, S., & Hummert, M. L. (2005). Enhancing communication with older adults: Overcoming elderspeak. *Journal of Psychosocial Nursing and Mental Health Services*, *43*(5), 12–16.

Williams Integracare Clinic. (n.d.). *Pros and cons of drinking with a straw.* https://integracareclinics.com/pros-and-cons-of-drinking-with-a-straw/

Wolffsohn, J. S., & Davies, L. N. (2019). Presbyopia: Effectiveness of correction strategies. *Progress in Retinal and Eye Research*, *68*, 124–143.

CHAPTER 3

Anderson, N. D. (1999). The attentional demands of encoding and retrieval in younger and older adults: Evidence from secondary task reaction time distributions. *Psychology and Aging*, *14*(4), 645–655.

Anstey, K. J., Wood, J., Lord, S., & Walker, J. G. (2005). Cognitive, sensory and physical factors enabling driving safety in older adults. *Clinical psychology review*, *25*(1), 45-65.

Arbuckle, T. Y., & Gold, D. P. (1993). Aging, inhibition, and verbosity. *Journal of Gerontology*, *48*, 225–232.

Aschenbrenner, A. J., & Balota, D. (2017). Dynamic adjustments of attentional control in healthy aging. *Psychology and Aging*, *32*(1), 1–15. https://dx.doi.org/10.1037/pag0000148

Atkinson, R. C., & Shiffrin, R. M. (1968). Human memory: A proposed system and its control processes. In K. W. Spence & J. T. Spence (Eds.), *Psychology of learning and motivation* (Vol. 2, pp. 89–195). Academic Press.

Ball, K., Edwards, J. D., Ross, L. A., & McGuin, G. (2010). Cognitive training decreases motor vehicle collision involvement of older drivers. *Journal of the American Geriatrics Society*, *58*(11), 2107–2113. https://www.doi.org/10.1111/j.1532-5415.2010.03138.x

Birren, J. E., Woods, A. M., & Williams, M. V. (1980). Behavioral slowing with age: Causes, organization, and consequences. In L. W. Poon (Ed.), *Aging in the 1980s: Psychological issues* (pp. 293–308). American Psychological Association. https://doi.org/10.1037/10050-021

Brébion, G. (2001). Language processing, slowing, and speed/accuracy trade-off in the elderly. *Experimental Aging Research*, *27*(2), 137–150.

Broadbent, D. E. (1956). Listening between and during practised auditory distractions. *British Journal of Psychology*, *47*, 51–60.

Bryan, J., & Luszcz, M. A. (1996). Speed of information processing as a mediator between age and free-recall performance. *Psychology of Aging*, *11*(1), 3–9.

Cerella, J., Poon, L. W., & Williams, D. M. (1980). Age and the complexity hypothesis. In L. W Poon (Ed.), *Aging in the 1980s: Psychological issues* (pp. 332–340). American Psychological Association.

Charlton, S. G., & Starkey, N. J. (2011). Driving without awareness: The effects of practice and automaticity on attention and driving. *Transportation Research Part F: Traffic Psychology and Behaviour*, *14*(6), 456–471.

Cohen-Shikora, E. R., Diede, N. T., & Bugg, J. M. (2018). The flexibility of cognitive control: Age equivalence with experience guiding the way. *Psychology and Aging*, *33*(6), 924–939. http://dx.doi.org/10.1037/pag0000280

Connelly, S. L., Hasher, L., & Zacks, R. T. (1991). Age and reading: The impact of distraction. *Psychology and Aging*, *6*(4), 533–541.

Dawson, J. D., Uc, E. Y., Anderson, S. W., Johnson, A. M., & Rizzo, M. (2010). Neuropsychological predictors of driving errors in older adults. *Journal of the American Geriatrics Society*, *58*(6), 1090–1096.

Edwards, J. D., Delahunt, P. B., & Mahncke, H. W. (2009). Cognitive speed of processing training delays driving cessation. *Journals of Gerontology Series A: Biomedical Sciences and Medical Sciences*, *64*(12), 1262–1267.

Edwards, J. D., Ruva, C. L., O'Brien, J. L., Haley, C. B., & Lister, J. J. (2013). An examination of mediators of the transfer of cognitive speed of processing training to everyday functional performance. *Psychology and Aging*, *28*(2), 314–321.

Edwards, J. D., Wadley, V. G., Vance, D. E., Roenker, D. L., & Ball, K. K. (2005). The impact of speed of processing training on cognitive and everyday performance. *Aging and Mental Health*, *9*, 262–271. https://doi.org/10.1080/13607860412331336788

Fozard, J. L., Vercruyssen, M., Reynolds, S. L., Hancock, P. A., & Quilter, R. E. (1994). Age differences and changes in reaction time: The Baltimore Longitudinal Study of Aging. *Journal of Gerontology*, *49*(4), P179–P189. https://doi.org/10.1093/geronj/49.4.P179

Frolov, N. S., Pitsik, E. N., Maksimenko, V. A., Grubov, V. V., Kiselev, A. R., Wang, Z., & Hramov, A. E. (2020). Age-related slowing down in the motor initiation in elderly adults. *PLOS One*, *15*(9), e0233942.

Giles, H., & Coupland, N. (1991). *Language: Context and consequences*. Brooks/Cole.

Gold, D. P., & Arbuckle, T. Y. (1995). A longitudinal study of off-target verbosity. *Journal of Gerontology*, *50B*, 307–315.

Hasher, L., & Zacks, R. T. (1988). Working memory, comprehension, and aging: A review and a new view. *Psychology of Learning and Motivation*, *22*, 193–225.

Hertzog, C. (2008). Theoretical approaches to the study of cognitive aging. In S. M. Hofer & D. F. Alwin (Eds.), *Handbook of Cognitive Aging: Interdisciplinary Perspectives* (pp. 34–49). SAGE.

Hoyer, W. J., & Touron, D. R. (2003). Learning in adulthood. In J. Demick & C. Andreoletti (Eds.), *Handbook of adult development* (pp. 23–41). Kluwer Academic/Plenum.

Huang, H. J., & Mercer, V. S. (2001). Dual-task methodology: Applications in studies of cognitive and motor performance in adults and children. *Pediatric Physical Therapy*, *13*(3), 133–140.

Hultsch, D. F., MacDonald, S. W., & Dixon, R. A. (2002). Variability in reaction time performance of younger and older adults. *The Journals of Gerontology Series B: Psychological Sciences and Social Sciences*, *57*(2), P101–P115.

James, L. E., Burke, D. M., Austin, A., & Hulme, E. (1998). Production and perception of "verbosity" in younger and older adults. *Psychology and Aging*, *13*, 355–367.

Jenkins, L., & Hoyer, W. J. (2000). Instance-based automaticity and aging: Acquisition, reacquisition, and long-term retention. *Psychology and Aging*, *15(3)*, 551–565.

Kahneman, D. (1973). *Attention and effort*. Prentice-Hill.

Kahneman, D., & Henik, A. (2017). Perceptual organization and attention. In M. Kubovy & J. R. Pomerantz (Eds.), *Perceptual organization* (pp. 181–211). Routledge.

Kemper, S., & Liu, C. J. (2007). Eye movements of young and older adults during reading. *Psychology and Aging*, *22*(1), 84–93.

Kemtes, K. A., & Kemper, S. (1997). Younger and older adults' on-line processing of syntactically ambiguous sentences. *Psychology and Aging*, *12*(2), 362–371.

Lien, M. C., Allen, P. A., Ruthruff, E., Grabbe, J., McCann, R. S., & Remington, R. W. (2008). Visual word recognition without central attention: Evidence for greater automaticity with advancing age. *Psychology and Aging*, *21*(3), 431–447.

Logan, G. D. (1992). Attention and preattention in theories of automaticity. *The American Journal of Psychology*, *105*(2), 317–339.

Logan, G. D., Taylor, S. E., & Etherton, J. L. (1999). Attention and automaticity: Toward a theoretical integration. *Psychological Research*, *62*(2–3), 165–181.

Maquetiaux, F., Lauge-Beauvais, M., Ruthroff, E., Hartley, A., & Bherer, L. (2010). Learning to bypass the central bottleneck: Declining automaticity with advancing age. *Psychology and Aging*, *25*(1), 177–192.

Margolin, S. J. (2018). Cognitively active older adults' comprehension and metacomprehension of negated text. *Experimental Aging Research*, *44*(4), 329–337. https://www.doi.org/10.1080/0361073X.2018.1475154

Margolin, S. J., & Abrams, L. (2009). *Not* may not be too difficult: The effects of negation on older adults' sentence comprehension. *Educational Gerontology*, *35*(4), 308–322.

Meinhardt, J., & Pekrun, R. (2003). Attentional resource allocation to emotional events: An ERP study. *Cognition and Emotion*, *17*(3), 477–500.

Myerson. J., Hale, S., Wagstaff, D, Poon, L. W, & Smith, G. A. (1990). The information-loss model: A mathematical theory of age-related cognitive slowing. *Psychological Review*, 97, 475–487.

National Highway Traffic Safety Administration. (2020). *Safety outcomes of licensing procedures for older drivers*. https://cdan.nhtsa.gov/SASStoredProcess/guest

Nicosia, J., Cohen-Shikora, E. R., & Balota, D. (2021). Re-examining age differences in the Stroop effect: The importance of the trees in the forest (plot). *Psychology and Aging*, *36*(2), 214–231. https://doi.org/10.1037/pag0000599

Posner, M. I., & Petersen, S. E. (1990). The attention system of the human brain. *Annual Review of Neuroscience*, *13*(1), 25–42.

Ratcliff, R., Thapar, A., & McKoon, G. (2001). The effects of aging on reaction time in a signal detection task. *Psychology and Aging*, *16*(2), 323–341. https://doi.org/10.1037/0882-7974.16.2.323

Rawson, K. A., & Touron, D. R. (2015). Reservation of memory-based automaticity in reading for older adults. *Psychology and Aging*, *20*(4), 809–823. http://dx.doi.org/10.1037//a0039652

Rayner, K., Yang, J., Schuett, S., & Slattery, T. J. (2013). Eye movements of older and younger readers when reading unspaced text. *Experimental Psychology*, *60*(5), 354–361.

Rey-Mermet, A., & Gade, M. (2018). Inhibition in aging: What is preserved? What declines? A meta-analysis. *Psychonomic Bulletin & Review*, *25*, 1695-1716. https://doi.org/10.3758/s13423-017-1384-7

Rey-Mermet, A., & Gade, M. (2020). Age-related deficits in the congruency sequence effect are task-specific: An investigation of nine tasks. *Psychology and Aging*, *35*(5), 744–764. https://doi-org.brockport.idm.oclc.org/10.1037/pag0000414

Roenker, D. L., Cissell, G. M., Ball, K. K., Wadley, V. G., & Edwards, J. D. (2003). Speed-of-processing and driving simulator training result in improved driving performance. *Human Factors*, *45*, 218–233.

Salthouse, T. A. (1980). Age and memory: Strategies for localizing the loss. In L. W. Poon, J. L. Fozard, L. Cermak, D. Arenberg, & L. W. Thompson (Eds.), *New directions in memory and aging* (pp. 47–65). Erlbaum

Salthouse, T. A. (1984). Effects of age and skill of typing. *Journal of Experimental Psychology: General*, *113*(3), 345–371.

Salthouse, T. A. (1996). The processing-speed theory of adult age differences in cognition. *Psychological Review*, *103*(3), 403–428. https://doi.org/10.1037/003295X.103.3.403

Schwebel, D. C., Ball, K. K., Severson, J., Barton, B. K., Rizzo, M., & Viamonte, S. M. (2007). Individual difference factors in risky driving among older adults. *Journal of Safety Research*, *38*(5), 501–509.

Scialfa, C. T., Guzy, L. T., Leibowitz, H. W., Garvey, P. M., & Tyrrell, R. A. (1991). Age differences in estimating vehicle velocity. *Psychology and Aging*, *6*(1), 60–66.

Servant, M., Cassey, P., Woodman, G. F., & Logan, G. D. (2018). Neural bases of automaticity. *Journal of Experimental Psychology: Learning, Memory, and Cognition*, *44*(3), 440–464. https://doi.org/10.1037/xlm0000454

Somberg, B. L., & Salthouse, T. A. (1982). Divided attention abilities in young and old adults. *Journal of Experimental Psychology: Human Perception and Performance*, *8*(5), 651–663.

Spelke, E., Hirst, W., & Neisser, U. (1976). Skills of divided attention. *Cognition*, *4*(3), 215–230.

Stanisław Jurecki, R., Lech Stańczyk, T., & Jacek Jaśkiewicz, M. (2017). Driver's reaction time in a simulated, complex road incident. *Transport*, *32*(1), 44–54.

Stine, E. A. L. (1990). On-line processing of written text by younger and older adults. *Psychology and Aging*, *5*, 68–78.

Stine-Morrow, E. A. L., Loveless, M. K., & Soederberg, L. M. (1996). Resource allocation in on-line reading by younger and older adults. *Psychology and Aging*, *11*, 475–486.

Stine-Morrow, E. A. L., Ryan, S., & Leonard, J. S. (2000). Age differences in on-line syntactic processing. *Experimental Aging Research*, *26*, 315–322.

Stine-Morrow, E. A. L., Soederberg Miller, L. M., Gagne, D. D., & Hertzog, C. (2008). Self-regulated reading in adulthood. *Psychology and Aging*, *23*(1), 131–153. https://doi.org/10.1037/0882-7974.23.1.131

Stone, M. (1960). Models for choice-reaction time. *Psychometrika*, *25*(3), 251–260.

Stroop, J. R. (1935). Studies of interference in serial verbal reactions. *Journal of Experimental Psychology*, *18*(6), 643–662. https://doi.org/10.1037/h0054651

Stroop, J. R. (1938). Factors affecting speed in serial verbal reactions. *Psychological Monographs*, *50*(5), 38–48. https://doi.org/10.1037/h0093516

Teichner, W. H., & Krebs, M. J. (1974). Laws of visual choice reaction time. *Psychological Review*, *81*(1), 75–98.

Traffic Safety Stats (2023). https://crashstats.nhtsa.dot.gov/Api/Public/ViewPublication/813448

Treisman, A. M. (1969). Strategies and models of selective attention. *Psychological Review*, *76*(3), 282–299.

Trunk, D. L., & Abrams, L. (2009). Do younger and older adults' communication goals influence off-topic speech in autobiographical narratives? *Psychology of Aging*, *24*(2), 324–337.

Tun, P. A., & Lachman, M. E. (2008). Age differences in reaction time and attention in a national telephone sample of adults: Education, sex, and task complexity matter. *Developmental Psychology*, *44*(5), 1421–1429.

Tun, P. A., & Wingfield, A. (1995). Does dividing attention become harder with age? Findings from the Divided Attention Questionnaire. *Aging, Neuropsychology, and Cognition*, *2*(1), 39–66. https://doi.org/10/1080/1300825589508256588

Tun, P. A., Wingfield, A., & Stine, E. A. (1991). Speech-processing capacity in young and older adults: A dual-task study. *Psychology and Aging*, *6*(1), 3–9. https://doi.org/10.1037/0882-7974.6.1.3

Uttl, B., & Graf, P. (1997). Color-word Stroop test performance across the adult life span. *Journal of Clinical and Experimental Neuropsychology*, *19*(3), 405–420.

Vance, D., Dawson, J., Wadley, V., Edwards, J., Roenker, D., Rizzo, M., & Ball, K. (2007). The accelerate study: The longitudinal effect of speed of processing training on cognitive performance of older adults. *Rehabilitation Psychology*, *52*(1), 89–96.

Wei, J., & Prater, C. D. (1962). The structure and analysis of complex reaction systems. In D. D. Eley, P. W. Selwood, P. B. Weisz, A. A. Balandin, J. H. De Boer, P. J. Debye, P. H. Emmett, J. Horiuti, W. Jost, G. Natta, E. K. Rideal, & H. S. Taylor (Eds.), *Advances in catalysis* (Vol. 13, pp. 203–392). Academic Press.

Wilkinson, R. T., & Allison, S. (1989). Age and simple reaction time: Decade differences for 5,325 subjects. *Journal of Gerontology, 44*(2), P29–P35.

Williams, B. R., Strauss, E. H., Hultsch, D. F., & Hunter, M. A. (2007). Reaction time inconsistency in a spatial Stroop task: Age-related differences through childhood and adulthood. *Aging, Neuropsychology, and Cognition, 14*(4), 417–439.

Wood, J. M., & Owsley, C. (2014). Useful field of view test. *Gerontology, 60*(4), 315–318.

Woods, D. L., Wyma, J. M., Yund, E. W., Herron, T. J., & Reed, B. (2015). Factors influencing the latency of simple reaction time. *Frontiers in Human Neuroscience, 9*, 131.

CHAPTER 4

Abrams, L., Trunk, D. L., & Margolin, S. J. (2007). Resolving tip-of-the-tongue states in young and older adults: The role of phonology. In L. O. Randal (Ed.), *Aging and the elderly: Psychology, sociology, and health* (pp. 1–41). Nova Science.

Amanullah, S., & Seeber, C. (2010). Niacin deficiency resulting in neuropsychiatric symptoms: A case study and review of literature. *Clinical Neuropsychiatry, 7*(1), 10–14.

Atkinson, R. C., & Shiffrin, R. M. (1968). Human memory: A proposed system and its control processes. In K. W. Spence & J. T. Spence (Eds.), *Psychology of learning and motivation* (Vol. 2, pp. 89–195). Academic Press.

Bailey, H., Dunlosky, J., & Kane, M. J. (2008). Why does working memory span predict complex cognition? Testing the strategy affordance hypothesis. *Memory & Cognition, 36*, 1383–1390. http://dx.doi .org/10.3758/MC.36.8.1383

Balota, D. A., Dolan, P. O., & Duchek, J. M. (2000). Memory changes in healthy young and older adults. In E. Tulving & F. I. M. Craik (Eds.), *The Oxford handbook of memory* (pp. 395–410). Oxford University Press.

Bassett, D. S., Zurn, P., & Gold, J. I. (2018). On the nature and use of models in network neuroscience. *Nature Reviews Neuroscience, 19*(9), 566–578.

Borella, E., Carretti, B., Sciore, R., Capotosto, E., Taconnat, L., Cornoldi, C., & De Beni, R. (2017). Training working memory in older adults: Is there an advantage of using strategies? *Psychology and Aging, 32*(2), 178–191. https://doi-org.brockport.idm.oclc.org/10.1037/pag0000155

Bradley, C., & Pearson, J. (2012). The sensory components of high-capacity iconic memory and visual working memory. *Frontiers in Psychology, 3*, 355.

Brehmer, Y., Westerberg, H., & Bäckman, L. (2012). Working-memory training in younger and older adults: Training gains, transfer, and maintenance. *Frontiers in Human Neuroscience, 6*, 63. http://dx.doi.org/10.3389/fnhum.2012.00063

Bröder, A., & Meiser, T. (2007). Measuring source memory. *Zeitschrift für Psychologie/Journal of Psychology, 215*(1), 52–60.

Brom, S. S., & Kliegel, M. (2014). Improving everyday prospective memory performance in older adults: Comparing cognitive process and strategy training. *Psychology and Aging, 29*(3), 744–755. https://doi.org/10.1037/a0037181

Brown, A. S., & Nix, L. A. (1996). Age-related changes in the tip-of-the-tongue experience. *The American Journal of Psychology, 109*(1), 79–91.

Brown, J. (1958). Some tests of the decay theory of immediate memory. *Quarterly Journal of Experimental Psychology, 10*(1), 12–21.

Brown, R., & McNeill, D. (1966). The "tip of the tongue" phenomenon. *Journal of Verbal Learning and Verbal Behavior, 5*(4), 325–337.

Brown, R. M., & Robertson, E. M. (2007). Off-line processing: Reciprocal interactions between declarative and procedural memories. *Journal of Neuroscience, 27*(39), 10468–10475.

Burke, D. M., Locantore, J. K., Austin, A. A., & Chae, B. (2004). Cherry pit primes Brad Pitt: Homophone priming effects on young and older adults' production of proper names. *Psychological Science, 15*(3), 164–170.

Burke, D. M., MacKay, D. G., & James, L. E. (2000). Theoretical approaches to language and aging. In T. J. Perfect & E. A. Maylor (Eds.), *Models of cognitive aging* (pp. 204–237). Oxford University Press.

Burke, D. M., MacKay, D. G., Worthley, J. S., & Wade, E. (1991). On the tip of the tongue: What causes word finding failures in young and older adults? *Journal of Memory and Language*, *30*(5), 542–579.

Carpenter, G. A. (2001). Neural-network models of learning and memory: Leading questions and an emerging framework. *Trends in Cognitive Sciences*, *5*(3), 114–118.

Carretti, B., Borella, E., & De Beni, R. (2007). Does strategic memory training improve the working memory performance of younger and older adults? *Experimental Psychology*, *54*, 311–320. http://dx.doi.org/10.1027/1618-3169.54.4.311

Chiarello, C., & Hoyer, W. J. (1988). Adult age differences in implicit and explicit memory: Time course and encoding effects. *Psychology and Aging*, *3*(4), 358–366. https://www.doi.org/10.1037/0882-7974.3.4.358

Churchill, J. D., Stanis, J. J., Press, C., Kushelev, M., & Greenough, W. T. (2003). Is procedural memory relatively spared from age effects? *Neurobiology of Aging*, *24*(6), 883–892.

Craik, F. I. (1994). Memory changes in normal aging. *Current Directions in Psychological Science*, *3*(5), 155–158.

Craik, F. I. M., Luo, L., & Sakuta, Y. (2010). Effects of aging and divided attention on memory for items and their contexts. *Psychology and Aging*, *25*(4), 968–979. https://www.doi.org/10.1037/a0020276

Collins, A. M., & Loftus, E. F. (1975). A spreading-activation theory of semantic processing. *Psychological Review*, *82*(6), 407–428. https://doi.org/10.1037/0033-295X.82.6.407

Connelly, S. L., Hasher, L., & Zacks, R. T. (1991). Age and reading: The impact of distraction. *Psychology and Aging*, *6*(4), 533–541.

Cuttler, C., & Graf, P. (2007). Personality predicts prospective memory task performance: An adult lifespan study. *Scandinavian Journal of Psychology*, *48*(3), 215–231.

de Guise, E., Gosselin, N., LeBlanc, J., Champoux, M. C., Couturier, C., Lamoureux, J., Dagher, J., Marcoux, J., Maleki, M., & Feyz, M. (2011). Clock drawing and mini-mental state examination in patients with traumatic brain injury. *Applied Neuropsychology*, *18*(3), 179–190.

Drury, J. L., Kinsella, G. J., & Ong, B. (2000). Age differences in explicit and implicit memory for pictures. *Neuropsychology*, *14*(1), 93–101.

Dywan, J., & Jacoby, L. (1990). Effects of aging on source monitoring: Differences in susceptibility to false fame. *Psychology and Aging*, *5*(3), 379–387.

Eich, T. S., Murayama, K., Castel, A. D., & Knowlton, B. J. (2014). The dynamic effects of age-related stereotype threat on explicit and implicit memory performance in older adults. *Social Cognition*, *32*(6), 559–570.

Einstein, G. O., McDaniel, M. A., Manzi, M., Cochran, B., & Baker, M. (2000). Prospective memory and aging: Forgetting intentions over short delays. *Psychology and Aging*, *15*, 671–683. https://www.doi.org/10.1037/0882-7974.15.4.671

Erickson, C. A., & Barnes, C. A. (2003). The neurobiology of memory changes in normal aging. *Experimental Gerontology*, *38*(1–2), 61–69.

Farrell, M. T., & Abrams, L. (2011). Tip-of-the-tongue states reveal age differences in the syllable frequency effect. *Journal of Experimental Psychology: Learning, Memory, and Cognition*, *37*(1), 277–285.

Federmeier, K. D., McLennan, D. B., De Ochoa, E., & Kutas, M. (2002). The impact of semantic memory organization and sentence context information on spoken language processing by younger and older adults: An ERP study. *Psychophysiology*, *39*(2), 133–146.

Fernandez-Romero, R., & Spica, D. M. (2021). Memory dysfunction. *CONTINUUM: Lifelong Learning in Neurology*, *27*(6), 1562–1585.

Folstein, M. F., Folstein, S. E., & McHugh, P. R. (1975). "Mini-mental state": A practical method for grading the cognitive state of patients for the clinician. *Journal of Psychiatric Research*, *12*(3), 189–198.

Hasher, L., & Zacks, R. T. (1988). Working memory, comprehension, and aging: A review and a new view. *Psychology of Learning and Motivation*, *22*, 193–225.

Hess, T. M., Auman, C., Colcombe, S. J., & Rahhal, T. A. (2003). The impact of stereotype threat on age differences in memory performance. *Journal of Gerontology: Psychological Sciences*, *58B*, 3–11.

Iachini, I., Iavarone, A., Senese, V. P., Ruotolo, F., & Ruggiero, G. (2009). Visuospatial memory in healthy elderly, AD and MCI: A review. *Current Aging Science*, *2*, 43–59.

James, L. E., & Burke, D. M. (2000). Phonological priming effects on word retrieval and tip-of-the-tongue experiences in young and older adults. *Journal of Experimental Psychology: Learning, Memory, and Cognition*, *26*(6), 1378–1391.

Jelicic, M. (1996). Effects of ageing on different explicit and implicit memory tasks. *European Journal of Cognitive Psychology*, *8*(3), 225–234.

Kamberis, N., Cavuoto, M. G., & Pike, K. E. (2021). The influence of subjective cognitive decline on prospective memory over 5 years. *Neuropsychology*, *35*(1), 78–89.

Kane, M. J., & Engle, R. W. (2000). Working-memory capacity, proactive interference, and divided attention: Limits on long-term memory retrieval. *Journal of Experimental Psychology: Learning, Memory, and Cognition*, *26*(2), 336–358.

Karni, A., & Korman, M. (2011). When and where in skill memory consolidation: Neurobehavioral constraints on the acquisition and generation of procedural knowledge. In *BIO web of conferences* (Vol. 1, p. 00047). EDP Sciences.

Kausler, D. H. (1994). *Learning and memory in normal aging*. Academic Press.

Korkki, S. M., Richter, F. R., Jeyarathnaraja, P., & Simoms, J. S. (2020). Healthy aging reduces the precision of episodic memory. *Psychology and Aging*, *35*(1), 124–142. http://dx.doi.org/10.1037/pag0000432

Kunimi, M., & Kojima, H. (2014). The effects of processing speed and memory span on working memory. *GeroPsych*, *27*(3), 109–114.

Lamarre, C. J., & Patten, S. B. (1991). Evaluation of the modified mini-mental state examination in a general psychiatric population. *The Canadian Journal of Psychiatry*, *36*(7), 507–511.

Light, L. L., & Singh, A. (1987). Implicit and explicit memory in young and older adults. *Journal of Experimental Psychology: Learning, Memory, and Cognition*, *13*(4), 531–541.

Loef, M., & Walach, H. (2013). The omega-6/omega-3 ratio and dementia or cognitive decline: A systematic review on human studies and biological evidence. *Journal of Nutrition in Gerontology and Geriatrics*, *32*, 1–23. http://dx.doi.org/10.1080/21551197.2012.752335

Lövdén, M., Rönnlund, M., Wahlin, Å., Bäckman, L., Nyberg, L., & Nilsson, L. G. (2004). The extent of stability and change in episodic and semantic memory in old age: Demographic predictors of level and change. *The Journals of Gerontology Series B: Psychological Sciences and Social Sciences*, *59*(3), P130–P134.

MacKay, D. G. (1987). *The organization of perception and action: A theory for language and other cognitive skills*. Springer-Verlag.

Maki, P. M., Zonderman, A. B., & Weingartner, H. (1999). Age differences in implicit memory: Fragmented object identification and category exemplar generation. *Psychology and Aging*, *14*(2), 284–294.

Margolin, S. J. (2018). Cognitively active older adults' comprehension and metacomprehension of negated text. *Experimental Aging Research*, *44*(4), 329–337. https://www.doi.org/10.1080/0361073X.2018.1475154

McClelland, J. L., & Rogers, T. T. (2003). The parallel distributed processing approach to semantic cognition. *Nature Reviews Neuroscience*, *4*(4), 310–322.

McClelland, J. L., Rumelhart, D. E., & Hinton, G. E. (1986). The appeal of parallel distributed processing. In A. Collins & E. E. Smith (Eds.), *Readings in cognitive science: A perspective from psychology and artificial intelligence* (pp. 52–72). Morgan Kaufmann.

McDaniel, M. A., & Einstein, G. O. (2007). *Prospective memory: An overview and synthesis of an emerging field*. SAGE.

Meyer, A. S., & Bock, K. (1992). The tip-of-the-tongue phenomenon: Blocking or partial activation? *Memory and Cognition*, *20*(6), 715–726.

Miller, G. A. (1956). The magical number seven, plus or minus two: Some limits on our capacity for processing information. *Psychological Review*, *63*(2), 81–97.

Mitchell, D. B. (1989). How many memory systems? Evidence from aging. *Journal of Experimental Psychology: Learning, Memory, and Cognition*, *15*(1), 31–49. https://doi-org.brockport.idm.oclc.org/10.1037/0278-7393.15.1.31

Mitchell, D. B., Brown, A. S., & Murphy, D. R. (1990). Dissociations between procedural and episodic memory: Effects of time and aging. *Psychology and Aging*, *5*(2), 264–276.

Mitchell, D. B., & Bruss, P. J. (2003). Age differences in implicit memory: Conceptual, perceptual, or methodological? *Psychology and Aging*, *18*(4), 807–822.

Moore, K., Hughes, C. F., Ward, M., Hoey, L., & McNulty, H. (2018). Diet, nutrition and the ageing brain: Current evidence and new directions. *Proceedings of the Nutrition Society*, *77*(2), 152–163.

Murre, J. M., Wolters, G., & Raffone, A. (2006). Binding in working memory and long term memory: towards an integrated model. In H. Zimmer (Ed.), *Handbook of binding and memory: Perspectives from cognitive neuroscience* (pp. 221–250). Oxford Academic.

National Institute on Aging. (2022). *Age-specific risk of dementia in the U.S. has declined over the past two decades*. https://www.nia.nih.gov/research/dbsr/age-specific-risk-dementia-u-s-has-declined-over-past-2-decades

Nilsson, L. G. (2003). Memory function in normal aging. *Acta Neurologica Scandinavica*, *107*, 7–13.

Park, D. C., Hertzog, C., Kidder, D. P., Morrell, R. W., & Mayhorn, C. B. (1997). Effect of age on event-based and time-based prospective memory. *Psychology and Aging*, *12*(2), 314–327.

Peich, M. C., Husain, M., & Bays, P. M. (2013). Age-related decline of precision and binding in visual working memory. *Psychology and Aging*, *28*(3), 729–743.

Perfect, T. J., & Hanley, J. R. (1992). The tip-of-the-tongue phenomenon: Do experimenter-presented interlopers have any effect? *Cognition*, *45*(1), 55–75.

Plassman, B. L., Langa, K. M., Fisher, G. G., Heeringa, S. G., Weir, D. R., Ofstedal, M. B., Burke, J. R., Hurd, M. D., Potter, G. G., Rodgers, W. L., Steffens, D. C., Willis, R. J., & Wallace, R. B. (2007). Prevalence of dementia in the United States: The aging, demographic, and memory study. *Neuroepidemiology*, *29*(1–2), 125–132. https://doi.org/10.1159/000109998

Ponjoan, A., Garre-Olmo, J., Blanche, J., Fages, E., Alves-Cabratosa, L., Marti-Lluch, R., Comas-Cofi, M., Parramon, D., Garci-Gil, M., & Ramos, R. (2019). Epidemiology of dementia: Prevalence and incidence estimates using validates electronic health records from primary care. *Clinical Epidemiology*, *11*, 217–228.

Rutherford, A., Gerasimos, M., Bruno, D., & Van den Bos, M. (2012). Long-term memory. In N. Braisby & A. Gellatly (Eds.), *Cognitive Psychology*, (2nd ed., pp. 229–265). Oxford University Press.

Salthouse, T. A. (1996). The processing-speed theory of adult age differences in cognition. *Psychological Review*, *103*(3), 403–428. https://doi.org/10.1037/003295X.103.3.403

Scarampi, C., & Gilbert, S. J. (2021). Age differences in strategic reminder setting and the compensatory role of metacognition. *Psychology and Aging*, *36*(2), 172–185. https://doi.org/10.1037/pag0000590

Schacter, D. L., Cooper, L. A., & Valdiserri, M. (1992). Implicit and explicit memory for novel visual objects in older and younger adults. *Psychology and Aging*, *7*(2), 299–308.

Schacter, D. L., Kaszniak, A. W., Kihlstrom, J. F., & Valdiserri, M. (1991). The relation between source memory and aging. *Psychology and Aging*, *6*(4), 559–568. https://doi.org/10.1037/0882-7974.6.4.559

Schryer, E., & Ross, M. (2013). The use and benefits of external memory aids in older and younger adults. *Applied Cognitive Psychology*, *27*(5), 663–671.

Shafto, M. A., Burke, D. M., Stamatakis, E. A., Tam, P. P., & Tyler, L. K. (2007). On the tip-of-the-tongue: Neural correlates of increased word-finding failures in normal aging. *Journal of Cognitive Neuroscience*, *19*(12), 2060–2070.

Shing, Y. L., Werkle-Bergner, M., Brehmer, Y., Müller, V., Li, S. C., & Lindenberger, U. (2010). Episodic memory across the lifespan: The contributions of associative and strategic components. *Neuroscience & Biobehavioral Reviews*, *34*(7), 1080–1091.

Siedlecki, K. L., Salthouse, T. A., & Berish, D. E. (2005). Is there anything special about the aging of source memory? *Psychology and Aging*, *20*(1), 19–32.

Sperling, G. (1960). The information available in brief visual presentations. *Psychological*

Monographs: General and Applied, 74(11), 1–29.

Sporns, O. (2014). Contributions and challenges for network models in cognitive neuroscience. *Nature Neuroscience, 17*(5), 652–660.

Stanton, A. (Director), & Walters, G. (Producer). (2003). *Finding Nemo* [Film]. Walt Disney Pictures; Pixar Animation Studios.

Strickland, L., Heathcote, A., Humphreys, M. S., & Loft, S. (2022). Target learning in event-based prospective memory. *Journal of Experimental Psychology: Learning, Memory, and Cognition, 48*(8), 1110–1126. https://doi.org/10.1037/xlm0000900

Sutterer, M. J., & Tranel, D. (2017). Neuropsychology and cognitive neuroscience in the fMRI era: A recapitulation of localizationist and connectionist views. *Neuropsychology, 31*(8), 972–980. https://doi.org/10.1037/neu0000408

Treisman, A. (1996). The binding problem. *Current Opinion in Neurobiology, 6*(2), 171–178.

Trott, C. T., Friedman, D., Ritter, W., & Fabiani, M. (1997). Item and source memory: Differential age effects revealed by event-related potentials. *NeuroReport, 8*(15), 3373–3378.

Tulving, E. (1987). Multiple memory systems and consciousness. *Human Neurobiology, 6*(2), 67–80.

Tye, M. (2006). Nonconceptual content, richness, and fineness of grain. In T. S. Gendler & J. Hawthorne (Eds.), *Perceptual experience* (pp. 504–530). Oxford Academic Press.

Unsworth, N., Spillers, G. J., & Brewer, G. A. (2012). Working memory capacity and retrieval limitations from long-term memory: An examination of differences in accessibility. *Quarterly Journal of Experimental Psychology, 65*(12), 2397–2410.

Varley, D., Henry, J. D., Gibson, E., Suddendorf, T., Rendell, P. G., & Redshaw, J. (2021). An old problem revisited: How sensitive is time-based prospective memory to age-related differences? *Psychology and Aging, 36*(5), 616–625.

Walsh, D. A., & Prasse, M. J. (2014, May). Iconic memory and attentional processes in the aged. In L. Poon, J. Fozard, L. Cermak, D. Arenberg, & L. Thompson (Eds.), *New directions in memory and aging (PLE: Memory): Proceedings of the George A. Talland Memorial Conference* (pp. 153–180). Psychology Press.

Ward, E., Berry, C., & Shanks, D. (2013). Age effects on explicit and implicit memory. *Frontiers in Psychology, 4*, 639.

West, R., & Craik, F. I. (2001). Influences on the efficiency of prospective memory in younger and older adults. *Psychology and Aging, 16*(4), 682–696.

White, K. K., & Abrams, L. (2002). Does priming specific syllables during tip-of-the-tongue states facilitate word retrieval in older adults? *Psychology and Aging, 17*(2), 226–235.

White, K. K., Abrams, L., & Frame, E. A. (2013). Semantic category moderates phonological priming of proper name retrieval during tip-of-the-tongue states. *Language and Cognitive Processes, 28*(4), 561–576.

Zacks, R. T., & Hasher, L. (2006). Aging and long-term memory: Deficits are not inevitable. In E. Bialystok & F. I. M. Craik (Eds.), *Lifespan cognition: Mechanisms of change* (pp. 162–177). Oxford Academic.

Zogg, J. B., Woods, S. P., Sauceda, J. A., Wiebe, J. S., & Simoni, J. M. (2012). The role of prospective memory in medication adherence: A review of an emerging literature. *Journal of Behavioral Medicine, 35*, 47–62.

CHAPTER 5

Arshiha, M. S., Talari, K. L., Noghani, F., Sedghi Goyaghaj, N., & Taghavi Larijani, T. (2016). The relationship between moral intelligence and communication skills among nursing students. *Iranian Journal of Medical Ethics and History of Medicine, 9*(3), 44–54.

Baltes, P. B. (1997). On the incomplete architecture of human ontogeny: Selection, optimization, and compensation as foundation of developmental theory. *American Psychologist, 52*, 366–380.

Baltes, P. B., & Willis, S. L. (1982). Plasticity and enhancement of intellectual functioning in old age: Penn State's Adult Enrichment Project (ADEPT) In F. I. M. Craik & S. Trehub (Eds.), *Aging and cognitive processes* (pp. 353–389). Springer.

Batey, M., & Furnham, A. (2006). Creativity, intelligence, and personality: A critical review of the scattered literature. *Genetic, Social, and General Psychology Monographs, 132*(4), 355–429.

Benedek, M., Jauk, E., Sommer, M., Arendasy, M., & Neubauer, A. C. (2014). Intelligence, creativity, and cognitive control: The common and differential involvement of executive functions in intelligence and creativity. *Intelligence, 46*, 73–83.

Bisiacchi, P. S., Borella, E., Bergamaschi, S., Carretti, B., & Mondini, S. (2008). Interplay between memory and executive functions in normal and pathological aging. *Journal of Clinical and Experimental Neuropsychology, 30*, 723–733. http://dx.doi.org/10.1080/13803390701689587

Blieszner, R., Willis, S. L., & Baltes, P. B. (1981). Training research in aging on the fluid ability of inductive reasoning. *Journal of Applied Developmental Psychology, 2*(3), 247–265.

Blyler, C. R., Gold, J. M., Iannone, V. N., & Buchanan, R. W. (2000). Short form of the WAIS-III for use with patients with schizophrenia. *Schizophrenia Research, 46*(2–3), 209–215.

Borella, E., Pezzuti, L., De Beni, R., & Cornoldi, C. (2020). Intelligence and working memory: Evidence from administering the WAIS-IV to Italian adults and elderly. *Psychological Research, 84*(6), 1622–1634.

Brody, N. (1997). Intelligence, schooling, and society. *American Psychologist, 52*(10), 1046–1050.

Cabello, R., Sorrel, M. A., Fernández-Pinto, I., Extremera, N., & Fernández-Berrocal, P. (2016). Age and gender differences in ability emotional intelligence in adults: A cross-sectional study. *Developmental Psychology, 52*(9), 1486–1492. https://doi.org/10.1037/dev0000191

Carpenter, S. M., Chae, R. L., & Yoon, C. (2020). Creativity and aging: Positive consequences of distraction. *Psychology and Aging, 35*(5), 654–662. https://doi.org/10.1037/pag0000470

Cattell, R. B. (1943). The measurement of adult intelligence. *Psychological Bulletin, 3*, 153–193.

Cattell, R. B. (1963). Theory of fluid and crystallized intelligence: A critical experiment. *Journal of Educational Psychology, 54*(1), 1–22.

Cattell, R. B., & Cattell, A. K. S. (1960). *Handbook for the individual or group culture fair intelligence test*. Institute for Personality and Ability Testing.

Costa, A., & Faria, L. (2018). Implicit theories of intelligence and academic achievement: A meta-analytic review. *Frontiers in Psychology, 9*, 829. https://doi.org/10.3389/fpsyg.2018.00829

Delhom, I., Satorres, E., & Meléndez, J. C. (2020). Can we improve emotional skills in older adults? Emotional intelligence, life satisfaction, and resilience. *Psychosocial Intervention, 29*(3), 133–139.

Delhom, I., Satorres, E., & Meléndez, J. C. (2022). Emotional intelligence intervention in older adults to improve adaptation and reduce negative mood. *International Psychogeriatrics, 34*(1), 79–89.

Delis, D. C., Kaplan, E., & Kramer, J. H. (2001). *Delis-Kaplan Executive Function System (D-KEFS)*. Psychological Corporation.

De Pergola, G., & D'Alessandro, A. (2018). Influence of Mediterranean diet on blood pressure. *Nutrients, 10*(11), 1700.

Dickens, W. T., & Flynn, J. R. (2001). Heritability estimates versus large environmental effects: The IQ paradox resolved. *Psychological Review, 108*(2), 346–369. https://doi.org/10.1037/0033-295X.108.2.346

Etezadi, S., & Pushkar, D. (2013). Why are wise people happier? An explanatory model of wisdom and emotional well-being in older adults. *Journal of happiness studies, 14*(3), 929-950.

Eysenck, H. J. (Ed.). (2012). *The measurement of intelligence*. Springer Science & Business Media.

Fastame, M. C. (2022). Are subjective cognitive complaints associated with executive functions and mental health of older adults? *Cognitive Processing, 23*(3), 503–512.

Féart, C., Samieri, C., & Barberger-Gateau, P. (2010). Mediterranean diet and cognitive function in older adults. *Current Opinion in Clinical Nutrition and Metabolic Care, 13*(1), 14–18.

Folstein, M. F., Folstein, S. E., & McHugh, P. R. (1975). "Mini-mental state": A practical method for grading the cognitive state of patients for the clinician. *Journal of Psychiatric Research*, *12*(3), 189–198.

Gard, T., Taquet, M., Dixit, R., Hölzel, B. K., de Montjoye, Y. A., Brach, N., Salat, D. H., Dickerson, B. C., Gray, J. R., & Lazar, S. W. (2014). Fluid intelligence and brain functional organization in aging yoga and meditation practitioners. *Frontiers in Aging Neuroscience*, *6*, 76.

Giorgio, A., Santelli, L., Tomassini, V., Bosnell, R., Smith, S., De Stefano, N., & Johansen-Berg, H. (2010). Age-related changes in grey and white matter structure throughout adulthood. *NeuroImage*, *51*(3), 943–951. https://doi.org/10.1016/j.neuroimage.2010.03.004

Gravetter, F. J., & Forzano, L.B. (2018). *Research methods for the behavioral sciences* (6th ed.). Cengage.

Henninger, D. E., Madden, D. J., & Huettel, S. A. (2010). Processing speed and memory mediate age-related differences in decision making. *Psychology of Aging*, *25*(2), 262–270. https://www.doi.org/10.1037/a0019096

Horn, J. L. (1982). The theory of fluid and crystallized intelligence in relation to concepts of cognitive psychology and aging in adulthood. In F. I. M. Craik & S. Trehub (Eds.), *Aging and cognitive processes* (pp. 237–278). Springer.

Jäncke, L., Sele, S., Liem, F., Oschwald, J., & Merillat, S. (2020). Brain aging and psychometric intelligence: A longitudinal study. *Brain Structure and Function*, *225*(2), 519–536.

Jauk, E., Benedek, M., & Neubauer, A. C. (2014). The road to creative achievement: A latent variable model of ability and personality predictors. *European Journal of Personality*, *28*(1), 95–105.

Kaufman, J. C., Plucker, J. A., & Baer, J. (2008). *Essentials of creativity assessment*. Wiley.

Lennick, D., & Kiel, F. (2007). *Moral intelligence: Enhancing business performance and leadership success*. Pearson Prentice Hall.

Lindenberger, U., Mayr, U., & Kliegl, R. (1993). Speed and intelligence in old age. *Psychology and Aging*, *8*(2), 207–220. https://doi.org/10.1037/0882-7974.8.2.207

Mackintosh, N. (2011). *IQ and human intelligence*. Oxford University Press.

Masunaga, H., & Horn, J. (2001). Expertise and age-related changes in components of intelligence. *Psychology and Aging*, *16*(2), 293–311.

Mayer, J. D. (2002). *MSCEIT: Mayer-Salovey-Caruso Emotional Intelligence Test*. Multi-Health Systems.

Mayer, J. D., Caruso, D. R., & Salovey, P. (1999). Emotional intelligence meets traditional standards for an intelligence. *Intelligence*, *27*, 267–298. http://dx.doi.org/10.1016/S0160-2896(99)00016-1

Mayer, J. D., & Salovey, P. (1997). What is emotional intelligence? In P. Salovey & D. Sluyter (Eds.), *Emotional development and emotional intelligence: Implications for educators* (pp. 3–31). Basic Books.

Meyers, J. E., Zellinger, M. M., Kockler, T., Wagner, M., & Miller, R. M. (2013). A validated seven-subtest short form for the WAIS-IV. *Applied Neuropsychology: Adult*, *20*(4), 249–256.

Morrow, D. G., Menard, W. E., Stine-Morrow, E. A. L., Teller, T., & Bryant, D. (2001). The influence of expertise and task factors on age differences in pilot communication. *Psychology and Aging*, *16*(1), 31–46. https://doi.org/10.1037/0882-7974.16.1.31

Naderi, H., Abdullah, R., Aizan, H. T., & Sharir, J. (2010). Intelligence and academic achievement: An investigation of gender differences. *Life Science Journal*, *7*(1), 83–87.

Paulhus, D. L., Wehr, P., Harms, P. D., & Strasser, D. I. (2002). Use of exemplar surveys to reveal implicit types of intelligence. *Personality and Social Psychology Bulletin*, *28*(8), 1051–1062.

Pfeifer, R., & Scheier, C. (2001). *Understanding intelligence*. MIT Press.

Piaget, J. (1929). *The child's conception of the world*. London: Routledge.

Plomin, R., & Von Stumm, S. (2018). The new genetics of intelligence. *Nature Reviews Genetics*, *19*(3), 148–159.

Ramchandran, K., Tranel, D., Duster, K., & Denburg, N. L. (2020). The role of emotional vs. cognitive intelligence in economic decision-making amongst older adults.

Frontiers in Neuroscience, *14*, 497.

Raven, J. C., Foulds, G., &, Forbes, A. (1973). *Advanced Progressive Matrices, Sets I and II: Plan and use of the scale with a report of experimental work*. Lewis.

Raz, N., Rodrigue, K. M., Kennedy, K. M., & Acker, J. D. (2007). Vascular health and longitudinal changes in brain and cognition in middle-aged and older adults. *Neuropsychology*, *21*(2), 149–157.

Robitaille, A., Piccinin, A. M., Muniz-Terrera, G., Hoffman, L., Johansson, B., Deeg, D. J., Aartsen, M. J., Comijs, H. C., & Hofer, S. M. (2013). Longitudinal mediation of processing speed on age-related change in memory and fluid intelligence. *Psychology and Aging*, *28*(4), 887–901.

Roth, B., Becker, N., Romeyke, S., Schäfer, S., Domnick, F., & Spinath, F. M. (2015). Intelligence and school grades: A meta-analysis. *Intelligence*, *53*, 118–137.

Runco, M. A., & Jaeger, G. J. (2012). The standard definition of creativity. *Creativity research journal*, *24*(1), 92-96.

Salthouse, T. A. (1984). Effects of age and skill of typing. *Journal of Experimental Psychology: General*, *113*(3), 345–371.

Salthouse, T. A. (1996). The processing-speed theory of adult age differences in cognition. *Psychological Review*, *103*(3), 403–428. https://doi.org/10.1037/003295X.103.3.403

Salthouse, T. A., & Saklofske, D. H. (2010). Do the WAIS-IV tests measure the same aspects of cognitive functioning in adults under and over age 65? In L. G. Weiss, D. H. Saklofske, D. L. Coalson, & S. Engi Raiford (Eds.), *Practical resources for the mental health professional* (pp. 217–235). Academic Press.

Schaie, K. W. (1994). The course of adult intellectual development. *American Psychologist*, *49*(4), 304–313. https://doi.org/10.1037/0003-06`

Schaie, K. W. (1996). *Intellectual development in adulthood: The Seattle longitudinal study*. Cambridge University Press.

Schaie, K. W. (2005). What can we learn from longitudinal studies of adult development? *Research in Human Development*, *2*(3), 133–158.

Schaie, K. W., & Willis, S. L. (1993). Age difference patterns of psychometric intelligence in adulthood: Generalizability within and across ability domains. *Psychology and Aging*, *8*(1), 44–55. https://doi.org/10.1037/0882-7974.8.1.44

Schaie, K. W., & Willis, S. L. (2010). The Seattle Longitudinal Study of adult cognitive development. *ISSBD Bulletin*, *57*(1), 24–29.

Schlinger, H. D. (2003). The myth of intelligence. *Psychological Record*, *53*(1), 15–32.

Shakeel, M. K., & Goghari, V. M. (2017). Measuring fluid intelligence in healthy older adults. *Journal of Aging Research*, *2017*, 8514582.

Sharma, S., & Babu, N. (2017). Interplay between creativity, executive function and working memory in middle-aged and older adults. *Creativity Research Journal*, *29*(1), 71–77.

Silbert, L. C., Nelson, C., Howieson, D. B., Moore, M. M., & Kaye, J. A. (2008). Impact of white matter hyperintensity volume progression on rate of cognitive and motor decline. *Neurology*, *71*(2), 108–113. https://www.doi.org/10.1212/01.wnl.0000316799.86917.37

Silverstein, A. T. (1985). Two- and four-subtest short forms of the WAIS-R: A closer look at validity and reliability. *Journal of Clinical Psychology*, *41*(1), 95–97.

Sinnott, J. D. (1981). The theory of relativity. *Human Development*, *24*(5), 293–311.

Sinnott, J. D. (1984). Postformal reasoning: The relativistic stage. In M. Commons, F. Richards & C. Armon (Eds.), *Beyond formal operations* (pp. 298–325). Praeger.

Sinnott, J., Hilton, S., Wood, M., & Douglas, D. (2020). Relating flow, mindfulness, cognitive flexibility, and postformal thought. *Journal of Adult Development*, *27*(1), 1–11.

Sternberg, R. J. (2006). The nature of creativity. *Creativity Research Journal*, *18*(1), 87–98.

Thorsen, C., Gustafsson, J. E., & Cliffordson, C. (2014). The influence of fluid and crystallized intelligence on the development of knowledge and skills. *British Journal of Educational Psychology*, *84*(4), 556–570.

Toprak, M., & Karakus, M. (2018). Teachers' moral intelligence: A scale adaptation into Turkish and preliminary evidence. *European Journal of Educational Research*, *7*(4), 901–911.

Tranter, L. J., & Koutstaal, W. (2008). Age and flexible thinking: An experimental demonstration of the beneficial effects of increased cognitively stimulating activity on fluid intelligence in healthy older adults. *Aging, Neuropsychology, and Cognition*, *15*(2), 184–207.

Tun, P. A., & Lachman, M. E. (2008). Age differences in reaction time and attention in a national telephone sample of adults: Education, sex, and task complexity matter. *Developmental Psychology*, *44*(5), 1421–1429.

Wechsler, D. (1981). *Wechsler Adult Intelligence Scale–Revised* (WAIS-R). Psychological Corporation.

Wechsler, D. (2008). *Wechsler Adult Intelligence Scale–Fourth Edition* (WAIS-IV). Pearson.

Willis, S. L., Blieszner, R., & Baltes, P. B. (1981). Intellectual training research in aging: Modification of performance on the fluid ability of figural relations. *Journal of Educational Psychology*, *73*(1), 41–50.

Willis, S. L., & Nesselroade, C. S. (1990). Long-term effects of fluid ability training in old-old age. *Developmental Psychology*, *26*(6), 905–910.

Willis, S. L., & Schaie, K. W. (1986). Training the elderly on the ability factors of spatial orientation and inductive reasoning. *Psychology and Aging*, *1*(3), 239–247. https://doi.org/10.1037/0882-7974.1.3.239

Worthy, D. A., Gorlick, M. A., Pacheco, J. L., Schnyer, D. M., & Maddox, W. T. (2011). With age comes wisdom: Decision making in younger and older adults. *Psychological Science*, *22*(11), 1375–1380.

Zaval, L., Li, Y., Johnson, E. J., & Weber, E. U. (2015). Complementary contributions of fluid and crystallized intelligence to decision making across the life span. In T. M. Hess, J. Strough, & C. E. Löckenhoff (Eds.), *Aging and decision making* (pp. 149–168). Elsevier Academic Press.

Zimprich, D., & Martin, M. (2002). Can longitudinal changes in processing speed explain longitudinal age changes in fluid intelligence? *Psychology and Aging*, *17*(4), 690–695.

CHAPTER 6

Adams, C., Smith, M. C., Pasupathi, M., & Vitolo, L. (2002). Social context effects on story recall in older and younger women: Does the listener make a difference? *Journal of Gerontology: Psychological Sciences*, *57B*, P28–P40.

Afshordi, N., & Liberman, Z. (2021). Keeping friends in mind: Development of friendship concepts in early childhood. *Social Development*, *30*(2), 331–342.

Amato, P. R. (2000). The consequences of divorce for adults and children. *Journal of Marriage and Family*, *62*(4), 1269–1287.

Andrews, G. J., Gavin, N., Begley, S., & Brodie, D. (2003). Assisting friendships, combating loneliness: User's views on a "befriending" scheme. *Ageing and Society*, *23*(3), 349–362.

Annie E. Casey Foundation. (2023). *Kids Count data book*. https://assets.aecf.org/m/resourcedoc/aecf-2023kidscountdatabook-2023.pdf

Asoodeh, M. H., Khalili, S., Daneshpour, M., & Lavasani, M. G. (2010). Factors of successful marriage: Accounts from self described happy couples. *Procedia-Social and Behavioral Sciences*, *5*, 2042–2046.

Backhouse, J. (2009). *Grandparents raising their grandchildren: impact of the transition from a traditional grandparent role to a grandparent-as-parent role* [Unpublished doctoral dissertation]. Southern Cross University.

Baker, F. C., De Zambotti, M., Colrain, I. M., & Bei, B. (2018). Sleep problems during the menopausal transition: Prevalence, impact, and management challenges. *Nature and Science of Sleep*, *10*, 73–95.

Bates, J. S., Taylor, A. C., & Stanfield, M. H. (2018). Variations in grandfathering: Characteristics of involved, passive, and disengaged grandfathers. *Contemporary Social Science*, *13*(2), 187–202.

Blieszner, R., & Adams, R. G. (1992). *Adult friendship*. SAGE.

Blieszner, R., & De Vries, B. (2001). Introduction perspectives on intimacy. *Generations*, *25*(2), 7–8.

Borchard, D. C., & Donohoe, P. A. (2008). *The joy of retirement: Finding happiness, freedom, and the life you've always wanted*. Amacom.

Bradbury, T. N. (1998). *The developmental course of marital dysfunction*. Cambridge University Press.

Bradbury, T. N., Fincham, F. D., & Beach, S. R. (2000). Research on the nature and determinants of marital satisfaction: A decade in review. *Journal of Marriage and Family, 62*(4), 964–980.

Buchanan, A., & Rotkirch, A. (2018). Twenty-first century grandparents: Global perspectives on changing roles and consequences. *Contemporary Social Science, 13*(2), 131–144.

Burton, L. M., & Bengston, V. L. (1985). Black grandmothers: Issues of timing and continuity of role. In V. L. Bengston & J. F. Robertson (Eds.), *Grandparenthood* (pp. 61–77). SAGE.

Centers for Disease Control and Prevention. (2024). *National Center for HIV, Viral Hepatitis, STD, and TB Prevention Atlas Plus: HIV, hepatitis, STD, TB, social determinants of health data*. https://www.cdc.gov/nchhstp/atlas/index.htm

Chan, A. C., Lee, S. K., Zhang, J., Banegas, J., Marsalis, S., & Gewirtz, A. H. (2022). Intensity of grandparent caregiving, health, and well-being in cultural context: A systematic review. *The Gerontologist, 63*(5), 851–873.

Cheung, S. Y., & Woo, L. (2021). Age stereotypes and the job suitability of older workers from hotel managers' perspectives. *International Journal of Hospitality Management, 95*, 102932.

Chevalier, S., Fouquereau, E., Gillet, N., & Demulier V. (2013). Development of the reasons for Entrepreneurs' Retirement Decision Inventory (RERDI) and preliminary evidence of its psychometric properties in a French sample. J. Career Assess. 21:572–86

Child Care Aware of America. (2024). *Cost of child care*. https://www.childcareaware.org/families/cost-child-care/

Chiu, C. Y. (1990). Normative expectations of social behavior and concern for members of the collective in Chinese society. *The Journal of Psychology, 124*(1), 103–111.

Choi, M., Sprang, G., & Eslinger, J. G. (2016). Grandparents raising grandchildren: A synthetic review and theoretical model for interventions. *Family and Community Health, 39*(2), 120–128. https://www.jstor.org/stable/48515472

Collins, G. A. (2003). Rethinking retirement in the context of an aging workforce. *Journal of Career Development, 30*(2), 145–157.

Condon, J., Luszcz, M., & McKee, I. (2018). The transition to grandparenthood: A prospective study of mental health implications. *Aging and Mental Health, 22*(3), 336–343.

Connidis, I. A. (2013). Intimate relationships: Learning from later life experience. In T. M. Calasanti & K. F. Slevin (Eds.), *Age matters: Re-aligning feminist thinking* (pp. 123–153). Routledge.

Cornwell, B., Laumann, E. O., & Schumm, L. P. (2008). The social connectedness of older adults: A national profile. *American Sociological Review, 73*(2), 185–203.

Cox, C. (2018). Cultural diversity among grandparent caregivers: Implications for interventions and policy. *Educational Gerontology, 44*(8), 484–491.

de Vaus, D., Wells, Y., Kendig, H., & Quine, S. (2007). Does gradual retirement have better outcomes than abrupt retirement? Results from an Australian panel study. *Ageing and Society, 27*(5), 667–682.

Dey, S., & Ghosh, J. (2016). Factors in the distribution of successful marriage. *International Journal of Social Sciences and Management, 3*(1), 60–64.

Duflos, M., & Giraudeau, C. (2022). Using the intergenerational solidarity framework to understand the grandparent-grandchild relationship: A scoping review. *European Journal of Ageing, 19*(2), 233–262.

Erikson, E. H. (1950). *Childhood and society*. Norton.

Farriol-Baroni, V., González-García, L., Luque-García, A., Postigo-Zegarra, S., & Pérez-Ruiz, S. (2021). Influence of social support and subjective well-being on the perceived overall health of the elderly. *International Journal of Environmental Research and Public Health, 18*(10), 5438.

Felmlee, D., & Muraco, A. (2009). Gender and friendship norms among older adults. *Research on Aging, 31*(3), 318–344. https://www.doi.org/10.1177/0164027508330719

Fitzroy, A. F., Kemp, C. L., & Burgess, E. O. (2022). "I'm not terribly lonely": Advancing the understanding of intimacy among older adults. *Journal of Aging Studies*, *61*, 101005.

Fleishman, J. M., Crane, B., & Koch, P. B. (2020). Correlates and predictors of sexual satisfaction for older adults in same-sex relationships. *Journal of Homosexuality*, *67*(14), 1974–1998.

Fuller-Thomson, E., & Minkler, M. (2001). American grandparents providing extensive child care to their grandchildren: Prevalence and profile. *The Gerontologist*, *41*(2), 201–209.

Gandaglia, G., Briganti, A., Jackson, G., Kloner, R. A., Montorsi, F., Montorsi, P., & Vlachopoulos, C. (2014). A systematic review of the association between erectile dysfunction and cardiovascular disease. *European Urology*, *65*(5), 968–978.

Geffen, R. M. (2014). The roles of American Jewish grandparents: An exploration of the intergenerational transmission of values. *Journal of Jewish Communal Service*, *89*(1), 55–60.

Gibson, H., Ashton-Shaeffer, C., Green, J., & Corbin, J. (2002). Leisure and retirement: Women's stories. *Loisir et Societe/Society and Leisure*, *25*, 257–284.

Giddens, A. (2020). Modernity and self-identity: Self and society in the late modern age. In S. Seidman & J. C. Alexander (Eds.), *The new social theory reader* (pp. 354–361). Routledge.

Gigy, L., & Kelly, J. B. (1993). Reasons for divorce: Perspectives of divorcing men and women. *Journal of Divorce & Remarriage*, *18*(1–2), 169–188.

Glenn, N. D. (1989). Duration of marriage, family, composition, and marital happiness. *National Journal of Sociology*, *3*, 3–24.

Grandparents: A Critical Child Care Safety Net. (2008). https://www.childcareaware.org/wp-content/uploads/2015/10/2008_grandparents_report-finalrept.pdf

Graziottin, A. (2010). Menopause and sexuality: Key issues in premature menopause and beyond. *Annals of the New York Academy of Sciences*, *1205*(1), 254–261.

Hall, E. D., Meng, J., & Reynolds, R. M. (2020). Confidant network and interpersonal communication associations with depression in older adulthood. *Health Communication*, *35*(7), 872–881.

Hall, J. A. (2011). Sex differences in friendship expectations: A meta-analysis. *Journal of Social and Personal Relationships*, *28*(6), 723–747.

Harris, S., Witt, P. J., & Thomas, T. (Executive Producers). (1985–1992). *The golden girls* [TV series]. Witt/Thomas/Harris Productions; Touchstone Television.

Hartwick, J., & Nagao, D. H. (1990). Social facilitation effects in recognition memory. *British Journal of Social Psychology*, *29*(3), 193–210.

Hawkins, A. J., Willoughby, B. J., & Doherty, W. J. (2012). Reasons for divorce and openness to marital reconciliation. *Journal of Divorce and Remarriage*, *53*(6), 453–463.

Hayslip, B., Jr., & Kaminski, P. L. (2005). Grandparents raising their grandchildren: A review of the literature and suggestions for practice. *The Gerontologist*, *45*(2), 262–269.

Hayslip, B., Jr., & Montoro-Rodriguez, J. (2023, October 10). First-time grandparenthood: Effects of on-timeness and off-timeness. *Journal of Intergenerational Relationships*. Advance online publication. https://doi.org/10.1080/15350770.2023.2267539

Helliwell, J. F., Layard, R., & Sachs, J. (Eds.). (2013). *World happiness report 2013*. United Nations Sustainable Development Solutions Network.

Holt-Lunstad, J. (2017). Friendship and health. In M. Hojjat & A. Moyer (Eds.), *The psychology of friendship* (pp. 233–248). Oxford University Press.

Holt-Lunstad, J., Smith, T. B., & Layton, J. B. (2010). Social relationships and mortality risk: A meta-analytic review. *PLoS Medicine*, *7*, e1000316. https://www.doi.org/10.1371/journal.ped.1000316

Hughes, M. E., & Waite, L. J. (2009). Marital biography and health at mid-life. *Journal of Health and Social Behavior*, *50*(3), 344–358.

Kaslow, F., & Robison, J. A. (1996). Long-term satisfying marriages: Perceptions of contributing factors. *American Journal of Family Therapy*, *24*(2), 153–170.

Kerstetter, D. L., Yarnal, C. M., Son, J. S., Yen, I. Y., & Baker, B. S. (2008). Functional support associated with belonging to the Red Hat Society®, a leisure-based social network. *Journal of Leisure Research*, *40*(4), 531–555.

Kruse, A., & Schmitt, E. (2012). Generativity as a route to active ageing. *Current Gerontology and Geriatrics Research, 2012*, 647650. https://doi.org/10.1155/2012/647650

Landry-Meyer, L., & Newman, B. M. (2004). An exploration of the grandparent caregiver role. *Journal of Family Issues, 25*(8), 1005–1025.

Leopold, T., & Skopek, J. (2015). The demography of grandparenthood: An international profile. *Social Forces, 94*(2), 801–832.

Liechty, T., Yarnal, C., & Kerstetter, D. (2012). "I want to do everything!": Leisure innovation among retirement-age women. *Leisure Studies, 31*(4), 389–408.

Lindau, S. T., Schumm, L. P., Laumann, E. O., Levinson, W., O'Muircheartaigh, C. A., & Waite, L. J. (2007). A study of sexuality and health among older adults in the United States. *New England Journal of Medicine, 357*(8), 762–774.

Liu, Q., Zhang, Y., Wang, J., Li, S., Cheng, Y., Guo, J., Tang, Y., Zeng, H., & Zhu, Z. (2018). Erectile dysfunction and depression: A systematic review and meta-analysis. *The Journal of Sexual Medicine, 15*(8), 1073–1082.

Margolin, S. J. (2018). Cognitively active older adults' comprehension and metacomprehension of negated text. *Experimental Aging Research, 44*(4), 329–337. https://www.doi.org/10.1080/0361073X.2018.1475154

Mayol-García, Y., Gurrentz, B., & Kreider, R. M. (2021). *Number, timing, and duration of marriages and divorces: 2016*. U.S. Department of Commerce.

McAdams, D. P., de St. Aubin, E., & Logan, R. L. (1993). Generativity among young, midlife, and older adults. *Psychology and Aging, 8*(2), 221–230. https://doi.org/10.1037/0882-7974.8.2.221

McNaught, W., & Barth, M. C. (1992). Are older workers "good buys"? A case study of Days Inns of America. *MIT Sloan Management Review, 33*(3), 53.

Meudell, P. R., Hitch, G. J., & Kirby, P. (1992). Are two heads better than one? Experimental investigations of the social facilitation of memory. *Applied Cognitive Psychology, 6*(6), 525–543.

Mjelde-Mossey, L. A. (2007). Cultural and demographic changes and their effects upon the traditional grandparent role for Chinese elders. *Journal of Human Behavior in the Social Environment, 16*(3), 107–120.

Minkler, M., & Roe, K. M. (1993). *Grandmothers as caregivers: Raising children of the crack cocaine epidemic*. SAGE.

National Association of Child Care Resource and Referral Agencies. (2008). *Grandparents: A critical child care safety net*. https://www.childcareaware.org/wp-content/uploads/2015/10/2008_grandparents_report-finalrept.pdf

Nussbaum, J. F. (1994). Friendship in older adulthood. In M. L. Hummert, J. M. Wiemann, & J. F. Nussbaum (Eds.), *Interpersonal communication in older adulthood: Interdisciplinary theory and research* (pp. 209–225). SAGE.

O'Dare, C. E., Timonen, V., & Conlon, C. (2019). Intergenerational friendships of older adults: Why do we know so little about them? *Ageing and Society, 39*(1), 1–16.

Pecchioni, L. L., & Croghan, J. M. (2002). Young adults' stereotypes of older adults with their grandparents as the targets. *Journal of Communication, 52*(4), 715–730.

Posadas, J., & Vidal-Fernandez, M. (2013). Grandparents' childcare and female labor force participation. *IZA Journal of Labor Policy, 2*, 14. https://doi.org/10.1186/2193-9004-2-14

Powdthavee, N. (2008). Putting a price tag on friends, relatives, and neighbours: using surveys of life satisfaction to value social relationships. *The Journal of Socio-Economics, 37*(4), 1459–1480.

Reed, C. (2015, April 5). Dutch nursing home offers rent-free housing to students. *PBS NewsHour.* www.pbs.org/newshour/world/dutch-retirement-home-offers-rent-free-housing-students-one-condition

Reis, H. T. (1990). The role of intimacy in interpersonal relations. *Journal of Social and Clinical Psychology, 9*(1), 15–30.

Rettberg, J. R., Yao, J., & Brinton, R. D. (2014). Estrogen: A master regulator of bioenergetic systems in the brain and body. *Frontiers in Neuroendocrinology, 35*(1), 8–30.

Riggle, E. D., Wickham, R. E., Rostosky, S. S., Rothblum, E. D., & Balsam, K. F. (2017). Impact of civil marriage recognition for long-term same-sex couples. *Sexuality Research and Social Policy, 14*(2), 223–232.

Robertson, J. F. (1976). Significance of grandparents: Perceptions of young adult grandchildren. *The Gerontologist, 16*, 137–140.

Santoro, N., & Randolph, J. F. (2011). Reproductive hormones and the menopause transition. *Obstetrics and Gynecology Clinics, 38*(3), 455–466.

Satici, B., & Deniz, M. E. (2020). Relational humor and marital satisfaction in married individuals. *International Journal of Psychology and Educational Studies, 7*(2), 72–78.

Scott, S. B., Rhoades, G. K., Stanley, S. M., Allen, E. S., & Markman, H. J. (2013). Reasons for divorce and recollections of premarital intervention: Implications for improving relationship education. *Couple and Family Psychology: Research and Practice, 2*(2), 131–145.

Sears, M. S., Repetti, R. L., Robles, T. F., & Reynolds, B. M. (2016). I just want to be left alone: Daily overload and marital behavior. *Journal of Family Psychology, 30*(5), 569–579. https://doi.org/10.1037/fam0000197

Sharifian, N., Kraal, A. Z., Zaheed, A. B., Sol, K., & Zahodne, L. B. (2020). The longitudinal association between social network composition and episodic memory in older adulthood: The importance of contact frequency with friends. *Aging & Mental Health, 24*(11), 1789–1795.

Smith, K. (2002). *Who's minding the kids? Child care arrangements: Spring 1997.* Current Population Reports, P70-86. U.S. Census Bureau.

Sonnega, A., & Weir, D. R. (2014). The Health and Retirement Study: A public data resource for research on aging. *Open Health Data, 2*(1), e7. http://doi.org/10.5334/ohd.am

Spanier, G. B. (1976). Measuring dyadic adjustment: New scales for assessing the quality of marriage and similar dyads. *Journal of Marriage and the Family, 38*(1), 15–28.

Stricker, G., & Hillman, J. L. (1996). Attitudes toward older adults: The perceived value of grandparent as a social role. *Journal of Adult Development, 3*, 71–79.

Strizzi, J. M., Ciprić, A., Sander, S., & Hald, G. M. (2021). Divorce is stressful, but how stressful? Perceived stress among recently divorced Danes. *Journal of Divorce and Remarriage, 62*(4), 295–311.

Svensson-Dianellou, A., Smith, P. K., & Mestheneos, E. (2010). Family help by Greek grandparents. *Journal of Intergenerational Relationships, 8*(3), 249–263.

Tavakol, Z., Nasrabadi, A. N., Moghadam, Z. B., Salehiniya, H., & Rezaei, E. (2017). A review of the factors associated with marital satisfaction. *Galen Medical Journal, 6*(3), 197–207.

Thiele, D. M., & Whelan, T. A. (2006). The nature and dimensions of the grandparent role. *Marriage & Family Review, 40*(1), 93–108.

Twenge, J. M., Campbell, W. K., & Foster, C. A. (2003). Parenthood and marital satisfaction: A meta-analytic review. *Journal of Marriage and Family, 65*(3), 574–583.

VanLaningham, J., Johnson, D.R., & Amato, P. (2001). Marital happiness, marital duration, and the U-shaped curve: Evidence from a five-wave panel study. *Social Forces, 79*(4), 1313–1341.

Walen, H. R., & Lachman, M. E. (2000). Social support and strain from partner, family, and friends: Costs and benefits for men and women in adulthood. *Journal of Social and Personal Relationships, 17*(1), 5–30.

Ward, R., Howorth, M., Wilkinson, H., Campbell, S., & Keady, J. (2012). Supporting the friendships of people with dementia. *Dementia-International Journal of Social Research and Practice, 11*(3), 287–303.

Weber, J. A., & Waldrop, D. P. (2000). Grandparents raising grandchildren: Families in transition. *Journal of Gerontological Social Work, 33*(2), 27–46.

Westrick-Payne, K. K. (2023). *Grandparents' characteristics by age*. Bowling Green State University. https://www.bgsu.edu/ncfmr/resources/data/family-profiles/westrick-payne-grandparents-characteristics-age-fp-23-02.html#

Willroth, E., & Hill, P. (2021). Social relationships in older adulthood and links with psychological and physical well-being. *Innovation in Aging, 5*(Suppl. 1), 212.

Winterich, J. A. (2003). Sex, menopause, and culture: Sexual orientation and the meaning of menopause for women's sex lives. *Gender and Society, 17*(4), 627–642.

Zhang, Z., & Hayward, M. D. (2006). Gender, the marital life course, and cardiovascular disease in late midlife. *Journal of Marriage and Family, 68*(3), 639–657.

Zhang, Z., Liu, H., & Yu, Y.-L. (2016). Marital biography and health in middle and late life. In J. Bookwala (Ed.), *Couple relationships in the middle and later years: Their nature, complexity, and role in health and illness* (pp. 199–218). American Psychological Association.

CHAPTER 7

Adams, C., Smith, M. C., Pasupathi, M., & Vitolo, L. (2002). Social context effects on story recall in older and younger women: Does the listener make a difference? *Journal of Gerontology: Psychological Sciences, 57B*, P28–P40.

Andersson, J., & Rönnberg, J. (1996). Collaboration and memory: Effects of dyadic retrieval on different memory tasks. *Applied Cognitive Psychology, 10*(2), 171–181.

Atkinson, R. C., & Shiffrin, R. M. (1968). Human memory: A proposed system and its control processes. In K. W. Spence & J. T. Spence (Eds.), *Psychology of learning and motivation* (Vol. 2, pp. 89–195). Academic Press.

Bailey, P. E., & Henry, J. D. (2008). Growing less empathetic with age: Disinhibition of the self-perspective. *Journal of Gerontology: Psychological Sciences, 63B*(4), P219–P226.

Barnier, A. J., & Sutton, J. (2008). From individual to collective memory: Theoretical and empirical perspectives. *Memory, 16*, 177–182. https://www.doi.org/10.3758/MC.38.3.255

Blair, I. V. (2013). Implicit stereotypes and prejudice. In G. B. Moskowitz (Ed.), *Cognitive social psychology* (pp. 354–369). Psychology Press.

Blanchard-Fields, F., & Norris, L. (1994). Causal attributions from adolescence through adulthood: Age differences, ego level, and generalized response style. *Aging, Neuropsychology, and Cognition, 1*, 67– 86. https://www.doi.org/10.1080/09289919408251451

Blumen, H. M., Rajaram, S., & Henkel, L. (2013) The applied value of collaborative memory research in aging: Behavioral and neural considerations. *Journal of Applied Research in Memory and Cognition, 2*, 107–117.

Burke, D. M., Locantore, J. K., Austin, A. A., & Chae, B. (2004). Cherry pit primes Brad Pitt: Homophone priming effects on young and older adults' production of proper names. *Psychological Science, 15*(3), 164–170.

Burke, D. M., MacKay, D. G., & James, L. E. (2000). Theoretical approaches to language and aging. In T. J. Perfect & E. A. Maylor (Eds.), *Models of cognitive aging* (pp. 204–237). Oxford University Press.

Burke, D. M., MacKay, D. G., Worthley, J. S., & Wade, E. (1991). On the tip of the tongue: What causes word finding failures in young and older adults? *Journal of Memory and Language, 30*(5), 542–579.

Castel, A. D. (2007). The adaptive and strategic use of memory by older adults: Evaluative processing and value-directed remembering. *Psychology of Learning and Motivation, 48*, 225–270.

Chasteen, A. L., Schwarz, N., & Park, D. C. (2002). The activation of aging stereotypes in young and older adults. *Journal of Gerontology Psychological Sciences, 57B*(6), P540–P547.

Chen, Y., & Blanchard-Fields, F. (1997). Age differences in stages of attributional processing. *Psychology of Aging, 12*(4), 694–703. https://www.doi.org/0882-7974/97/53.00

Chen, Y., & Blanchard-Fields, F. (2000). Unwanted thought: Age differences in the correction of social judgments. *Psychology of Aging, 15*(3), 475–482. https://www.doi.org/10.1037//0882-7974.14.3.475

Coats, A. H., & Blanchard-Fields, F. (2013). Making judgments about other people: Impression formation and attributional processing in older adults. *International Journal of Ageing and Later Life, 8*(1), 97–110.

Erber, J. T., Szuchman, L. T., & Rothberg, S. T. (1990). Everyday memory failure: Age differences in appraisal and attribution. *Psychology and Aging, 5*(2), 236–241. https://doi.org/10.1037/0882-7974.5.2.236

Fiske, S. T., Cuddy, A. C., Glick, P., & Xu, J. (2002). A model of (often mixed) stereotype content: Competence and warmth respectively follow from perceived status and competition. *Journal of Personality and Social Psychology*, *82*, 878–902.

Funder, D. C. (1982). On the accuracy of dispositional versus situational attributions. *Social Cognition*, *1*(3), 205–222.

Galinsky, A. D., & Moskowitz, G. B. (2007). Further ironies of suppression: Stereotype and counterstereotype accessibility. *Journal of Experimental Social Psychology*, *43*(5), 833–841.

Haghighi, P., & Oremus, M. (2023). Examining the association between functional social support, marital status, and memory: a systematic review. *BMC Geriatrics*, *23*(1), 290.

Hasher, L., & Zacks, R. T. (1988). Working memory, comprehension, and aging: A review and a new view. *Psychology of Learning and Motivation*, *22*, 193–225.

Henkel, L. A., & Rajaram, S. (2011). Collaborative remembering in older adults: Age-invariant outcomes in the context of episodic recall deficits. *Psychology and Aging*, *26*(3), 532–545. https://www.doi.org/10.1037/a0023106

Hertzog, C., & Hultsch, D. F. (2000). Metacognition in adulthood and old age. In F. I. M. Craik & T. A. Salthouse (Eds.), *The handbook of aging and cognition* (pp. 417–466). Erlbaum.

Hess, T. M., & Auman, C. (2001). Aging and social expertise: The impact of trait-diagnostic information on impressions of others. *Psychology and Aging*, *16*, 497–510. https://www.doi.org/10.1037/0882-7974.16.3.497

Hess, T. M., Auman, C., Colcombe, S. J., & Rahhal, T. A. (2003). The impact of stereotype threat on age differences in memory performance. *The Journals of Gerontology: Series B*, *58*(1), P3–P11. https://doi.org/10.1093/geronb/58.1.P3.

Hess, T. M., Hinson, J. T., & Statham, J. A. (2004). Explicit and implicit stereotype activation effects on memory: Do age and awareness moderate the impact of priming? *Psychology and Aging*, *19*(3), 495–505.

Hess, T. M., & Smith, B. T. (2014). Aging and the impact of irrelevant information on social judgments. *Psychology and Aging*, *29*(3), 542–553.

Hilton, D. J., Smith, R. H., & Kin, S. H. (1995). Processes of causal explanation and distributional attribution. *Journal of Personality and Social Psychology*, *68*(3), 377–387.

Hummert, M. L., Garstka, T. A., Shaner, J. L., & Stratham, S. (1994). Stereotypes of the elderly held by young, middle-aged, and elderly adults. *Journal of Gerontology: Psychological Sciences*, *49*, P240–P249.

Kelly, M. E., Duff, H., Kelly, S., McHugh Power, J. E., Brennan, S., Lawlor, B. A., & Loughrey, D. G. (2017). The impact of social activities, social networks, social support and social relationships on the cognitive functioning of healthy older adults: A systematic review. *Systematic Reviews*, *6*(1), 1–18.

Krendl, A. C., Rule, N. O., & Ambady, N. (2014). Does aging impair first impression formation accuracy? Differentiating emotion recognition from complex social inferences. *Psychology and Aging*, *29*(3), 482–490.

Levy, B. (1996). Improving memory in old age through implicit self-stereotyping. *Journal of Personality and Social Psychology*, *71*(6), 1092–1107. https://www.doi.org/0022-3514/96/$3.00

Levy, B. R., Chung, P. H., Bedford, T., & Navrazhina, K. (2014). Facebook as a site for negative age stereotypes. *The Gerontologist*, *54*(2), 172–176.

Levy, B., & Langer, E. (1994). Aging free from negative stereotypes: Successful memory in China and among the American deaf. *Journal of Personality and Social Psychology*, *66*, 989–997.

MacKay, D. G. (1987). *The organization of perception and action: A theory for language and other cognitive skills*. New York: Springer-Verlag.

Macrae, C. N., Milne, A. B., & Bodenhausen, G. V. (1994). Stereotypes as energy-saving devices: A peek inside the cognitive toolbox. *Journal of personality and Social Psychology*, *66*(1), 37–47.

Nosek, B. A., Smyth, F. L., Hansen, J. J., Devos, T., Lindner, N. M., Ranganath, K. A., Tucker Smith, C., Olson, K. R., Chugh, D., Greenwald, A. G., & Banaji, M. R. (2007). Pervasiveness and correlates of implicit attitudes and stereotypes. *European Review of Social Psychology*, *18*(1), 36–88.

Oremus, M., Tyas, S. L., Maxwell, C. J., Konnert, C., O'Connell, M. E., & Law, J. (2020). Social support availability is positively associated with memory in persons aged 45–85 years: A cross-sectional analysis of the Canadian Longitudinal Study on Aging. *Archives of Gerontology and Geriatrics*, *86*, 103962.

Radvansky, G. A., Copeland, D. E., & Von Hippel, W. (2010). Stereotype activation, inhibition, and aging. *Journal of Experimental Social Psychology*, *46*(1), 51–60.

Rahhal, T. A., Hasher, L., & Colcombe, S. J. (2001). Instructional manipulations and age differences in memory: Now you see them, now you don't. *Psychology and Aging*, *16*(4), 697–706.

Rey-Mermet, A., & Gade, M. (2018). Inhibition in aging: What is preserved? What declines? A meta-analysis. *Psychonomic Bulletin and Review*, *25*, 1695–1716. https://doi.org/10/3758/s13423-017-1384-7

Salthouse, T. A. (1984). Effects of age and skill of typing. *Journal of Experimental Psychology: General*, *113*(3), 345–371.

Salthouse, T. A. (1996). The processing-speed theory of adult age differences in cognition. *Psychological Review*, *103*(3), 403–428. https://doi.org/10.1037/003295X.103.3.403

Stewart, B. D., von Hippel, W., & Radvansky, G. A. (2009). Age, race, and implicit prejudice. *Psychological Science*, *20*, 164–168. https://www.doi.org/10.1111/j.1467-9280.2009.02274.x

Stewart, T. L., Latu, I. M., Kawakami, K., & Myers, A. C. (2010). Consider the situation: Reducing automatic stereotyping through situational attribution training. *Journal of Experimental Social Psychology*, *46*(1), 221–225.

von Hippel, W., Silver, L. A., & Lynch, M. E. (2000). Stereotyping against your will: The role of inhibitory ability in stereotyping and prejudice among the elderly. *Personality and Social Psychology Bulletin*, *26*, 523–532.

Wang, M., & Chen, Y. (2004). Age differences in the correction processes of context-induced biases: When correction succeeds. *Psychology and Aging*, *19*(3), 536–540. https://www.doi.org/10.1037/0882-7974.19.3.536

Weiss, D., Sassenberg, K., & Freund, A. M. (2013). When feeling different pays off: How older adults can counteract negative age-related information. *Psychology and Aging*, *28*(4), 1140–1146. https://www.doi.org/10.1037/a0033811

Weldon, M. S. (2001). Remembering as a social process. In D. L. Medin (Ed.), *The psychology of learning and motivation: Advances in research and theory* (pp. 67–120). Academic Press.

Yoon, C., Hasher, L., Feinberg, F., Rahhal, T. A., & Winocur, G. (2000). Cross-cultural differences in memory: The role of culture-based stereotypes about aging. *Psychology and Aging*, *15*, 694–704.

CHAPTER 8

Al-Ani, M., & Winchester, D. E. (2015). Prevalence and overlap of noncardiac conditions in the evaluation of low-risk acute chest pain patients. *Critical Pathways in Cardiology*, *14*(3), 97–102.

Alpert, J. E., & Fava, M. (1997). Nutrition and depression: The role of folate. *Nutrition Reviews*, *55*(5), 145–149.

Alzheimer's Association. (2023). *Alzheimer's disease facts and figures*. https://www.alz.org/alzheimers-dementia/facts-figures

Alzheimer's Disease International. (n.d.). *Vascular dementia*. https://www.alzint.org/about/dementia-facts-figures/types-of-dementia/vascular-dementia

American Association for Geriatric Psychiatry. (2022, October 27). *Anxiety and older adults: Overcoming worry and fear*. https://www.aagponline.org/index.php?src=gendocs&ref=anxiety

Anxiety and Depression Association of America. (2024). *Anxiety disorders: Facts and statistics*. https://adaa.org/understanding-anxiety/facts-statistics

Bagyinszky, E., Youn, Y. C., An, S. S. A., & Kim, S. (2014). The genetics of Alzheimer's disease. *Clinical Interventions in Aging*, *9*, 535–551.

Barry, L. C., Thorpe, R. J., Jr., Penninx, B. W., Yaffe, K., Wakefield, D., Ayonayon, H. N., Satterfield, S., Newman, A. B., & Simonsick, E. M. (2014). Race-related differences in depression onset and recovery in older persons over time: The health, aging, and body composition study. *The American Journal of Geriatric Psychiatry*, *22*(7), 682–691. https://doi.org/10.1016/j.jagp.2013.09.001

Beck, A. T., Ward, C. H., Mendelson, M., Mock, J., & Erbaugh, J. (1961). An inventory for measuring depression. *Archives of General Psychiatry*, *4*, 53–63.

Bellenguez, C., Grenier-Boley, B., & Lambert, J. C. (2020). Genetics of Alzheimer's disease: Where we are, and where we are going. *Current Opinion in Neurobiology*, *61*, 40–48.

Bertram, L., & Tanzi, R. E. (2012). The genetics of Alzheimer's disease. *Progress in Molecular Biology and Translational Science*, *107*, 79–100.

Bhugra, D., Till, A., & Sartorius, N. (2013). What is mental health?. *International Journal of Social Psychiatry*, *59*(1), 3–4.

Blennow, K., de Leon, M. J., & Zetterberg, H. (2006). Alzheimer's disease. *Lancet*, *368*(95331), 387–403.

Borelli, C. M., Grennan, D., & Muth, C. C. (2020). Causes of memory loss in elderly persons. *JAMA*, *323*(5), 486–486.

Boucher, L. A. (1999). Disruptive behaviors in individuals with Alzheimer's disease: A behavioral approach. *American Journal of Alzheimer's Disease*, *14*(6), 351–356.

Bower, E. S., Wetherell, J. L., Mon, T., & Lenze, E. J. (2015). Treating anxiety disorders in older adults: Current treatments and future directions. *Harvard Review of Psychiatry*, *23*(5), 329–342.

Brown, T. A., Campbell, L. A., Lehman, C. L., Grisham, J. R., & Mancill, R. B. (2001). Current and lifetime comorbidity of the *DSM-IV* anxiety and mood disorders in a large clinical sample. *Journal of Abnormal Psychology*, *110*(4), 585–599. https://doi.org/10.1037/0021-843X.110.4.585

Bunt, S., Steverink, N., Olthof, J., Van Der Schans, C. P., & Hobbelen, J. S. M. (2017). Social frailty in older adults: A scoping review. *European Journal of Ageing*, *14*, 323–334.

Carleton, R. N., Duranceau, S., Freeston, M. H., Boelen, P. A., McCabe, R. E., & Antony, M. M. (2014). "But it might be a heart attack": Intolerance of uncertainty and panic disorder symptoms. *Journal of Anxiety Disorders*, *28*(5), 463–470.

Carr, C. P., Martins, C. M. S., Stingel, A. M., Lemgruber, V. B., & Juruena, M. F. (2013). The role of early life stress in adult psychiatric disorders: A systematic review according to childhood trauma subtypes. *The Journal of Nervous and Mental Disease*, *201*(12), 1007–1020.

Choi, S. H., Na, D. L., Lee, B. H., Hahm, D. S., Jeong, J. H., Yoon, S. J., Yoo, K. H., Ha, C.-K., & Han, I. W. (2001). Estimating the validity of the Korean version of expanded clinical dementia rating (CDR) scale. *Journal of the Korean Neurological Association*, *19*(6), 585–591.

Cramer, A. O., Van Borkulo, C. D., Giltay, E. J., Van Der Maas, H. L., Kendler, K. S., Scheffer, M., & Borsboom, D. (2016). Major depression as a complex dynamic system. *PlOS One*, *11*(12), e0167490.

Crowe, M., Andel, R., Pedersen, N. L., Johansson, B., & Gatz, M. (2003). Does participation in leisure activities lead to reduced risk of Alzheimer's disease? A prospective study of Swedish twins. *The Journals of Gerontology Series B: Psychological Sciences and Social Sciences*, *58*(5), P249–P255.

Dan, S., Sharma, D., Rastogi, K., Shaloo, Ojha, H., Pathak, M., & Singhal, R. (2022). Therapeutic and diagnostic applications of nanocomposites in the treatment Alzheimer's disease studies. *Biointerface Research in Applied Chemistry*, *12*(1), 940–960.

Dauncey, M. J. (2009). New insights into nutrition and cognitive neuroscience: Symposium on "Early nutrition and later disease: Current concepts, research and implications." *Proceedings of the Nutrition Society*, *68*(4), 408–415.

DeLong, G. R. (1993). Effects of nutrition on brain development in humans. *The American Journal of Clinical Nutrition*, *57*(2), S286–S290.

Domschke, K., & Maron, E. (2013). Genetic factors in anxiety disorders. *Anxiety Disorders*, *29*, 24–46.

Donahue, J. J. (2020). Fight-flight-freeze system. In V. Zeigler-Hill & T. K. Shackelford (Eds.), *Encyclopedia of personality and individual differences* (pp. 1590–1595). Springer.

Donovan, R. J., Henley, N., Jalleh, G., Silburn, S. R., Zubrick, S. R., & Williams, A.

(2007). People's beliefs about factors contributing to mental health: Implications for mental health promotion. *Health Promotion Journal of Australia*, *18*(1), 50–56.

Féart, C., Samieri, C., & Barberger-Gateau, P. (2010). Mediterranean diet and cognitive function in older adults. *Current Opinion in Clinical Nutrition and Metabolic Care*, *13*(1), 14–18.

Fiske, A., Wetherell, J. L., & Gatz, M. (2009). Depression in older adults. *Annual Review of Clinical Psychology*, *5*, 363–389.

Folstein, M. F., Folstein, S. E., & McHugh, P. R. (1975). "Mini-mental state": A practical method for grading the cognitive state of patients for the clinician. *Journal of Psychiatric Research*, *12*(3), 189–198.

Fusar-Poli, P., de Pablo, G. S., De Micheli, A., Nieman, D. H., Correll, C. U., Kessing, L. V., Pfenning, A., Bechdolf, A., Borgwardt, S., Arango, C., & van Amelsvoort, T. (2020). What is good mental health? A scoping review. *European Neuropsychopharmacology*, *31*, 33–46.

Gallagher, D., Nies, G., & Thompson, L.W. (1992). Reliability of the Beck Depression Inventory with older adults. *Journal of Consulting and Clinical Psychology*, *50*(1), 152–153.

Gallo, J. J., Anthony, J. C., & Muthén, B. O. (1994). Age differences in the symptoms of depression: A latent trait analysis. *Journal of Gerontology*, *49*(6), P251–P264.

García-Portilla, P., de la Fuente Tomás, L., Bobes-Bascarán, T., Jiménez Treviño, L., Zurrón Madera, P., Suárez Álvarez, M., Menéndez Miranda, I., García Álvarez, L., Sáiz Martínez, P. A., & Bobes, J. (2021). Are older adults also at higher psychological risk from COVID-19? *Aging and Mental Health*, *25*(7), 1297–1304.

Geerlings, S. W., Beekman, A. T., Deeg, D. J., & Van Tilburg, W. (2000). Physical health and the onset and persistence of depression in older adults: An eight-wave prospective community-based study. *Psychological Medicine*, *30*(2), 369–380

German, L., Kahana, C., Rosenfeld, V., Zabrowsky, I., Wiezer, Z., Fraser, D., & Shahar, D. R. (2011). Depressive symptoms are associated with food insufficiency and nutritional deficiencies in poor community-dwelling elderly people. *The Journal of Nutrition, Health and Aging*, *15*, 3–8.

Girgus, J. S., Yang, K., & Ferri, C. V. (2017). The gender difference in depression: Are elderly women at greater risk for depression than elderly men? *Geriatrics*, *2*(4), 35.

Goetz, C. G., Emre, M., & Dubois, B. (2008). Parkinson's disease dementia: Definitions, guidelines, and research perspectives in diagnosis. *Annals of Neurology: Official Journal of the American Neurological Association and the Child Neurology Society*, *64*(S2), S81–S92.

Gow, A. J., Corley, J., Starr, J. M., & Deary, I. J. (2013). Which social network or support factors are associated with cognitive abilities in old age? *Gerontology*, *59*(5), 454–463.

Grainger, S. A., Crawford, J. D., Kochan, N. A., Mather, K. A., Chander, R. J., Draper, B., Brodaty, H., Sachdev, P. S., & Henry, J. D. (2020). An investigation into early-life stress and cognitive function in older age. *International Psychogeriatrics*, *32*(11), 1325–1329.

Gratwicke, J., Jahanshahi, M., & Foltynie, T. (2015). Parkinson's disease dementia: A neural networks perspective. *Brain, 138(6)*, 1454–1476.

Green, R. C., Cupples, L. A., Go, R., Benke, K. S., Edeki, T., Griffith, P. A., Williams, M., Hipps, Y., Graff-Radford, N., Bachman, D., Farrer, L. A., & MIRAGE Study Group. (2002). Risk of dementia among white and African American relatives of patients with Alzheimer disease. *JAMA*, *287*(3), 329–336.

Guesnet, P., & Alessandri, J. M. (2011). Docosahexaenoic acid (DHA) and the developing central nervous system (CNS): Implications for dietary recommendations. *Biochimie*, *93*(1), 7–12. https://www.doi.org/10.1016/j.biochi.2010.05005

Harbottle, L. (2019). The effect of nutrition on older people's mental health. *British Journal of Community Nursing*, *24*(7), S12–S16.

Hettema, J. M., Prescott, C. A., Myers, J. M., Neale, M. C., & Kendler, K. S. (2005). The structure of genetic and environmental risk factors for anxiety disorders in men and women. *Archives of General Psychiatry*, *62*(2), 182–189.

Hovens, J. G., Wiersma, J. E., Giltay, E. J., Van Oppen, P., Spinhoven, P., Penninx, B. W., & Zitman, F. G. (2010).

Childhood life events and childhood trauma in adult patients with depressive, anxiety and comorbid disorders vs. controls. *Acta Psychiatrica Scandinavica, 122*(1), 66–74.

Hudson, A., & Hudson, P. (2021). Risk factors for cannabis-related mental health harms in older adults: A review. *Clinical Gerontologist, 44*(1), 3–15.

Huhn, S., Kharabian Masouleh, S., Stumvoll, M., Villringer, A., & Witte, A. V. (2015). Components of a Mediterranean diet and their impact on cognitive functions in aging. *Frontiers in Aging Neuroscience, 7*, 132.

Iavarone, A., Ziello, A. R., Pastore, F., Fasanaro, A. M., & Poderico, C. (2014). Caregiver burden and coping strategies in caregivers of patients with Alzheimer's disease. *Neuropsychiatric Disease and Treatment, 10*, 1407–1413.

Iqtidar, N., & Chaudary, M. N. (2012). Misdiagnosed vitamin B12 deficiency a challenge to be confronted by use of modern screening markers. *Journal of the Pakistan Medical Association, 62*(11), 1223–1229.

Jiang, Y., Yang, H., Zhao, J., Wu, Y., Zhou, X., & Cheng, Z. (2020). Reliability and concurrent validity of Alzheimer's disease assessment scale–Cognitive subscale, Chinese version (ADAS-Cog-C) among Chinese community-dwelling older people population. *The Clinical Neuropsychologist, 34*(Supp. 1), 43–53.

Kalaria, R. (2002). Similarities between Alzheimer's disease and vascular dementia. *Journal of the Neurological Sciences, 203–204*, 29–34.

Katz, S., Ford, A. B., Moskowitz, R. W., Jackson, B. A., & Jaffe, M. W. (1963). Studies of illness in the aged: the index of ADL: A standardized measure of biological and psychosocial function. *JAMA, 185*(12), 914–919.

Korczyn, A. D., Vakhapova, V., & Grinberg, L. T. (2012). Vascular dementia. *Journal of the Neurological Sciences, 322*(1–2), 2–10.

Krause, N. (1986). Social support, stress, and well-being among older adults. *Journal of Gerontology, 41*(4), 512–519.

Krause, N., Shaw, B. A., & Cairney, J. (2004). A descriptive epidemiology of lifetime trauma and the physical health status of older adults. *Psychology of Aging, 19*(4), 637–648. https://www.doi.org/10.1037/0882-7974.19.4.637

Krendl, A. C., & Perry, B. L. (2021). The impact of sheltering in place during the COVID-19 pandemic on older adults' social and mental well-being. *The Journals of Gerontology: Series B, 76*(2), e53–e58.

Ku, P. W., Steptoe, A., & Chen, L. J. (2017). Prospective associations of exercise and depressive symptoms in older adults: The role of apolipoprotein E4. *Quality of Life Research, 26*(7), 1799–1808.

Kumar, N., Kumar, V., Anand, P., Kumar, V., Dwivedi, A. R., & Kumar, V. (2022). Advancements in the development of multi-target directed ligands for the treatment of Alzheimer's disease. *Bioorganic & Medicinal Chemistry, 61*, 116742.

Lanius, R. A., Vermetten, E., & Pain, C. (2010). *The impact of early life trauma on health and disease: The hidden epidemic*. Cambridge University Press.

Leggieri, M., Thaut, M. H., Fornazzari, L., Schweizer, T. A., Barfett, J., Munoz, D. G., & Fischer, C. E. (2019). Music intervention approaches for Alzheimer's disease: A review of the literature. *Frontiers in Neuroscience, 13*, 132.

Lewis, M. S., Miller, L. S., Johnson, M. A., Dolce, E. B., Allen, R. H., & Stabler, S. P. (2005). Elevated methylmalonic acid is related to cognitive impairment in older adults enrolled in an elderly nutrition program. *Journal of Nutrition for the Elderly, 24*(3), 47–65.

Lubben, J. E. (1988). Assessing social networks among elderly populations. *Family and Community Health, 11*, 42–52.

Luo, M. S., Chui, E. W. T., & Li, L. W. (2020). The longitudinal associations between physical health and mental health among older adults. *Aging and Mental Health, 24*(12), 1990–1998.

Mackenzie, C. S., Reynolds, K., Cairney, J., Streiner, D. L., & Sareen, J. (2012). Disorder-specific mental health service use for mood and anxiety disorders: Associations with age, sex, and psychiatric comorbidity. *Depression and Anxiety, 29*(3), 234–242.

Mackenzie, C. S., Scott, T., Mather, A., & Sareen, J. (2008). Older adults' help-seeking attitudes and treatment beliefs concerning mental health problems. *The American Journal of Geriatric Psychiatry, 16*(12), 1010–1019.

Maggi, S., Ticinesi, A., Limongi, F., Noale, M., & Ecarnot, F. (2023). The role of nutrition and the Mediterranean diet on the trajectories of cognitive decline. *Experimental Gerontology, 173*, 112110.

Maschi, T., Baer, J., Morrissey, M. B., & Moreno, C. (2013). The aftermath of childhood trauma on late life mental and physical health: A review of the literature. *Traumatology, 19*(1), 49–64.

McKitrick, L. A., Camp, C. J., & Black, F. W. (1992). Prospective memory intervention in Alzheimer's disease. *Journal of Gerontology, 47*(5), P337–P343.

Melzer, T. M., Manosso, L. M., Yau, S. Y., Gil-Mohapel, J., & Brocardo, P. S. (2021). In pursuit of healthy aging: Effects of nutrition on brain function. *International Journal of Molecular Sciences, 22*(9), 5026.

Merikangas, K. R., & Low, N. C. (2004). The epidemiology of mood disorders. *Current Psychiatry Reports, 6*(6), 411–421.

Monti, J. M., Moulton, C. J., & Cohen, N. J. (2015). The role of nutrition on cognition and brain health in ageing: A targeted approach. *Nutrition Research Reviews, 28*(2), 167–180.

National Institute of Mental Health. (2023, July). *Major depression*. https://www.nimh.nih.gov/health/statistics/major-depression

National Institutes of Health. (2022, July 18). *Office of Dietary Supplements: Omega-3 fatty acids* (Fact sheet). ods.od.nih.gov/factsheets/Omega3FattyAcids-Consumer/

National Institutes of Health. (2023, December 15). *Office of Dietary Supplements: Vitamin B12* (Fact sheet). ods.od.nih.gov/factsheets/VitaminB12-Consumer/

Newsom, J. T., & Schulz, R. (1996). Social support as a mediator in the relationship between functional status and quality of life in older adults. *Psychology and Aging, 11*(1), 34–44. https://www.doi.org/10.1037/0882-7974.11.1.34

Payne, M. (2010). Nutrition and late-life depression: Etiological considerations. *Aging Health, 6*(1), 133–143.

Pelletier, A., Barul, C., Féart, C., Helmer, C., Bernard, C., Periot, O., Dilharreguy, B., Dartigues, J.-F., Allard, M., Barberger-Gateau, P., Catheline, G., & Samieri, C. (2015). Mediterranean diet and preserved brain structural connectivity in older subjects. *Alzheimer's and Dementia, 11*(9), 1023–1031.

Perez-Cornago, A., Sanchez-Villegas, A., Bes-Rastrollo, M., Gea, A., Molero, P., Lahortiga-Ramos, F., & Martinez-Gonzalez, M. Á. (2017). Relationship between adherence to Dietary Approaches to Stop Hypertension (DASH) diet indices and incidence of depression during up to 8 years of follow-up. *Public Health Nutrition, 20*(13), 2383–2392.

Petkus, A. J., Gatz, M., Reynolds, C. A., Kremen, W. S., & Wetherell, J. L. (2016). Stability of genetic and environmental contributions to anxiety symptoms in older adulthood. *Behavior Genetics, 46*(4), 492–505.

Pillemer, S. C., & Holtzer, R. (2016). The differential relationships of dimensions of perceived social support with cognitive function among older adults. *Aging and Mental Health, 20*(7), 727–735. https://doi.org/10.1080/13607863.2015.1033683

Pingol, E. (2023, December 10). *Katz Index of Independence in Activities of Daily Living*. Care Patron. https://www.carepatron.com/templates/katz-index-of-independence-in-activities-of-daily-living

Pini, L., Pievani, M., Bocchetta, M., Altomare, D., Bosco, P., Cavedo, E., Galluzzi, S., Marizzoni, M., & Frisoni, G. B. (2016). Brain atrophy in Alzheimer's disease and aging. *Ageing Research Reviews, 30*, 25–48.

Poulakis, K., Pereira, J. B., Mecocci, P., Vellas, B., Tsolaki, M., Kłoszewska, I., Soininen, H., Lovestone, S., Simmons, A., Wahlund, L.-O., & Westman, E. (2018). Heterogeneous patterns of brain atrophy in Alzheimer's disease. *Neurobiology of Aging, 65*, 98–108.

Prado, E. L., & Dewey, K. G. (2014). Nutrition and brain development in early life. *Nutrition Reviews, 72*(4), 267–284.

Qiu, C., Kivipelto, M., & Von Strauss, E. (2022). Epidemiology of Alzheimer's disease: Occurrence, determinants, and strategies toward intervention. *Dialogues in Clinical Neuroscience, 11*(2), 111–128.

Radloff, L. S. (1977). The CES-D scale: A self-report depression scale for research in the general population. *Applied Psychological Measurement, 1*, 385–401.

Rathod, R., Kale, A., & Joshi, S. (2016). Novel insights into the effect of vitamin B12 and omega-3 fatty acids on brain function. *Journal of Biomedical Science*, *23*, 1–7.

Reiss, A. B., Ahmed, S., Dayaramani, C., Glass, A. D., Gomolin, I. H., Pinkhasov, A., Stecker, M. M., Wisniewski, T., & De Leon, J. (2022). The role of mitochondrial dysfunction in Alzheimer's disease: A potential pathway to treatment. *Experimental Gerontology*, *164*, 111828.

Richardson, T. J., Lee, S. J., Berg-Weger, M., & Grossberg, G. T. (2013). Caregiver health: Health of caregivers of Alzheimer's and other dementia patients. *Current Psychiatry Reports*, *15*, 1–7.

Sartorius, N. (2002). *Fighting for mental health*. Cambridge University Press.

Shapiro, A. M., Benedict, R. H., Schretlen, D., & Brandt, J. (1999). Construct and concurrent validity of the Hopkins Verbal Learning Test–revised. *The Clinical Neuropsychologist*, *13*(3), 348–358.

Skoog, I., Waern, M., Duberstein, P., Blennow, K., Zetterberg, H., Börjesson-Hanson, A., Östling, S., Guo, X., Kern, J., Gustafson, D., Gudmundsson, P., Marlow, T., & Kern, S. (2015). A 9-year prospective population-based study on the association between the APOE* E4 allele and late-life depression in Sweden. *Biological Psychiatry*, *78*(10), 730–736.

Snowden, D. D. A, Greiner, L. H., Mortimer, J. A., Riley, K. P., Greiner, P. A., & Markesbery, W. R. (1997). Brain infarction and the clinical expression of Alzheimer disease: The Nun Study. *JAMA*, *277*, 813–817.

Tombaugh, T. N., & McIntyre, N. J. (1992). The Mini–Mental State Examination: A comprehensive review. *Journal of the American Geriatrics Society*, *40*(9), 922–935.

Torres, S. J., & Nowson, C. A. (2012). A moderate-sodium DASH-type diet improves mood in postmenopausal women. *Nutrition*, *28*(9), 896–900.

Trifu, S. C., Trifu, A. C., Aluaș, E., Tătaru, M. A., & Costea, R. V. (2020). Brain changes in depression. *Romanian Journal of Morphology and Embryology*, *61*(2), 361–370.

Uauy, R., & Dangour, A. D. (2006). Nutrition in brain development and aging: Role of essential fatty acids. *Nutrition Reviews*, *64*(Suppl. 2), S24–S33.

Vahia, I. V., Jeste, D. V., & Reynolds, C. F. (2020). Older adults and the mental health effects of COVID-19. *JAMA*, *324*(22), 2253–2254.

Varesi, A., Pierella, E., Romeo, M., Piccini, G. B., Alfano, C., Bjørklund, G., Oppong, A., Ricevuti, G., Esosito, C., Chirumbolo, S., & Pascale, A. (2022). The potential role of gut microbiota in Alzheimer's disease: From diagnosis to treatment. *Nutrients*, *14*(3), 668.

Vellone, E., Piras, G., Talucci, C., & Cohen, M. Z. (2008). Quality of life for caregivers of people with Alzheimer's disease. *Journal of Advanced Nursing*, *61*(2), 222–231.

VibrantGreen. (2018, April 22). *What is the role of acetylcholinesterase at a synapse?* https://socratic.org/questions/what-is-the-role-of-acetylcholinesterase-at-a-synapse-1

Wang, S. Y., & Kim, G. (2020). The relationship between physical-mental comorbidity and subjective well-being among older adults. *Clinical Gerontologist*, *43*(4), 455–465.

Webb, L. M., & Chen, C. Y. (2022). The COVID-19 pandemic's impact on older adults' mental health: Contributing factors, coping strategies, and opportunities for improvement. *International Journal of Geriatric Psychiatry*, *37*(1). https://www.doi.org/10.1002/gps.5647

Wetherell, J. L., Petkus, A. J., White, K. S., Nguyen, H., Kornblith, S., Andreescu, C., Zisook, S., & Lenze, E. J. (2013). Antidepressant medication augmented with cognitive-behavioral therapy for generalized anxiety disorder in older adults. *American Journal of Psychiatry*, *170*(7), 782–789.

Wolitzky-Taylor, K. B., Castriotta, N., Lenze, E. J., Stanley, M. A., & Craske, M. G. (2010). Anxiety disorders in older adults: A comprehensive review. *Depression and Anxiety*, *27*(2), 190–211.

World Health Organization. (2023, March 15). *Dementia*. https://www.who.int/news-room/fact-sheets/detail/dementia

Yesavage, J. A., Brink, T. L., Rose, T. L., Lum, O., Huang, V., Adey, M. B., & Leirer, V. O. (1983). Development and validation of a geriatric depression screening scale: A preliminary report. *Journal of Psychiatric Research, 39*, 37–49.

Yu, F., Kolanowski, A. M., Strumpf, N. E., & Eslinger, P. J. (2006). Improving cognition and function through exercise intervention in Alzheimer's disease. *Journal of Nursing Scholarship, 38*(4), 358–365.

Zarit, S. H., & Zarit, J. M. (2011). *Mental disorders in older adults: Fundamentals of assessment and treatment.* Guilford Press.

Zilberman, M. (2009). Substance abuse across the lifespan in women. In K. Brady, S. Back, & S. Greenfield (Eds.), *Women and addiction: A comprehensive handbook* (pp. 3–13). Guilford Press.

CHAPTER 9

Arnett, J. J. (2000). Emerging adulthood: A theory of development from the late teens through the twenties. *American Psychologist, 55*(5), 469.

Asebedo, S. D., Wilmarth, M. J., Seay, M. C., Archuleta, K., Brase, G. L., & MacDonald, M. (2019). Personality and saving behavior among older adults. *Journal of Consumer Affairs, 53*(2), 488–519.

Atkinson, R. C., & Shiffrin, R. M. (1968). Human memory: A proposed system and its control processes. In K. W. Spence & J. T. Spence (Eds.), *Psychology of learning and motivation* (Vol. 2, pp. 89–195). Academic Press.

Bouchard, T. J., Jr., Lykken, D. T., McGue, M., Segal, N. L., & Tellegen, A. (1990). Sources of human psychological differences: The Minnesota study of twins reared apart. *Science, 250*(4978), 223–228.

Campbell, L., Simpson, J. A., Stewart, M., & Manning, J. (2003). Putting personality in social context: Extraversion, emergent leadership, and the availability of rewards. *Personality and Social Psychology Bulletin, 29*(12), 1547–1559.

Caspi, A., & Moffitt, T. E. (1993). When do individual differences matter? A paradoxical theory of personality coherence. *Psychological Inquiry, 4*(4), 247–271.

Caspi, A., & Roberts, B. W. (2001). Personality development across the life course: The argument for change and continuity. *Psychological Inquiry, 12*(2), 49–66.

Chapman, B. P., Duberstein, P. R., Sörensen, S., Lyness, J. M. (2006). Personality and perceived health in older adults: The five factor model in primary care. *Journal of Gerontology: Psychological Sciences, 61B*, P362–P365.

Chapman, B. P., Duberstein, P. R., Sörensen, S., & Lyness, J. M. (2007). Gender differences in Five Factor Model personality traits in an elderly cohort. *Personality and Individual Differences, 43*(6), 1594–1603.

Chatterjee, S., & Fan, L. (2021). Older adults' life satisfaction: The roles of seeking financial advice and personality traits. *Journal of Financial Therapy, 12*(1), 51–78.

Chiu, R. K., & Francesco, A. M. (2003). Dispositional traits and turnover intention: Examining the mediating role of job satisfaction and affective commitment. *International Journal of Manpower, 24*(3), 284–298.

Cloninger, C. R. (1994). Temperament and personality. *Current Opinion in Neurobiology, 4*(2), 266–273.

Colquitt, J. A., & Simmering, M. J. (1998). Conscientiousness, goal orientation, and motivation to learn during the learning process: A longitudinal study. *Journal of Applied Psychology, 83*(4), 654–665. https://doi.org/10.1037/0021-9010.83.4.654

Costa, P. T., Jr., & McCrae, R. R. (1985). *The NEO Personality Inventory manual*. Psychological Assessment Resources.

Costa, P. T., Jr., & McCrae, R. R. (1988). From catalog to classification: Murray's needs and the five-factor model. *Journal of Personality and Social Psychology, 55*(2), 258–265.

Costa, P. T., Jr., & McCrae, R. R. (1994). Stability and change in personality from adolescence through adulthood. In C. F. Halverson, Jr., G. A. Kohnstamm, & R. P. Martin (Eds.), *The developing structure of temperament and personality from infancy to adulthood* (pp. 139–150). Erlbaum.

Costa, P. T., Jr., & McCrae, R. R. (2006). Trait and factor theories. In M. Hersen & J. C. Thomas (Eds.), *Comprehensive handbook of personality and psychopathology* (Vol. 1, pp. 96–115). Wiley.

Costa, P. T., Jr., Terracciano, A., & McCrae, R. R. (2001). Gender differences in personality traits across cultures: Robust and surprising findings. *Journal of Personality and Social Psychology, 81*(2), 322–331. https://doi.org/10.1037/0022-3514.81.2.322

Cox, K. S., Wilt, J., Olson, B., & McAdams, D. P. (2010). Generativity, the Big Five, and psychosocial adaptation in midlife adults. *Journal of Personality, 78*(4), 1185–1208.

Cumberland-Li, A., Eisenberg, N., Champion, C., Gershoff, E., & Fabes, R. A. (2003). The relation of parental emotionality and related dispositional traits to parental expression of emotion and children's social functioning. *Motivation and Emotion, 27*(1), 27–56.

Donnellan, M. B., & Lucas, R. E. (2008). Age differences in the Big Five across the life span: Evidence from two national samples. *Psychology and Aging, 23*(3), 558–566.

Ebaugh, H. R. F. (1988). *Becoming an ex: The process of role exit*. University of Chicago Press.

Erikson, E. (1959). *Identity and the life cycle*. International Universities Press.

Friedman, B., Veazie, P. J., Chapman, B. P., Manning, W. G., & Duberstein, P. R. (2013). Is personality associated with health care use by older adults? *The Milbank Quarterly, 91*(3), 491–527.

George, J. M., & Zhou, J. (2001). When openness to experience and conscientiousness are related to creative behavior: An interactional approach. *Journal of Applied Psychology, 86*(3), 513–524. https://doi.org/10.1037/0021-9010.86.3.513

George, L. K. (1993). Sociological perspectives on life transitions. *Annual Review of Sociology, 19*, 353–373.

Gillen, M., & Kim, H. (2014). Older adults' receipt of financial help: Does personality matter? *Journal of Family and Economic Issues, 35*(2), 178–189.

Herero, V. G., & Extremera, N. (2010). Daily life activities as mediators of the relationship between personality variables and subjective well-being among older adults. *Personality and Individual Differences, 49*(2), 124–129.

Hosseinkhanzadeh, A. A., & Taher, M. (2013). The relationship between personality traits with life satisfaction. *Sociology Mind, 3*(1), 99–105.

Kotov, R., Watson, D., Robles, J. P., & Schmidt, N. B. (2007). Personality traits and anxiety symptoms: The multilevel trait predictor model. *Behaviour Research and Therapy, 45*(7), 1485–1503.

Lang, F. R., Staudinger, U. M., & Carstensen, L. L. (1998). Perspectives on socioemotional selectivity in late life: How personality and social context do (and do not) make a difference. *The Journals of Gerontology Series B: Psychological Sciences and Social Sciences, 53*(1), P21–P30.

McAdams, D. P. (1996). Personality, modernity, and the storied self: A contemporary framework for studying persons. *Psychological Inquiry, 7*(4), 295–321.

McAdams, D. P. (2003). Identity and the life story. In R. Fivush & C. A. Haden (Eds.), *Autobiographical memory and the construction of a narrative self* (pp. 203–224). Psychology Press.

McAdams, D. P. (2006). The role of narrative in personality psychology today. *Narrative Inquiry, 16*(1), 11–18.

McAdams, D. P., Anyidoho, N. A., Brown, C., Huang, Y. T., Kaplan, B., & Machado, M. A. (2004). Traits and stories: Links between dispositional and narrative features of personality. *Journal of Personality, 72*(4), 761–784.

McAdams, D. P., & Olson, B. D. (2010). Personality development: Continuity and change over the life course. *Annual Review of Psychology, 61*, 517–542.

McCrae, R. R., & Costa, P. T., Jr. (1989). More reasons to adopt the five-factor model. *American Psychologist, 44*(2), 451–452.

Roberts, B. W., & DelVecchio, W. F. (2000). The rank-order consistency of personality from childhood to old age: A quantitative review of longitudinal studies. *Psychological Bulletin, 126*, 3–25.

Roberts, B. W., & Jackson, J. J. (2008). Sociogenomic personality psychology. *Journal of Personality, 76*(6), 1523–1544.

Roberts, B. W., & Wood, D. (2006). Personality development in the context of the neo-socioanalytic model of personality. In D. K. Mroczek & T. D. Little (Eds.), *Handbook of personality development* (pp. 11–39). Erlbaum.

Rostami, M., Ahmadboukani, S., & Saleh Manijeh, H. (2022). Big five personality traits and predicting mental health among Iranian older adults. *Gerontology and Geriatric Medicine, 8*, 23337214221132365.

Rothbart, M. K. (2007). Temperament, development, and personality. *Current Directions in Psychological Science, 16*(4), 207–212.

Saucier, G., & Simonds, J. (2006). The structure of personality and temperament. In D. K. Mroczek & T. D. Little (Eds.), *Handbook of personality development* (pp. 109–128). Erlbaum.

Saulsbury, M. D., Brown, U. J., Heyliger, S. O., & Beale, R. L. (2011). Effect of dispositional traits on pharmacy students' attitude toward cheating. *American Journal of Pharmaceutical Education, 75*(4), 69.

Shyer, C. (Director), & Meyers, N. (Producer). (1995). *Father of the bride part II* [Film]. Touchstone Pictures.

Sörensen, S., Duberstein, P. R., Chapman, B., Lyness, J. M., & Pinquart, M. (2008). How are personality traits related to preparation for future care needs in older adults? *The Journals of Gerontology Series B: Psychological Sciences and Social Sciences, 63*(6), P328–P336.

Specht, J. (Ed.). (2017). *Personality development across the lifespan*. Academic Press.

Stewart, A. J., & Ostrove, J. M. (1998). Women's personality in middle age: Gender, history, and midcourse corrections. *American Psychologist, 53*(11), 1185–1194.

Stewart, A. J., & Vandewater, E. A. (1999). "If I had it to do over again . . .": Midlife review, midcourse corrections, and women's well-being in midlife. *Journal of Personality and Social Psychology, 76*(2), 270–283.

Tate, C. C. (2014). Gender identity as a personality process. In B. L. Miller (Ed.), *Gender identity: Disorders, developmental perspectives and social implications* (pp. 1–22). Nova Science.

Tauber, B., Wahl, H.-W., & Schröder, J. (2016). Personality and life satisfaction over 12 years: Contrasting mid- and late life. *GeroPsych: The Journal of Gerontopsychology and Geriatric Psychiatry, 29*(1), 37–48. https://doi.org/10.1024/1662-9647/a000141

Tkach, C., & Lyubomirsky, S. (2006). How do people pursue happiness? Relating personality, happiness-increasing strategies, and well-being. *Journal of Happiness Studies, 7*(2), 183–225.

Torges, C. M., Stewart, A. J., & Duncan, L. E. (2008). Achieving ego integrity: Personality development in late midlife. *Journal of Research in Personality, 42*(4), 1004–1019.

Torges, C. M., Stewart, A. J., & Nolen-Hoeksema, S. (2008). Regret resolution, aging, and adapting to loss. *Psychology and Aging, 23*(1), 169–180. https://doi.org/10.1037/0882-7974.23.1.169

Triandis, H. C., & Suh, E. M. (2002). Cultural influences on personality. *Annual Review of Psychology, 53*(1), 133–160.

U.S. Government Accountability Office. (2011, June 7). *Retirement income: Ensuring income throughout retirement requires difficult choices* (GAO-11-400). https://www.gao.gov/products/gao-11-400

Versey, H. S., Stewart, A. J., & Duncan, L. E. (2013). Successful aging in late midlife: The role of personality among college-educated women. *Journal of Adult Development, 20*(2), 63–75.

Webster, M. M., & Ward, A. J. (2011). Personality and social context. *Biological Reviews, 86*(4), 759–773.

Weisberg, Y. J., DeYoung, C. G., & Hirsh, J. B. (2011). Gender differences in personality across the ten aspects of the Big Five. *Frontiers in Psychology, 2*, 178.

Williams, P. G., Suchy, Y., & Kraybill, M. L. (2010). Five-factor model personality traits and executive functioning among older adults. *Journal of Research in Personality, 44*(4), 485–491.

Wrzus, C., & Roberts, B. W. (2017). Processes of personality development in adulthood: The TESSERA framework. *Personality and Social Psychology Review, 21*(3), 253–277.

Zia, M. H., Ahmed, H., & Ishaque, A. (2019). Conscientiousness, extraversion and project success: Does emotional intelligence matter? *Peshawar Journal of Psychology and Behavioral Sciences, 5*(1), 19–37.

CHAPTER 10

Acierno, R., Ruggiero, K. J., Kilpatrick, D. G., Resnick, H. S., & Galea, S. (2006). Risk and protective factors for psychopathology among older versus younger adults after the 2004 Florida hurricanes. *The American Journal of Geriatric Psychiatry*, *14*(12), 1051–1059.

Averill, P. M., & Beck, J. G. (2000). Posttraumatic stress disorder in older adults: A conceptual review. *Journal of Anxiety Disorders*, *14*(2), 133–156.

Barrera, M., Sandler, I., & Ramsay, T. (1981). Preliminary development of a scale of social support: Studies on college students. *American Journal of Community Psychology*, *9*, 435–447.

Ben-Zur, H. (2020). Emotion-focused coping. In V. Zeigler-Hill & T. K. Shakelford (Eds.), *Encyclopedia of personality and individual differences* (pp. 1343–1345). Springer.

Biondi, M., & Picardi, A. (1996). Clinical and biological aspects of bereavement and loss-induced depression: a reappraisal. *Psychotherapy and psychosomatics*, *65*(5), 229-245.

Blackburn, E. H. (2000). Telomere states and cell fates. *Nature*, *408*(6808), 53–56.

Butcher, S. K., & Lord, J. M. (2004). Stress responses and innate immunity: Aging as a contributory factor. *Aging Cell*, *3*(4), 151–160.

Clarkson, K. (2012). Stronger (What doesn't kill you) [Song]. On *Stronger*. RCA.

Conklin, Q. A., Crosswell, A. D., Saron, C. D., & Epel, E. S. (2019). Meditation, stress processes, and telomere biology. *Current Opinion in Psychology*, *28*, 92–101.

Cook, J. M., & Simiola, V. (2017). Trauma and PTSD in older adults: Prevalence, course, concomitants and clinical considerations. *Current Opinion in Psychology*, *14*, 1–4.

Crane, M. F., Kangas, M., Karin, E., Searle, B., & Chen, D. (2020). Leveraging the experience of stressors: The role of adaptive systematic self-reflection. *Anxiety, Stress, and Coping*, *33*(3), 231–247.

Crane, M. F., & Searle, B. J. (2016). Building resilience through exposure to stressors: The effects of challenges versus hindrances. *Journal of Occupational Health Psychology*, *21*(4), 468–479.

Dhabhar, F. S. (2009). Enhancing versus suppressive effects of stress on immune function: Implications for immunoprotection and immunopathology. *Neuroimmunomodulation*, *16*(5), 300–317.

Dhabhar, F. S. (2014). Effects of stress on immune function: The good, the bad, and the beautiful. *Immunologic Research*, *58*, 193–210. https://doi.org/10.1007/s12026-014-8517-0

Dhabhar, F. S., Saul, A. N., Holmes, T. H., Daugherty, C., Neri, E., Tillie, J. M., Kusewitt, D., & Oberyszyn, T. M. (2012). High-anxious individuals show increased chronic stress burden, decreased protective immunity, and increased cancer progression in a mouse model of squamous cell carcinoma. *PLoS One*, *7*(4), e33069.

Epel, E. S., Blackburn, E. H., Lin, J., Dhabhar, F. S., Adler, N. E., Morrow, J. D., & Cawthon, R. M. (2004). Accelerated telomere shortening in response to life stress. *Proceedings of the National Academy of Sciences*, *101*(49), 17312–17315.

Epel, E., Daubenmier, J., Moskowitz, J. T., Folkman, S., & Blackburn, E. (2009). Can meditation slow rate of cellular aging? Cognitive stress, mindfulness, and telomeres. *Annals of the New York Academy of Sciences*, *1172*(1), 34–53.

Epel, E. S., Lin, J., Wilhelm, F. H., Wolkowitz, O. M., Cawthon, R., Adler, N. E., Dolbier, C., Mendes, W. B., & Blackburn, E. H. (2006). Cell aging in relation to stress arousal and cardiovascular disease risk factors. *Psychoneuroendocrinology*, *31*(3), 277–287.

Fali, T., Vallet, H., & Sauce, D. (2018). Impact of stress on aged immune system compartments: Overview from fundamental to clinical data. *Experimental Gerontology*, *105*, 19–26.

Folkman, S., Lazarus, R. S., Pimley, S., Novacek, J. (1987). Age differences in stress and coping processes. *Psychology and Aging*, 2, 171–184. https://www.doi.org/10.1037/0882-7974.2.2.171

Folkman, S., & Moskowitz, J. T. (2007). Positive affect and meaning-focused coping during significant psychological stress. *The Scope of Social Psychology: Theory and Applications*, *10*, 193–208.

Franceschi, C., & Campisi, J. (2014). Chronic inflammation (inflammaging) and its potential contribution to age-associated diseases. *Journals of Gerontology Series*

A: Biomedical Sciences and Medical Sciences, *69*(Suppl. 1), S4–S9.

Godbout, J. P., & Glaser, R. (2006). Stress-induced immune dysregulation: Implications for wound healing, infectious disease and cancer. *Journal of Neuroimmune Pharmacology*, *1*(4), 421–427.

Harrison, T., Kahn, D., & Hsu, M. (2004). A hermeneutic phenomenological study of widowhood for African American women. *Journal of Death and Dying*, *50*, 131–149. https://www.doi.org/10.2190/U122-9K12-3CLMAJ9W

Hayflick, L. (1965). The limited in vitro lifetime of human diploid cell strains. *Experimental Cell Research*, *37*(3), 614–636.

Hoppes, S., Bryce, H., Hellman, C., & Finlay, E. (2012). The effects of brief mindfulness training on caregivers' well-being. *Activities, Adaptation & Aging*, *36*, 147–166. https://www.doi.org/10.1080/01924788.2012.673154

Inoue, Y., Stickely, A., Yazawa, A., Aida, J., Koyanagi, A., & Kondo, N. (2022). Childhood adversities, late-life stressors and the onset of depressive symptoms in community dwelling older adults. *Aging and Mental Health*, *26*(4), 828–833.

Irwin, M., Patterson, T., Smith, T. L., Caldwell, C., Brown, S. A., Gillin, J. C., & Grant, I. (1990). Reduction of immune function in life stress and depression. *Biological Psychiatry*, *27*(1), 22–30.

Jennings, P. A., Aldwin, C. M., Levenson, M. R., Spiro, A., III, & Mroczek, D. K. (2006). Combat exposure, perceived benefits of military service, and wisdom in later life: Findings from the Normative Aging Study. *Research on Aging*, *28*(1), 115–134.

Kadri, A., Gracey, F., & Leddy, A. (2022, February 9). What factors are associated with posttraumatic growth in older adults? A systematic review. *Clinical Gerontologist*. Advance online publication. https://www.doi.org/10.1080/07317115.2022.2034200

Koenig, H. (2009). Research on religion, spirituality and mental health: A review. *The Canadian Journal of Psychiatry*, *54*, 283–291.

Koenig, H. G. (2012). Religion, spirituality, and health: The research and clinical implications. *International Scholarly Research Network Psychiatry*, *2012*, 278730. http://dx.doi.org/10.5402/2012/278730

Krause, N. (1986). Social support, stress, and well-being among older adults. *Journal of Gerontology*, *41*(4), 512–519.

Kurth, F., Cherbuin, N., & Luders, E. (2017). Promising links between meditation and reduced (brain) aging: An attempt to bridge some gaps between the alleged fountain of youth and the youth of the field. *Frontiers in Psychology*, *8*, 860.

Lazarus, R. S., & Folkman, S. (1984). *Stress, appraisal, and coping*. Springer.

Manuck, S. B., Cohen, S., Rabin, B. S., Muldoon, M. F., & Bachen, E. A. (1991). Individual differences in cellular immune response to stress. *Psychological Science*, *2*(2), 111–115.

Marketon, J. I. W., & Glaser, R. (2008). Stress hormones and immune function. *Cellular Immunology*, *252*(1–2), 16–26.

McEwen, B. S. (2017, April 10). Neurobiological and systemic effects of chronic stress. *Chronic Stress*, *1*. https://doi.org/10.1177/2470547017692328

McEwen, B. S. (2022). Protective and damaging effects of stress mediators: Central role of the brain. *Dialogues in Clinical Neuroscience*, *8*(4), 367–381.

McLemore, K. A. (2018). A minority stress perspective on transgender individuals' experiences with misgendering. *Stigma and Health*, *3*(1), 53–64. https://doi.org/10.1037/sah0000070

Meléndez, J. C., Mayordomo, T., Sancho, P., & Tomás, J. M. (2012). Coping strategies: Gender differences and development throughout life span. *The Spanish Journal of Psychology*, *15*(3), 1089–1098.

Moos, R. H. (1993). *Coping Responses Inventory: CRI Adult Form*. Psychological Assessment Resources.

Moos, R. H., Brennan, P. L., Schutte, K. K., & Moos, B. S. (2006). Older adults' coping with negative life events: Common processes of managing health, interpersonal, and financial/work stressors. *The International Journal of Aging and Human Development*, *62*(1), 39–59.

Nakamura, J. S., Kim, E. S., Rentscher, K. E., Bower, J. E., & Kuhlman, K. R. (2022). Early life stress, depressive symptoms, and inflammation: The role of social factors.

Aging and Mental Health, 26(4), 843–851.

Navarro, A. B., & Bueno, B. (2005). Efectos del sexo, el nivel educativo y el nivel económico en el afrontamiento de los problemas en personas muy mayores. *Revista Española de Geriatría y Gerontología, 40*(1), 34–43.

Nieto, M., Romero, D., Ros, L., Zabala, C., Martínez, M., Ricarte, J. J., Serrano, J. P., & Latorre, J. M. (2020). Differences in coping strategies between young and older adults: The role of executive functions. *The International Journal of Aging and Human Development, 90*(1), 28–49.

Norris, F. H., & Murrell, S. A. (1988). Prior experience as a moderator of disaster impact on anxiety symptoms in older adults. *American Journal of Community Psychology, 16*(5), 665–683.

O'Donovan, A., Tomiyama, A. J., Lin, J., Puterman, E., Adler, N. E., Kemeny, M., Wolkowitz, O. M., Blackburn, E. H., & Epel, E. S. (2012). Stress appraisals and cellular aging: A key role for anticipatory threat in the relationship between psychological stress and telomere length. *Brain, Behavior, and Immunity, 26*(4), 573–579.

Park, C. L. (2005). Religion as a meaning-making framework in coping with life stress. *Journal of Social Issues, 61*, 707–729. http://dx.doi.org/10.1111/j.1540-4560.2005.00428.x

Peacock, E. J., & Wong, P. T. (1990). The stress appraisal measure (SAM): A multidimensional approach to cognitive appraisal. *Stress Medicine, 6*(3), 227–236.

Pless Kaiser, A., Cook, J. M., Glick, D. M., & Moye, J. (2019). Posttraumatic stress disorder in older adults: A conceptual review. *Clinical Gerontologist, 42*(4), 359–376.

Pruett, S. B. (2003). Stress and the immune system. *Pathophysiology, 9*(3), 133–153.

Puterman, E., Lin, J., Blackburn, E., O'Donovan, A., Adler, N., & Epel, E. (2010). The power of exercise: Buffering the effect of chronic stress on telomere length. *PLOS One, 5*(5), e10837.

Raabe, F. J., & Spengler, D. (2013). Epigenetic risk factors in PTSD and depression. *Frontiers in Psychiatry, 4*, 80.

Reisman, S. (1997, May). Measurement of physiological stress. In J. R. LaCourse (Ed.), *Proceedings of the IEEE 23rd Northeast Bioengineering Conference* (pp. 21–23). IEEE.

Rozlog, L. A., Kiecolt-Glaser, J. K., Marucha, P. T., Sheridan, J. F., & Glaser, R. (1999). Stress and immunity: Implications for viral disease and wound healing. *Journal of Periodontology, 70*(7), 786–792.

Saul, A. N., Oberyszyn, T. M., Daugherty, C., Kusewitt, D., Jones, S., Jewell, S., Malarkey, W. B., Lehman, A., Lemeshow, S., & Dhabhar, F. S. (2005). Chronic stress and susceptibility to skin cancer. Journal of the National Cancer Institute, *97*(23), 1760–1767. https://www.doi.org/10.1093/jnci/dji401

Schryer, E., & Ross, M. (2012). Evaluating the valence of remembered events: The importance of age and self-relevance. *Psychology and Aging, 27*, 237–242. https://www.doi.org/10.1037/a0023283

Sin, F., Berger, S., Kim, I. J., & Yoon, D. (2021). Digital social interaction in older adults during the COVID-19 pandemic. *Proceedings of the ACM on Human-Computer Interaction, 5*(CSCW2), 1–20.

Sorrell, J. (2015). Meditation for older adults: A new look at an ancient intervention for mental health. *Journal of Psychosocial Nursing and Mental Health Services, 53*(5), 15–19.

Stokes, J. P., & Wilson, D. G. (1984). The inventory of socially supportive behaviors: Dimensionality, prediction and gender differences. *American Journal of Community Psychology, 12*(1), 53–69.

Stroebe, W., Zech, E., Stroebe, M. S., & Abakoumkin, G. (2005). Does social support help in bereavement? *Journal of Social and Clinical Psychology, 24*(7), 1030–1050.

Tedeschi, R G., & Calhoun. L. G. (2004). Posttraumatic growth: Conceptual foundations and empirical evidence. *Psychological Inquiry, 15*, 1–18.

Teichner, W. H. (1968). Interaction of behavioral and physiological stress reactions. *Psychological Review, 75*(4), 271–291. https://doi.org/10.1037/h0020281

Thapa, D. K., Visentin, D. C., Kornhaber, R., & Cleary, M. (2020). Prevalence and factors associated with depression, anxiety, and stress symptoms among older adults: A cross-sectional population-based study. *Nursing & Health Sciences, 22*(4), 1139–1152.

Thorp, S. R., Sones, H. M., & Cook, J. M. (2011). Posttraumatic stress disorder among older adults. *Clinical Gerontologist, 42*(4), 359–376.

Tiihonen Möller, A., Bäckström, T., Söndergaard, H. P., & Helström, L. (2014). Identifying risk factors for PTSD in women seeking medical help after rape. *PloS One, 9*(10), e111136.

Tolahunase, M., Sagar, R., & Dada, R. (2017). Impact of yoga and meditation on cellular aging in apparently healthy individuals: A prospective, open-label single-arm exploratory study. *Oxidative Medicine and Cellular Longevity, 2017*, 7928981. https://doi.org/10.1155/2017/7928981

Treadway, M. T., & Lazar, S. W. (2010). Meditation and neuroplasticity: Using mindfulness to change the brain. In R. Baer (Ed.), *Assessing mindfulness and acceptance processes in clients: Illuminating the theory and practice of change* (pp. 185–206). Context Press.

Vannini, P., Gagliardi, G. P., Kuppe, M., Dossett, M. L., Donovan, N. J., Gatchel, J. R., Quiroz, Y. T., Premnath, P. Y., Amariglio, R. Sperling, R. A., & Marshall, G. A. (2021). Stress, resilience, and coping strategies in a sample of community-dwelling older adults during COVID-19. *Journal of Psychiatric Research, 138*, 176–185.

Whitehead, B. R., & Bergeman, C. S. (2020). Daily religious coping buffers the stress-affect relationship and benefits overall metabolic health in older adults. *Psychology of Religion and Spirituality, 12*(4), 393–399. http://dx.doi.org/10.1037/rel0000251

CHAPTER 11

Allers, R., Minkoff, R. (Directors), Mecchi, I., Roberts, J., Woolverton, L. (Screenwriters), & Hahn, D. (Producer). (1994). *The lion king* [Film]. Walt Disney Pictures; Walt Disney Feature Animation.

Allumbaugh, D. L., & Hoyt, W. T. (1999). Effectiveness of grief therapy: A meta-analysis. *Journal of Counseling Psychology, 46*(3), 370–380.

American Psychiatric Association. (1994). *Diagnostic and statistical manual of mental disorders* (4th ed.). American Psychiatric Association.

American Psychiatric Association. (2022). *Diagnostic and statistical manual of mental disorders* (5th ed., text rev.). American Psychiatric Association.

Anderson, H. (2010). Common grief, complex grieving. *Pastoral Psychology, 59*(2), 127–136.

Appelbaum, P. S. (2017). Should mental disorders be a basis for physician-assisted death? *Psychiatric Services, 68*(4), 315–317.

Arizmendi, B. J., & O'Connor, M. F. (2015). What is "normal" in grief? *Australian Critical Care, 28*(2), 58–62.

Azari, N. P., Nickel, J., Wunderlich, G., Niedeggen, M., Hefter, H., Tellmann, L., Herzog, H., Stoerig, P., Birnbacher, D., & Seitz, R. J. (2001). Neural correlates of religious experience. *European Journal of Neuroscience, 13*(8), 1649–1652.

Bartrop, R. W., Lazarus, L., Luckhurst, E., Kiloh, L. G., & Penny, R. (1977). Depressed lymphocyte function after bereavement. *The Lancet, 309*(8016), 834–836.

Bonanno, G. A. (2005). Resilience in the face of potential trauma. *Current Directions in Psychological Science, 14*(3), 135–138.

Bonanno, G. A., Wortman, C. B., Lehman, D. R., Tweed, R. G., Haring, M., Sonnega, J., Carr, D., & Nesse, R. M. (2002). Resilience to loss and chronic grief: A prospective study from preloss to 18-months postloss. *Journal of Personality and Social Psychology, 83*(5), 1150–1164.

Bosma, H., Apland, L., & Kazanjian, A. (2010). Cultural conceptualizations of hospice palliative care: More similarities than differences. *Palliative Medicine, 24*(5), 510–522.

Bowlby, J. (1980). *Attachment and loss* (Vol. 3). Basic Books.

Bruinsma, S. M., Tiemeier, H. W., Heemst, J. V. V., van der Heide, A., & Rietjens, J. A. (2015). Risk factors for complicated grief in older adults. *Journal of Palliative Medicine, 18*(5), 438–446.

Buckley, T., Mihailidou, A. S., Bartrop, R., McKinley, S., Ward, C., Morel-Kopp, M. C., Spinaze, M., & Tofler, G. H. (2011). Haemodynamic changes during early bereavement: Potential contribution to increased cardiovascular risk. *Heart, Lung and Circulation, 20*(2), 91–98.

Buss, M. K., Rock, L. K., & McCarthy, E. P. (2017, February). Understanding palliative care and hospice: A review for primary care providers. *Mayo Clinic Proceedings*, *92*(2), 280–286.

Carlson, M. D., Morrison, R. S., Holford, T. R., & Bradley, E. H. (2007). Hospice care: What services do patients and their families receive? *Health Services Research*, *42*(4), 1672–1690.

Cerney, M. S., & Buskirk, J. R. (1991). Anger: The hidden part of grief. *Bulletin of the Menninger Clinic*, *55*(2), 228–237.

Cruz-Ortega, L. G., Gutierrez, D., & Waite, D. (2015). Religious orientation and ethnic identity as predictors of religious coping among bereaved individuals. *Counseling and Values*, *60*(1), 67–83.

Davis, B. A., Burns, J., Rezac, D., Dillard, B., Kieffner, E., Gargus, J., Tiberi, A. A., & Waters, J. (2005). Family stress and advance directives: A comparative study. *Journal of Hospice and Palliative Nursing*, *7*(4), 219–227.

Ditto, P. H., Danks, J. H., Smucker, W. D., Bookwala, J., Coppola, K. M., Dresser, R., Fagerlin, A., Gready, R. M., Houts, R. M., Lockhart, L. K., & Zyzanski, S. (2001). Advance directives as acts of communication: A randomized controlled trial. *Archives of Internal Medicine*, *161*(3), 421–430.

Dominick, S. A., Irvine, A. B., Beauchamp, N., Seeley, J. R., Nolen-Hoeksema, S., Doka, K. J., & Bonanno, G. A. (2010). An internet tool to normalize grief. *OMEGA—Journal of Death and Dying*, *60*(1), 71–87.

Effiong, A., & Effiong, A. I. (2012). Palliative care for the management of chronic illness: A systematic review study protocol. *BMJ Open*, *2*(3), e000899.

Elison, J., & McGonigle, C. (2003). *Liberating losses: When death brings relief*. Da Capo Press.

Fliedner, M., Zambrano, S., Schols, J. M., Bakitas, M., Lohrmann, C., Halfens, R. J., & Eychmüller, S. (2019). An early palliative care intervention can be confronting but reassuring: A qualitative study on the experiences of patients with advanced cancer. *Palliative Medicine*, *33*(7), 783–792.

Friedman, R., & James, J. W. (2008). The myth of the stages of dying, death and grief. *Skeptic*, *14*(2), 37–42.

Galatzer-Levy, I. R., & Bonanno, G. A. (2012). Beyond normality in the study of bereavement: Heterogeneity in depression outcomes following loss in older adults. *Social Science and Medicine*, *74*(12), 1987–1994.

Gerra, G., Monti, D., Panerai, A. E., Sacerdote, P., Anderlini, R., Avanzini, P., Zaimovic, A., Brambilia, F., & Franceschi, C. (2003). Long-term immune-endocrine effects of bereavement: Relationships with anxiety levels and mood. *Psychiatry Research*, *121*(2), 145–158.

Groenewoud, J. H., Van Der Maas, P. J., Van Der Wal, G., Hengeveld, M. W., Tholen, A. J., Schudel, W. J., & Van Der Heide, A. (1997). Physician-assisted death in psychiatric practice in the Netherlands. *New England Journal of Medicine*, *336*(25), 1795–1801.

Haun, M. W., Estel, S., Ruecker, G., Friederich, H. C., Villalobos, M., Thomas, M., & Hartmann, M. (2017). Early palliative care for adults with advanced cancer. *Cochrane Database of Systematic Reviews*, *6*(6), CD011129.

Hays, J. C., & Hendrix, C. C. (2008). The role of religion in bereavement. In M. S. Stroebe, R. O. Hansson, H. Schut, & W. Stroebe (Eds.), *Handbook of bereavement research and practice: Advances in theory and intervention* (pp. 327–348). American Psychological Association. https://doi.org/10.1037/14498-016

Holland, J. M., Currier, J. M., Coleman, R. A., & Neimeyer, R. A. (2010). *Integration of Stressful Life Experiences Scale (ISLES)* [Database record]. APA PsycTests.

Horowitz, M., Wilner, N., & Alvarez, W. (1979). Impact of Event Scale: A measure of subjective stress. *Psychosomatic Medicine*, *41*(3), 209–218.

Huang, F. Y., Hsu, A. L., Chao, Y. P., Shang, C. M. H., Tsai, J. S., & Wu, C. W. (2021). Mindfulness-based cognitive therapy on bereavement grief: Alterations of resting-state network connectivity associate with changes of anxiety and mindfulness. *Human Brain Mapping*, *42*(2), 510–520.

Irwin, M., Daniels, M., Smith, T. L., Bloom, E., & Weiner, H. (1987). Impaired natural killer cell activity during bereavement. *Brain, Behavior, and Immunity, 1*(1), 98–104.

Jacobs, S. (1993). *Pathologic grief: Maladaptation to loss*. American Psychiatric Association.

Kelley, M. M., & Chan, K. T. (2012). Assessing the role of attachment to God, meaning, and religious coping as mediators in the grief experience. *Death Studies, 36*(3), 199–227.

Kim, S. Y., & Lemmens, T. (2016). Should assisted dying for psychiatric disorders be legalized in Canada? *CMAJ, 188*(14), E337–E339.

Kitson, G. C. (2000). Adjustment to violent and natural deaths in later and earlier life for black and white widows. *The Journals of Gerontology Series B: Psychological Sciences and Social Sciences, 55*(6), S341–S351.

Kleinpell, R., Vasilevskis, E. E., Fogg, L., & Ely, E. W. (2019). Exploring the association of hospice care on patient experience and outcomes of care. *BMJ Supportive & Palliative Care, 9*(1), e13–e13.

Kübler-Ross, E. (1973). *On death and dying*. Routledge.

Landry, J. T., Foreman, T., & Kekewich, M. (2015). Ethical considerations in the regulation of euthanasia and physician-assisted death in Canada. *Health Policy, 119*(11), 1490–1498

Lichtenthal, W. G., Burke, L. A., & Neimeyer, R. A. (2011). Religious coping and meaning-making following the loss of a loved one. *Counseling and Spirituality, 30*(2), 113–135.

Maciejewski, P. K., Zhang, B., Block, S. D., & Prigerson, H. G. (2007). An empirical examination of the stage theory of grief. *JAMA, 297*(7), 716–723.

Mayo Clinic Staff. (2022, August 2). *Living wills and advance directives for medical decisions*. www.mayoclinic.org/healthy-lifestyle/consumer-health/in-depth/living-wills/art-20046303

Meier, D. E., & Brawley, O. W. (2011). Palliative care and the quality of life. *Journal of Clinical Oncology, 29*(20), 2750–2752.

Meier, D. E., Emmons, C. A., Litke, A., Wallenstein, S., & Morrison, R. S. (2003). Characteristics of patients requesting and receiving physician-assisted death. *Archives of Internal Medicine, 163*(13), 1537–1542.

Moon, J. R., Glymour, M. M., Vable, A. M., Liu, S. Y., & Subramanian, S. V. (2014). Short- and long-term associations between widowhood and mortality in the United States: Longitudinal analyses. *Journal of Public Health, 36*(3), 382–389.

Morris, R. I., & Christie, K. M. B. (1995). Initiating hospice care: Why, when, and how. *Home Healthcare Now, 13*(5), 21–26.

Neimeyer, R. A. (1999). Narrative strategies in grief therapy. *Journal of Constructivist Psychology, 12*(1), 65–85.

Newson, R. S., Boelen, P. A., Hek, K., Hofman, A., & Tiemeier, H. (2011). The prevalence and characteristics of complicated grief in older adults. *Journal of Affective Disorders, 132*(1–2), 231–238.

Nseir, S., & Larkey, L. K. (2013). Interventions for spousal bereavement in the older adult: An evidence review. *Death Studies, 37*(6), 495–512.

Oregon Health Authority. (n.d.). *Death with Dignity Act*. https://www.oregon.gov/oha/ph/providerpartnerresources/evaluationresearch/deathwithdignityact/pages/index.aspx

Pargament, K. I., Smith, B. W., Koenig, H. G., & Perez, L. (1998). Patterns of positive and negative religious coping with major life stressors. *Journal for the Scientific Study of Religion, 37*(4), 710–724.

Peacock, E. J., & Wong, P. T. (1990). The stress appraisal measure (SAM): A multidimensional approach to cognitive appraisal. *Stress Medicine, 6*(3), 227–236.

Prigerson, H. G., Maciejewski, P. K., Reynolds III, C. F., Bierhals, A. J., Newsom, J. T., Fasiczka, A., Frank, E., Doman, J., & Miller, M. (1995). Inventory of Complicated Grief: A scale to measure maladaptive symptoms of loss. *Psychiatry Research, 59*(1–2), 65–79.

ProCon.org. (2023, August 9). *States with legal medical aid in dying (MAID)*. https://euthanasia.procon.org/states-with-legal-physician-assisted-suicide/

Ramachandran, V. S., Hirstein, W. S., Armel, K. C., Tecoma, E., & Iragui, V. (1997, October). The neural basis of religious experience. *Society for Neuroscience Abstracts, 23*(2), p. 1316.

Rao, J. K., Anderson, L. A., Lin, F. C., & Laux, J. P. (2014). Completion of advance directives among US consumers. *American Journal of Preventive Medicine, 46*(1), 65–70.

Rosenblatt, P. C. (1988). Grief: The social context of private feelings. *Journal of Social Issues, 44*(3), 67–78.

Schlick, C. J. R., & Bentrem, D. J. (2019). Timing of palliative care: When to call for a palliative care consult. *Journal of Surgical Oncology, 120*(1), 30–34.

Shaffer, C. S., Cook, A. N., & Connolly, D. A. (2016). A conceptual framework for thinking about physician-assisted death for persons with a mental disorder. *Psychology, Public Policy, and Law, 22*(2), 141–157. https://doi.org/10.1037/law0000082

Shear, M. K. (2012). Getting straight about grief. *Depression and Anxiety, 29*(6), 461–464.

Shear, M. K., Ghesquiere, A., & Glickman, K. (2013). Bereavement and complicated grief. *Current Psychiatry Reports, 15*(11), 1–7.

Shuchter, S. R., & Zisook, S. (1993). The course of normal grief. In M. S. Stroebe, W. Stroebe, & R. O. Hansson (Eds.), *Handbook of bereavement: Theory, research, and intervention* (pp. 23–43). Cambridge University Press.

Silveira, M. J., Kim, S. Y., & Langa, K. M. (2010). Advance directives and outcomes of surrogate decision making before death. *New England Journal of Medicine, 362*(13), 1211–1218.

Silver, R. C., & Wortman, C. B. (2007). The stage theory of grief. *JAMA, 297*(24), 2692–2694.

Smith, K. A., Harvath, T. A., Goy, E. R., & Ganzini, L. (2015). Predictors of pursuit of physician-assisted death. *Journal of Pain and Symptom Management, 49*(3), 555–561.

Snyder, S., Hazelett, S., Allen, K., & Radwany, S. (2013). Physician knowledge, attitude, and experience with advance care planning, palliative care, and hospice: Results of a primary care survey. *American Journal of Hospice and Palliative Medicine®, 30*(5), 419–424.

Stroebe, M., Schut, H., & Stroebe, W. (2007). Health outcomes of bereavement. *The Lancet, 370*(9603), 1960–1973.

Stroebe, W., Zech, E., Stroebe, M. S., & Abakoumkin, G. (2005). Does social support help in bereavement? *Journal of Social and Clinical Psychology, 24*(7), 1030–1050.

Teno, J. M., Gruneir, A., Schwartz, Z., Nanda, A., & Wetle, T. (2007). Association between advance directives and quality of end-of-life care: A national study. *Journal of American Geriatric Society, 55*(2), 189–194.

Tilden, V. P., Tolle, S. W., Nelson, C. A., Fields, J. (2001). Family decision-making to withdraw life-sustaining treatments from hospitalized patients. *Nursing Research, 50*(2), 105–115.

Yoo, Y. S., & Kang, H. Y. (2006). Effects of a bereavement intervention program on depression and life satisfaction in middle aged widows in Korea. *Journal of Korean Academy of Nursing, 36*, 1367–1373.

Yun, Y. H., Rhee, Y. S., Nm, S. Y., Chae, Y. M., Heo, D. S., Lee, S. W., Hong, Y. S., Kim, S. Y., & Lee, K. S. (2004). Public attitudes toward dying with dignity and hospice. palliative care. *Journal of Hospice and Palliative Care, 7*(1), 17–28.

AUTHOR INDEX

SUBJECT INDEX